CHAUCER'S CULTURAL GEOGRAPHY

Basic Readings in Chaucer and His Time
Christian K. Zacher and Paul E. Szarmach, *Series Editors*

CHAUCER'S CULTURAL GEOGRAPHY

EDITED BY
KATHRYN L. LYNCH

Routledge
Taylor & Francis Group

LONDON AND NEW YORK

Published in 2002 by
Routledge
711 Third Avenue
New York, NY 10017

Published in Great Britain by
Routledge
2 Park Square, Milton Park
Abingdon, Oxfordshire
OX14 4RN

First issued in paperback 2014

Copyright © 2002 by Kathryn L. Lynch

Routledge is an imprint of the Taylor & Francis Group, an informa business

Cataloguing-in-Publication Data is available from the Library of Congress.

ISBN 978-0-415-93001-7 (hbk)
ISBN 978-0-415-76227-4 (pbk)

Contents

Acknowledgments

My gratitude goes to all the authors and editors who generously shared their work so that I could put together this volume, and especially to Kenneth Bleeth and Suzanne Akbari for their insight and efficiency—not only in the essays they wrote for this collection, which any reader will be able to appreciate, but also in the sage and tactful advice that each offered behind the scenes and in their cheer and promptness. My thanks go as well to John Fyler, whose conversations helped me shape the project at its inception; to my two research assistants, Elizabeth Coe and Emily See; to the always reliable staff of the Wellesley College Library; and to the editorial staff at Routledge. This collection would not have been possible without the generous assistance of a series of research grants from Wellesley College.

My largest debt, as ever, is to my family, and especially to my husband, Robert McDonnell. As well as being my emotional and spiritual support, he provides me with a model of logical rigor and spare prose. It is a model I wish I could reach more often than I do. Finally, this book is dedicated to the memory of my mother. Like Geoffrey Chaucer himself, she was simultaneously the most provincial and the most cosmopolitan of travelers. Her wit and judgment, much missed, continue to guide me in my life journey.

Introduction

KATHRYN L. LYNCH

Mapping the Middle Ages

It may seem a paradox that a collection of essays like this one, focusing on the topic of geography, should be plagued by geographical problems: the difficulties of mapping territory, locating boundaries, setting limits. But such is the case—and perhaps the situation is less paradoxical than it might at first seem. It is instead probably inevitable that isolating geography as a subject for investigation should uncover the definitional problems that make any mapping or geographical enterprise a less than transparent process. Is the mapping to be governed by predetermined worldviews or destinations? Is it, in short, to be a Christian mapping as medieval maps were, a Eurocentric mapping, or a mapping informed by modern-day multicultural politics and the goals of diversity?

This basic question leads to others: Is something like an objective geography possible or desirable? Is Chaucer's geography to be inspected through the lens of the present day, with its many global histories of imperialist incursions and racist exclusions? Or is it to be strictly regarded from the historical perspective of the Middle Ages, to the extent that such a perspective can be recreated? Is our focus to be on Chaucer's incorporation, his use and understanding, of the cultural attitudes and achievements of *other* parts of his world—on, say, Arabic science or Asian trade routes—or is it to be on the set of attitudes that *he* displays, on his attempts to control, dominate, or otherwise come to terms with cultural difference? In trying to navigate my way through and around such questions, I have tried to set a course that avoids definitive answers to them, one that rather steers around them, like an explorer or maybe more like a tour guide, with the aim of exposing as much of the landscape to the reader as possible. I have thus tried to choose essays for inclusion here that represent as expansive and various a set of approaches to Chaucer's "cultural geography," and as wide a range of Chaucerian texts, as possible.

1

Before introducing these essays in more detail, a small excursus may be in order. Consider the following facts: The English word *geography* is itself an anachronism (it did not come into use until 150 years after Chaucer's time). Even in Latin, the Greek-derived word *geographia* was rare during the late classical and medieval periods, when study and measurement of the earth were more commonly considered aspects of scriptural or philosophical study, as for Augustine or Cassiodorus, or of geometry, as for Martianus Capella.[1] Nor, indeed, was the English word *map* yet in use, either as a noun or a verb. The Middle English word *mapamounde,* which Chaucer himself employed ("To Rosemounde," line 2),[2] meant simultaneously both a map of the world and the world itself. Similarly, the common word for a geographical border, a *march(e),* derived from a natural feature of the landscape that created the frontier, that is, the marshland or wetland that distinguishes ocean from shore. And *orient* meant the direction east, the point on the globe where the sun rises. Rather than an absolute space, the space of the "orient" was relative; in the late fifteenth century, an "Oriental" could even be "a resident of the eastern parts of England" (*MED*). And it was by such a natural transference again that the noun *orient* came to signify brilliance, as possessed by the sun or the pearl that came from the east.

These linguistic conflations reflect what we might think of as a more organic relationship to earthly space. As Sylvia Tomasch shows in her essay "*Mappae Mundi* and 'The Knight's Tale'," medieval maps embodied a frankly Christian and fully symbolic way of looking at the world, one that collapsed distinctions between geographical and temporal space, and between the divine body and the physical world. Medieval travelogues did not chart a process of objective "discovery," as we know it; rather, objective description and visual possession collapse into a narration that presents past events as if they were perpetually present, and landscape becomes, in Mary Campbell's phrase, "transcendently referential."[3] Relatively speaking, little was known and much was yet to be discovered about the actual space of the world, which was thus ripe for imaginary and speculative projections. Human understanding of physical space was more fluid, more changeable, less sharply distinct from and more comfortably linked to imaginative space than it would be even a few hundred years later, and the medieval understanding of geography was thus far different from our own. At the same time, this understanding can still be placed on a continuum with our own.

We might think, in fact, of the medieval relationship to global space as analogous to modern-day speculations about what we call provocatively "outer space" or more simply just "space"; this "space" is an area for serious scientific study to be sure, but it is also the property of poets and the writers of science fiction and film. Space in the modern age, like the *mundus* of the medievals, is still profoundly open: to the most advanced dazzling and dizzying speculations of cosmographers and theorists of universal origin or ultimate fate as well as to conspiracy fantasies and theories of extraterrestrial invasion. The heavens today are a "space" where fact and fiction may implode into one another—just as they did in medieval fantasies about the far reaches of the earth. In an ironical historical contrast, the Middle Ages was more functional and scientific in its mapping of the stars than in its mapping of earthly space, while our age today is the reverse.

While I don't want to reify or romanticize such potential historical differences, I do hope that the essays in this book can help to challenge and complicate our thinking about the boundary between medieval and modern. As several of the essays in this volume suggest, this temporal borderline need not be a sharply drawn one. We do share much with our medieval predecessors. Specific modern attitudes toward the exotic East find their historical roots in the past, and reflect as well enduring features of the way the human psyche copes with what is culturally alien or strange. To this end, Edward Said's influential book *Orientalism*, though it is chiefly based on features of post-Enlightenment imperialism, has also proven useful to medievalists. Said paved the way for this use of his theories when he located precedents in the Middle Ages for later Orientalist attitudes.[4] As Said notes, medieval writers schematize, demystify, domesticate, and generally remake the far away into the familiar just as they mark it as different from and decidedly inferior to European culture, and in ways clearly similar to those found in later writers.

At the same time, authors like Dante and Chaucer *were* writing before the Age of Discovery, and, lacking a full history of successful colonialism, their views of cultural "Others," like Muslims and Mongols, could not be so securely superior as those of their successors. On the one hand, medieval Christians revealed their shameful loathing of the culturally different in fantasies of Saracens as horrible and monstrous; on the other hand, such panic reflects the fear of the conquered, not the security of the conqueror.[5] Despite temporary early gains, the Crusades were ultimately unsuccessful in maintaining control of Jerusalem, and by the middle of the fifteenth century, even the Christian city of Constantinople had fallen to the Muslims. The vow of the new ruler, Mehmed II, that Rome would follow serves as a reminder to us of the insecurity European Christians must have felt in the face of Ottoman power.[6] Indeed, the Christian Crusader cannot be seen in any meaningful sense as the forerunner of the later European explorer: His religious motivation differed sharply from the more fully and frankly imperialistic aims of the later adventurer, and his activities, broadly viewed, played little part in laying the foundation for later commercial relations between Europe and the Middle East or the political dominance of Europe over other parts of the world.[7] In most cases, Crusading was a far from money-making proposition—indeed, it was often financially devastating—and was generally undertaken from a sincere desire to defend the faith.[8]

As to that faith, it is important to remember as well that both Christianity and Islam are religions that convey a universalist message. Well before there was anything but the most primitive and perfunctory notion of "Europe" as a location with a cultural significance, the notion "Christendom" had great power.[9] While, of course, the ideal rarely coincides with the reality, the goal of Christian conquest was conversion, in which all—both conqueror and conquered—can theoretically participate. Even the category of color, seemingly intractable to modern readers, could be erased by conversion.[10] Thus, however various and even monstrous the geographic and cultural "Other" might seem, there is no "Other" that is ultimately and fundamentally "Other" to Christianity (the notable exception being the Jews).[11] This is a lesson conveyed by travel narratives like Mandeville's *Travels*, which reveals the world as a continuum of marvels. Mandeville, as Iain Higgins has shown, maps the "Other" onto a universalist Christian landscape, a "universal world": "an overarching scheme within which the East's marvelous abundance of customs, manners, and diversities can be contained, made sense of, and contemplated with calm pleasure rather than bewilderment or fear, and for secular and spiritual instruction rather than distraction or condemnation."[12] Similarly, the embedding of the entire physical world within the divine body in the thirteenth-century Ebstorf map (Tomasch, figure 7), framed by the head, hands, and feet of Christ, visually underscores this divinely authorized diversity.

None of this should be taken to imply that the European Middle Ages were a unitary "Golden Age," a time of relative innocence, of purer motives, before Enlightenment Imperialism (itself a phenomenon about which it is too easy to be simplistic) took over. Rather, ruptures and deficiencies in our understanding of the relationship between past and present—those that challenge our ideas of progress as well as those that reinforce them—suggest that we need to open ourselves to complications in the master historical narrative. Just as we cannot accept uncritically a body of scholarly literature that was built on the dominance and control of Western European cultures over the rest of the world, as Said has convincingly shown, so we cannot just turn that scholarship on its head without returning to look more carefully at its first principles. Even Said, as Kathleen Biddick has pointed out, "tells the history of Orientalism according to the highly conventionalized chronologies of an Enlightenment history of progress."[13] In this narrative, the Middle Ages has a special role, both as self and Other—both as the source of later attitudes toward difference and as the origin that stands prior to them, against which the "enlightened" present can be defined. Awkwardly thrust into this corner, medievalists are well positioned to resist the binary of self/other, to call attention to the difficulties involved in such a straightforward narrative and the gains that can follow from extricating ourselves from it.

As just one example, let us consider the binary that divides self/other into the geographic dichotomy West/East. Is this a dichotomy that can withstand historical scrutiny? How can our mapping of the Middle Ages help us to refine and revise the history that puts West/East at its center?[14] My earlier remarks on the structure and motivations of the Crusades suggest that Christian/Muslim would have been a more accurate formulation within a medieval context. At the same time, even the opposition Christian/Muslim represents an ideological distortion of the complex and interlocking relationships among many different Mediterranean cultures during most of the Middle Ages. The binary Christian/Muslim, in short, was a feature of Crusader propaganda, which is not even true to the complexity of a medieval ethnography that included pagans and idolaters[15] as well as Saracens and Christians, including those of various sects like the Nestorians. Instead, a more careful scrutiny suggests a richer and more dialogic, rather than sharply oppositional, relationship between the cultures we think of as "West" and "East" throughout much of the Middle Ages, especially the early centuries.

During this period, what we tend to think of now as the crown jewels of "Western" learning and civilization—especially the works of Greek science and philosophy—were being preserved and transmitted by "Eastern" powers. Greco-Roman learning was first preserved by the political power of the Byzantine empire, the true successor of Rome, and then transmitted by Muslim, Arabic editions, and its wisdom and first principles thus exercised as profound an influence on those "Eastern" cultures as they were later to do on "Western" philosophy. In a recent study of the foundations of the Western intellectual tradition, Marcia Colish imagines a hypothetical traveler through the "cultural capitals of the Mediterranean world and Northern Europe" around the year 1100; "[h]ad such a traveller been asked to predict which of these societies [Islam, Byzantium, Europe] would produce a scientific revolution in the seventeenth century and an Enlightenment in the eighteenth, chances are that he or she would have bet on Islam."[16] It is not my purpose here either to affirm or to question the assumptions about Western intellectual or scientific development after the Middle Ages that inform Colish's speculation; it is enough, I think, to note that medieval history renders the narrative of that development geographically and chronologically more complicated than we are usually led to believe.

As the historical "Other," whose existence is often ignored by combatants in the culture wars, the Middle Ages tells a story that puts these complications of the West/East binary into dialogue with the more straightforward narrative of "Western" enlightenment progress that holds sway in modern "Western" schools, for at least most nonspecialists. The cultural geography of the Middle Ages discloses that "Western" culture, far from being the property of Europe, was tracing a complicated route throughout the Mediterranean world,[17] and indeed that some of its most cherished values, like religious tolerance, were mapped onto the far East, with the great Mongol leaders like Kubilai Khan, who had a reputation for listening to the wise men of many cultures. These Middle Ages are both different from and linked to the historical periods that would follow in complex and often uncharted ways. Uncoupling the values of liberal, rationalist thought from the divisive and provocative politics of geography may be a liberating step for "Eastern-ers" and "Westerners" alike, and a step that, in our increasingly unstable and polarized world, we badly need to take. As Salman Rushdie eloquently laments, "I, too, have ropes around my neck, I have them to this day, pulling me this way and that, East and West, the nooses tightening, commanding, *choose, choose.* I buck, I snort, I whinny, I rear, I kick. Ropes, I do not choose between you. Lassoes, lariats, I choose neither of you, and both. Do you hear? I refuse to choose."[18] Some of these ropes are woven from a story that strangles and suppresses the Middle Ages; to the extent that we can unbraid and reweave that historical record, our work can lead forward to a more accu-rate and more productive narrative for the future.

Mapping Chaucer

The essays selected for inclusion in this collection do not present a coherent or unified picture of Chaucer's "cultural geography." I think of them more as a set of mirrors, which, when held up to his work, will reveal and illuminate different angles and aspects of his perspective. Those angles will not consti-tute a final or complete vision, but will, I hope, suggest the need for further inspection and point to areas of the subject that require clarification and offer opportunities for further understanding. I hope also that recent scholarly dis-cussion of Chaucer will not stop with or be of interest only to Chaucerians. Both because of his gifts as a poet and intellectual and because of his pro-found influence on later English and European poetry, Chaucer makes an excellent case study in medieval cultural geography, although until recently his poems were rarely approached with this topic in mind. Biographically, Chaucer was ideally situated to reflect and reflect on cultural difference. As a soldier, diplomat, and civil servant, he was widely traveled and cosmopolitan for his age; as the essays gathered here show, he was attracted to the topic of cultural geography in all its forms, knowledgeable about related issues that range from heresy to the Crusades.

Chaucer brought English poetry to the continent and continental poetry to England. In the process he also brought English poetry into contact with the world of the Eastern Mediterranean already engaged by his classical sources, for example, in the *Legend of Good Women*, where various Eastern queens wear the crown of "good woman" uneasily; in the Knight's Tale, built upon Boccaccio's retelling of Theseus's victory over the eastern Amazons; or in his various retellings of Aeneas's distraction by the Carthaginian Queen Dido. The entire known world was Chaucer's palette, and even when he was not working from a single set of recognizable texts, he dipped his brush in every color group available to him. He sets, for example, the Prioress's Tale not in Europe where one might expect to find it,[19] but in Asia. He exploits the irony of assigning to the Squire, whose "chyvachie" has been limited to

Europe (I.85–86), an exotic oriental tale. And he displays as well his fine ear for cultural difference closer to home, in the Miller's Tale and the Reeve's Tale, set respectively in Oxford and Cambridge, in the latter of which we find the first example of the use of dialect in English for the purposes of characterization (e.g., I.4026–33). Travel is a governing metaphor of his work, especially of the *Canterbury Tales*, which counterpoints literal and metaphorical forms of pilgrimage, sketching specific geographical references onto a haunting symbolic landscape. Few poets have as profound a sense of place as Chaucer; few have contributed to their national poetry as sharp an understanding of the relationship between geography and human identity. In this context, it is something of a mystery that he wrote little about the city of his birth, London, which David Wallace has thus dubbed "the absent city."[20] It is in this complex and contradictory Chaucer, this cosmopolitan poet of "Englishness," that I hope to interest the reader through the essays reprinted here.

These essays are simply a representative sampling of work, and there are thus several excellent pieces that I was not able to use. For example, there is much good work that has been done on Chaucer's relationship to Europe and continental culture, for instance by David Wallace.[21] My focus, however, is more tightly on spaces that correspond to the binary of self/other, a choice that shifts attention away from the intermediate landscape of continental Europe. Moreover, though representative, the essays collected here are mostly quite recent. The earliest piece is an excerpt from Dorothee Metlitzki's ground-breaking book *The Matter of Araby in Medieval England*, published in 1977, and fully half the essays I have chosen were published in the 1990s. This preference for relatively recent work reflects the fact that, before the past twenty years or so, an approach to Chaucer through the study of either his geography or his attitudes to different cultures was rare. There is, however, one notable exception to this generalization, in scholarly work that treats the Squire's Tale, which, as I have noted elsewhere, remains the "locus classicus of Chaucer's orientalism."[22] Given the relatively large body of material on the Squire's Tale that fits our theme and its temporal priority, it seems right to begin this collection with a separate section devoted to this tale, and this section offers a chance to study the evolution of the "oriental" analysis of Chaucer across time. After a newly commissioned essay that introduces general themes, in each of the two major divisions of this book critical essays are reproduced chronologically so that the reader can trace some of the development within the field.

Kenneth Bleeth's new essay, "Orientalism and the Critical History of the Squire's Tale," leads off the opening section of the volume with a discussion of the importance of "Orientalism" in the record of critical response to the Squire from the late eighteenth century forward to the present. While agreeing with previous scholars that Gardiner Stillwell's 1948 essay, "Chaucer in Tartary," marks an important turning point in criticism of the tale,[23] Professor

Bleeth also recognizes that Stillwell reinscribes traditional Western attitudes toward the "orient" as a romantic and fantastic wonderland, merely reversing Chaucer's posture toward this "venture into foreign territory" from enthusiasm to nervousness. Orientalist assumptions are still "at work," as they continue to be in criticism from succeeding decades by Donald Howard, E. T. Donaldson, Robert P. Miller, and others. Only in the last 15 years does Bleeth distinguish a self-consciousness coming into discussions of the tale, under the influence of Said's important book; in the most recent work on the subject, Bleeth notes a new self-critical attitude even in the application of Said's work, a more nuanced approach that he expects is likely to characterize future studies of the topic.

Bleeth's essay provides the background for the three essays on the Squire's Tale selected for reprinting here. The first of these, John M. Fyler's "Domesticating the Exotic in the Squire's Tale," links the concerns of Orientalism to genre and to the psychological categories that genre encodes and erodes. Through the youthful Squire, Chaucer explores the limits and values of romance, as Professor Fyler puts it, "a naive as well as compelling genre." Romance in its quest for "the forbidden erotic" suggests the possibility that taboos, especially the incest taboo, might be abolished. In the Squire's sometimes clumsy rendition, Chaucer explores the comic potential of this yearning for the erasure of the lines between self and other, to pick up the phrase from Fyler's title, in "domesticating the exotic." But literal birds do not serve comfortably as metaphorical humans, nor does the male Squire as a disinterested partisan of women, so the Squire's vision must give way to that of the more mature Franklin. At the same time, of Chaucer's three tales that "attempt to imagine the world beyond the bounds of Christendom," the Squire's is the most sympathetic.

Vincent J. DiMarco's essay, "The Historical Basis of Chaucer's Squire's Tale," takes a sharply different approach, examining what happens when one looks beyond the romance of the tale to historical realities in the Eastern world that would have been known to Chaucer and that might have informed his telling of this "oriental" tale. Professor DiMarco reads the Squire's Tale as an imaginative recasting of actual medieval political negotiations occurring between emissaries of the Egyptian Mamluk empire and the Mongol Khan Özbeg during the first half of the fourteenth century. Although the alliance between Mongol and Egyptian–Islamic forces was to remain fragile, these negotiations would have reminded Chaucer's European audience of a whole web of Eastern alliances—between the Mamluks and Ilkhanids as well as between the Mamluks and the Golden Horde—that would have prevented any realistic Mongol–Christian partnership to regain the Holy Land throughout the fourteenth century. The Squire in his tale thus gently, and perhaps unconsciously, rebukes the Crusading spirit of his father the Knight, and points toward a more sophisticated and tolerant understanding not only of medieval geopolitical realities but of "alien" cultures themselves. Although their approaches are quite different, in this conclusion DiMarco and Fyler come together in agreement.

The last of the essays in the Squire's Tale section, my own "East Meets West in Chaucer's Squire's and Franklin's Tales," looks outward from the Squire's Tale to the tale's position within the *Canterbury Tales*—and thus, I hope, makes a bridge to the concerns of the remainder of the collection. Like Fyler, I see the tale's type—an oriental romance on the model of the tales of the *Thousand and One Nights*—as central to its meaning, especially as that meaning is later brought under correction by the Franklin. Moreover, I argue that this oriental romance is specifically marked as "feminine" writing, bringing the issue of woman as "Other" into the circle of Orientalist concerns. As we will see, the "other" gender often overlaps with the "other" culture, which perhaps explains the frequency with which feminist approaches are brought to bear on Chaucer's cultural geography (see later chapters; e.g., Delany, Schibanoff). Thus, the successors to the Squire (a kind of Shahrazad manqué) as narrator are Dorigen in the Franklin's Tale and Virginia in the Physician's Tale, and Chaucer's own complex and problematic attitudes toward the unregulated play of fiction can be traced in the fates of those two heroines. In this analysis, the East is not chiefly a geographical place, as it was for DiMarco, or even a psychological category, as it was for Fyler, but a self-conscious poetic device—a way of talking about art and fiction making.

In the first essay of the second section of the collection, "Orientation and Nation in Chaucer's *Canterbury Tales*," Suzanne Conklin Akbari puts Chaucer's practice in dialogue with a larger universe of texts and "discourses," both medieval and modern. Professor Akbari's broad view allows her to speak directly to several of the specific essays collected here; in her analysis, commissioned for this volume, she engages with Sylvia Tomasch's discussion of the structural importance of cartography to Chaucer especially in the Knight's Tale, Katharine S. Gittes's reflections on the relevance of the tale collection as a genre, and Derek Pearsall's arguments against medieval English nationalism, and thus she complicates the discussion of each of these topics. Similarly, like Bleeth, Delany, and Schibanoff, she inspects the centrality of Edward Said's work to discussions of medieval "Orientalism," specifically pondering the question of whether either the Foucauldian term *discourse* or the academic term *Orientalist* is appropriately descriptive for the Middle Ages and Chaucer. She focuses both on the larger structural level of the pilgrimage frame in the *Canterbury Tales* and on a number of individual tales, and she tests the heuristic value of different lenses—geographic and national—in sharpening that focus.

By situating the *Canterbury Tales* within the medieval encyclopedic and chorographic traditions, Akbari illustrates the usefulness of thinking of Chaucer's work as a kind of fictional "discourse," as an effort to impose order, which in the Knight's Tale is literally mapped onto the world of the tale. This is not, however, to imply that order is the *point* of the Knight's Tale; "what is excluded" there from the geographic order—"the dangerous heat of the South"—is not permanently repressed, but returns later in the "luxurious warmth" and chaotic libidinal impulses of the Squire's Tale. If the ordering impulses of these two tales, however, suggest the value of thinking of Chaucer's texts as "discourse," it is less clear that his is a discourse of Orientalism. The South, not the East, is the direction that is missing from the triangulations of the the Knight's Tale, and that is, in turn, supplied by the Squire's Tale. It is the South that then forms a more distinct binary with the cool rationalism of the Franklin's Tale. In contrast to the discourse of Orientalism, ideas in nation and nationalism have greater explanatory power and medieval warrant, as shown by the Man of Law's Tale, where the romance language of "the monstrous, strange, or unnatural" is reinforced by being set in strange and familiar nations. In this and other Canterbury tales, nation emerges as a central term in the process of constructing difference, even as it is redefined by other distinctions, like those based on class and religion; hence the medieval "discourse" of nation becomes a more accurate and less anachronistic way to describe medieval global, political, and social diversity than Orientalism.

With "Scientific Imagery in Chaucer," an excerpt from Dorothee Metlitzki's *The Matter of Araby in Medieval England*, we turn from Chaucer's attitudes *toward* the world outside Europe and, as with DiMarco, back to how his knowledge *of* that world finds its way into his poetry. Professor Metlitzki meticulously studies the range of Arabic science that informs Chaucer's discussion of alchemy in the Canon's Yeoman's Tale, and the complicated lines of descent that made it available to him. At the same time, there is a definite stable vocabulary—as Metlitzki puts it, "a uniformity of designation"—upon which Chaucer is drawing that securely links his usage to a defined alchemical tradition derived from Arabic Islamic philosophy. Through the works of Arnold of Villa Nova, and others in the Latin West, Chaucer had access to an Arabic scientific allegory that symbolically represented the mystery of an alchemical reaction in the incestuous marriage of Mercury and Sulphur— also identified with the sun and the moon, or gold and silver. Chaucer's sources also reflect the need for secrecy between alchemical master and student (and author and reader) that links the alchemical tradition to Islamic mysticism and marks alchemy as "the most important worldly science." While Metlitzki stops short of offering a fully developed theory of the meaning of the Canon's Yeoman's Tale, her work definitively shows that any interpretation that does not take into account the Islamic philosophers will be incomplete.

Katharine Slater Gittes's essay "The *Canterbury Tales* and the Arabic Frame Tradition" also shows the way that Chaucer incorporates non-Western traditions, this time formal rather than substantive. Working from an eighth-century Indian–Arabic work, the *Panchatantra*, Gittes suggests that the open-ended frame of that work, which encloses more tightly unified Indian tales, derived from its Arabic translations and reflects an aesthetic that stands in sharp contrast to the drive toward unity and closure embodied in, for example, the Greek poetics of Aristotle or Horace. This sort of frame—architecturally more similar to the Arabic mosque than the Gothic cathedral—might have reached Chaucer through its imitators in medieval Spain, where the *Panchatantra* would have influenced Petrus Alfonsi's twelfth-century *Disciplina Clericalis*, to which Chaucer refers several times in the Tale of Melibee. Although Gittes' provocative essay skirts close to essentializing culture and raised some eyebrows at its first publication,[24] it offers a useful and important way of thinking about the way Chaucer's use of form distinguishes him from other contemporary European authors, like Gower and Boccaccio, and may signal his openness to influences from beyond Europe.

Louise O. Fradenburg's analysis of space in the Prioress's Tale, excerpted from her essay "Criticism, Anti-Semitism, and the Prioress's Tale," suggestively blurs the lines between interior and exterior spaces, between the body and the world it inhabits, and between temporal and physical spaces, taking us to a "place" of pre-Oedipal infancy and speechlessness where borderlines dissolve. The tale defends against growth, learning, and change, and thus against language and narrative. Its style, praised by many critics for its artistry, rather exemplifies the emptiness of pure formalism. In this context, the challenges posed by the Prioress's Tale's cartography—its location, for example, in a Jewry, in Asia, its many entrances and exits—represent the challenges of a temporal world, an Other, which the tale will decisively reject in favor of repetition, immobility, and lifelessness. This movement is linked as well to the tale's anti-Semitism, in which the New Law itself becomes a substitution, a replacement of a law of constraint with one of "magical possession," although of course in its violent retribution against the Jews in the tale the New Law becomes the Old and enacts sameness rather than difference. To restate these points again in the language of space, an initial concern with the space outside the body is displaced onto a desire to "colonize" the space inside, an increasingly urgent "desire for the crisis that will bring about the end of change," and thus becomes a need for the spectacle that will "master abjection." The hopelessness and corruptness of this desire are reminders to critics of the importance of their task *as* critics, open to change, progress, and historicity.

While Professor Fradenburg's analysis focuses on a symbolic, interior cartography, the next essay, Sylvia Tomasch's "*Mappae Mundi* and 'The Knight's Tale': The Geography of Power, the Technology of Control," turns our attention to the actual physical maps of medieval cartography. Following a useful survey of some of the most common kinds of medieval maps that would have been known to Chaucer, Professor Tomasch argues that Chaucer shows an awareness not only of contemporary geography but also of the ways in which mapmaking and world making collide, rendering all geographic perception a construction rather than a transparent reflection of reality. Although her focus is ultimately on the Knight's Tale, Tomasch takes detours into the *House of Fame* and *Troilus and Criseyde*, to demonstrate Chaucer's attentiveness to problems of perspective, and again into several of the Canterbury tales—among them the Pardoner's Tale, the Monk's Tale, and the Wife of Bath's Tale—to show Chaucer's knowledge of the scope of the inhabited world and the central place of Jerusalem. Within her analysis, Theseus of the Knight's Tale becomes the mapmaker par excellence, the amphitheater he builds a kind of T-O map or *imago mundi*, and the slippages in his control of the action represent both the inevitable failures of all mapmaking and specifically the defectiveness of a pre-Christian map lacking a center, like Jerusalem, that can hold it together; that center finally emerges in the destination of the tales, Canterbury, which as a type of Jerusalem retrospectively gives meaning to the whole.

A broad knowledge of the world and a willingness to build artistically on that knowledge, however, do not necessarily imply the openness to or sympathy for other cultures that we saw hinted at by Fyler and DiMarco. In her essay "Geographies of Desire: Orientalism in Chaucer's *Legend of Good Women*," Sheila Delany debates the question of Chaucer's attitude toward the Islamic infidel by considering his poetic response to the kinds of crusades that were still part of English foreign policy in the late fourteenth century. In part, Professor Delany also sets up this debate as a vehicle for testing the applicability of Said's theory of Orientalism to Chaucer. While, on the one hand, there were plenty of medieval critics of crusading adventures, foreign aspirations had their energetic apologists too, like Philippe de Mézières. Placing Chaucer on this continuum is not a simple manner, as the complex ironies and counterironies of the *Legend of Good Women* demonstrate. Just as this poem's counterpoint of victim and villain works simultaneously to undermine the virtue of both men and women, so it also casts its oriental characters—both male and female—under a shadow of excess and irrationality. The result is to make Chaucer, in Delany's view, a prime example of a medieval Orientalist, in the several senses in which Edward Said deploys that term. Indeed, in contrast to Woman whose difference from Man dissolves under the aspect of eternity, the Oriental is for Chaucer an unredeemable Other.

Feminist concerns also take center stage in Susan Schibanoff's "Worlds Apart: Orientalism, Antifeminism, and Heresy in Chaucer's Man of Law's Tale." For both Professors Schibanoff and Delany the misogyny of Chaucer's poetry and its religious chauvinism are mutually reinforcing, although Schibanoff to an extent reverses Delany in seeing the sexual category of woman as ultimately more inassimilable than the religious category of Muslim. Building on Jonathan Dollimore's theories of "transgressive proximity,"[25] Schibanoff positions the Islamic Other in opposition to the pagan

Others in the tale: Defined as a heretic by such medieval authorities as Peter the Venerable, the Muslim served as the most dangerous kind of religious Other, possessing a threatening proximity to the Christian, which required decisive and energetic repudiation. Women were likewise condemned by a "rhetoric of proximity," the more "mannish" (like the mothers-in-law in Chaucer's tale) the more deplorable. In comparison with Chaucer's sources, the ease of the Syrian Muslims' conversion, in Schibanoff's reading, contrasts with the tale's dramatic presentation of religious difference once Custance arrives in Northumberland. Similarly, the most dangerous women in the tale are those who impersonate men. Schibanoff extends this reading to the tale's endlink, where she connects up the concern with heresy (in Harry Bailly's remarks about the Parson's Lollady) to the restoration of "fraternal ties" in the *Canterbury Tales*; as is frequently the case in this complex work, Chaucer manages to have it both ways, implicating the Man of Law's hearty religio-sexual *communitas* while at the same time reinscribing it.

The *Canterbury Tales*, as the essays gathered here show, includes places both literal and figurative, both undeniably actual and deeply symbolic. If the "Asia" of the Prioress remains a shadowy entity, intimating fears of the unknown, the outside, growth, and change, the Oxford and Cambridge of the Miller's Tale and the Reeve's Tale emerge as distinctively realized locales familiar to the poet and easily recognizable to his audience. If the classical world described by the Knight carries with it the weight of cultural tradition, the Mongol Empire narrated by his son displays Chaucer's knowledge of the political realities of a world within his memory. For the *Tales* themselves a return journey was planned, one that would culminate in a meal at a specific tavern in a specific suburb of London, Southwark, that had its own unseemly reputation,[26] but this is a journey that, by accident or design, never occurs, and the *Tales*, as we have them, end instead just outside Canterbury, in a nameless "thrope" (X.12) with clearly apocalyptic overtones. It thus seems appropriate to this rhythm of point and counterpoint to end our own journey through Chaucer's places by imitating that return that never happens, by bringing Chaucer home to England by way of all the places, foreign in time and space, through which he travels in his verse.

Derek Pearsall's "Chaucer and Englishness," the final and most recently published essay in the book, maintains this tension between distance and closeness, and between literal and symbolic, in its perspective on "Englishness." In this analysis by an Englishman contemplating his home from abroad, "Englishness" is regarded from the outside in and from the inside out. Perhaps not surprisingly, the sense of cultural estrangement that leads to such an objectification of national character was not strange to Chaucer and his time (or indeed to any time), as Professor Pearsall traces a pattern of xenophobia and prenational communalism in the English language and in medieval English behavior toward Others, like the Flemish. But xenophobia has little to do with national character, as Pearsall demonstrates first by arguing that no usefully developed sense of English "nationhood" existed at Chaucer's time (in this he differs from Akbari), and second by showing that Chaucer's reputation as a poet of "Englishness" was never decisively established until the nineteenth century and then only in England. Stranger anxiety is a universal, rather than a cultural, phenomenon, at least until people make it so. If Pearsall denies the existence of a fourteenth-century "Englishness," however, he does not turn his back on all forms of cultural identity formation. In American culture and its lack of interest in Chaucer's "Englishness," Pearsall finds evidence of a "national consciousness" based on democratic and transcendental values, values that may also be reflected in Professor Pearsall's own (rather un-"English") observation that Chaucer was a "European rather than an Anglocentric poet."

It pleases me to end with Pearsall's essay for another reason, too. His cosmopolitan and universalist speculations suggest that a lively concern with the diversities of place and culture in the writings of Chaucer (or of any other author) does not necessarily lead to balkanizing or parochial conclusions. Chaucer was a man of his time, just as we are citizens of our own places and generations, and all times bring with them their peculiar narrownesses of vision, their prejudices, their disingenuous bids for power. As the essays printed here make clear, Chaucer—in his sly misogyny, his aspirations as a poet of the Greco-Roman classical past, his dehumanization of Jews and Muslims, his comic mockery of Celtic and Mongol storytelling—puts his own limitations on display. There can be no denying the moments when such shadows cut across Chaucer's verse, but there are also moments when the shadows lift, when Chaucer's distinctive self-consciousness reminds us of how much he actually and miraculously understood of what he was doing. Our recognition of the uneasy tension between these two Chaucers represents an important act of cross-cultural understanding, though across time rather than space, and reflects a faith in our shared humanity that I like to think he would have appreciated.

Notes

1. Natalia Lozovsky, *"The Earth Is Our Book": Geographical Knowledge in the Latin West* (Ann Arbor: University of Michigan Press, 2000), 6–34.
2. References to Chaucer's poetry are taken from *The Riverside Chaucer*, 3rd ed., ed. Larry D. Benson (Boston: Houghton Mifflin, 1987).
3. Mary B. Campbell, "Landscape, Writing, and Early Medieval Pilgrimage," in *Discovering New Worlds: Essays on Medieval Exploration and Imagination*, ed. Scott D. Westrem (New York: Garland, 1991), 11.
4. See, for example, Said's discussion of Dante in *Orientalism* (New York: Random House, 1978), 68–70.

5. For fantasies of Islam and Muslims as monstrous, see, for example, Michael Uebel, "Unthinking the Monster: Twelfth-Century Responses to Saracen Alterity," in *Monster Theory: Reading Culture*, ed. Jeffrey Jerome Cohen (Minneapolis: University of Minnesota Press, 1996), 264–91. Specifically for the link between Saracens and the race of dog-headed men, see also John Block Friedman, *The Monstrous Races in Medieval Art and Thought* (Cambridge, MA: Harvard University Press, 1981), 67–69, and Jeffrey Jerome Cohen, *Of Giants: Sex, Monsters, and the Middle Ages* (Minneapolis: University of Minnesota Press, 1999), 132–33.

6. Thomas F. Madden, *A Concise History of the Crusades* (Lanham, MD: Rowman & Littlefield), 202.

7. See the chapter "Commerce and the Crusades," in J. R. S. Phillips, *The Medieval Expansion of Europe* (Oxford: Oxford University Press, 1988), 26–55.

8. Madden, 11–14. As Madden explains, new developments in the analysis of the historical record reveal the limitations of earlier theories that the Crusades were often undertaken by younger sons desiring land and profit: "In short, most noblemen who joined the crusade did so from a simple and sincere love of God. As is still true, people gladly march off to horrible wars if they believe that the cause for which they fight is noble, true, and greater than themselves" (13).

9. Phillips, 32–33. See also Benedict Anderson, *Imagined Communities: Reflections on the Origin and Spread of Nationalism*, rev. ed. (London: Verso, 1991), 12–19.

10. This is not to say that color was unimportant in the medieval discourse of difference, or to deny that it was negatively charged; see, for example, Geraldine Heng, "The Romance of England," in *The Postcolonial Middle Ages*, ed. Jeffrey Jerome Cohen (New York: St. Martin's Press, 2000), 140–41, 163–64 nn. 7–8. As Heng herself notes, however, "baptism often whitens the skin color of blacks and partial blacks, indicating that the spiritual essence conferred by religion can have priority over the genetic essence conferred by the biologism of color" (163 n.7).

11. Jews, of course, could and did convert to Islam and Christianity during the Middle Ages; I refer here to the virulence of medieval anti-Semitism and to the lack of a messianic or territorial destiny for medieval Judaism. See also *Chaucer and the Jews*, ed. Sheila Delany (New York: Routledge, forthcoming).

12. Iain Higgins, *Writing East: The "Travels" of Sir John Mandeville* (Philadelphia: University of Pennsylvania Press, 1997), 79. See also Higgins's unblinking account of *The Book* [of Sir John Mandeville]'s profound anti-Semitism (79–81).

13. Kathleen Biddick, "Coming out of Exile: Dante on the Orient Express," in *The Postcolonial Middle Ages*, 36. See also Biddick's comments on the ways that medievalists reproduce the problems of Said's historical narrative by either deploying the objective distances of modernity against the Middle Ages or by rehabilitating the Middle Ages as "a non-Orientalist Golden Age" (39). Also useful for rethinking the temporal marginalization of the Middle Ages are Kathleen Davis's and John M. Ganim's essays in the same volume:

respectively, "Time Behind the Veil: The Media, the Middle Ages, and Orientalism Now," 105–22, and "Native Studies: Orientalism and Medievalism," 123–34.

14. Or even, as Suzanne Conklin Akbari argues, the dichotomy North/South; see "From Due East to True North: Orientalism and Orientation," in *The Postcolonial Middle Ages*, 19–34.

15. Idolaters were composed chiefly of Hindus and Buddhists; see, for example, Marco Polo, *The Travels*, trans. Ronald Latham (Harmondsworth: Penguin, 1958), 85–92, 247–58.

16. Marcia L. Colish, *Medieval Foundations of the Western Intellectual Tradition, 400–1400* (New Haven, CT: Yale University Press, 1997), xi.

17. See, for example, Part III of Colish's study, cited above; "Early Medieval Civilizations Compared," 113–72.

18. Salman Rushdie, "The Courter," in *East, West* (New York: Pantheon, 1994), 211.

19. Most versions of this tale do not specifically name the setting as does Chaucer; see the explanatory note to VII.488, in the *Riverside Chaucer*, 914.

20. David Wallace, "Chaucer and the Absent City," in *Chaucer's England: Literature in Historical Context*, ed. Barbara A. Hanawalt (Minneapolis: University of Minnesota Press, 1992), 59–90. A revised version of this essay appears as Chapter 6 of Wallace's *Chaucerian Polity: Absolutist Lineages and Associational Forms in England and Italy* (Stanford, CA: Stanford Univeristy Press, 1997), 156–81.

21. See, for example, "The Absent City," cited earlier; also, "In Flaundres," *Studies in the Age of Chaucer* 19 (1997): 63–91, and *Chaucerian Polity*, cited above.

22. Kathryn L. Lynch, "East Meets West in Chaucer's Squire's and Franklin's Tales," *Speculum* 70 (1995): 531; see also Bleeth, this volume.

23. Gardiner Stillwell, "Chaucer in Tartary," *Review of English Studies* 24 (1948): 177–88.

24. See the responses in *PMLA*, Forum, 98 (1983): 902–4, and 99 (1984): 109–12.

25. Jonathan Dollimore, *Sexual Dissidence: Augustine to Wilde, Freud to Foucault* (Oxford: Clarendon Press, 1991).

26. Wallace, "The Absent City," 59–61.

Selected Bibliography

The following bibliography is not comprehensive. It does not present all the sources used by each of the essays in this collection; for these, see the full bibliographic references provided in the notes to each essay. Instead, this bibliography includes a representative selection of some of the most useful and influential sources that might be consulted by a student or scholar seeking to situate him- or herself in the field of Chaucer studies and medieval geographic and cross-cultural scholarship, not including those made available in this volume. It is offered as a kind of starting bibliography in the field. For primary sources no attempt is made to compile a complete list of scholarly editions and translations; rather, the most easily accessible, authoritative English translations are listed. Brief annotations are included when a book's title is not explanatory.

Primary Sources

Boccaccio, Giovanni. *Decameron*. Trans. John Payne, rev. Charles S. Singleton. Berkeley: University of California Press, 1982.

Chaucer, Geoffrey. *The Riverside Chaucer*. 3rd edition. Gen. ed. Larry D. Benson. Boston: Houghton Mifflin, 1987.

Dawson, Christopher, ed. *Mission to Asia*. Medieval Academy Reprints for Teaching 8. Toronto: University of Toronto Press, 1980. [Originally published as *The Mongol Mission*. London: Sheed and Ward, 1955. Includes the travel narratives of John of Plano Carpini and William of Rubruck, who journeyed to Mongolia in the mid thirteenth century, as well as excerpts from letters written by John of Monte Corvino, Andrew of Perugia, and Brother Peregrine, which are of lesser importance.]

Gower, John. *Confessio Amantis*. In *The English Works of John Gower*. Ed. G. C. Macaulay. EETS, e.s. 81–82. 1900–1. Rpt. Oxford: Oxford University Press, 1979.

Haddawy, Husain, trans. *The Arabian Nights*. New York: W. W. Norton, 1990.

Moseley, C. W. R. D., trans. *The Travels of Sir John Mandeville.* Harmondsworth: Penguin, 1983.

Petrus Alfonsi. *The Disciplina Clericalis.* Trans. and ed. Eberhard Hermes. English trans. P. R. Quarrie. Berkeley: University of California Press, 1977.

Polo, Marco. *The Travels.* Trans. Ronald Latham. Harmondsworth: Penguin, 1958.

Slessarev, Vsevolod, ed. and trans. *Prester John: The Letter and the Legend.* Minneapolis: University of Minnesota Press, 1959. [A modern English translation of a fifteenth-century French version of this letter from the mythical Indian Christian King Prester John to the rulers of Europe. Includes a useful historical introduction to the *Letter.*]

Stoneman, Richard, ed. *Legends of Alexander the Great.* London: J. M. Dent, 1994. [Translations of various short, but influential texts describing episodes in the career of Alexander the Great, including "Alexander's Letter to Aristotle," "The Letter of Pharasamanes to Hadrian (on the Wonders of the East)," an excerpt from the *Chronicle* of George the Monk, Palladius's "On the Life of the Brahmans," the Correspondence of Alexander and Dindimus, and a version of Alexander's journey to Paradise. The latest of these texts dates from before 1175, though an appendix shows their influence on early English literature.]

Yule, Henry, ed. *Cathay and the Way Thither, Being a Collection of Medieval Notices of China.* Vol. 2. London: Hakluyt Society, 1913. [Contains the Travels of Friar Odoric of Pordenone.]

Secondary Sources

Akehurst, F. R. P., and Stephanie Cain Van D'Elden, eds. *The Stranger in Medieval Society.* Medieval Cultures, 12. Minneapolis: University of Minnesota Press, 1997. [Essay collection.]

Anderson, Benedict. *Imagined Communities: Reflections on the Origin and Spread of Nationalism.* Rev. ed. London: Verso, 1991.

Asín Palacios, Miguel. *Islam and the Divine Comedy.* Ed. and trans. Harold Sutherland. London: Cass, 1968.

Atiya, Aziz S. *The Crusade in the Later Middle Ages.* 2nd ed. 1938. Rpt. New York: Kraus Reprint Corporation, 1965.

Beazley, C. Raymond. *The Dawn of Modern Geography.* Vol. 3. *A History of Exploration and Geographical Science from the Middle of the Thirteenth Century to the Early Years of the Fifteenth Century (c. A. D. 1260–1420).* Oxford: Clarendon Press, 1906.

Campbell, Mary. *The Witness and the Other World: Exotic European Travel Writing, 400–1600.* Ithaca, NY: Cornell University Press, 1988.

Cohen, Jeffrey Jerome. *Of Giants: Sex, Monsters, and the Middle Ages.* Medieval Cultures, 17. Minneapolis: University of Minnesota Press, 1999.

———, ed. *The Postcolonial Middle Ages.* New York: St. Martin's Press, 2000. [Essay collection.]

Colish, Marcia L. *Medieval Foundations of the Western Intellectual Tradition, 400–1400.* New Haven, CT: Yale University Press, 1997.

Cornelia, Marie. "Chaucer's Tartarye." *Dalhousie Review* 57 (1977): 81–89.

Daniel, Norman. *Islam and the West: The Making of an Image*. Edinburgh: University Press, 1962.

Delany, Sheila. "Chaucer's Prioress, the Jews, and the Muslims." *Medieval Encounters: Jewish, Christian and Muslim Culture in Confluence and Dialogue* 5 (1999): 199–213.

———. *The Naked Text: Chaucer's Legend of Good Women*. Berkeley: University of California Press, 1994.

Friedman, John Block. *The Monstrous Races in Medieval Art and Thought*. Cambridge, MA: Harvard University Press, 1981.

Fyler, John M. "Chaucerian Romance and the World beyond Europe." In *Literary Aspects of Courtly Culture*. ed. Donald Maddox and Sara Sturm-Maddox. Cambridge, England: D. S. Brewer, 1994. 257–63.

Gittes, Katharine S. *Framing the Canterbury Tales: Chaucer and the Medieval Frame Narrative Tradition*. New York: Greenwood Press, 1991.

Hanawalt, Barbara A., ed. *Chaucer's England: Literature in Historical Context*. Minneapolis, University of Minnesota Press, 1992. [Essay collection.]

Harley, J. B., and David Woodward. *The History of Cartography*. Vol. 1. *Cartography in Prehistoric, Ancient, and Medieval Europe and the Mediterranean*. Chicago: University of Chicago Press, 1987.

Higgins, Iain Macleod. *Writing East: The "Travels" of Sir John Mandeville*. Philadelphia: University of Pennsylvania Press, 1997.

Howard, Donald R. *Writers and Pilgrims: Medieval Pilgrim Narratives and Their Posterity*. Berkeley: University of California Press, 1980.

Ingham, Patricia Clare. *Sovereign Fantasies: Arthurian Romance and the Making of Britain*. Philadelphia: University of Pennsylvania Press, 2001.

Jordan, Carmel. "Soviet Archaeology and the Setting of the Squire's Tale." *The Chaucer Review* 22 (1987): 128–40.

Kimble, George H. T. *Geography in the Middle Ages*. New York: Russell & Russell, 1938.

Kritzeck, James. *Peter the Venerable and Islam*. Princeton: Princeton University Press, 1964.

Lewis, Bernard. *Islam and the West*. New York: Oxford University Press, 1993.

Lynch, Kathryn L. "Storytelling, Exchange, and Constancy: East and West in Chaucer's Man of Law's Tale." *The Chaucer Review* 33 (1999): 409–22.

Madden, Thomas F. *A Concise History of the Crusades*. Lanham, MD: Rowman & Littlefield, 1999.

Magoun, Francis Peabody. *A Chaucer Gazetteer*. Chicago: University of Chicago Press, 1961. [Comprehensive dictionary of names in Chaucer with geographical connections.]

Menocal, Maria Rosa. *The Arabic Role in Medieval Literary History: A Forgotten Heritage*. Philadelphia: University of Pennsylvania Press, 1987.

Metlitzki, Dorothee. *The Matter of Araby in Medieval England*. New Haven, CT: Yale University Press, 1977.

Ridley, Florence H. *The Prioress and the Critics*. English Studies, 30. Berkeley: University of California Press, 1965. [A discussion of earlier criticism, focusing in part on the conventionalism of the Prioress's anti-semitism.]

Romm, James S. *The Edges of the Earth in Ancient Thought: Geography, Exploration, and Fiction.* Princeton, NJ: Princeton University Press, 1992.

Said, Edward W. *Culture and Imperialism.* New York: Alfred A. Knopf, 1993.

————. *Orientalism.* New York: Random House, 1994. [First published in 1978; this edition includes Said's afterword, which discusses his reflections on the book's reception.]

Schildgen, Brenda Deen. *Pagans, Tartars, Moslems, and Jews in Chaucer's Canterbury Tales.* Gainsville, FL: University Press of Florida, 2001.

Southern, R. W. *Western Views of Islam in the Middle Ages.* Cambridge, MA: Harvard University Press, 1962.

Tomasch, Sylvia, and Sealy Gilles, eds. *Text and Territory: Geographical Imagination in the European Middle Ages.* Philadelphia: University of Pennsylvania Press, 1998. [Essay collection.]

Wallace, David. "In Flaundres." *Studies in the Age of Chaucer* 19 (1997): 63–91. [1996 Biennial Chaucer Lecture on the significance of Flanders in Chaucer's writing, as a kind of border territory that both distinguishes the English from and links them to the European continent.]

Westrem, Scott D., ed. *Discovering New Worlds: Essays on Medieval Exploration and Imagination.* New York: Garland, 1991. [Essay collection.]

Wright, John Kirtland. *The Geographical Lore of the Time of the Crusades: A Study in the History of Medieval Science and Tradition in Western Europe.* 1925. Rpt. [expanded] New York: American Geographical Society, 1965.

Zacher, Christian K. *Curiosity and Pilgrimage: The Literature of Discovery in Fourteenth-Century England.* Baltimore, MD: Johns Hopkins University Press, 1976.

Orientalism and the Critical History of the Squire's Tale

KENNETH BLEETH

The history of the Squire's Tale's reception has been surveyed twice—by David Lawton in *Chaucer's Narrators* (1985), and by Donald Baker in his 1990 Variorum edition.[1] Although both Lawton and Baker touch on what Kathryn Lynch calls the tale's "aura of exotic alterity," neither addresses directly the connections between its critical fortunes and its oriental subject matter.[2] In what follows, I examine some representative responses to the poem from the late eighteenth century to the 1970s, and suggest that Orientalist discourse—the ways of imagining and describing the East that have been given their most influential formulation in Edward Said's *Orientalism* (1978)—has left its mark on the study of virtually all aspects of the tale.[3] I conclude by looking briefly at several commentaries written since the appearance of Said's book. In contrast to the earlier body of criticism, in which Orientalist assumptions remain largely unexamined, these more recent assessments of the Squire's Tale engage directly with the issues raised by Said's work and the extensive literature that has grown up around it, arguing, among other things, that Chaucer's poem reflects, and reflects upon, attitudes toward the East that Said restricts to the post-Enlightenment period. Indeed, the most recent work on the Squire's Tale takes this trend a step further, by complicating and interrogating Said's own assumptions.

Several of the themes that figure prominently in later critical responses to the Squire's Tale's Eastern setting are already present in the first substantial comment on the poem, that of Thomas Warton in his *History of English Poetry* (1774–1806). In describing the Squire's Tale as an "Arabian fiction engrafted on Gothic chivalry," Warton imagines the work as an encounter between East and West, one in which the motifs and styles of medieval romance have been artfully adapted to accommodate oriental material. Warton's fascination with the tale's "imagination" (which he explicitly distinguishes from "arbitrary fancy") is evident in the dozen pages he devotes to

21

the "wonderful discoveries and mysterious inventions" of Eastern learning
that constitute analogues to the gifts that the stranger knight brings from the
king of Arabia and India, and in his tracing of the magical elements in Western romance to accounts of Arabian astrology and magic. But his admiration
of the glamorous surface of Part 1 of the Squire's Tale is qualified by his
ambivalence about the objects that appear in the court of the Tartar king
Cambyuskan. On the one hand, the horse, ring, mirror, and sword are
instances of natural magic, "a favorite pursuit of the Arabians, by which they
imposed false appearances on the spectator." On the other hand, he remarks
of the horse of brass that "by such inventions we are willing to be deceived.
These are the triumphs of deception over truth."[4] Warton's observations
exemplify in condensed form two opposed impulses displayed at greater
length in Western narratives of the orient before and since: an attitude of
wonder before the marvels of the East, and a skeptical or rationalist need to
demystify the marvelous.

Some 80 years after Warton, the Reverend John Jephson, in his notes to
Robert Bell's edition of Chaucer (1854–1856), displays a similarly divided
response to the Squire's Tale's oriental subject. Jephson likens the poem's
appeal to that of the *Arabian Nights*—for much of the eighteenth and nineteenth centuries the *locus classicus* for images of Eastern exoticism—and
praises Chaucer's "marvellous powers of *picture-writing*," his skill in "faithfully preserv[ing]" the "special attributes of Oriental fiction" by bringing the
"gorgeous details and fantastical enchantments" of the Eastern scene before
the mind's eye. At the same time, Jephson resists surrendering to the pleasures of the text: "brilliancy of fancy the Easterns certainly possess, but it is
the fancy of the opium-eater; their highest aspirations never contemplate any
enjoyment beyond that of sensuality or power . . . the radical defects of this
style of fiction [are] its want of aim and mere sensuousness." The essentializing of the "Easterns" in this passage, the conflation of aesthetic and moral
judgments, the figures of speech associating the East with waywardness and
sensuality are familiar features of Orientalist discourse in the nineteenth century and the early years of the twentieth century. Also, insofar as the orient
can be understood as textually constructed by Western writers, Jephson participates in this construction by locating the East's fundamental differences
from the West in the respective literary productions of the two cultures: the
dazzling descriptive skill of the oriental fabulists is limited by their inability
to rise above the material ("the dignity of suffering virtue finds no responsive
chord in their hearts, which are of the earth, earthy"); the author of the *Quest
of the Holy Grail* and the Chaucer of the Man of Law's Tale, on the other
hand, are "impressed with a feeling of responsibility, and of the immutability
of the law of right and wrong, which gives an elevation even to their most
extravagant flights. Such moral elevation is sought for in vain in Eastern
romance."[5] By establishing the East as the West's binary opposite, Jephson is

able to represent certain defining qualities of the European character as precisely what the corresponding oriental texts lack.

Jephson's observations, written at the high tide of British colonial expansion, are characteristic of their historical moment. Although the overt xenophobia displayed here is absent from later commentary on the Squire's Tale, post-Victorian scholarship on the tale (and not only British scholarship) attests to the persistence of the beliefs about oriental otherness that inform Jephson's remarks. A recurrent motif is the tale's uniqueness among the poet's works; "so unlike anything else [Chaucer] wrote," in Alfred Pollard's phrase, it is frequently defined by its marginal relation to the dominant concerns of the *Canterbury Tales*.[6] In contrast to those texts that deal with marriage, commerce, and class conflict, the Squire's narrative of feasting, magic, and talking birds promises a short-term escape from the serious business of life. In his fervently nationalistic *Chaucer's England*, published in 1869, Matthew Browne praises Chaucer's embodiment of the English domestic ethos, the "fixed centre" of the family hearth that is the true "heart of England."[7] Writing of the Squire's Tale some 40 years later, John Matthews Manly similarly endows spatial terms with an ethical resonance; if Chaucer's England—and the West more generally—define what is known and valued, then this "curious . . . flight of the oriental imagination," set "in the remote east . . . beyond the Christian pale," lies "beyond the central realm of sober experience."[8] The image of the East as (in Mary Campbell's phrase) "essentially 'Elsewhere,' " at the distant periphery of a center that is England, is implied as well in Lilian Winstanley's admiring comments on Chaucer's transformation of human lovers into birds in Part 2 of the poem ("Chaucer adds an element of the remote and fantastic to the tale, which puts it in perfect accord with the Eastern spirit . . . reproduc-[ing] the true feeling of the more primitive and less civilised East"), and in John Livingston Lowes's sketch of Chaucer "turning for a moment [in the Squire's Tale] from his world of wool and hides and ditches" to a realm of "magic and illusion and enchanted princesses, in that remote and mysterious orient where anything may happen."[9] In this little vignette, the unpredictable events and evanescent phenomena of Chaucer's Eastern romance define by contrast the essential Chaucerian reality as rooted in a solid world of hard work and unglamorous material facts.

The notion that Lowes advances in passing—that the Squire's Tale is a temporary truancy from Chaucer's proper subjects—serves as the governing idea of Gardiner Stillwell's "Chaucer in Tartary" (1948). As both Lawton and Baker suggest, in its alertness to tone, Stillwell's essay may be thought of as marking the beginning of modern criticism of the poem.[10] But Stillwell's conception of the poet is a thoroughly traditional one; the tale's humor and irony are produced, in his account, by a clash between Chaucer's "humanity" and "commonsense point of view"—characteristic attributes of the quintessentially English figure created by nineteenth-century readers—and the exoticism of the tale's Eastern setting.[11] Questioning the dominant interpretation of the poem as "a romantic joy-ride to a Tartary of golden atmosphere and magic trappings" (177), Stillwell imagines it instead as an aborted travel narrative in which Chaucer the Tourist discovers that "all is not well with him in these strange regions" (188) and stages a strategic withdrawal. In Stillwell's view, Chaucer's uneasiness at the spectacle of oriental difference is partly a matter of temperament. But cultural conditioning plays a role as well. The observation that Chaucer is "not altogether at home in Tartary" (179) reminds us that the personal traits Stillwell attributes to him—he is "realistic . . . sensible, pragmatic" (179, 187)—are also national ones, products of the identity-endowing properties of place. As Said points out, one possible textual response to the variety and strangeness of the orient is disengagement; describing Edward Lane's control of his protean material in *An Account of the Manners and Customs of the Modern Egyptians* (1836), Said observes that the author's "capacity to rein in his profuse subject matter with an unyielding bridle of discipline and detachment depends on his cold distance from Egyptian life."[12] In Stillwell's scenario, Chaucer (unlike Lane) is unable to maintain the disinterested stance appropriate to the European spectator of oriental marvels. Aware of his unsuitability to the task before him, the poet intrudes nervously into his narrative, treating his subject with "elvish elusiveness" (183), "ironic understatement" (183), and "whimsical *occupatio*" (188). Such devices of self-presentation, elsewhere in Chaucer's works hallmarks of his sophistication, produce in this Eastern tale only "artistic confusion" (188). For Stillwell, Chaucer's departure from his familiar topics proves to be a false step: "precisely those traits we love most in Chaucer—sagacious realism, humour, critical intellect, subtlety of mood, and natural human gusto—keep him from maintaining the wide-eyed *naiveté* and quaint curiosity required by his theme, and make him realize that it is better to abandon his attempt to force an entrance into fairyland than to get stuck in a magic casement" (188). In his figure of the poet as a burglar or housebreaker, Stillwell represents the writing of the Squire's Tale as a transgressive act, one that (as the Keatsian echoes imply) constitutes an escape into romantic fantasy that goes against the grain of Chaucer's clear-minded genius.[13]

Stillwell is interested primarily in the effect on the poem's verbal texture of Chaucer's venture into foreign territory. Several more recent discussions evaluate the implications of the Squire's Tale's Eastern setting in broadly social terms. In his 1973 article "Chaucer's *Squire's Tale* and the Decline of Chivalry," Stanley Kahrl discovers in the poem symptoms of the waning Middle Ages. Contrasting the Squire's "incoherent" narrative with the Knight's "celebration of classical order in the chivalric world," Kahrl links the Squire's "penchant for the exotic" with a more widespread "impulse toward exoticism and disorder at work in the courts of late medieval Europe."[14] In *The Idea of the Canterbury Tales* (1976), Donald Howard interprets the Squire's flirtation with the strange and the remote as Chaucer's comment on the hollowness of contemporary aristocratic "fads and fashions." As "the only tale in which we get the exotic Mandevillian world of oriental travel which had already captured the imagination of Chaucer's contemporaries," the Squire's narrative adds something new to the work as a whole. But the ineptness of "this fantastical fragment" suggests that the taste for "hearsay tales of distant princes" is "empty and jejune."[15]

Although Stillwell makes no distinction between narrator and author, Kahrl and Howard read the tale dramatically, laying the blame for the tale's perceived inadequacies at the Squire's rather than the poet's door. The limitations of the dramatic principle for a reading of the Squire's Tale have been persuasively outlined by Lawton; among other things, this approach creates a narrator whose supposed character flaws include, inter alia, lechery, triviality, intellectual incapacity, and (more benignly) the callowness of youth.[16] In some of the observations about the Squire's youthfulness and its accompanying superficiality, we can see Orientalist assumptions at work. According to Nevill Coghill, the "young Squire," whose "head is full of wonders, horses of brass, magic mirrors, and swords . . . [is] still in the tapestry world of Chaucer's own youthful vision," which the poet had since "passed beyond . . . into the common light of day."[17] E. T. Donaldson suggests that the tale is perhaps a product of Chaucer's own early years, and finds it "graced by a kind of youthful enthusiasm and enterprise." But he wonders whether an "oriental romance, full of magic and marvels and plot upon plot," could have engaged the mature poet's serious commitment.[18] And Robert P. Miller, contrasting the tale's "air of fantasy" with the historical and geographical solidity of the Knight's Tale, views its romantic aura as "a reflection of the yet-undisciplined emblematic youth whose dreams and desires do not yet conform to what Chaucer thought of as life's deeper realities."[19] As historians of the oriental tale have shown, a taste for exotic stories was regularly taken in the eighteenth and early nineteenth centuries as a sign of an immature and unruly imagination; the "wild and diversified incidents" of the *Arabian Nights*, Richard Hole writes in 1797, "are seldom thoroughly relished but by children."[20] In the comments I've just cited from three twentieth-century critics, we see the persistence of these beliefs about the specialized appeal of oriental fables. Building on the ostensible connection between Eastern marvels and adolescent fantasies, Coghill, Donaldson, and Miller place the Squire's Tale in the context of Chaucer's career and assess its literary merits; the poet's pleasure in exotic fictions is projected retrospectively onto the Squire, while Chaucer himself, leaving behind such unformed enthusiasms, evolves into the father of English verse.

The impulse to explain, control, or restructure oriental difference is visible not only in responses to the Squire's Tale's subject matter and narrative voice, but also in discussions of its sources and form. Although numerous Eastern analogues to the tale's plot motifs were collected at an early date, Chaucerians in search of the poet's immediate models were frustrated by the absence of any clear body of sources such as existed for almost all the other *Canterbury Tales*. The possibility that Chaucer might have assembled the Squire's Tale from what Robert K. Root rather dismissively calls "scraps of knowledge about Tartary and the Far East [that] he had picked up in reading or conversation" was conceded—but only reluctantly.[21] In place of such ephemeral and fragmentary origins, more authoritative sources—now lost—were proposed: Manly believed that Chaucer drew on a single Eastern tale, translated into French or English; Lilian Winstanley thought it probable that Chaucer was "directly following some unknown original" in Latin or Italian; H. R. Hinckley goes Manly and Winstanley one better, positing the existence of an entire "Genghis cycle of romance (similar to the cycles of Alexander and Charlemagne)."[22] For scholars bent on discovering antecedents for all of Chaucer's poems, his oriental tale presented a problem: "the genesis of the Squire's Tale," Pollard remarks in the introduction to his 1899 edition, "has baffled investigation more than any other."[23] One way out of the impasse was to minimize the uncertainties surrounding this genesis by remaking it on familiar Western patterns.

The challenge that the Squire's Tale poses for positivistic source study is paralleled by scholarly puzzlement about its structure; the précis of future events inserted by the Squire at the end of Part 2 suggests one story generating another apparently unrelated one, an organizational principle "unique in Chaucer's work."[24] This structural singularity has been connected with Chaucer's (or the Squire's) imitation of an Eastern literary type. In his 1942 article "The Genre of Chaucer's *Squire's Tale*," Haldeen Braddy argued that the synopsis of further adventures implies a continuation modeled on the "box within a box" shape of the oriental framing tale, in which a principal story serves as the frame and is followed by several intercalated incidents before the framing tale is resumed and concluded.[25] Noting that the Squire's excessively leisurely narration recalls the atmosphere of the *Arabian Nights*, Harry Berger, Jr., observes that the poem's listeners are "threatened by a prospectus that would have surely exhausted the combined lung-power of Scheherazade and Ariosto"; in contrast to the Knight's carefully structured narration, "the *Squire's Tale* displays a failure of control."[26] Derek Pearsall also links the young pilgrim's narrative gaucheries with his attempt to reproduce an Eastern form: in the "staggering synopsis" of coming attractions we see the tale "growing . . . almost of [its] own will, into a monstrous oriental saga, and the Squire is no longer in control."[27]

Behind these images of the oriental tale as a many-limbed beast that threatens the youthful Squire with loss of control is the motif of the East as insidiously dangerous, striving to undermine rationality with its excesses. This familiar mythology makes itself felt in a well-known suggestion about what is perhaps the most vexed question in Squire's Tale scholarship—that of the tale's apparent incompleteness. At the conclusion of his essay, Braddy observes that the Squire's prospectus seems to imply that Cambalo wedded his sister Canacee, and that the closest analogue to the Canacee–falcon episode appears in a section of the *Arabian Nights* that includes a prominent account of incest. Braddy argues that the abrupt termination of the Squire's Tale is connected with the poet's discovery of "this unattractive theme" in his source: "we may presume that as a man Chaucer would not tolerate the idea of incest, because as a poet he certainly speaks against it"—Braddy's evidence for the latter assertion being the Pardoner's allusion to Lot, who in his drunkenness lay unwittingly by his two daughters, and the Man of Law's observation that Chaucer (presumably unlike Gower) wrote no word of "thilke wikke ensample of Canacee, / That loved hir owene brother synfully" (Introduction to the Man of Law's Tale, II.78–79).[28] In his translation of the *Arabian Nights* (1839–1841), Edward Lane excluded the lengthy incest narrative because it "depends upon incidents of a most objectionable nature."[29] The Chaucer evoked by Braddy shares Lane's Victorian scruples; in his high-minded refusal to follow his oriental model where it might lead, he is a belated incarnation of the "healthy-souled man" "free from . . . uncontrollable irregularity of thought" prominent in popular conceptions of the poet in the late nineteenth and early twentieth centuries.[30] As Said has shown, European narratives of the orient often waver between a fascination with its novelty and suggestiveness and a need to contain this threatening otherness. Braddy's hypothesis that the poet stumbled unawares upon incest in his source story, which Lawton calls "fanciful, thinly based, and . . . unduly influential," has nevertheless maintained its hold on the critical imagination, in part because it allows readers to imagine a version of Chaucer who shares these contradictory impulses: Drawn ever more deeply into his sources by the lure of the exotic, the poet encounters the East at its most alien and unsettling, gathers his wits about him, and beats a hasty retreat.[31]

In the scholarship and criticism I have examined up to this point, observations about the Squire's Tale's Eastern setting and subject matter incorporate a set of mostly tacit assumptions about the orient and its relation to European culture. Over the past 15 years or so, several critics have taken a fresh look at the tale's cultural geography, but with a more nuanced sense of what's at stake in Chaucer's refashioning of Eastern romance—a self-awareness prompted in part by Said's book and the published responses to it. Although John Fyler's "Domesticating the Exotic in the *Squire's Tale*" (1988) makes no direct reference to Said's work, Fyler's reading demonstrates that some of the impulses Said locates in modern Orientalist discourse—the wish to control or assimilate the Other and the corresponding resistance of the exotic to demystification, the vacillation between the alien and the familiar—are present as well in Chaucer's tale, reflecting both the paradoxes of romance as a genre and the ambivalent motives of the Squire as a storyteller.[32] In a brief but suggestive commentary that builds on Fyler's observations, Susan Crane introduces gender into the tale's program for managing the exotic: Although Cambyuskan's daughter Canacee "is an instance of the exotic for the narrator," her own relation to the marvelous is contrasted with the masculine desire for appropriation and control.[33] Gender is also one of the subjects of Kathryn Lynch's "East Meets West in Chaucer's Squire's and Franklin's Tales"; examining the ways in which Chaucer consciously "out-Easts the East" in the former work, Lynch sees the Squire as "setting up an argument about women, pleasure, and the East that the Franklin will dismantle."[34] Finally, in an essay that seeks to revise and historicize Said's paradigm of East and West as mirroring binaries, Suzanne Akbari argues that the dominant medieval world division was tripartite (Asia, Europe, and Africa), and uneven; Chaucer's pairing of the Squire's Tale and the Franklin's Tale forms part of her evidence for the gradual emergence, in the late fourteenth century, of the soon-to-be-standard dichotomy—a "cold, dispassionate, northerly Occident" that is the mirror image of an orient associated with heat and the sun.[35]

In their engagement, implicit and explicit, with the issues raised by Said's work, these four responses form part of a larger ongoing scholarly conversation about the usefulness of postcolonial methodologies for the study of the Middle Ages. (As Akbari's interrogation of one of Said's central ideas suggests, future contributions to this conversation are more likely to arise from a productive friction with Said's perspective rather than, as has been the case until recently, by employing him as a bulwark or authority.[36]) Unlike criticism of other Chaucerian texts, which has only in the past decade taken up the topic of Chaucer's Orientalism, readers of the Squire's Tale have traditionally shown an interest in Chaucer's adoption of the culturally alien Eastern romance. This record of attention offers an unusually full picture of the unspoken premises that have shaped attitudes toward the Squire's Tale's oriental subject over time, and provides a historical perspective from which we can judge the impact, both realized and potential, of recent work in cultural studies on the reception of Chaucer's text.

Notes

1. David Lawton, *Chaucer's Narrators* (Cambridge: Brewer, 1985), 106–129; Geoffrey Chaucer, *The Squire's Tale*, ed. Donald C. Baker (Norman: University of Oklahoma Press, 1990), 59–74.
2. Kathryn L. Lynch, "East Meets West in Chaucer's Squire's and Franklin's Tales," *Speculum* 70 (1995): 531.
3. Edward W. Said, *Orientalism* (New York: Pantheon, 1978).

4. Thomas Warton, *The History of English Poetry* (London: Dodsley, 1778), 1: 398, 400, 402, 415.

5. *The Poetical Works of Geoffrey Chaucer*, ed. Robert Bell, assisted by John M. Jephson (London: Griffin, [1870]), 2: 200–01. On Orientalism and textuality, see Said, 92–95.

6. Geoffrey Chaucer, *The Squire's Tale*, ed. A.W. Pollard (London: Macmillan, 1899), ix.

7. Matthew Browne, pseud. [William Rands], *Chaucer's England* (London: Hurst and Blackett, 1869), 1: 249–251.

8. John Matthews Manly, "A Knight Ther Was," *Transactions and Proceedings of the American Philological Association* 38 (1907): 91, 90 n.1.

9. Mary B. Campbell, *The Witness and the Other World: Exotic European Travel Writing, 400–1600* (Ithaca: Cornell University Press, 1988), 48; Geoffrey Chaucer, *The Clerkes Tale and the Squieres Tale*, ed. Lilian Winstanley (Cambridge: Cambridge University Press, 1908), cxiv, cxxiii; John Livingston Lowes, *Geoffrey Chaucer and the Development of his Genius*. (Boston: Houghton Mifflin, 1934), 225–226.

10. Lawton, 110; Baker, 64–65.

11. Gardiner Stillwell, "Chaucer in Tartary," *Review of English Studies* 24 (1948): 179, 183 (subsequent references to Stillwell's essay will be cited in the body of my text). On the creation of Chaucer's Englishness, see Derek Pearsall, "Chaucer and Englishness," in *1998 Lectures and Memoirs. Proceedings of the British Academy* (Oxford, Oxford University Press, 1999), 77–99; and Steve Ellis, "English Chaucer," in *Chaucer at Large: The Poet in the Modern Imagination* (Minneapolis: University of Minnesota Press, 2000), 58–79.

12. Said, 162.

13. Stillwell was perhaps remembering Roger Sherman Loomis's romantic reverie in the opening sentence of *Celtic Myth and Arthurian Romance* (New York: Columbia University Press, 1927), 1: "To think of Medieval Romance is to gaze through magic casements opening on the foam of perilous seas in faery lands forlorn."

14. Stanley J. Kahrl, "Chaucer's *Squire's Tale* and the Decline of Chivalry," *Chaucer Review* 7 (1973): 195.

15. Donald R. Howard, *The Idea of the Canterbury Tales* (Berkeley: University of California Press, 1976), 266–267.

16. Lawton, 111–115; lechery: Chauncey Wood, "The Significance of Jousting and Dancing as Attributes of Chaucer's Squire," *English Studies* 52 (1971): 116–118; triviality: Joyce E. Peterson, "The Finished Fragment: A Reassessment of the *Squire's Tale*," *Chaucer Review* 5 (1970): 67; intellectual incapacity: Robert P. Miller, "Chaucer's Rhetorical Rendition of Mind: *The Squire's Tale*," in *Chaucer and the Craft of Fiction*, ed. Leigh A. Arrathoon (Rochester, Mich.: Solaris, 1986), 221 and passim; youthfulness: Derek Pearsall, "The Squire as Story-Teller," *University of Toronto Quarterly* 34 (1964): 83–84.

17. Nevill Coghill, *The Poet Chaucer* (London: Oxford University Press, 1949), 167.

18. *Chaucer's Poetry: An Anthology for the Modern Reader*, ed. E. T. Donaldson, 2nd ed. (New York: Ronald, 1975), 1086.

19. Miller, 219.

20. Richard Hole, *Remarks on the Arabian Nights' Entertainments* (1797), quoted in Brian Alderson, "Scheherazade in the Nursery," in *The* Arabian Nights *in English Literature: Studies in the Reception of* The Thousand and One Nights *into British Culture*, ed. Peter L. Caracciolo (New York: St. Martin's, 1988), 82; see also Peter L. Caracciolo, "Introduction," 3–4. At the beginning of Chapter 3 of his *Tales and Popular Fictions* (London: Whittaker, 1834), in which he speculates on the *Squire's Tale*'s possible oriental sources, Thomas Keightley notes the predilection of "the youthful mind" for the East and its wonders (32). As Said points out, "childlike/mature" is one of the pairs of terms typically used by British colonialist writers to express the relation of East to West (40).

21. Robert Kilburn Root, *The Poetry of Chaucer* (Boston: Houghton Mifflin, 1906), 270. The presumed orality of the *Squire's Tale*'s sources, implicitly or explicitly contrasted with written "auctoritee," is noted by Raymond Preston: "It seems to me that the man who was once amused by oriental magic gifts . . . such as the Squire speaks about, had now heard more than enough of them from traders, sailors, and preachers" (*Chaucer* [London: Sheed and Ward, 1952], 271); and Kahrl: "Chaucer stressed [in the prologue to *The Legend of Good Women*] that [the] historical matter which he derived from books was the fit subject for poetry rather than verbal reports because at least you can believe what you read in books" (199).

22. John Matthews Manly, "Marco Polo and the *Squire's Tale*," *PMLA* 11 (1896): 363; Winstanley, ci; Henry Barrett Hinckley, *Notes on Chaucer: A Commentary on the Prolog and Six Canterbury Tales* (Northampton, MA: Nonotuck, 1907), 211.

23. Pollard, vii.

24. Helen Cooper, *The Canterbury Tales*, 2nd ed. (Oxford: Oxford University Press, 1996), 223.

25. Haldeen Braddy, "The Genre of Chaucer's *Squire's Tale*," *Journal of English and Germanic Philology* 41 (1942): 279–290.

26. Harry Berger, Jr., "The F-Fragment of the *Canterbury Tales*: Part I," *Chaucer Review* 1 (1966): 88, 91.

27. Pearsall, "Squire as Story-Teller," 88, 90 (but see Pearsall's partial retraction of this dramatic ironic interpretation, in *The Canterbury Tales* [London: George Allen & Unwin, 1985], 140).

28. Braddy, 289. The citation is from *The Riverside Chaucer*, 3rd ed., ed. Larry D. Benson (Boston: Houghton Mifflin, 1987).

29. *The Arabian Nights' Entertainments; or The Thousand and One Nights*, trans. Edward William Lane (New York: Pickwick, 1927), 1069.

30. On the "healthy Chaucer," see Ellis, 17–31 passim. (The quoted phrases, from F. J. Furnivall and Percy W. Ames, are cited by Ellis, 20.)

31. Lawton, 109.

32. John M. Fyler, "Domesticating the Exotic in the *Squire's Tale*," *ELH* 55 (1988): 1–26.

33. Susan Crane, *Gender and Romance in Chaucer's* Canterbury Tales (Princeton: Princeton University Press, 1994), 145.

34. Lynch, 541, 530.
35. Suzanne Conklin Akbari, "From Due East to True North: Orientalism and Orientation," in *The Postcolonial Middle Ages*, ed. Jeffrey Jerome Cohen (New York: St. Martin's, 2000), 29–30.
36. For two additional examples of dissent from and dialogue with Said, see Kathleen Biddick, "Coming out of Exile: Dante on the Orient Express," in Cohen, *Postcolonial Middle Ages*, 35–52, and Kathleen Davis, "Time Behind the Veil: The Media, the Middle Ages, and Orientalism Now," ibid., 105–22.

Domesticating the Exotic in the Squire's Tale

JOHN M. FYLER

To the memory of Donald R. Howard

Surely one of the most curious features of romance as a genre is its preoccupation with incest. This most ancient of taboos is succumbed to or narrowly avoided in a number of medieval English romances, among them *Sir Degaré, Sir Eglamour of Artois, Huon of Burdeux*, and Malory's *Morte Darthur*; it survives to threaten Tom Jones.[1] It appears, Chaucer's Man of Law reminds us, in *Apollonius of Tyre* and in the *Confessio Amantis*; it also appears in the earliest sources of the Man of Law's own sanitized tale, where the heroine flees to escape her father's unwelcome advances.[2] In the Squire's Tale, incest is much closer to the surface: the Squire's heroine is the namesake of the Canacee whose "wikke ensample" the Man of Law castigates (II.78); and when the Squire outlines the missing bulk of his tale, he seems to promise that his Canacee too will be incestuous.[3] Incest, or the threat of incest, shows up in so many romances linked otherwise by nothing except their genre that it must answer compelling needs of romance narration and satisfy the most deeply seated impulses of the romantic imagination. It offers, above all, the frisson of narrowly avoided peril, the thrill of the forbidden exotic. It also, as in *Tom Jones*, may mark the threat of the experiential fallen world to the providentially ruled world of innocence. Although incest, as Lévi-Strauss tells us, is the primal taboo, some romances dangle before us the suggestion that there was a time before this first of laws, an Eden beyond its constraint on human desire. For one of the most basic elements of romance, Northrop Frye suggests, is a nostalgic yearning for an Edenic youth of erotic innocence, where the incest prohibition marks the border between Golden Age and fallen world or, as we might say now, between nature and culture.[4]

This essay first appeared in *ELH* 55 (1988): 1–26. Reprinted by permission of the Johns Hopkins University Press.

At its heart, the incest taboo forbids us to treat the same as if it were other, and it insists on the need for deciding which is which. This insistence gives it a particular affinity with romance as a literary genre because of the romantic tropes that most vividly mimic its structure—doubling and repetition, which likewise play on the distinction between same and other, and translate it into narrative terms as expansion and collapse. Doubling, repetition, and incest are so recurrent in romance that one can hardly say which of them came first: it seems not so much a question of the chicken and the egg, as of the yolk and white of the one shell. They all embody the most distinctive concerns of romance narrative: questions of identity, complicated by disguise or igno-rance; distinctions between self and other; the difficulties of making discrimi-nations in a mysterious, magical world. And their tendency to dilation—the permutations in kinship structures, the countless doublings and repetitions the romance plot requires for its resolution, the length of time it takes for the dis-covery of true identity to ward off threatened incest—typify the romantic elu-sion of clarity, the reluctance of romance narrative to reach its ending.[5]

Chaucer is much aware of these devices, and his own romances make some use of them. The Man of Law doubles his narrative and finds not one but two wicked mothers-in-law to torment his heroine. Sir Thopas is about to repeat his tentative foray into fairyland when he is rescued by Harry Bailly's interruption. In the heap of bodies at Thebes, Palamon and Arcite lie "Bothe in on armes" (I.1012), anonymous and identical, before they shift violently from blood brotherhood to mortal enmity. Diomede copies the stages of Troilus's courtship, but in the parodic haste of double or triple time; Pan-darus's fictional fabrications are echoed in fact. In all of these instances, Chaucer brings a characteristic self-consciousness to his use of literary form, and implicitly comments on generic conventions even as he employs them.

The Squire's Tale, more than any other of Chaucer's romances, examines the wellsprings of the romantic impulse itself at the same time that it examines the motives of the Squire as storyteller. For the paradox of romance, from a mature and disenchanted perspective, is that it is a naive as well as compelling genre. Its nostalgic yearning for the forbidden erotic is part of its quest for identity, simplicity, and unity; yet the delays that prevent their achievement do not serve simply to titillate us with postponed delight, but also to comment on the possibility of the quest itself. If the incest taboo prohibits treating the same as if it were other, Chaucer shows that there are corresponding difficulties, and comic potentialities, in treating the other as if it were the same—that is, in domesticating the exotic too readily. Chaucer highlights such questions in the Squire's Tale by the countervailing pressures so evident within it. The debunk-ing response of the "vulgar many" to its marvels, and the Squire's own occa-sional disenchantment, prepare us to look questioningly at his own innocence as a romance narrator. To his chagrin, the Squire finds that disenchantment and the declining world threaten the innocent wonders of his romance. But he also reveals despite himself that his own effort to domesticate the exotic asserts identity between incomparables, and that the exotic—however much apparently tamed—is always ready to declare its otherness once again.

I

The most immediate threats of disenchantment are to the four marvelous presents that Cambyuskan receives on his birthday. Two of them are explicitly devices for *translatio*: the horse can travel everywhere in the world within a day; the ring allows its wearer to understand any bird's speech "openly and pleyn, / And answere hym in his langage ageyn" (151–52). The other two gifts are also aids to translation, if in a less direct sense: like the horse and ring, they close gaps, recover unities, pull together what has been dispersed. The sword offers the only means possible of healing the armor-piercing wounds it inflicts; the mirror allows its possessor to make doubleness and hypocrisy transparent (as John Stevens says, it allows "political foresight and amorous insight" by revealing traitors and false lovers).[6] These are gifts from an innocent world to a fallen one: they offer the means of reintegration, of recapturing a lost world of freshness, transparency, and clarity. Their purpose is to make the distant or obscure accessible or the exotic familiar, to unmask doubleness or hypocrisy. But the sword, capable of both healing mayhem and wreaking it, epitomizes the problematic quality of the others as innocent gifts in a world of experience. By their nature they mirror what romance itself attempts to do but also has most difficulty doing. For as Northrop Frye points out, romance always plays off identity against alienation, reality against illusion, and its own existence depends on a gap that is not quite closed, indeed, not quite capable of being closed. Identity, the goal of the romantic quest, is also its negation: "all its meanings in romance," Frye says, "have some connection to a state of existence in which there is nothing to write about. It is existence before 'once upon a time' and subsequent to 'and they lived happily ever after.' "[7]

The Squire protects the innocence and elegance of his exotic world with the inexpressibility topos: he cannot describe Canacee's beauty (34–41) or reproduce the envoy's word-perfect speech (99–109). But alienation and disenchantment enter the tale through its characters when "the peple" confront the marvelous gifts, to which they refuse to grant innocence or exotic otherness. Their unvarying response denies the possibility of white magic, of an innocent marvel: either the magic is sinister, or it may be explained in scientific, debunking terms, or its mystery dissipates under the sour wisdom of precedent: "Nothing under the sun is new, neither is any man able to say: Behold, this is new: for it hath already gone before in the ages that were before us" (Eccles. 1:10). The horse is "a fairye, as the peple semed" (201), like Pegasus or the Trojan Horse, but it must be a trick, whether of magic or of military strategy:

> As lewed peple demeth comunly
> Of thynges that been maad moore subtilly
> Than they kan in hir lewednesse comprehende;
> They demen gladly to the badder ende.
>
> (221–24)[8]

The mirror provokes amazement, or a scientific explanation of its workings, "Naturelly, by composiciouns / Of anglis and of slye reflexiouns" (229–30). The sword may be explained away by the precedent of Telephus—wounded and then healed by Achilles' spear—and also by a discussion of the science of tempering metal (236–46). The "craft of rynges" is mysterious because the expertise of Moses and Solomon is lost in the distant past; even this most unprecedented marvel, however, may be explicable:

> But nathelees somme seiden that it was
> Wonder to maken of fern-asshen glas,
> And yet nys glas nat lyk asshen of fern;
> But, for they han yknowen it so fern,
> Therfore cesseth hir janglyng and hir wonder.
> As soore wondren somme on cause of thonder,
> On ebbe, on flood, on gossomer, and on myst,
> And alle thyng, til that the cause is wyst.
> Thus jangle they, and demen, and devyse
> Til that the kyng gan fro the bord aryse.
>
> (253–62)[9]

The final couplet is the Squire's aristocratic comment on the vulgar many. Before then it is not entirely clear when he is reporting their views and when expressing his own: in a passage where the *rime riche* of "fern" and "fern" insists on distinctions within the seemingly identical, the narrator appropriates the "jangle" of 261 from the skeptics' word "janglyng" in their indirect discourse (257); and the "wondren somme" of 258 at first sight seems to be the narrator's remark, in parallel sequence with "somme seiden" (253), instead of constituting part of what those "somme" said. This blurring of voices is fitting in the Squire's Tale. If writers of romance conventionally introduce cynical characters in order to confront their jaded responses head-on, the Squire himself exhibits some disenchantment, even as he strenuously tries to escape it and to protect his romance from it.[10] His most distinctive quality as a historical character—-implied in the General Prologue and openly evident in the way he tells his tale—is his strong sense of belated-ness: his father's Crusades have dwindled to his own "chyvachie" (I.85) in Flanders.[11] This apprehension of belatedness is attended by a simultaneous nostalgia for and impatience with the past. The Squire's father can say "Ther is no newe gyse that it nas old" (I.2125), and his tale, significantly, is of ancient Greece and claims the authority of "olde stories" (I.859) for its telling. The Squire, by contrast, both longs for and resents the cachet of chivalric tradition and the weight of the "olde poetries" and "olde geestes" (206–11) that authenticate but also devalue his magic horse.

His ambivalence explains his choice of a story about exotic thirteenth-century Tartary, and the way in which he relates that story to the European chivalric tradition. "No man but Launcelot" could describe the dances and dalliance at Cambyuskan's court, "and he is deed" (287). The envoy from the King of Araby and India speaks so well

> That Gawayn, with his olde curteisye,
> Though he were comen ayeyn out of Fairye,
> Ne koude hym nat amende with a word.
>
> (95–97)

Does the phrase "olde curteisye" imply that "modern" courtesy is nonexistent or at best a pale copy? Is the "Fairye" where Gawain now resides not the Isle of Avalon but never-never land?[12] Is true courtesy to be found only among virtuous heathens? The Squire's ambiguous comments here evoke the referential, intertextual quality of romance and its double-edged effect. On the one hand, he owes his very story to "knightes olde" (69), and he needs to bring in Gawain and Lancelot— however old or dead—to establish its proper eminence. On the other, the mob uses "thise olde poetries" (206) and "thise olde geestes" (211) to empty his marvels of their exoticism by searching out dismal precedents for them or—more worrisome to the Squire—debunking them as the stale leavings of an outworn tradition:

> Swich wondryng was ther on this hors of bras
> That syn the grete sege of Troie was,
> Theras men wondreden on an hors also,
> Ne was ther swich a wondryng as was tho.
>
> (305–8)

As in these lines, which try with half-hearted vivacity to pump up our excitement, the Squire's Tale is a repeated warning that familiarity breeds indifference if not contempt. Once the secret of fern ash transformed to glass is known, its wonder cannot survive. The tercelet, having won the falcon's love, quickly becomes bored and takes off with a kite. The Squire himself must look far afield for a story fresh enough to be worth the telling. This constant threat is much like that of dead metaphor. Indeed, the Squire shows the linguistic version of the problem—the inevitable devaluation of verbal currency as it is worn by use—when he uses two famous phrases from the Gospels to describe the fickle tercelet as a whited sepulchre (518–19) and as

the most consummate of traitors: no man, the falcon proclaims, "were worthy unbokelen his galoche, / Ther doubleness or feynyng sholde approche"
(555–56). These allusions to Matthew and Mark raise the decibel level of
diatribe considerably; they also constitute a shocking debasement of reference.

Yet the problem raised here is an intractable one. If familiarity must
lead to devaluation, the vulgar skeptics at Cambyuskan's court nonetheless
exhibit an almost irresistible human impulse to explain the exotic, to
domesticate it, by recourse to the familiar—or alternatively, to worry about
its possible virulence. Chaucer implies that Tartar suspicions about the
magic brass flying horse are at least prudent, for according to medieval tradition, the Trojan Horse was made of brass.[13] How can one experience the
otherness of the exotic, the Squire asks, without trusting its innocence and
giving in freely to its attractive power? How can one be certain, the skeptics
respond, that its power is in fact innocent? As if to support their skepticism,
Chaucer translates a verse—"Thus seyn the peple and drawen hem apart"
(252)—from book 2 of the *Aeneid* (39), where an overly credulous popu-
lace, not suspicious enough of exotic Greek gifts, admit the Trojan Horse to
their own destruction. The larger issue of the Squire's Tale, our mental difficulty in confronting and assimilating the other, is augmented here by a
vigorous reminder that there may also be physical risks in such a confrontation.

Nor does the Squire himself, despite his concerns, avoid reducing the
marvelous to the mundane. Canacee sees the falcon "Amydde a tree, for drye
as whit as chalk" (409), where the bird has beaten herself "so pitously / With
bothe hir wynges til the rede blood / Ran endelong the tree ther-as she stood"
(414–16). This tree is a miniature of a famous ancient marvel, heavily
charged with symbolic meaning: the Arbre Sec, or Dry Tree.[14] But its suit-
ability to the Squire's Tale is the effect of an afterthought. Machaut's *Dit dou
Lyon* mentions "l'Aubre sec, / Ou li oisel pendent au bec [the Dry Tree,
where the birds hang by their beaks]," and the *Epistola Presbyteri Johannis*
identifies the Dry Tree as the Arbor Seth, in which there is a "diversitas
avium omnium, quae sub coelo sunt [profuse variety of all the birds that live
beneath the heaven]."[15] The Dry Tree's primary purpose, however, is not to
support fainting birds: according to Sir John Mandeville and his source, Vincent of Beauvais, it is a tree "of Abrahamis tyme," which died on the day of
the Crucifixion, and will return to life only when

> a lord and a prynce of the west shal conquere the Holy Lond with helpe of
> othere Cristene, and he shal do synge a masse vndyr that drie ok, and aftyr
> that it shal waxen grene ayen and bere leuys and freut. And thour vertu of
> that ilke merakele ther shal manye, as wel Iewes as Sarasynys, ben conuer-
> tyd and turne to the Cristene lawe. . . . And thow it be callid the dreye tre,
> neuertheles ther is gret vertue therin; who so bere ony porcioun therof on

hym, he shal neuere ben trauayled with the fallynge euyl, ne his hors shal neuere ben foundered whil he hath it on hym.[16]

In the thirteenth-century *Queste del Saint Graal*, Sir Bors has a vision of the Dry Tree, and of Christ as the pelican who sacrifices itself for the sake of its young. I quote from Malory's translation:

> And so a litill frome thens he loked up into a tre and there he saw a passynge grete birde uppon that olde tre. And hit was passyng drye, withoute leyffe; so she sate above and had birdis whiche were dede for hungir. So at the laste he smote hymselffe with hys beke which was grete and sherpe, and so the grete birde bledde so faste that he dyed amonge hys birdys. And the yonge birdys toke lyff by the bloode of the grete birde.[17]

In Malory's phrasing, "by the bare tre betokenyth the worlde, whych ys naked and nedy, withoute fruyte, but if hit com of oure Lorde."[18] The Squire's dry tree reduces the nakedness and need of the as yet unredeemed fallen world to the lovesick achings of a bird.

In the Squire's narration of his tale, there are in fact repeated reminders of how readily a marvel dwindles to the more-or-less everyday: fresh beginnings always succumb, and rapidly, to disenchantment or ruined hopes.[19] The tale begins in spring, against the somber background of Cambyuskan's wars, in which "many a doughty man" died (11), and the birds' bitter memory of winter:

> Ful lusty was the weder and benigne,
> For which the foweles, agayn the sonne sheene,
> What for the sesoun and the yonge grene,
> Ful loude songen hire affecciouns.
> Hem semed han geten hem protecciouns
> Agayn the swerd of wynter, keene and coold.
>
> (52–57)

The new year asserts its force here even more emphatically than it does in the opening lines of the General Prologue. Cambyuskan's birthday, as befits its mood of magic and innocent celebration, is on March 15, just after the spring equinox in the medieval calendar. His description, moreover, is startlingly like that of the Squire himself in the General Prologue: "Yong, fressh, and strong, in armes desirous / As any bacheler of al his hous" (23–24)—as if the Squire has successfully grafted his own high spirits and vitality onto a much older man.[20] Yet this mood of youthful energy gives way quickly to the people's sour skepticism about marvels and the drunken torpor of the Tartar men. Likewise, as in the Prologue to the *Legend of Good Women*, the birds' touching forgetfulness of winter cannot wholly cancel our awareness that winter will come again. Indeed, the "lusty" weather they celebrate threatens to darken even more rapidly, for the magical mirror is to protect Canacee "ageyn this lusty someres tyde" (142), a time of amatory "tresoun" and "subtiltee" that is near at hand:

> Who koude telle yow the forme of daunces
> So unkouthe, and swiche fresshe contenaunces,
> Swich subtil lookyng and dissymulynges
> For drede of jalouse mennes aperceyvynges?
> No man but Launcelot, and he is deed.
>
> (283–87)

The "fresshe contenaunces" of springtime youth coexist here with the "subtil lookyng and dissymulynges" that characterize the Ovidian world of jealous duped husbands (and dead Lancelots). Because of its very nature courtly dalliance threatens this world of innocent delight.

The most startling of these aborted beginnings opens part 2 of the tale. Against the background of alcoholic "fumositee" and the drunken sleep that has overtaken the Tartar men, Canacee is early to bed, early to rise in the freshness of a spring morning:

> Up riseth fresshe Canacee hireselve,
> As rody and bright as dooth the yonge sonne,
> That in the Ram is foure degrees up ronne—
> Noon hyer was he whan she redy was.
>
> (384–87)

These lines are overloaded with youngness, as they press simile towards doubling or identity: young, fresh Canacee is like the young sun, four degrees into Aries (that is, just beyond the equinox), and also four degrees above the horizon (that is, just after dawn).[21] But then:

> The vapour which that fro the erthe glood
> Made the sonne to seme rody and brood;
> But nathelees it was so fair a sighte
> That it made alle hire hertes for to lighte,
> What for the seson and the morwenynge,
> And for the foweles that she herde synge.
> For right anon she wiste what they mente
> Right by hir song, and knew al hire entente.
> The knotte why that every tale is toold,
> If it be taried til that lust be coold
> Of hem that han it after herkned yoore,

> The savour passeth ever lenger the moore,
> For fulsomnesse of his prolixitee;
> And by the same resoun, thynketh me,
> I sholde to the knotte condescende,
> And maken of hir walkyng soone an ende.
>   (393–408)

Many others have remarked on the irony of these lines in a tale that promises to be nearly endless. But what is most striking here is the way that the fear of tedium interrupts this fresh beginning before it has time to wear out its welcome. In a split second fresh morning becomes dusty afternoon: the magical fusions of sun, zodiacal sign, and heroine, of woman and singing bird, separate out into the cold distinctions of the everyday.

II

This repeated sequence of marvels debunked and fresh beginnings aborted, of spoilsport skeptics and nervous disenchantment, contrasts with the Squire's own persisting innocence as a teller of romance and calls it into question. The Squire repeatedly leaves us at the line between sameness and otherness, innocence and experience, the familiar and the exotic. More than many medieval romances, his tale constitutes a full deployment of what Fredric Jameson and Patricia Parker note as a central impulse in romance, the projection of the other.[22] But the Squire's Tale also contains repeated counterweights to that exotic imagining. At every level of the poem, from its conspicuous *rimes riches* to the broad outlines of its plot, we find twinned terms, doubles that we are invited to consider identical or equivalent, but that then separate into nonrelation. The other proves to be at once imaginable and inaccessible or untranslatable; and the Squire either retreats into the familiar, with realistic displacements of the fantastic, or—to some extent despite himself—reveals the impossibility of entering fully into an alien consciousness.

The particular vividness of this paradox is no doubt due in part to Chaucer's interest in the relation between tale and teller, and in the difficulties of impersonating an alien voice. As Marshall Leitester has said, the "enterprise" of the *Canterbury Tales* "involves the continual attempt, continually repeated, to see from another's point of view, to stretch and extend the self by learning to speak in the voices of others."[23] And one form of Chaucer's moral commentary on his pilgrims calibrates their ability, or willingness, to "stretch and extend the self" in this way. Of the tales that attempt to imagine the world beyond the bounds of Christendom— those of the Man of Law, Squire, Prioress, and Second Nun—only the Squire's does so sympathetically. But in the Squire's tale, as in many of the *Canterbury Tales,* self-enclosure and self-interest preclude a fully successful imagining of otherness. Translating a bird's "leden" (435–36), its language, is possible only by magic, and the Squire's rhetoric is, he says, not up to translating the envoy's speech (99–109). Other forms of translation in the tale prove to be as difficult to bring off.

Chaucer's meaning—the link between the skeptically received marvels and the Squire's problematic efforts to imagine the other—is in part to be explained by his source for the transformation of fern ash into glass. This passage from Jean de Meun, which comes just before Nature's confession in the *Roman de la Rose*, is of unusual importance, I think, for it elucidates the Canon's Yeoman's tale as well as the Squire's. Jean describes Nature's work in the fallen world as an unending battle against death and corruption, her strategy being to fill the world with every form of life. She gives true forms in coins of various currencies ["donne formes veroies / En coins de diverses monnoies"] (16015–16), and these forms serve as models for Art.[24] But Art, however closely it apes Nature, cannot make things that are alive, however natural they seem ["ne puet fere choses vives, / Ja si ne sembleront naïves"] (16033–34). Whatever the care with which it paints knights, beasts, flowers, lovers in spring, caged birds, courtly dances, and in whatever medium, its creations are at best pallid, lifeless, imperfect doubles of Nature's vital forms. Jean then compares art to alchemy, which is itself, he says, a true art, capable of great marvels ["granz merveilles"] (16086). Even if art were to learn from alchemy, it could never change one species to another ("les especes remuer" or "transmuer") unless it knew how to reduce them first to their primordial matter ["les ramene / A lor matire premerene"] (16068–70). But even if Art could do this, it would still need an elixir with exactly the right catalyst to make the transmutation occur; it would have to distinguish the differences that separate species from one another ["devise entr'eus les sustances / Par especiaus differences"] (16079–80). Yet if species cannot change, individual bodies have some ability to move from one species to another (16087–95). The transformation of ferns to fern ash to glass is one such marvel, created by art: "Si n'est pas li voirres fogieres / Ne fogiere ne rest pas voirre [But glass is not fern, nor is fern glass]" (16100–101). Another is Nature's work: the way in which a thundercloud can produce, and drop, a stone. One could transmute metals too, Jean says, if one were able to put them in pure form according to their affinities ["complexions voisines"] (16117), because they are all made of one matter beneath their various appearances, born in their several ways from sulfur and quicksilver (16113–24).

Jean's shift from Nature to Art to alchemy is more than a little confusing, though exceptionally suggestive. It is of a piece with one of Nature's digressions, which Chaucer also makes use of in the Squire's Tale (228–35): a master of mirrors, she says, can make many things be born of one (18177–78); mirrors can make things that are far apart seem to be contiguous ["conjointes e prochaines"] (18212), or make one thing seem to be two. When we think about these various collapses of many into one and fracturings of one into many, we may profitably recall the thoughts of two modern writers on this subject—Jung, who speaks of incest and alchemy in the same breath in *The Psychology of the Transference*, and Derrida, who argues that "Society, language, history, articulation, in a word supplementarity, are born at the same time as the prohibition of incest."[25] These modern comments share the dominant schema of their medieval predecessors: an original state (real or nostalgically imagined) of unity and integration; a fallen state of fragmentation, alienation, *différance*; and a border between them marked by anxious needs for definition and uncertain dangers of transgression. Chaucer himself, in the Canon's Yeoman's Tale, suggests that the multiplication of metals and the multiplication of words are analogous phenomena: the alchemist's nostalgia, from his world of confusion, proliferative materials, and opaque jargon, is in some part a longing for the world of transparent language before Babel. The Squire's Tale, if less vividly than the Canon's Yeoman's, shows that reintegration—the quest of romance—is not fully achievable, that the other finally resists integration with the self.

In the plot of the tale, there are three interrelated attempts to imagine the other, and in each instance we are made aware of both similarity and irreducible difference. The three—a man imagining a woman, a Christian European imagining a heathen Tartar, and a human being imagining a falcon—build on one another, and their cumulative effect is to make each of them seem problematic. To be precise, the egregiously precarious nature of the second and third—European and Mongol, person and bird—leads us to realize that the first—male and female—is, perhaps surprisingly, no less difficult. When a young noble male European imagines the sentiments of a *gentil* female bird "of fremde land" (429), as these are made evident in her colloquy with a Mongolian princess, we are assured that a basic impulse of romance, asserting and then overcoming distance, is being pushed to its furthest limits.

The Tartar court, as the Squire describes it, is both comfortably familiar and convincingly exotic. We might expect a conventional romance plot in which, as in *Bevis of Hampton*, a Saracen princess must be converted to Christianity in order to marry the hero. Instead, cultural relativism allows a less strenuously enforced community by granting Cambyuskan the status of a virtuous heathen—"He kepte his lay, to which that he was sworn" (18)— and giving the Tartar religion the unexceptionable propriety of the everyday. After dinner, the court goes "Unto the temple, as reson was" (296); and there is no rush to convince it of the unreasonableness of its ways. On the other hand, beneath this placid surface of toleration there are hints of the truly outlandish in the Squire's allusions to Mongol customs as they are reported in thirteenth- and fourteenth-century accounts. He is not alone in his interest in

Tartar exoticism: Juliet Vale has documented a Cheapside tournament in 1331 at which the participants were "*larvati ad similitudinem Tartorum*, disguised in masks painted with Tartars' faces and appropriate head-dresses," and, she argues, the "fairly detailed knowledge" required for making such masks "indicates a familiarity with," indeed "a strong English interest" in, "travellers' accounts."[26] But these accounts repeatedly remind us of the terrifying barbarity of the Mongols, however tamed in the European imagination by several generations of acquaintance and by the ebb in their tidal wave of conquest. Even the habits of Mongol daily life resist easy assimilation. The Squire reports: "Ther is som mete that is ful deynte holde, / That in this lond men recche of it but smal" (70–71). The narratives of the Franciscan missionaries John of Plano Carpini and William of Rubruck, which Christopher Dawson has edited in *The Mongol Mission*, agree on the extreme drunkenness of the Mongols and on their repulsive diet.[27] According to Vincent of Beauvais (who borrows from John of Plano Carpini) and Sir John Mandeville, these Mongolian delicacies include hounds, lions, rats, and mice.[28] Culinary squeamishness, as we guess the contents of their "strange sewes" (67), may indeed overbalance any desire to assimilate the mysterious East.

The Franciscan missionaries also number incest among the Mongols' outlandish practices, and the Squire's ambiguous phrasing must lead us to wonder whether Canacee will marry her brother Cambalo.[29] The problem the Squire creates is one of doubled names. The Man of Law had made much of Chaucer's refusal to tell the stories of Apollonius of Tyre or of Canacee, "That loved hir owene brother synfully— / Of swiche cursed stories I sey fy—"(II.79–80). The Squire's heroine Canacee is no doubt a different woman, though the coincidence of names evidently influenced the early scribal editors of the *Canterbury Tales*, the great majority of whom name the Squire as the speaker who is to follow the Man of Law.[30] Spenser's completion of the tale, in book 4 of the *Faerie Queene*, resolves the issue by preserving legal distance at its closest approach to identity: in a textbook case of elegant exogamy, Cambell and Triamond trade their sisters Canacee and Cambina.[31] But we must wonder if the Squire's Canacee is to follow the example of her classical namesake, especially since he promises to tell of Cambalo, "That faught in lystes with the bretheren two / For Canacee er that he myghte hire wynne" (668–69). The editions of Skeat and Baugh are quick to note that this Cambalo must be someone other than Canacee's brother Cambalo, and that the "bretheren two" are no doubt her brothers; but this second doubling of names is more than awkward. Indeed, Haldeen Braddy suggests that Chaucer left the *Squire's Tale* unfinished because he discovered halfway through copying his source that it was a story about incest.[32] The process of demystification involved in making necessary distinctions—giving up the titillation of incest for a less exotic licit story, deciding that "Canacee" is not "Canacee," nor "Cambalo" "Cambalo"—is much like the rationalizing, realistic displacement by which the members of the Tartar court explain away the magical horse, mirror, sword, and ring. Such confusions test our hearts' desire and minds' ability, to find similitudes and make discriminations—in effect, to tell a hawk from a handsaw.

We are, as a matter of fact, asked to do almost exactly that, for the Squire rehearses the complaint of a peregrine falcon "of fremde land" (429) (a tautological doubling of "peregrine," as Dorothy Bethurum notes), whose avian language we can understand because of Canacee's magic ring.[33] Canacee's gentility, the falcon says, is a less exotic though equally welcome bridge between woman and bird:

> "That pitee renneth soone in gentil herte,
> Feelynge his similitude in peynes smerte,
> Is preved alday, as men may it see,
> As wel by werk as by auctoritee;
> For gentil herte kitheth gentillesse."
>
> (479–83)

Her gender is as important as her gentility: the falcon, appealing to Canacee's "verray wommanly benignytee" (486), implies that a female human being can feel the sorrow of a female bird more readily than a male could (and, indeed, she seems to be correct, since Canacee has already guessed the source of her sorrow). According to the editions of Skeat and Baugh, this falcon, who refers to herself at one point as a woman, is in fact a princess who has been magically transformed into a bird.[34] But there is no reason to believe that this bird is not a bird, and, as in the Nun's Priest's Tale and the *Parliament of Fowls*, the imperfect homology of human and avian terms repeatedly has jarring comic effects. As Talbot Donaldson says, "it is hard to believe that the creator of Chauntecleer and Pertelote could with a straight face describe a hawk as a 'tigre' who falls on his knees to his love."[35] And, one might add, it is especially hard to believe this because the Squire has already conceded that tigers are not like people, or birds, in their capacity for sentiment:

> ther nys tygre, ne noon so crueel beest
> That dwelleth outher in wode or in forest,
> That nolde han wept, if that he wepe koude,
> For sorwe of hire, she shrighte alwey so loude.
>
> (419–22)

Magic ring or not, there are limits to Canacee's ability to find similitude by an act of *gentil* sympathy: in a failure of communication that Harry Berger has remarked, Canacee holds out the lap of her garment to catch the swooning falcon, but the bird misses and drops to the ground.[36]

These questions of gender and species come up most forcefully when the falcon, using a Boethian commonplace, berates her lover for abandoning her:

> That 'alle thyng, repeirynge to his kynde,
> Gladeth hymself;' thus seyn men, as I gesse.
> Men loven of propre kynde newefangelnesse,
> As briddes doon that men in cages fede.
> For though thou nyght and day take of hem hede,
> And strawe hir cage faire and softe as silk,
> And yeve hem sugre, hony, breed and milk,
> Yet right anon as that his dore is uppe
> He with his feet wol spurne adoun his cuppe,
> And to the wode he wole and wormes ete;
> So newefangel been they of hire mete,
> And loven novelries of propre kynde,
> No gentillesse of blood ne may hem bynde.
>
> (608–20)

In the *Consolation of Philosophy*, this example of "kindly enclynyng" is one of several metaphors for the natural inclination of the soul, however much distracted by worldly things, to move to its proper place in heaven.[37] It has prompted some implausible Boethian readings of the Squire's Tale. Robert Haller notes that in Boethius "a clear distinction is made between men and birds. The *exemplum* is literally true of birds," but "applies by analogy to man." By erasing this distinction, the Squire shows, according to Haller, that he has not understood Boethius, and "the *exemplum* works ironically" in his tale. "By identifying 'gentillesse of blood' with the delicate food, the hawk has made such gentillesse into a false good. . . . And in her preference for this delicate food, she has indicated that she is going against 'kynde'; the Squire makes a similar error.[38]

But as Richard Leighton Greene has argued in response to Haller's essay, the falcon's application of the exemplum is carefully circumscribed: "The point is that the faithless male falcon is being spoken of as if a man, a male human being, and not as if representative of both sexes of *genus homo*. . . . Male human beings are then likened to *cage-birds*, not to falcons at all. Falcons are not caged, definitely do not eat sugar, honey, bread, and milk, and when freed do not go to the wood and eat worms!"[39] Though Greene makes an important point here, the exemplum is nonetheless more comic, and more confused, than he suggests. In the Manciple's Tale, Chaucer uses it as part of a joke, with the warrant of La Vieille's discourse in the *Roman de la Rose* (13941–14158). Along with the cat who craves mice and the she-wolf in heat, the bird who would rather "in a forest that is rude and coold / Goon ete wormes and swich wrecchednesse" (1X.170–71) is an analogue for the unrestrainable sexual appetite of women; but the Manciple then shifts its reference: "Alle thise ensamples speke I by thise men / That been untrewe, and nothyng by wommen" (1X.187–88). In the Squire's version of the exemplum, tenor and vehicle, number and gender keep reversing and dissolving into each other. The metaphorical equivalence of human beings and birds becomes a literal statement about a particular bird; "men" and "birds" both become terms that have within themselves double meanings, imperfectly distinguished. In the phrase "thus seyn men, as I gesse" or "briddes . . . that men in cages fede", "men" refers, or can refer, to both men and women; in the single verse that separates these two phrases, "Men loven of propre kynde newefangelnesse," "men" are, as Greene says, males, and they suffer the obloquy directed against all amorous males in the Squire's Tale. Likewise, though falcons are not songbirds, when the abstract "briddes" and "hem" of the exemplum turn into "his" and "he," the particular bird who spurns his cup and goes to eat worms in the wood is pretty closely identified with the fickle tercelet.[40] As in the *Parliament of Fowls*, the literal threatens the metaphorical, humanized birds threaten to become simply birds; and the falcon does not advance her case much by using the natural propensities of wild birds to accuse her lover. If a bird's nature is to be wild, we must suspect—whether or not falcons actually eat worms, and even if a *gentil* princess can respond intuitively to a *gentil* falcon—that it is silly to apply human notions of love or gentility to *any* species of birds.[41] The uncertain difference between "man" and "man" (that is to say, between "man" and "woman") or between "bird" and "bird" (songbird and raptor), let alone the one between "man" and "bird," hovers between harmonic resolution and absolute disjunction.

Like many other romances, the Squire's Tale promises to end in reintegration and a recovery of the lost innocent world: the fragmentary tale ends with a forecast of the tercelet's repentance and reunion with the falcon, "By mediacion of Cambalus" (656). The Squire makes up for the tercelet's male insouciance by performing his own version of mediation. He has been asked by the Host to "sey somwhat of love, for certes ye / Konnen theron as muche as any man" (2–3); and the request is fitting. As the General Prologue describes him, "So hoote he lovede that by nyghtertale / He sleep namoore than dooth a nyghtyngale" (I.97–98). (The Squire has his own affinity with birds.) Like Troilus, the Squire fights "In hope to stonden in his lady grace" (I.88); and he fights in his tale on behalf of a woman's view of love's perils. His romance has almost nothing good to say about men, and everything to say on behalf of women. He describes the magic mirror, which can warn a woman of her lover's treachery, "His newe love, and al his subtiltee" (140), and presages what may happen to Canacee, to whom the mirror is given, with the falcon's extended complaint against the perfidy of men. Yet, as in the *Legend of Good Women*, male villainy is somewhat overstated, as the Squire rushes to celebrate the "trouthe that is in wommen sene" (645). While all the men in the Tartar court get drunk and stay up all night, Canacee goes to bed early and sober, because she is "ful mesurable, as wommen be" (362). The falcon reaches back not only to Jason and Paris but to the beginning of history for her case against male duplicity—to Lamech, "that alderfirst bigan / To loven two" (550–51). And in the Ellesmere and Cambridge Gg manuscripts, the falcon calls her own fairness into question when she adds the name of Troilus himself, improbably, to this list of false male lovers.[42]

In its extreme partisanship on behalf of women in the battle of the sexes, the Squire's Tale is like two other works of Chaucer's, the *Legend of Good Women* and the unfinished *Anelida and Arcite* (to which the tale is much indebted). But it is unlike them in one very interesting respect; both of the other narrators praise women extravagantly because they have to. The god of love orders Chaucer to write saints' lives of love's martyrs in penance for having written of Criseyde; and the *Legends*, often hilariously, delete every unsavory detail in their effort to say nothing bad about any woman.[43] The narrator of *Anelida and Arcite* is constrained by his sources: "First folowe I Stace, and after him Corynne" (21). Statius provides the martial setting of Thebes; Corinna, Ovid's torment now given her own pen, provides the energy of Anelida's complaint from a female poet's perspective.[44] (At last, the Wife of Bath might exclaim, a lion is doing the painting!) But at first glance, it is certainly odd that the Squire, purely of his own volition, should make so extreme a leap of sympathy. If he is a lover courting his lady, does he not risk defeating his own amorous purposes by dwelling on male perfidy? If no man is to be trusted, why should he be?

Chaucer raises this last question in his own person when, at the end of *Troilus and Criseyde*, he commands the women in his audience: "Beth war of men, and herkneth what I seye!" (V.1785); and his general interest in sexual politics gives a particular force to his examination of the Squire's motives. One of the effects of the Squire's exaggerated sympathy with women, as he seems to be more or less aware, is to make a distinct contrast with his father's point of view as it appears in the Knight's Tale.[45] If the Knight identifies with Theseus, Canacee is the closest to a surrogate for the Knight's son. His sympathy with her is his most explicit challenge to his father's perspective, and it serves to redefine the purposes of romance as more narrowly romantic. The Knight treats women gingerly, with humor or at most a bemused detachment: their lament for Arcite's death is ludicrously beside the point; they are always weeping; Emelye's maiden rites are a female mystery that "I dar nat telle," for "it is good a man been at his large" (I.2284–88). Though not so programmatically as in the *Teseida*, Femenye is a territory that must be subjugated to rational control. The Squire's interest in Canacee, by contrast, is an act of sympathy—his *gentillesse* responding to hers—that is equivalent to what she herself does when she feels pity for the wounded falcon. Even so, like his own European imagining of the Tartars or Canacee's womanly imagining of a bird, the Squire's male imagining of Canacee founders and must seem, if not false, an attempt to bridge the unbridgeable.

As Chaucer makes us increasingly realize, the Squire's sympathy cannot be fully disinterested, precisely because he is a lover; and his one-sided praise of women has an end in view. For he follows to the letter Amor's advice in the *Roman de la Rose*, in a passage that also mentions Gawain's famed courtesy (*Romaunt* 2210). Amor warns that the lover must shun "vilayn speche," and must serve women wholeheartedly:

> And alle wymmen serve and preise,
> And to thy power her honour reise;
> And if that ony myssaiere
> Dispise wymmen, that thou maist here,
> Blame hym, and bidde hym holde hym stille.
> And [set] thy myght and all thy wille
> Wymmen and ladies for to please,
> And to do thyng that may hem ese,
> That they ever speke good of thee,
> For so thou maist best preised be.
>
> (2229–38)

The trouble with this advice, of course, is that a lover is hardly capable of disinterested benevolence: in a joke that goes back to Ovid, Amor's concern for gentility, euphemism, and decorous sentiment always has an ulterior motive. Chaucer makes exactly this joke in the *Legend of Good Women* (once again playing on the two meanings of the word "man"), when his narrator's attacks on his own sex establish his credentials as the woman's man who is alone to be trusted:

> Be war, ye wemen, of youre subtyl fo,
> Syn yit this day men may ensaumple se;
> And trusteth, as in love, no man but me.
>
> (2559–61)[46]

The Squire too hopes for a reward, and the rewards for such service are not all verbal. In terms that Amor would understand—witness the euphemisms of pilgrim's staff, sacred relics, and rosebuds at the end of the *Roman de la Rose*—the Squire's tale may be summed up as his effort to put himself in a woman's place.

The quality that most distinguishes the *Canterbury Tales* from other frame narratives of the fourteenth century is Chaucer's interest in using a tale to characterize its teller, and to shed light on his or her preoccupations, insights, and habitual blindnesses.[47] This defining quality is perhaps most apparent in tales with sources or analogues in Gower's *Confessio Amantis*—among them, the tales of the Man of Law, Physician, Wife of Bath, and

Manciple. In each case, Gower's version is relatively freestanding and independent of context; indeed, we often feel an unproductive disproportion between a complex story and the simple moral sentence it is supposed to illustrate. Chaucer deflects and narrows Gower's stories to the dramatic self-revelations of particular, idiosyncratic tellers; and in each case, he self-consciously considers the ideological implications of genre. In the Squire's Tale Chaucer gives romance narrative and the romance narrator their most searching examination. The conventional trappings of the genre—threatened incest, doublings, binary terms that are fused together with only limited success—serve primarily to comment on the Squire's own comportment as a lover. His enthusiastic innocence, a large part of his narrative verve, reveals itself to be in part an overly confident and naive appropriation of the female to male concerns. Love's code of service, which seems at first sight to be a cruel device for women to torment men, also serves male purposes and satisfies male desires—and a lover's success, as the falcon's narrative reveals, can quickly turn to sullen indifference. The Squire, as favorably as he is treated in the General Prologue, and however sympathetically we may view him as the teller of his tale, exhibits a lover's blindness to the self-interest within his professedly disinterested sympathy with women.

But if this characterization is the most piquant result of domesticating the exotic in the Squire's Tale, it is by no means the only one: in larger terms, Chaucer uses the Squire and his tale to make a genial comment on his own favorite myth, that of the Golden Age and declining world. The Squire's Tale, with a great deal of delicacy and wit, shows how fully romance reflects a basic human desire for reintegration, for abolishing the distance caused by alienating categories; and it also shows how vigorously such categories resist their own dissolution. In the Franklin's Tale, which immediately follows the Squire's, the hints of a golden past (which surface even in the names Orleans and Aurelius) find their fullest expression in the construction of an ideal sexual relationship between equals, in which the divisive effects of hierarchical categories have been dissipated. But the "mature innocent wisdom" of that tale contrasts with the more adolescent vision of the Squire's, just as the Franklin's ideal of marital equality contrasts with the Squire's mixture of innocent delight and jaded disenchantment, of boundaries crossed or reasserted—a mixture summed up by that central preoccupation of romance: incest.[48]

Notes

I read part of the present essay, in somewhat different form, at a Special Session of the 1982 MLA Convention, and I am grateful to Susan Crane for the opportunity to have done so.

1. For a catalogue of various types of incest as they appear in Middle English romance, see Margaret Adlum Gist, *Love and War in the Middle English Romances* (Philadelphia: University of Pennsylvania Press, 1947), 50–55.

2. See Margaret Schlauch, "The Man of Law's Tale," in *Sources and Analogues of Chaucer's Canterbury Tales* (Chicago: University of Chicago Press, 1941), 155–57; and Laura A. Hibbard, *Mediaeval Romance in England* (New York: Oxford University Press, 1924), 23–34.

3. All quotations from Chaucer are from *The Riverside Chaucer*, ed. Larry D. Benson, 3rd ed. (Boston: Houghton Mifflin, 1987).

4. Claude Lévi-Strauss, *The Elementary Structures of Kinship*, trans. James Harle Bell and John Richard von Sturmer, rev. ed. (Boston: Beacon Press, 1969), 8–25; Northrop Frye, *Anatomy of Criticism* (Princeton: Princeton University Press, 1957), 200.

5. Patricia Parker is especially interesting on the ways in which romance "simultaneously quests for and postpones a particular end, objective, or object" *(Inescapable Romance* [Princeton: Princeton University Press, 1979], 4). For a suggestive account of this ambivalence in Greek romance, see Arthur Heiserman, *The Novel Before the Novel* (Chicago: University of Chicago Press, 1977).

6. John Stevens, *Medieval Romance: Themes and Approaches* (London: Hutchinson University Library, 1973), 100.

7. Northrop Frye, *The Secular Scripture* (Cambridge: Harvard University Press, 1976), 54.

8. The *Riverside Chaucer* reading "a fairye" changes Robinson's "of Fairye": see the textual note on p. 1129 of the *Riverside Chaucer*, and F. N. Robinson, ed., *The Works of Geoffrey Chaucer*, 2nd ed. (Boston: Houghton Mifflin, 1957), 130. Either reading works well in context. The tonal complications of this passage are well sensed but not fully explained by Gardiner Stillwell, "Chaucer in Tartary," *Review of English Studies* 24 (1948): 186–87. One of Chaucer's probable sources, the romance *Cléomadès* (quoted in Schlauch [note 2], 367), also attacks the "lewed peple" for their suspicion:

> Gent de petit entendement
> Demandent à la fois comment
> Tels choses pueënt estre faites
> Que je vous ai ici retraites.
> Aucun en sont tout esbahi.
> Et savez vous que je leur di?
> Je leur di que nigromancie
> Est moult merveilleuse clergie;
> Car mainte merveille en a on
> Faite pieça, bien le set on.
> (1639–48)

[People of little understanding ask immediately how such things as I have told you of here could be made. Some of them are completely frightened. And do you know what I tell them? I tell them that necromancy is truly astonishing knowledge; for one has long since made many a marvel with it, as we well know.] For some interesting general comments on the impulse toward the rationalization of marvels, see Tzvetan Todorov, *Introduction à la Littéra-ture Fantastique* (Paris: Seuil, 1970), esp. 29 and 46–49.

9. Such skepticism about marvels appears elsewhere: William of Rubruck ques-tions the accounts that Solinus and Isidore give of the wonders of the East *(The Mongol Mission,* ed. Christopher Dawson [London: Sheed and Ward, 1955], 170). And Sir John Mandeville often adopts a skeptical pose; see the useful comments of Donald R. Howard, *Writers and Pilgrims: Medieval Pil-grimage Narratives and Their Posterity* (Berkeley and Los Angeles: Univer-sity of California Press, 1980), 62–65, and C. W. R. D. Moseley, *The Travels of Sir John Mandeville* (Harmondsworth: Penguin, 1983), 17–18.

10. Malory's Sir Dinadan and Arthur's court in *Sir Gawain and the Green Knight* are the most notable cynics to be challenged. Chaucer's Franklin warns the skeptical "heep" of us in his audience to wait and see if innocence is rewarded (V.1493).

11. See Alan Gaylord, "A 85–88: Chaucer's Squire and the Glorious Campaign," *Papers of the Michigan Academy of Science, Arts, and Letters* 45 (1960): 341–60; and Stanley J. Kahrl, "Chaucer's *Squire's Tale* and the Decline of Chivalry," *Chaucer Review* 7 (1973): 194–209.

12. The Knight's veneration of the past is characteristic of fourteenth-century romance, for which "olde bookes" grant authenticity; see Howard R. Patch, "Chaucer and Mediaeval Romance," in *Essays in Memory of Barrett Wendell* (Cambridge: Harvard University Press, 1926), 96. Josephine Waters Bennett argues that the Squire's "knyghtes olde" is a reference to Sir John Mandeville *(The Rediscovery of Sir John Mandeville* [New York: Modern Language Association, 1954], 225–26).

The Squire's ambivalence about the past is the more sharply defined by its contrast with the Franklin's response. Although they share the view that, in Europe at least, the days of magic are over, for the Squire this is a matter of regret, for the Franklin one of relief. In the Franklin's Tale, magic is

> swich folye
> As in oure dayes is nat worth a flye—
> For hooly chirches feith in oure bileve
> Ne suffreth noon illusioun us to greve.
> (V. 1131–34)

Romance itself is a form of magic that may delude as much as delight: the phantoms that Aurelius sees in the magician's study are a stock list of romantic desires—scenes of hunting and falconry, knights jousting, and Aurelius's own "lady on a daunce, / On which hymself he daunced, as hym thoughte" (1200–1201). The Squire, young and amorous, is still in this dance, and if his tale reveals the precariousness of romantic phantoms, it also seeks them out.

13. See Guido de Columnis, *Historia Destructionis Troiae*, ed. Nathaniel Edward Griffin (Cambridge: Mediaeval Academy of America, 1936), 230; and John Gower, *Confessio Amantis*, ed. G. C. Macaulay (Oxford: Clarendon Press, 1901), I.1087 and 1131.

14. See Rose Jeffries Peebles, "The Dry Tree: Symbol of Death," *Vassar Mediaeval Studies*, ed. Christabel Forsythe Fiske (New Haven: Yale University Press, 1923), 59–79; and M. R. Bennett, "The Legend of the Green Tree and the Dry," *Archaeological Journal* 83 (1926): 21–32. See especially G. V. Smithers's notes to *Kyng Alisaunder*, Early English Text Society 237 (1957), 146 n. 6755.

15. *Oeuvres de Guillaume de Machaut*, ed. Ernest Hoeppffner, Société des Anciens Textes Français (Paris: Firmin Didot, 1911), 2: 209, lines 1437–38, quoted by John L. Lowes, "The Dry Sea and the Carrenare," *Modern Philology* 3 (1905–6): 8; *Epistola Presbyteri Johannis*, quoted by Lowes, "The Squire's Tale and the Land of Prester John," *Washington University Studies* 1, Part 2, No. 1 (1913), 14. Also see Esther Casier Quinn, *The Quest of Seth for the Oil of Life* (Chicago: University of Chicago Press, 1962), esp. 103–14.

16. *The Bodley Version of Mandeville's Travels*, ed. M. C. Seymour, Early English Text Society 253 (London: Oxford University Press, 1963), 46–49. Also see Henry Yule, ed., *The Book of Ser Marco Polo, the Venetian*, 2nd ed. (London: John Murray, 1875), 1: 132–45.

17. *The Works of Sir Thomas Malory*, ed. Eugene Vinaver (Oxford: Clarendon Press, 1947), 2: 956. For the thirteenth-century French text, see *La Queste del Saint Graal*, ed. Albert Pauphilet, Classiques Français du Moyen Age (Paris: Champion, 1923), 167–68.

18. Malory, 2: 967; *La Queste del Saint Graal:* "Li arbres sanz foille et sanz fruit senefie apertement le monde, ou il n'avoit alors se male aventure non et povreté et soufreté" (184).

19. The contrast with *Sir Gawain and the Green Knight* is instructive: the Gawain poet doubles the mood of new beginnings and fresh innocence—the story takes place at Christmas and New Year's Day; Arthur's court is in its "first age"—and then plays it against an inevitable tragic downfall, the cyclical change in the seasons and in human history. In the Franklin's Tale, the symbolic resonances of the Christmas season work less ambiguously, offering release from threatened horrors.

20. Compare General Prologue I.80 ("a lusty bacheler"), 84 ("of greet strengthe"), and 92 ("He was as fressh as is the month of May"). There is yet another teasing hint of the Squire's narrative investment in the Tartar king: Cambyuskan has ruled for twenty years (V.43), the Squire's age (I.82). These echoes bring to mind Chaucer's frequent device of the narrator's having a surrogate or double within his tale. But in the Squire's Tale narrative sympathy shifts quite noticeably to Canacee, as her father recedes into the mass of the drunken Tartar men: "Hir liste nat appalled for to be, / Ne on the morwe unfeestlich for to se" (365–66). This shift begins to occur when the Squire seems to aver (as F. N. Robinson [note 8] points out, 719) that he is not the teller of this tale, although he, of all the pilgrims, is uniquely fitted to tell it:

> He moste han knowen love and his servyse
> And been a feestlych man as fressh as May,
> That sholde yow devysen swich array.
> (280–82)

Canacee, as "feestlych" and "fressh" as the one ideally suited to describe her, henceforth commands his sympathetic attention.

21. Compare the remarks of J. C. Eade, *The Forgotten Sky: A Guide to Astrology in English Literature* (Oxford: Clarendon Press, 1984), 143–44.

22. Fredric Jameson, "Magical Narratives: Romance as Genre," *New Literary History* 7 (1975–76): 161; Patricia Parker (note 5) quotes this essay as she begins her own theoretical discussion, 4. Also see Jameson's reworking of "Magical Narratives" in *The Political Unconscious: Narrative as a Socially Symbolic Act* (Ithaca: Cornell University Press, 1981), 103–50.

23. H. Marshall Leicester, Jr., "The Art of Impersonation: A General Prologue to the *Canterbury Tales*," *PMLA* 95 (1980): 221.

24. All references to Jean de Meun are to *Le Roman de la Rose,* ed. Daniel Poirion (Paris: Garnier-Flammarion, 1974).

25. C. G. Jung, *The Psychology of the Transference,* in *The Practice of Psychotherapy,* 2nd ed., trans. R. F. C. Hull (New York: Pantheon, 1966), especially 167–201. I am indebted to James Nohrnberg, *The Analogy of "The Faerie Queene"* (Princeton: Princeton University Press, 1976), 622–23, for his mention of Jung's work in the context of the Canacee–Cambalo story. For the quotation from Jacques Derrida, see *Of Grammatology,* trans. Gayatri Chakravorty Spivak (Baltimore and London: Johns Hopkins University Press, 1976), 265. Barbara Johnson uses this quotation as an epigraph in *The Critical Difference* (Baltimore and London: Johns Hopkins University Press, 1980), 25, in an exceptionally interesting discussion of the relation between sexual difference and literature; see particularly 13, and her remarks on Baudelaire's "Invitation au Voyage," 28. Also see Patricia Parker's (note 5) fine comments on romance and modern linguistics, 220 ff.

26. Juliet Vale, *Edward III and Chivalry* (Woodbridge, Suffolk: Boydell, 1982), 70–72. Also see Millard Meiss, *French Painting in the Time of Jean de Berry: The Boucicaut Master* (New York: Phaidon, 1968), fig. 83, for a pictorial representation of "festivities at the court of the Great Khan" (from Paris, Bibliothèque Nationale, MS Fr. 2810: *Le livre des merveilles*).

27. See Dawson (note 9) for reports of Mongol drunkenness (15–16, 97, 163) and diet (16—where they are accused of cannibalism—and 100). Matthew Paris also accuses them of cannibalism (*Matthew Paris's English History,* trans. J. A. Giles [London: H. G. Bohn, 1852–54], 1: 312–14).

28. See the *Riverside Chaucer* notes (890) for the correspondences between the Squire's Tale, Sir John Mandeville, and Mandeville's source, Vincent of Beauvais's *Speculum Historiale,* 30.78 (*Bibliotheca Mundi Vincenti Burgundi* [Douay, 1624; reprint, Graz: Akademische Druck-u.-Verlagsanstalt, 1964]).

29. On incest among the Mongols, see Dawson, 7 and 104.

30. See E. T. Donaldson, "The Ordering of the Canterbury Tales," in *Medieval Literature and Folklore Studies: Essays in Honor of Francis Lee Utley,* ed. Jerome Mandel and Bruce A. Rosenberg (New Brunswick: Rutgers University Press, 1970), 195.

31. There is an interesting discussion of Spenser's meaning in Jonathan Goldberg, *Endlesse Worke: Spenser and the Structures of Discourse* (Baltimore

and London: Johns Hopkins University Press, 1981), 114–17; Goldberg's remarks on the Squire's Tale (36–41) are a great deal more removed from the likely meanings of the text. Also see Nohrnberg (note 25), 622–23.

32. Haldeen Braddy, *Geoffrey Chaucer: Literary and Historical Studies* (Port Washington: Kennikat Press, 1971), 93.

33. See Dorothy Bethurum, ed., *The Squire's Tale* (Oxford: Clarendon Press, 1965), note to 428. Chaucer's conspicuous doubling of names and terms in the Squire's Tale—another instance of which is "For ye youreself upon yourself yow wreke" (454)—has much in common with a common trick of Ovidian irony, as in Marsyas' agonized cry "quid me mihi detrahis? [Why do you tear me from myself?]" or Daedalus's pitiable condition: "at pater infelix, nec iam pater [the unhappy father, now no longer a father]" (*Metamorphoses* 6.385, 8.231).

34. See the note to 499 in the editions of Walter W. Skeat (Oxford: Clarendon Press, 1894) and Albert C. Baugh (New York: Appleton-Century-Crofts, 1963).

35. E. T. Donaldson, ed., *Chaucer's Poetry*, 2nd ed. (New York: Ronald Press, 1975), 1086. There are other examples of this comically imperfect homology. At some points we may forget that the falcon is not a woman: her cage is decorated "In signe of trouthe that is in wommen sene" (645; see also 559). But when she says that she took her faithless lover "by the hond" (596), we are closer to the jarring details of the *Nun's Priest's Tale*, where Pertelote's beautiful eyes are set in "scarlet reed" (VII.3161), and the *Parliament of Fowls*.

36. Harry Berger, Jr., "The F-Fragment of the *Canterbury Tales*: Part I," *Chaucer Review* 1 (1966): 91.

37. Boece 3, m. 2 and pr. 3. The other examples of natural inclination are the lion, apparently tamed, that returns to its carnivorous habits; "the yerde of a tree, that is haled adoun by myghty strengthe" and springs back as soon as it is released; and the Sun, setting in the west, but returning to its accustomed rising place.

38. Robert S. Haller, "Chaucer's *Squire's Tale* and the Uses of Rhetoric," *Modern Philology* 62 (1965): 292–93.

39. Richard Leighton Greene, " 'Foules of ravyne' and 'foules smale' in Chaucer's 'Squire's Tale,' " *Notes & Queries* 210 (1965): 447.

40. Karl Heinz Göller notes this shift in number, but offers a different explanation for it: "Chaucer's 'Squire's Tale': 'The knotte of the tale,' " in *Chaucer und seine Zeit: Symposion für Walter E Schirmer*, ed. Arno Esch (Tübingen: Niemeyer, 1968), 185.

41. The falcon tells her sad tale "to maken othere be war by me, / As by the whelp chasted is the leon" (490–91); we may wonder if these cross-species lessons really work. They do, the Squire implies, by providing a universal catalogue of sexual difference: the male falcon is a "tygre" and is also comparable to Jason and Paris (542–48).

42. See John M. Manly and Edith Rickert, eds., *The Text of "The Canterbury Tales," Studied on the Basis of All Known Manuscripts* (Chicago: University of Chicago Press, 1940), 6: 557.

43. Chaucer certainly had the Prologue to the *Legend* in mind as he wrote the Squire's Tale, for he twice copies from his long excursus on the birds' delight at the coming of spring (F 125–70), once at the beginning of the tale (52–57), and again at the end, when the hawk's "mewe," covered with "veluettes blewe, / In signe of trouthe that is in wommen sene" (644–45), is painted green on the outside, with such "false fowles, / As ben thise tidyves, ter-celettes, and owles" (647–48). The emphasis on women's "trouthe" recalls one of Chaucer's most repeated words in the *Legend*; see esp. F 260, 267, 297, 668, and 1041.

44. John Norton-Smith is, I believe, the only one who has noticed this, and his remarks on Corinna are similar to mine; see "Chaucer's *Anelida and Arcite*," in *Medieval Studies for J. A. W. Bennett*, ed. P. L. Heyworth (Oxford: Claren-don Press, 1981), 95–96.

45. The contrast with the Knight's Tale has other ramifications. Canacee and Emelye are described in quite similar terms, and several of their similarities have been noted by Marie Neville, "The Function of the *Squire's Tale* in the Canterbury Scheme," *Journal of English and Germanic Philology* 50 (1951): 173. They are both early risers (both are up with the sun [I.1040, 1051, 2273; V.384–87]), and they both go for early morning walks in gardens. But the very different treatments they receive are the most striking signs of more general differences between the two tales.

46. For a further ironic dimension in this shift of gender, see Lee Patterson, "For the Wyves love of Bathe": Feminine Rhetoric and Poetic Resolution in the *Roman de la Rose* and the *Canterbury Tales*," *Speculum* 58 (1983): "The 'men' of the penultimate line presumably means 'everyone,' but in the context its more specific, generic meaning predominates: men, the line disturbingly claims, are a subtle foe precisely *because* ('syn') they continually see examples of male tyranny. Far from dissuading men from treachery, the legendary form provides them with models" (689).

47. It will be apparent that I disagree with some recent works on this subject; see David Lawton, *Chaucer's Narrators* (Cambridge: D. S. Brewer, 1985), Derek Pearsall, *The Canterbury Tales* (London: George Allen & Unwin, 1985), and C. David Benson, *Chaucer's Drama of Style* (Chapel Hill: University of North Carolina Press, 1986).

48. The phrase "mature innocent wisdom" is Northrop Frye's, *Anatomy of Criticism*, 202.

The Historical Basis of Chaucer's Squire's Tale

VINCENT J. DIMARCO

This essay is dedicated to the memory of Robert A. Pratt.

"For all that appears to the contrary, the world has been right for the last five hundred years in regarding the Squire's Tale as nothing more or less than a romance"—thus the crushing pronouncement of Kittredge, delivered at the close of his masterful, point-by-point demolition of Brandl's attempt to understand the tale as a historical allegory of contemporary events centered on the family of Edward III.[1] But has the world been right, if that is in fact how the tale has been regarded? That the dominant impression of the Squire's Tale is of a miscellany of various motifs and allusions, bits of pseudoscientific lore, oriental story pattern, and the reminiscences of travelers' accounts, no fair-minded reader can deny. Further, the fragmentary state of the poem, plus the undeniable rhetorical shortcomings (and excesses) of its youthful narrator, naturally supports speculation that Chaucer never intended to finish the story, but aimed instead for the Franklin politely to interrupt and declare the tale successfully concluded. For at the very least we may suspect that left to his own devices, and judging from the narrative plan he announces in lines 651–70,[2] the Squire (and Chaucer) would otherwise be embarking on a performance of several thousand lines. There are various ends, but no clear means, in sight.

Not every miscellany is a hodgepodge, however; and while it is clear that one fifteenth-century reader, Jean of Angoulême, and a number of twentieth-century critics following the lead of Gardiner Stillwell's influential study[3] have pronounced upon the tale's absurdity, we may do well nonetheless to investigate to what extent the ambitious, perhaps ultimately unmanageable fantasies of the Squire are rooted in a perception shared with his audience of certain geographical, political, and historical realities that suggest the story's significance. So to proceed, even to the extent of identifying actual individu-

This essay first appeared in *Edebiyât* 1 (1989): 1–22. Reprinted by permission.

als who served as the models, clear or faint, of the characters in the tale is not
to enlist the fiction in the service of an ingenious commentary on the conditions of the English court, as did Brandl or, later, Tupper.[4] I wish instead
merely to suggest, as in the case of Cambyuskan's patently magic mirror,
which finds its actual scientific prototype in the reflecting lens of the Pharos
lighthouse of Alexandria, that the Squire's Tale as a whole seeks to effect
through romance a magical transformation of real knowledge, experience,
and history.[5] For I will argue that, regardless of the poem's ultimate disposition, the romantic wonderland of the Squire's Tale is composed on the basis
of, and with constant reference to, a geopolitical situation of immediate and
well-realized significance. The tale prompts questions of no less importance
than the feasibility and ultimate value of the crusade against the heathen; and
by inference it may well suggest an alternative, more tolerant, and realistic
modus vivendi.

We may begin with the emissary of the "kyng of Arabe and of Inde,"
who rides into Cambyuskan's court at Sarai, much in the manner of the *grene
gome* riding into Camelot, as if he comes from the world of faerie or, as
Fisher puts it, from "simply exotic Eastern regions; not territories particularly associated with the Mongol Hordes."[6] Alone among commentators on
the poem, Robert A. Pratt has denied the purely imaginary status of this kingdom and has identified it as Middle India or India Minor, consisting chiefly,
he says, of Southern Arabia, which from 1252–1382 "was under the control
of the Bahri Mamluks at Cairo."[7] To document this assertion we should note,
first, the classical tradition of various "Indies"; second, the existence of one
India on the African continent in a region (Ethiopia) that in the fourteenth
century was contested by the Egyptian Mamluks, who did in fact control
much of Arabia; third, the medieval disposition to extend the definition and
boundaries of Arabia to lands on both sides of the Red Sea, and hence to
associate it even further with the kingdom of Mamluk Egypt; and fourth, the
geographical tradition that extended the notion of one of the Indies to
encompass the territory all the way from Arabia to the Indus delta.

The absence of any significant body of geographical knowledge of India
among the ancient Greeks,[8] the continuing ignorance of the width and extent
of this distant and mysterious land, a mistaken identification of the Nile
(when thought of as the Biblical Physon) with the Indus, and the geographical ambiguity of certain familiar Biblical verses all combined to establish and
perpetuate throughout the Middle Ages a tradition of various Indies, often
three, one of which was regularly identified with Ethiopia (Abyssinia).[9]
Homer seems to confuse Ethiopia and India, as do most certainly Virgil, his
commentator Servius, Procopius, Epiphanius, Socrates Scholasticus, and
Gervase of Tilbury, *et al.*[10] So venerable a tradition easily accommodated and
rationalized the relocation in the mid-fourteenth century of the kingdom of
Prester John, Rex Indiorum, from its various supposed sites in Central Asia,

to Ethiopia, especially since the Coptic Christians of that land were then
engaged in active opposition to their immediate neighbors, the Moslem
Mamluks of Egypt.[11] At a time (1384) contemporaneous with Chaucer's
writing, the Florentine traveler Simon Sigoli, repeating the common rumor
that Prester John controlled the course of the Nile from his Ethiopian
domain, gives evidence that Ethiopia was regularly considered by Europeans,
in Silverberg's words, "a limb of India":

> Questo signore Presto Giovanni abita in India, ed è cristiano, e possiede
> molte terre di cristiani, e ancche d'infedeli. E la cagione perchè il Soldano
> fa omaggio a costui se è, che ogni volta che questo Presto Giovanni facesse
> aprire certe cateratte di un fiume, allagherebbe il Cairo e Allessandria e
> tutto quel paese; e dicesi che questo fiume è il Nilo il quale corre allato al
> Cairo . . . e il Soldano è á confini con questo Presto Giovani col suo ter-
> reno.[12]

Thus did a flexible notion of India in the Middle Ages, resting on venerable precedent, allow for situating that land elsewhere than on the Indian sub-
continent, and regularly placed it on the African continent, which in
Chaucer's time was in the sphere of direct Mamluk influence. Equally relevant to our purposes is the explicit connection of India, thus conceived, and
Arabia, by Benjamin of Tudela (fl. ca. 1173) who identifies Aden (present-
day South Yemen, on the southern Arabian peninsula) with Middle India, but
who locates this "Aden" on the *western* shore of the Red Sea, in a region
almost certainly corresponding to Ethiopia. So too for Marco Polo, whose
Middle India, Abash (Abyssinia), is in conflict with an Aden that has likewise been misplaced westward. As both Wright and Beazley conclude, the
effect of Benjamin's and Polo's ignorance of the true extent of the Red Sea is
to define an India composed of Ethiopia and southern Arabia.[13] Indeed, the
rather fluid sense during the Middle Ages of what constituted Arabia shakes
any easy confidence we might have that Chaucer, in the opinion of Magoun,
means by "Arabe" only the Arabian peninsula.[14] In his 1789 translation of
Father Jerome Lobo's *Voyage to Abyssinia*, Samuel Johnson remarks that the
"Ancients called all the countries that extend beyond Egypt on each side of
the Red Sea, India or Ethiopia, indifferently."[15] He then goes on to identify
the land of the Midianites as "in Arabia, or the eastern Ethiopia." The Cotton
Mandeville similarly sketches the contours of an Arabia that lies on both
sides of the Red Sea, and that encompasses territories beyond the Arabian
peninsula that certainly include the northern coast of Africa:

> And wyteth wel that the rewme of Arabye is a fulle gret contree. . . . Arabye
> dureth fro the endes of the reme of Caldee [Chaldea] vnto the laste ende of
> Affryk and marcheth to the lond of Ydumme [Idumea] toward the ende of
> Botron [Bozrah, south of Damascus]. And in Caldee the chief cytee is Bal-
> dak [Baghdad]. And of Affryk the chief cytee is Cartage, that Dydo that was

Eneas wif founded, the whiche Eneas was of the cytee of Troye and
after was kyng of Itaylle.[16]

Even more tellingly, Roger Bacon, who also knows the tradition of the
"African India" and who, following Pliny, identifies one of the Ethiopian
tribes as the "Indi," offers a description of an expansive Arabia that in the fourteenth century would be seen to conform closely with the Mamluk empire and
sphere of influence, in its conjunction of Ethiopia/"India," Egypt, and Arabia:

> Et inveniemus apud Plinium sexto libro, et Alfraganus concordat, et
> Lucanus quod antiqui vocabant partem Arabiae totum quod habitatur a mari
> Aethiopico et meridie descendendo per Meroen et Syenem, ita etiam quod
> Heliopolis Aegypti, de qua dictum est, in Arabia computetur; et ideo totum
> quod habitatur a Meroe et Syene et Heliopoli versus orientem inter mare
> Rubrum et mare Aethiopicum sub Arabia continetur. . . . Et non solum hoc,
> sed quicquid est circa linguam, id est, extremitatem maris Rubri et super lit-
> tus ejus versus orientem a cuspide linguae usque ad sinum ejus Persicum.
> Et extendit se a mare Rubro usque ad Pelusium Aegypti ad occidentem, et
> dilatat se ad septentrionem per totum desertum, in quo vagati sunt filii
> Israelis usque ad terram Philistinorum super mare nostrum conterminam
> Aegypto, et extensam ad orientem donec occurrat Amalechitarum regio,
> quae est ad orientem terrae Philistiim, et usque ad terram Edom, seu Idu-
> maeam, que est ad orientem Amalech et usque ad terram Moab.[17]

Then, Bacon adds, Arabia turns northward as far as Lebanon, Cilicia (Lesser
Armenia), and the Euphrates.

In the last of a train of associations that give currency to Chaucer's col-
location *of Arabe and of Inde*, again with reference to Mamluk holdings and
activity in the fourteenth century, we may cite evidence of a geographical tradition that understood one of the Indies as extending from Arabia to the delta
of the Indus. As we have seen, both Benjamin of Tudela and Marco Polo construe India to include southern Arabia, while Mandeville, in the opinion of
his most recent editor, faithfully mirrors contemporary cartographical practice in this regard, with the *Metrical Version* of the *Travels* identifying the
Dead Sea as marking the boundary between "Litille Ynde and Araby," and
the *Cotton Version* also identifying *Emlak* (*Euilac* in the French text), corresponding to Havilah of Gen. 2:14 (modern Obillah on the lower Euphrates),
as India.[18] Such an identification merely echoes Peter Comestor, "Hevilath,
id est Indiam."[19] Similarly, Odoric of Podernone recounts his visit to "inland
India" (*India quae est infra terram*), which is almost certainly to be located at
the head of the Persian Gulf in the area around Basrah.[20] Moreover, under the
rubric "des contrees d'"Ynde' in MS B.N. fonds français 574 (the *Image du
monde*) is described Arabia, along with Palestine, Babylonia, and Chaldea.[21]
And finally we may note how in the Hereford *Mappa mundi* the pictorial representation of the fabulous beast the *Eale* (the yale) is placed on the borders

of Egypt and Arabia Petraea, along with an inscription from Solinus that clearly announces the Indian provenance of the beast.[22]

We cannot doubt, then, that in Chaucer's time the kingdom "of Arabe and of Inde," however conceived, would have been identified with the Mamluk empire, which, centered in Egypt at Cairo, and in full possession since 1291 of the entire Holy Land and what was once the Crusading States, was eager to extend its influence, by diplomacy or force of arms, into Nubia and Ethiopia, while retaining its considerable holdings down the Arabian coast as far as what is today South Yemen and continuing to exert significant influence over the tribes of the interior Arabian peninsula. Giacomo di Verano, describing in his *Liber peregrinationis* a visit to the Holy Land in 1335, offers a representative understanding of the vastness of the Mamluks' holdings (and also, incidentally, places Mecca [Lamech] in India):

> In primis sciendum est, quod Soldanus totam Egiptum possidet, Arabiam, Palestinam, Terram promissionis et totam Asyriam. Sui confines sunt ab Alexandria per Nilum fluvium ascendentes usque ad Ethiopiam per XV dietas; super litus vero Maris Magni versus orientem perveniunt usque Anthiochiam, que contigua est Armenie. . . . De Alexandria autem ascenditur ad Kayrum at Babiloniam, que distant per CC miliaria; et de Kayro ascenditur per Arabiam usque Lamech, qui est sepultus ille pessimus Mahometh, que civitas Lamech est magna [urbs] Indie, et distat Lamech a Kayro et Babilonia per XXX dietas et plus; de Antiochia vero, que habet confinem omnem Armeniam, ascenditur per regnum Aaman, sive Aleph, usque ad Tartaros, per XII dietas, et ille rex Aaman est unus de regibus Asyrie subjectus Soldano. Infra hos terminos continetur Damascus, Terra promissionis, desertum magnum Arabie, Moab et Amon, Palestina, que omnia sunt sub potestate Soldani.[23]

Mandeville, only slightly more conservatively, identifies the Mamluk sultan as "lord of v. kyngdoms"—viz., Egypt, Jerusalem, Syria, Aleppo, and Arabia; he then goes on to add that through vassals "many othere londes he holdeth in his hond."[24]

We are now in a position to investigate the historical basis of the Squire's Tale, which features the appearance at the court of "Sarray, in the land of Tartarye" (correctly identified as Sarai, capital of the Golden Horde, by Francis Thynne in 1599)[25] of an emissary of Mamluk Egypt who comes bearing gifts, one of which, a magic ring, is given to Canacee, daughter of the reigning Mongol monarch, Cambyuskan. That this embassy will lead to Canacee's betrothal we can have little doubt, given the romantic atmosphere occasioned by the stranger's arrival (lines 276–90), Canacee's involvement in the amatory problems of the falcon in Part Two of the fragment, the forecast (lines 667–69) that Canacee's brother will have to combat two individuals for her and, finally, the story-line of the closest analogues. Chaucer would have found a visitor from a foreign court bearing gifts that included both a flying horse and, like the magic mirror, a *salvatio urbis* in either of two thirteenth-century Old French romances, the *Cléomadès* of Adenet le Rois and the *Méliacin* or *Cheval de fust* of Girard d'Amiens.[26] I am personally convinced that in respect to certain details of setting and narration the *Méliacin* presents a version of the story closer to Chaucer's poem, but for present purposes it hardly matters, since in both of these independent treatments of the tale of the Enchanted Horse collected in the *Thousand and One Nights* (as well as in that ultimate source-story itself) the princess is demanded in marriage, as a result of the monarch's rash boon, by the visitor who has brought the magic horse.

We should resist the natural temptation to search for the Mamluk–Mongol diplomacies thus figured in the situation of the Squire's Tale in events closely contemporaneous with the composition of the *Tales of Canterbury*, for although much of the Eastern lore of the Squire's Tale may well have come to Chaucer orally, from merchants and seamen whom he would have encountered in his post as Controller of Customs in the Port of London, it is a fact that from about the middle of the fourteenth century both the Mamluk empire and the Khanate of the Golden Horde, ruled by a succession of impotent monarchs, drastically waned in influence and power. Moreover, with the collapse of the Ilkhanid dynasty in Persia ca. 1340, perhaps the most important reason in the first place for such alliances between Egypt and Sarai had vanished. Now in the case of the Knight's campaigns—more than one of which are indirectly related to the events depicted in the Squire's Tale— Chaucer clearly expects his audience to understand allusions to crusading enterprises over the past half-century. But by the same token, we cannot presume that in the absence of popular written sources Chaucer or his audience would have anything other than a hazy knowledge of Mamluk–Mongol relations of the preceding century. Nevertheless, it is useful to point out, if only as background to a later, more immediately relevant diplomacy, an early exchange of envoys (1261–63) between Sultan Baibars of Cairo (Mandeville's Bendochare or Melech Dare) and Berke, Khan of the Golden Horde, an ardent sympathizer of Islam, in an effort toward an alliance against Hülegü and the Ilkhanids of Persia who had taken Baghdad in 1258 and abolished the Caliphate. As in the Squire's Tale, the Mamluks brought presents to the Mongol court on the Volga: "There was a throne inlaid with carved ebony and ivory, a silver chest, choice prayer-carpets, curtains, cushions innumerable, fine swordblades and silver hilts, saddles from Khwarizm, bows from Damascus, Arabian javelins, silver and enamelled lamps and chandeliers, a priceless Koran in a gold-embroidered case, black eunuchs, cooks, Arab horses, dromedaries, mules, wild asses, giraffes, apes, parrots, etc." The alliance may well have been sealed when Berke sent his daughter in marriage to Baibars.[27] The diplomatic union was continued during the sultanate of el-Mansur Seyf ed-din Qala'un (Elphy, to Mandeville), who in 1287 sent to Töde-Möngke, Khan of the Golden Horde, costly material to furnish a mosque constructed in the Crimea.[28]

But we are on much firmer footing, I believe, if we look for the occasion depicted in the Squire's Tale in this alliance as it was preserved and developed in the reigns of the Mamluk sultan el-Melik en-Nasir (Mandeville's Malech Nassar; ruled 1291–92, 1298–1308, 1309–40) and Khan Özbeg (variously Uzbeck, Usbeck; ruled 1313–41), each of whom led his respective empire to its political, cultural, and military apogee. It is virtually impossible that Chaucer would not have known of Nasir, who maintained active diplomatic relations with Philip VI of France, Pope John XXII, Jaime II of Aragon, and the emperors of Byzantium, as well as with the kings of Ethiopia and Yemen, the Merenids of North Africa (Chaucer's Belmarye), even the rulers of Bulgaria and Hindustan, and who also forged commercial arrangements with Venice, Pisa, and Genoa.[29] Indeed, it is Nasir whose three reigns correspond to that of the Sultan of Egypt or "Babylon" (i.e., Fostat, old Cairo) in much of the fourteenth-century crusading propaganda circulating through western Europe, as for example in the *Secreta fidelium crucis* of Marino Sanuto, the memoir of Henri II de Lusignan (which advocated a route of attack on Alexandria later followed by Chaucer's Knight in the service of Peter II de Lusignan), the *Liber de acquisitione terrae sanctae* of Ramon Lull, the *Directorium* of Burcard(?), etc.[30] Mandeville, who knows the details of Nasir's regaining power in 1309, concludes that he "renede longe and gouerned wisely so that his eldest sone was chosen after him Melech Mader," and in fact it is Mandeville's knowledge of Nasir and his successors, representing material not available in his extant sources, that has been cited to make a claim for that author's actual presence in Egypt.[31] To Hayton the Armenian, Nasir, the sultan reigning at the time of the composition of the widely circulated *Flos historiarum*, was a man of strong, albeit suspicious character, whose empire, although not invulnerable, was buttressed by alliances with the Golden Horde.[32] Ibn Battūta, who visited Egypt in 1326, describes Nasir as of noble character and great virtues, beneficent to pilgrims and assiduous in hearing complaints and appeals in person, farsighted, forceful, devoted to the arts, and the center of a splendid court to which flocked representatives of many lands.[33] Lane-Poole summarizes his character and accomplishments thus: "This self-possessed, iron-willed man,—absolutely despotic, ruling alone—physically insignificant, small of stature, lame of a foot, and with a cataract in the eye,—with his plain dress and strict morals, his keen intellect and unwearied energy, . . . his shrewd diplomacy degenerating into fruitless deceit, his unsleeping suspicion and cruel vengefulness, his superb court, his magnificent buildings,—is one of the most remarkable characters of the Middle Ages. His reign was certainly the climax of Egyptian culture and civilization."[34]

When we consider that the long reign of Özbeg Khan of the Golden Horde at Sarai (1313–41) marked what is universally considered the Golden Age of that Mongol dynasty, and that Özbeg, too, was well known to Western Europe, the relevance to the Squire's Tale of Mongol–Mamluk relations during this period becomes all the more intriguing. We note first Özbeg's special relevance to "Sarray," or New Sarai, which, although founded by Berke (near present-day Volgograd, on the Akhtuba branch of the Volga) only became the capital and court city of the Horde with Özbeg's accession to the throne, and grew during his reign to a population of 100,000.[35] Second, with regard to Cambyuskan's campaigns against "Russye / Thurgh which ther dyde many a doughty man,"[36] evidence here too points to Özbeg. Warfare in Russia continued intermittently long after Batu's successful invasion in 1236–37 and 1240–41, as the various Russian states, though seriously divided, steadily gained ground against the suzerainty of the Horde. Özbeg had cunningly played off the interests of Moscow against those of Tver, but an uneasy peace was shattered in 1317–18 when Michael of Tver defeated Iuri of Moscow, and Özbeg invaded, re-confirming Michael's right to rule while at the same time devastating the greater part of Russia with the exception of Novgorod and Pleskau. It was also during Özbeg's reign that Mongol might was brought to bear in western Russia, Volynia, and Galicia, against an emerging power in Lithuania, Prince Gedmyn, while in the late 1330s under the influence of Lithuania, Smolensk on the Dneiper briefly rose in revolt against the Horde and had to be subdued militarily.[37]

Considering next Chaucer's description of Cambyuskan's religious conviction, "As of the secte of which that he was sworn / He kepte his lay, to which that he was born,"[38] I suggest that here a minor lack of analogy to Özbeg paradoxically argues that this particular individual provided the model of Chaucer's character. For Özbeg, although apparently brought up with the usual Mongol shamanistic beliefs, is remarkable for having converted to Islam, and thus by his accession to the throne is responsible for having instituted Islam as the official religion of the Golden Horde, albeit not without some resistance from the old, entrenched Mongol lines. Özbeg is regularly praised by Moslem historians for his vigorous propagation of the faith; a mosque he built in Solkhat in the Crimea (1314) was still standing in the twentieth century; Ibn Battūta, who met Özbeg and visited Sarai in 1332–33, remarks on his dutiful religious observance and counts at least thirteen mosques in his capital; and William Adam notes to the West the favor the Khan showed to "Saracen monks."[39] But if Özbeg was known as a devout Moslem, he also enjoyed, rightly or wrongly, the reputation in western Europe of tolerance toward Christians. While a list of Franciscan houses in

Tartary, assembled by an anonymous Englishman in 1314, shows a foundation already at Sarai, it was doubtless the favorable notice of Özbeg and his court contained in William Adam's *De modo Sarracenos extirpandi* (completed soon after 1313) that led to John XXII's complimentary correspondence with Özbeg in 1317, praising him for his benevolent treatment of his Christian subjects.[40] Other papal letters, urging the Khan to protect the Christians in his realm from strictures imposed by Moslems, and to the Christians themselves to remain steadfast in the faith, were dispatched in 1321, 1323, and 1330.[41] Writing in 1335, Pascal of Vittoria mentions the papal indulgence available to those laboring in missionary activity in Özbeg's lands. Benedict XII continued friendly correspondence with Özbeg and his son in 1338, and in that same year the papal legate John of Marignolli presented Özbeg at Sarai with, among other things, a great war horse, rich clothing, and cordial waters.[42] In 1340 Özbeg sent as personal envoy to Avignon a Hungarian Minorite, Elias, to testify to the Khan's good favor toward his Christian subjects; in his replies to this embassy, Benedict shows considerable knowledge of events in Özbeg's court, and during the same time he writes directly to Özbeg's wife and son to stress the advantages of conversion to the Christian faith.[43]

However unrealistic the prospect of Özbeg's conversion to Christianity, and however inflated the reports of his benevolence toward Christians, such efforts by the various popes and the missionaries reporting to them must be seen as part of the Church's efforts to neutralize, by whatever means possible, the power of Mamluk Egypt. Even before the decisive battle of Ain Jalut (1260), where Egypt had arrested the westward thrust of the Ilkhanid Mongols of Persia, there had been enmity between the Mamluks and those infidels on their borders; and even when the Ilkhanids officially adopted Islam at the accession of Ghazan Khan in 1295 their territorial ambitions on Mamluk Syria did not abate, nor did the hope in the West of a Christian–Mongol alliance against Egypt. Such an alliance is the persistent theme of fourteenth-century crusading propaganda circulating in the West, of the kind that would have stimulated Chaucer's Knight as well as his favorite crusader, Peter of Cyprus. Edward I of England had acted on such a rumored sympathy to Christianity among the Ilkhanids when he dispatched a delegation headed by Geoffrey de Langley to Arghun Khan in 1297.[44] Prince Hayton of Armenia, whose unfortunate kingdom of Cilicia was regularly ravaged by the Mamluks (all the more so, it would happen, in the years after Peter of Cyprus' raid on *Lyas* [Lajazzo] in 1365), detailed in the first part of his *Flos historiarium* the record of hostility of Egypt to Mongol Persia, then in the second part issued an enthusiastic call for a resumption of the crusade against Egypt based on the apparent desire of the Ilkhanids to ally with the West. William Adam, who intimately knew both the courts of Sarai and Tabriz, likewise argued that the best way to interdict traffic between the Mamluks and their allies in the Crimea was to join with the Persian Mongols. Marino Sanuto argued that Mamluk Syria would fall to the Christians if attacked by the Ilkhanids, and that such an alliance would also help to relieve the economic hardships placed on the West by a resumption of the Egyptian crusade. And the *Directorium*, written later during the reigns of Nasir, Özbeg, and the Ilkhanid Abu Said (1317–35), made a similar argument for a Christian–Mongol joint enterprise.[45]

Such antagonism between Mamluk Egypt and Mongol Persia was real enough, as we have seen, and persistent; it traditionally involved, for both the Mamluks and the Golden Horde, the continuing possibility of joint defense against the common enemy whose lands lay between them. But in the situation depicted in the Squire's Tale, Chaucer offers an image of the strength of Mamluk Egypt and the shrewdness of its foreign policy that would render null and void any such hopes to encourage destructive disunity among the enemy infidels, and make a resumption of the struggle to regain the Holy Land folly to consider.

Soon after assuming the throne of Sarai, Özbeg had written to Nasir as defender of Islam to announce boldly, and with considerable exaggeration, that in Özbeg's vast empire there were now only believers in Islam, all subjects having been either converted or put to the sword. Apparently provoked by a border incursion by a vassal-prince of the Ilkhanids, and concerned by what appeared gestures on Nasir's part toward a rapprochement with Tabriz, Özbeg dispatched in 1314 a large embassy to Cairo. In a spirit of solidarity Nasir accepted the slaves sent as gifts with this mission, and sent back costly presents to Özbeg.[46] In 1316 Nasir dispatched envoys demanding in marriage a princess descended from Chingis Khan himself; this embassy, too, bore rich presents to Sarai. Nasir's ambassador was at first denied an audience with the Khan, while the Mongols pretended to be shocked by the prospect of sending one so royal all the way to Egypt; one day later, after suitable gifts had been proffered, they acceded to the request, but insisted that four full years elapse, with suitable time for negotiations, presents, and preparations, before the marriage itself could take place. The incredible sum of one million dinars was demanded along with a large number of horses, armor, and so forth, and a cortège of Mongols was arranged to accompany the royal bride-to-be. Nasir, who had less need for the alliance than Özbeg, let the matter slip, but it was re-introduced by Özbeg to a later envoy of Nasir, Seif-ud-din, who was at Sarai on other matters. Özbeg declared himself prepared to furnish a princess of the house of Chingis, sprung from Berke, for the customary marriage gift of 20,000 dinars; when Seif-ud-din protested that he was neither empowered nor equipped to carry on such negotiations, Özbeg had the Moslem merchants of Sarai advance the money, as well as additional sums for entertainment. Princess Tulunbeg (Arab.: Dulunbija) embarked from Sarai on 17 October 1319, laying over for a few days at Constantinople where the wedding party was lavishly entertained by Emperor Andronicus II, and arrived at Alexandria the following April, the trip having been prolonged by unfavorable winds. She proceeded to Cairo under a tent of golden tissue that was placed on a carriage dragged by Mamluks. At Cairo she was received by Nasir's lieutenant and the chief emirs, and carried on their shoulders in a covered litter to a silken pavilion. Three days later Nasir granted an audience to the Mongols, Greeks, and Georgians who had accompanied her and, after the marriage contract had been signed, Princess Tulunbeg was conducted to her apartments in the palace that "had been decorated in a fashion hitherto unknown among the Mussulmans."[47]

The marriage, like the alliance that Özbeg hoped it would formalize, proved less than satisfactory. Five years later (1325) travelers reported to Özbeg that Nasir had divorced Tulunbeg after only a few days; that she had been given by him to one of his emirs; and that she had subsequently died. Özbeg's embassies to Cairo in 1332 and 1335 to demand an explanation proved fruitless, as Nasir refused to extend any formal apology, content instead to account for what had happened as the will of Allah. And when Özbeg offered to marry one of Nasir's daughters he was told that none, alas, had yet reached marriageable age. Özbeg, under pressure by Abu Said's forces in the mid 1320s, at one point threatened to cut off the export of slaves to the Mamluk court that had not supported him against the Ilkhanids to a degree he would have desired; he even went so far as to execute a Genoese merchant who was a personal friend of the Egyptian sultan.[48] But Nasir, doubtless cognizant of Özbeg's dependence, and mindful of protecting his own territory, rather than completely breaking off relations with the Golden Horde merely left them in suspension, and moved instead to cement a peaceful arrangement independently with the Ilkhanids. The resulting treaty of Nasir and Abu Said, signed in 1323, was in the main honored by both sides until the latter's death in 1335, at which time the Ilkhanate began to slip into a chaos from which it never really emerged. Nasir's Egypt had neutralized the threat posed by its closest and most powerful enemy without seriously damaging its traditional alliance with that enemy's own greatest adversary, the Golden Horde. In the face of such a coalition with Egypt at its center, the European dream of a Mongol–Christian alliance to defeat Egypt and regain the Holy Land was irrevocably shattered, for all the fervent imagining that had so long sustained it. The best that could realistically be expected now of crusading ventures from the middle of the century were the melancholy and temporary successes enumerated in the portrait of the Knight—the ultimately inconsequential campaigns in North Africa and Moorish Spain; the rape, then abandonment of Alexandria; raids in Asia Minor and beleaguered Cilicia (which was to be destroyed in reprisal by the Mamluks in the 1370s and 1380s); and, finally, the redirection of crusading activity by the Teutonic Order to a theatre far indeed from the Holy Land, against (among others) the Orthodox Christians of the Baltic North. The portrait of Chaucer's Knight presents an idealized, though not impossible career spanning four decades of service "in his lordes werre," in eloquent testimony to Christian idealism in a cause by that time long lost. It seems a remarkable irony, then, that in the half-told tale "of Cambyuskan the bold" of that same Knight's son, Chaucer depicts through historical hindsight a situation whose implications suggest the ultimate failure of such later crusading enterprises. But at the same time can we not appreciate in this fragmentary yet provocative fiction the Squire's exclusively "Saracen" orientation—an orientation that, presented without comparison to any Western European norm, offers in its honorific treatment of such "infidels" a sophisticated outlook and understanding, not only of late-medieval historical and political realities, but of the worth, the integrity of "alien" cultures as well?[49]

Appendix: Notes on the Names of the Ruling House of the Golden Horde in Chaucer's Squire's Tale

Chaucer's Cambyuskan (var. Cambynskan, Kambynskan) has been understood since Thynne's *Animadversions*[50] to correspond to Camius (Cāius Khan), latinized name of Chingis, or Genghis Khan (cf. Hayton's Changuis Can; Mandeville's Changuys). Chingis, of course, never came close to Russia, the invasion being accomplished by his grandson Batu (Hayton's Baitho, Bayto; Mandeville's Batho). But Chaucer's Cambyuskan could well represent a garbled version of Khan Usbekkhan, or some such appellation.

Cambyuskan is depicted as future father-in-law of Theodora, a not unfamiliar name in Byzantine history, which testifies, I believe, to the poet's knowledge of Orthodox Christian alliances through marriage with the Mongols. It should be noted that in 1257 Prince Gleb of the Russian principality of Rostov took in marriage the daughter of the Great Khan Möngke; she was baptized Theodora. This Prince Gleb was a frequent visitor to the Golden Horde.[51] Somewhat farther afield but closer in time to the composition of the Squire's Tale and the events on which it is based, as brought forward in this essay, is the marriage in 1346 of Theodora, daughter of John VI Cantacuzenus, to the Ottoman Sultan Orkhan.[52] But perhaps more relevant to our inquiries is the fact that Özbeg gave in marriage his own sister Konchak (Konchaka) to the Orthodox Prince Iuri of Moscow; her name at baptism became Agatha.[53] Furthermore, Özbeg's third wife, who adopted at marriage the Turkish name Bayalun, was the daughter of the Byzantine Emperor Andronicus III. Ibn Battūta, on a visit to Özbeg's court in 1332–33, accompanied this woman on a journey to Constantinople. Apparently displeased with her marriage and her conversion to Islam, she chose not to return to Sarai.[54]

Cambyuskan is represented as the father of two sons, Algarsyf and Cambalo, and one daughter, Canacee. Ibn Battūta likewise reports of Özbeg's three children, his two sons Tïnibeg (Tina Bak) and Janibeg (Jani Bak), and his daughter Ĩt kujujuk.[55] Some slight support of Hinckley's speculation that the name of Algarsyf represents a corruption of the Russian Iaroslav, a name "of frequent occurrence in the Russian house of Rurik,"[56] is furnished by the special importance enjoyed by Iaroslav I (father of Alexander Nevsky) in the estimation of Batu Khan, who made him his personal envoy to the election of the Great Khan in Karakorum in 1246. John of Plano Carpini, who was also present at this electoral *kuriltay*, mentions Iaroslav often in his narrative.[57]

Skeat thought Cambalo to be derived from Cambalus, Kublai Khan's capital; Robinson preferred as a source for the name Kambala (properly, Kammala), who was Kublai's grandson. But closer to Chaucer's concern in this tale is Cembalo, modern Balaklava on the Crimean peninsula, an important trading center that was ceded by Özbeg to the Venetians.[58]

Astrological explanations of the names of Cambyuskan and his family have elsewhere been proposed.[59]

The suggestion of an incest-motif in the announcement, at the end of the fragment, of a later episode involving Cambalo's struggle to "wynne" Canacee, as well as the associations of the story of Canace (Κανάκη), sister of Marcaeus, suggests to Braddy a possible reason for Chaucer's abandoning the tale.[60] But an interesting sidelight on the problem is offered by knowledge of the Mongol custom, reported to the West by John of Plano Carpini (and, dependent on him, Mandeville), of marriage sanctioned between a son and daughter of the same father, but of different mothers.[61] In what is probably no more than an intriguing coincidence, Ibn Battūta reports that Özbeg's daughter Ĩt kujujuk was not of the same mother as his two sons, Tïnibeg and Janibeg.[62]

Notes

1. George Lyman Kittredge, "Supposed Historical Allusions in the Squire's Tale," *ESt* 13 (1890), 1–24, in rebuttal to A. Brandl, "Über einige historische Anspielungen in den Chaucer-Dichtungen," *ESt* 12 (1889), 161–86, esp. pp. 161–74. Brandl understands Cambyuskan to stand for Edward III; his two sons Algarsyf and Cambalo, Edward the Black Prince and John of Gaunt, respectively; and his daughter Canacee, Edward's daughter-in-law, Constance of Castille. The falcon in Part Two of the story supposedly represents Elizabeth, daughter of Henry of Lancaster; this Elizabeth was divorced by John of Hastings in favor of Phillipa, sister of Roger Mortimer, Earl of March.

2. The edition used throughout is *The Riverside Chaucer*, Larry D. Benson, gen. ed. (Boston: Houghton Mifflin, 1987). The present essay seeks to

enlarge upon and develop a number of points included by the author in the Explanatory Notes to the Squire's Tale, pp. 890–95. SqT VII.651–70 are as follows:

> Thus lete I Canacee hir hauk kepyng;
> I wol namoore as now speke of hir ryng
> Til it come eft to purpos for to seyn
> How that this faucon gat hire love ageyn
> Repentant, as the storie telleth us,
> By mediacion of Cambalus,
> The kynges sone, of which I yow tolde.
> But hennesforth I wol my proces holde
> To speken of aventures and of batailles
> That nevere yet was herd so grete mervailles.
> First wol I telle yow of Cambyuskan,
> That in his tyme many a citee wan;
> And after wol I speke of Algarsif,
> How that he wan Theodora to his wif,
> For whom ful ofte in greet peril he was,
> Ne hadde he ben holpen by the steede of bras;
> And after wol I speke of Cambalo,
> That faught in lystes with the bretheren two
> For Canacee er that he myghte hire wynne.
> And ther I lefte I wol ayeyn bigynne.

3. Jean's comment on the Squire's Tale is quoted by Paul Strohm, "Jean of Angoulême: A Fifteenth-Century Reader of Chaucer," *NM* 72 (1971), 72: "Ista fabula est valde absurda in terminis et ideo ad presens pretermittatur nec utlterius de ea procedatur." With Gardiner Stillwell, "Chaucer in Tartary," *RES* 24 (1948), 177–88, ought to be compared John P. McCall, "The Squire in Wonderland," *ChauR* 1 (1966), 103–9; Harry Berger, Jr., "The F-Fragment of the *Canterbury Tales*: Part I," *ChauR* 1 (1966), 88–102, esp. pp. 88–95; and, with particular attention to the narrator, D. A. Pearsall, "The Squire as Story-Teller," *UTQ* 34 (1964), 82–92, and Robert S. Haller, "Chaucer's *Squire's Tale* and the Uses of Rhetoric," *MP* 62 (1965), 285–95. That the Franklin interrupts the Squire's Tale has been thoughtfully questioned by John W. Clark, "Does the Franklin Interrupt the Squire?," *ChauR* 7 (1972), 160–161, and David M. Seaman, " 'The Wordes of the Frankeleyn to the Squier': An Interruption?," *ELN* 24 (1986), 12–18.

4. Frederick Tupper, "Chaucer's Tale of Ireland," *PMLA* 36 (1921), 186–222, esp. pp. 196–99.

5. For the Pharos Lighthouse, one of the wonders of the classical and medieval world, and the legends surrounding its technological wonders, see Hermann Thiersch, *Pharos, Antike, Islam und Occident* (Leipzig and Berlin: B. G. Teubner, 1904), esp. pp. 39–63. Chaucer unmistakably points us toward a scientific explanation of the "magic" mirror in lines 228–35 of the tale; see in this regard John W. Spargo, *Virgil the Necromancer* (Cam-

bridge: Harvard University Press, 1934), p. 135. The topic deserves separate treatment.

6. John H. Fisher, ed., *The Complete Poetry and Prose of Geoffrey Chaucer* (New York: Holt, Rinehart and Winston, 1977), p. 190, note to line 110.

7. Robert A. Pratt, ed., *The Tales of Canterbury* (Boston: Houghton Mifflin, 1972), p. 375, note to line 110.

8. See, for instance, J. W. McCrindle, *Ancient India as Described by Megasthenês and Arrian*, rev. ed. (Calcutta: Chuckervertty, Chatterjee, 1926), pp. 1–29.

9. As for example Cosmas Indicopleustes, *Christian Topography* 11, lines 331–40, ed. and tr. J. W. McCrindle (London: Hakluyt Society, 1897), pp. 372–73. The land of Cush, moreover, through which the Gihon was said (Gen. 2:13) to flow, was regularly and mistakenly identified with the homonymous biblical name for Ethiopia. And Ugo Monneret de Villard, "Le Leggende orientali sui Magi Evangelici," *Studi e Testi* 163 (1952), p. 219n., plausibly suggests the influence of Esther 1:1 and 8:9, which include India and Ethiopia in the kingdom of the Persians.

10. Homer, *Iliad* 1, line 423, ed. and tr. A. T. Murray (Cambridge: Harvard University Press [Loeb], 1924); Virgil, *Georgics* 4.291–93, tr. H. Rushton Fairclough; Servius on Virgil, "Indiam omnem plagam Aethiopiae accipimus," quoted by C. Raymond Beazley, *The Dawn of Modern Geography* (1906; rpt. New York: Peter Smith, 1949), vol. 3, p. 151; Procopius, *Buildings* 6.1.6, ed. and tr. Glanville Downey (London: Heinemann [Loeb], 1940), p. 363; Epiphanius, *De gemmis*, ed. Robert P. Blake and Henri de Vis, *Studies and Documents* 2, London, 1934, pp. 107–9 (where the Physon is identified with both the Indus and the Ganges); Socrates Scholasticus, *The Ecclesiasticall Historie of Socrates Scholasticus*, 15 (corresponding to ch. 19 of the original), tr. M[eredith] H[anmer] (London, 1576); Gervaise of Tilbury, *Otia imperialia*, in *Scriptores rervm brvnsvicensivm*, ed. G. W. Leibniz (Hanover: N. Foerster, 1710), 2: 759–60.

11. The earliest written identification of the Ethiopian Prester John was apparently made by the Italian geographer Giovanni da Carignano, who in 1306 interviewed Ethiopian envoys of King Wedem Ar'ad as they passed through Genoa on their return from Avignon. His treatise has not survived, but an abstract is included in Jacopo Filippo Foresti's *Supplementum Chronicarum*, published in Venice in 1483; for the history of citations of the African Prester John, see Robert Silverberg, *The Realm of Prester John* (Garden City, NY: Doubleday, 1972), pp. 163–92.

12. Simon Sigoli, *Viaggi al Monte Sinai*, in *Viaggi in Terrasanta*, ed. Cesare Angelini (Florence: F. Le Monnier, 1944), p. 213. "This potentate Prester John dwells in India, and is Christian, and he possesses many cities, both of Christians and of infidels. And the reason why the Sultan [of Egypt] pays him homage is this, that whenever this Prester John chooses to open certain river sluices he can drown Cairo and Alexandria and all that entire country; and it is said that this river is the Nile which flows by Cairo . . . and the Sultan's lands are bordered by Prester John." See Silverberg, *Realm of Prester John*, pp. 178–79. As a matter of fact, King 'Amda-Seyon (1314–44) threatened to do

this very thing. John of Marignolli, whose mission to the "Tartars" began in 1338, reports the same legend of the Sultan's tribute paid to Prester John, and earlier in the century Hayton the Armenian, without mentioning Prester John, had suggested that the surest way to capture Alexandria was to interrupt the water supply carried by conduit from the Nile. See Hayton, *Flos historiarum Terre Orientis* 4.10, *Recueil des historiens des Croisades*, Vol. 2: *Documents Arméniens* (Paris: Imprimerie nationale, 1906), pp. 348–49; and Henry Yule, ed., *Cathay and the Way Thither*, rev. Henri Cordier (London: Hakluyt Society 38, 1915), vol. 3, pp. 222–23, for a conjecture as to the origin of the legend.

13. Benjamin of Tudela, *Travels*, tr. Manuel Komroff, in *Contemporaries of Marco Polo* (New York: Liveright, 1928), p. 312; *The Book of Ser Marco Polo, the Venetian, concerning the Kingdom and Marvels of the East*, tr. Colonel Sir Henry Yule, 3rd ed., rev. Henri Cordier (London: J. Murray, 1903), vol. 2, pp. 433–35. See also Beazley, *The Dawn of Modern Geography*, vol. 3, pp. 150–52, and John Kirtland Wright, *The Geographical Lore of the Time of the Crusades* (1925; rpt. New York: Dover, 1965), p. 292.

14. Francis P. Magoun, Jr., *A Chaucer Gazetteer* (Chicago: University of Chicago Press, 1961), s.v. "Arab(y)e," p. 19.

15. *A Voyage to Abyssinia by Father Jerome Lobo*, tr. Samuel Johnson (London: Elliot & Kay; Edinburgh: Eliot, 1789), pp. 196–97.

16. *Mandeville's Travels*, ed. M. C. Seymour (Oxford: Clarendon, 1967), pp. 29–30.

17. *The "Opus Majus" of Roger Bacon*, ed. John Henry Bridges (1900; rpt. Frankfurt/Main: Minerva, 1964), vol. 1, pp. 325–26, translated in *The Opus Majus of Roger Bacon*, tr. Robert Belle Burke (New York: Russell and Russell, 1962), vol. 1, pp. 343–44: "We shall find in Pliny in the sixth book, Alfraganus and Lucan also agreeing, that the ancients called part of Arabia all the land which is inhabited from the Aethiopic Sea and the south passing through Meroë and Syene, so also that the Heliopolis of Egypt, of which mention has been made, is reckoned in Arabia; and therefore all that country which is inhabited from Meroë, Syene, and Heliopolis toward the east between the Red Sea and the Aethiopic Sea is included under Arabia . . . and not only this section, but whatever there is around the tongue, that is, the extremity of the Red Sea and beyond its shore eastward from the point of its tongue to its Persian Gulf. It extends from the Red Sea as far as Pelusium in Egypt to the west, and spreads to the north through the whole of the desert in which the children of Israel wandered as far as the land of the Philistines above our sea bounded by Egypt, and extending eastward until the region of the Amalechites is reached, which lies to the east of the land of Philistia, as far as the land of Edom, or Idumaea, lying to the east of Amalech and reaching as far as the land of Moab."

18. *The Metrical Version of Mandeville's Travels*, ed. M. C. Seymour, EETS, OS 269 (London: Oxford University Press, 1973), lines 1240–45; *Mandeville's Travels*, ed., Seymour, p. 115. For the French text, see *The Buke of John Maundeuill being The Travels of Sir John Mandeville, Knight 1322–1356* (*Egerton MS. 1982*), ed. George F. Warner (London: Roxburghe Club, 1889), pp. 79–80.

19. Petrus Comestor, *Historia Scholastica*, Gen. 14, in *PL* 198: 1068.

20. Yule-Cordier, *Cathay and the Way Thither*, vol. 3, p. 111, where it is noted that Talmudic writers and Arabs identify the Lower Euphrates region as Hind, i.e., India, perhaps because it was the point of rendezvous for Indian vessels.

21. Wright, *Geographical Lore*, p. 467, n. 102.

22. W. L. Bevan and H. W. Phillott, *Mediaeval Geography: An Essay in Illustration of the Hereford Mappa Mundi* (1873: rpt. Amsterdam: Meridian, 1969), p. 43. For the Yale, see T. H. White, *Bestiary: The Book of Beasts* (New York: G. P. Putnam's Sons, 1960), pp. 54–55. Note also that the Hereford cartographer-illustrator places the *Rinosceros*, also identified from Solinus as of Indian provenance, on the border of Ethiopia.

23. Giacomo di Verona, *Liber peregrinationis*, ed. R. Röhricht, *Revue de l'Orient Latin* 3 (1895), 247–48.

24. *Mandeville's Travels*, ed. Seymour, pp. 24–25.

25. *Francis Thynne's Animadversions upon Speght's first (1598 A.D.) edition of Chaucer's Works*, ed. G. H. Kingsley, rev. F. J. Furnivall, EETS, OS 9, (1875; rpt. London: Oxford University Press, 1965), pp. 53–54.

26. Albert Henry, ed., *Les Oeuvres d'Adenet le Roi*, Vol. 5, *Cléomadès* (Brussels: Presses Universitaires de Bruxelles, 1971); Girard d' Amiens, *Le Roman du Cheval de Fust, ou de Méliacin*, ed. Paul Aebischer (Geneva: Droz, 1974).

27. For Baibars' character and career, see Stanley Lane-Poole, *A History of Egypt*, Vol. 6: *The Middle Ages* (New York: Charles Scribner's Sons, 1901), pp. 262–75; and Steven Runciman, *A History of the Crusades*, Vol. 3: *The Kingdom of Acre and the Later Crusades* (1954; rpt. New York: Harper and Row, 1967), pp. 315–48. Accounts of the Egyptian-Mongol embassy are given by Bertold Spuler, *History of Mongols*, tr. Helga and Stuart Drummond (Berkeley and Los Angeles: University of California Press, 1972), pp. 181–82; Lane-Poole, *History of Egypt*, pp. 265–66; B. Grekov and A. Iakoubovski, *La Horde d'Or*, tr. François Thuret (Paris: Payot, 1939), pp. 79–80; and Henry H. Howorth, *History of the Mongols from the 9th to the 19th Century*, Vol. 2: *The So-called Tartars of Russia and Central Asia* (London: Longmans, Green, 1880), pp. 115–23. The marriage is noted by Stanley Lane-Poole, *The Story of Cairo* (London: J. M. Dent, 1902), pp. 205–6; I have not found it elsewhere recorded.

28. Grekov and Iakoubovski, *La Horde d'Or*, p. 84.

29. For Nasir's biography and reign, see G. Weil, *Geschichte des Abbasiden Chalifats in Aegypten* (Stuttgart: J. B. Metzler, 1860–62), vol. 1, pp. 191–98 (first reign); vol. 2, pp. 272–79 (second reign); and vol. 3, pp. 297–412 (third reign); and Lane-Poole, *History of Egypt*, pp. 288–318. For specialized studies of particular diplomacies, see M. Canard, "Les relations entre les Merenides et les Mameloukes au XIVe siècle," *Annales de l'Institut d'Etudes Orientales* 5 (1939–41), 41–81; and Aziz Suryal Atiya, "Egypt and Aragon," *Abhandlungen für die Kunde des Morgenlandes* 8 (1938), 7–71; W. [von] Heyd, *Histoire du commerce du Levant au môyen age* (Leipzig: Otto Harrossowitz, 1888), vol. 2, pp. 23–45.

30. Martinvs Sanvtvs, *Liber secretorvm fidelivm crvcis super Terrae Sanctae*

(1609; rpt. Jerusalem: Massada Press, 1972); for Ramon Lull, *Liber de acquisitione Terrae Sanctae*, see Aziz S. Atiya, *The Crusade in the Later Middle Ages*, 2nd ed. (1938; rpt. New York: Kraus, 1970), pp. 84–85; Henri II de Lusignan, "Informatio ex parte nunciorum regis Cypri pro subsidio Terre Sancte et passagio, consilium regis Cypri pro passagio faciendo," ed. René de Mas Latrie, in *Documents nouveaux servant de preuves à l'histoire de l'ile de Chypre sous le règne des princes de la maison de Lusignan* (Paris: Imprimerie nationale, 1882), pp. 118–28; for the *Directorium*, see Atiya, *Crusade in the Later Middle Ages*, pp. 99–113.

31. See Robert Fazy, "Jehan de Mandeville: ses voyages et son séjour discuté en Egypte," *Etudes asiatiques* 3 (1949), 30–54, and the discussion of the matter by Dorothee Metlitzki, *The Matter of Araby in Medieval England* (New Haven, CT: Yale University Press, 1977), pp. 233–39. Metlitzki also prints (p. 237) a letter interpolated in four MSS of the *Travels*, purportedly by Melech-masser (Nasir's eldest son?) in which he describes himself as "the soudan of the Babylonians, Assyrians, Egyptians, Amaricans, Medes, Alexandrians, Parthians and Ethiopians[,] . . . provost of the Earthly Paradise and guardian of the Sepulchre of the Crucified, king of Jerusalem, of Africa and Asia, lord of Barbary from East to West, king of kings and prince of princes, offspring of the gods, standard of Mahomet," etc.

32. Hayton, *Flos historiarum*, 4, ch. 2.

33. *The Travels of Ibn Battūta A. D. 1325–1354*, tr. H. A. R. Gibb (Cambridge: Hakluyt Society, 2nd ser. 110, 1958), 1, pp. 26–28.

34. Lane-Poole, *History of Egypt*, pp. 316–17.

35. For New Sarai, see Grekov and Iakoubovski, *La Horde d'Or*, pp. 70–71, 135–47.

36. SqT VII.10–11.

37. For these campaigns, see George Vernadsky, *The Mongols and Russia* (New Haven, CT: Yale University Press, 1953), pp. 195–208; Henry H. Howorth, *History of the Mongols*, vol. 2, pp. 148–72; Jeremiah Curtin, *The Mongols in Russia* (Boston: Little, Brown, 1908), pp. 298–336, and Bertold Spuler, *Die Goldene Horde; die Mongolen in Russland* (Wiesbaden: Otto Harrassowitz, 1965), pp. 85–99.

38. SqT VII.17–18.

39. See Vernadsky, *Mongols in Russia*, pp. 196, 198; *Travels of Ibn Battūta*, tr. Gibb, vol. 2, pp. 482–85, 515–16; Guillelmus Adae, *De modo Sarracenos extirpandi*, p. 530.

40. See Beazley, *Dawn of Modern Geography*, vol. 3, pp. 236ff.

41. Beazley, *Dawn of Modern Geography*, vol. 3, pp. 236ff.

42. Luke Wadding, *Annales Minorum* (Rome: R. Bernabo, 1733), vol. 7, pp. 213, 217, 218.

43. Wadding, *Annales Minorum*, vol. 7, pp. 227–28, 229–30; James Muldoon, *Popes, Lawyers, and Infidels* (Philadelphia: University of Pennsylvania Press, 1979), pp. 84–85.

44. See T. Hudson Turner, "Unpublished Notices of the Times of Edward I, Especially of His Relations with the Moghul Sovereigns of Persia," *Archaeological Journal* 8 (1851), 44–51; Runciman, *History of the Crusades*, vol. 3, pp.

346–47; and Denis Sinor, "The Mongols and Western Europe," in *A History of the Crusades*, Vol. 3: *The Fourteenth and Fifteenth Centuries*, ed. Harry W. Hazard (Madison: University of Wisconsin Press, 1975), pp. 531–32.

45. Hayton, *Flos historiarum*, 4.12–13; Guillelmus Adae, *De modo Sarracenos extirpandi*, pp. 534–35; Marinvs Sanvtvs, *Liber secretorvm*, pp. 32–33; for the *Directorium*, see Atiya, *Crusade in the Later Middle Ages*, p. 107.

46. For the history of these diplomacies, see Howorth, *History of the Mongols*, vol. 2, pp. 149–51; Spuler, *Die Goldene Horde*, pp. 92–95; S. Zakirov, *Diplomaticheskie otnosheniia Zolotoi Ordy s Egiptom* (XIII–XIV vv.) (Moscow, 1966), pp. 74–82. My thanks to Professor Robert Rothstein, University of Massachusetts (Amherst), for the translation of this last source.

47. Howorth, *History of the Mongols*, vol. 2, p. 151, translating Novairi.

48. Spuler, *Die Goldene Horde*, pp. 96–97; Vernadsky, *The Mongols in Russia*, pp. 197–98.

49. See, for example, the stimulating essay by Morton W. Bloomfield, "Chaucer's Squire's Tale and the Renaissance," *Poetica* (Japan) 8 (1981), 28–35, which reminds us that Cambyuskan exemplifies natural (non-Christian) man who displays noble virtues.

50. Thynne, *Animadversions*, p. 54.

51. Vernadsky, *The Mongols and Russia*, pp. 168–70.

52. See Herbert Adams Gibbons, *The Foundation of the Ottoman Empire* (Oxford: Clarendon, 1916), pp. 92–94; and *Cambridge Medieval History*, vol. 4 (New York: Macmillan; Cambridge: Cambridge University Press, 1927), pp. 757–59.

53. Spuler, *Die Goldene Horde*, pp. 88–89; Howorth, *History of the Mongols* vol. 2, pp. 151–52; Vernadsky, *The Mongols in Russia*, pp. 199–200. As a result of the death of this woman, who had been captured by the forces of Tver, Michael, Prince of Tver, was executed, and Michael's sons were forced to recognize Iuri as Grand Duke. For the form of the woman's name, see Paul Pelliot, *Notes sur l'histoire de la Horde d'Or* (Paris: Libraire d'Amérique et Orient, 1949), pp. 95–96.

54. This is described in the *Travels of Ibn Battūta*, tr. Gibb, vol. 2, pp. 502–6. Given what we hear in the Squire's Tale of Cambalo's efforts to "wynne" his sister in combat "with the bretheren two" (lines 668–69), it is interesting to note that on her arrival in her father's realm near Constantinople this woman was met by her brother at the head of 5,000 armed horsemen. For the name "Bayalun," see Pelliot, *Notes sur l'histoire de la Horde d'Or*, pp. 83–85.

55. See the *Travels of Ibn Battūta*, pp. 489–90. Howorth, *History of the Mongols*, vol. 2, p. 172, notes two other sons (unknown to Ibn Battūta), Timur and Khidrbeg. After Özbeg's death Tïnibeg ruled briefly, then was murdered by his younger brother Janibeg.

56. Henry Barrett Hinckley, *Notes on Chaucer* (1907, rpt. New York; Haskell House, 1964), p. 215.

57. See Christopher Dawson, *Mission to Asia* (New York: Harper and Row, 1966), pp. 10, 15, 39, 58, 62, 65, and 70–71; and Vernadsky, *Mongols in Russia*, pp. 61, 142–43, and 381. Iaroslav was indeed a well-known figure: his biography, which Vernadsky terms "perhaps the highest achievement of

Russian literature of the early Mongol period," has been published in its fragmentary state by M. Gorlin, "Le dit de la ruine de la terre Russe et de la mort du Grand-Prince Jaroslav," *Revue des études slaves* 32 (1947), 1–33.

58. See A. J. de H. Bushnell, "Names and Sources of Chaucer's Squire's Tale," *Blackwoods* 187 (1910), 654–57; and Michel Balard, *La Romanie Génoise (XIIe–Début du XVe siècle)* (Genoa: Atti della società ligure storia patria, 1978), p. 157.

59. See *Canterbury Tales by Geoffrey Chaucer*, ed. John Matthews Manly (New York: Henry Holt, 1928), p. 598n; J. D. North, "Kalenderes Enlumyned Ben They: Some Astronomical Themes in Chaucer," *RES* 20 (1969), 129–54, 257–83, 418–44, esp. pp. 257–62; and Metlitzki, *Matter of Araby*, pp. 75–80.

60. Haldeen Braddy, "Two Chaucer Notes," *MLN* 62 (1947), 173–79.

61. For John of Plano Carpini, see Dawson, *Mission to Asia*, p. 7; and cf. *Mandeville's Travels*, ed. Seymour, p.177: "In that contree [the realm of the Great Khan] sum man hath an c. wyfes, summe lx., summe mo, summe lesse. And thei taken the nexte of hire kyn to hire wyfes, saf only that thei out take hire modres, hire doughtres, and hire sustres of the moder syde. But hire sustres on the fadir syde of another womman thei may wel take, and hire bretheres wyfes also after here deth, and here stepmodres also in the same wyse." Mongol marriage customs are often remarked upon by Europeans: William of Rubruck, *Travels*, ch. 7 (Dawson, *Mission to Asia*, p. 104) notes that the Mongols observe the first and second degrees of consanguinity but no degree of affinity; hence, they can even be married to two sisters at the same time, and a son often takes for his wives all the wives of his deceased father, except his own mother; Vincent of Beauvais, *Speculum Historiale*, 29.76 (1624; rpt. Graz, Austria, 1965), p. 1211, echoes Rubruck. Marco Polo (tr. Yule, vol. 1, pp. 221–22) reports that the Mongols marry their cousins, the widowed wives of their fathers (again excepting their own mothers), and the widowed wives of their brothers. See also Hayton, *Flos historiarum*, 3, ch. 49.

62. *Travels of Ibn Battūta*, vol. 2, p. 486.

East Meets West in Chaucer's Squire's and Franklin's Tales

KATHRYN L. LYNCH

Near the conclusion of the so-called marriage group in the *Canterbury Tales* sits Chaucer's Squire's Tale, a strange hybrid narrative of love and betrayal located in the Mongol empire.[1] Surprisingly, however, none of the many modern readers of the tale has made a study of how the Squire's Tale's setting in the East is connected to its view of the subject that dominates Fragments IV and V of the *Canterbury Tales*: love, power, and the negotiation of a settlement in the prolonged war between the sexes. The omission is especially perplexing when the Squire's Tale is read in combination with its companion narrative, the Franklin's Tale. Indeed, the relation of Squire to Franklin is normally seen as old money to new, aristocrat to parvenu, without reference either to the question of female power or to the geographical and cultural oppositions upon which the stories also insist. When the Squire is understood as making a contribution to the conversation initiated by the Wife of Bath and carried on at least through the Franklin's Tale, it is generally on the subject of true nobility, chivalry, or *gentillesse*—not on the "gentle sex." Donald Baker even goes so far as to rechristen G. L. Kittredge's marriage group a "gentillesse group" in order to include the Squire in its discussion.[2]

A closer examination of the cultural geography of the Squire's and the Franklin's Tales will show that, rather than undermining false social pretensions in his upstart Franklin, Chaucer is more interested in commenting on a different sort of excess here: an excess of female sexual power connected by both the Squire and Franklin with the exotic East. To be sure, I do not deny that the Squire and Franklin are characters well suited to dramatize and discipline this surplus of female power. But I will not be arguing that therefore the point of either tale is the narrator's reflection in it. The Squire sets up an

This essay first appeared in *Speculum* 70 (1995): 530–51. Reprinted by permission of the Medieval Academy of America.

argument about women, pleasure, and the East that the Franklin will dismantle, and the Franklin's argument will in turn be put under the correction of the
Physician; in each phase, we regard the teller as well as the tale. But our
analysis should never stop with the teller, whose limitations may be seen as
merely heuristic, taken in the context of his total performance.[3]

If the narrator is not the primary focus, what *does* seem immediately
important about the Squire's Tale? A quick look at both the tale itself and widespread reader response suggests an answer in its Orientalism. The first two
lines contain three references to locations in the East ("Sarray," "Tartarye," and
"Russye"); the characters' names, beginning with Cambyuskan in the fourth
line, are largely of Eastern origin, and the poet almost immediately makes reference to the alien law that binds the king (line 18).[4] Correspondingly, the
Squire's Tale has long been viewed as the locus classicus of Chaucer's Orientalism. Thomas Warton in the late eighteenth century and Richard Wharton in
the early nineteenth refer matter in the tale respectively to Mandeville and
Marco Polo. Arguments have since been offered for the importance of the legends of Prester John, the Byzantine epic *Digenes Akrites*, astronomical treatises, a lost romance of Arabic origins, more than one individual tale from the
Arabian or *Thousand and One Nights* collection, and the general structure of
frame tales in the Persian and Indian traditions.[5] Some scholars maintain that
Chaucer worked from a single source, others that his method here was syn-
thetic and highly original. And Jennifer R. Goodman has recently called the
Squire's Tale a "composite romance," a European type characterized by "a
fondness for Oriental detail without reference to any single Oriental source."[6]
But what all these theories of origin share—and what their sheer weight and
persistence support—is the centrality of the Oriental motif to the Squire's Tale;
the tale wraps itself in an aura of exotic alterity, an insistent Orientalism in
much the sense that Edward Said has defined that term.[7]

Although the "Orientalism" that Said discusses in his book-length study
is primarily limited to the period after the late eighteenth century, it has its
roots, as Said also makes clear, in much earlier times, stretching back to the
Middle Ages and beyond. The character of Western Orientalism changed, of
course, after the late Renaissance, with the beginning, as Said puts it, of "the
period of extraordinary European ascendancy,"[8] just as it altered further with
the objectivist and scientific impulses of the Enlightenment. But many features of Orientalism were clearly present in Chaucer's day as well: the Orient, so called even by Chaucer (e.g., Monk's Tale, line 2314), as monstrous,
mysterious, exotic, sensual, sexually deviant. If the East was still a serious
military threat to the West during the Middle Ages, its superior technologies
only made its power more exasperating and inscrutable. More importantly,
Chaucer's world shares with later Western culture a particular way of
approaching the East through domination and moral judgment. First setting
up a strange, different, and dehumanized Other, Said's Orientalist—whether

Chaucer or H. A. R. Gibb—then attempts to erase that difference, to domesticate, disenchant, contain, even to incorporate the Other.[9] Cultural scapegoating, of course, is not limited to the West; the West itself could be exoticized and defined as Other by regions outside, and Europe was not the only part of the medieval world to create an imaginary of cultural distance from India, Africa, and China.[10] Orientalism, however, is the expression of Western power over the space outside its cultural perimeter, space that bears only an oblique relationship to its real geographical counterpart. Indeed, the transactions that constitute Orientalism are primarily, as Said insists, textual ones, participating in a tradition of discourse about and images of the Orient that themselves enact the Orientalist's will to power. The Squire's Tale and the Franklin's Tale, as we will see, are both texts that so attempt to reorganize and gain control over the imaginary world of the East by re-presenting its relationship to a culturally ascendant West.

Before turning to the Squire's Tale itself, however, we need to consider some more specific points about the content of medieval Orientalism and especially about its complex relationship to gender. If the East is geographically and culturally Other to the West, it is also made sexually strange, especially acting as the site where gender distinctions are blurred, the threat of the feminine more explicitly acknowledged, and the relationship between the sexes subtly but fundamentally redefined. I can most easily describe these exchanges by tuning to the frame story of that most famous of Eastern narratives, the *Arabian* or *Thousand and One Nights* (later I will argue these same points about gender and geography from Western sources like Mandeville and Boccaccio). I believe, for reasons discussed below, that Chaucer knew the *Thousand and One Nights*, but I would not insist on the point. Although some of the tales in the *Thousand and One Nights* clearly circulated in Europe during Chaucer's time and have indeed been named as possible sources for the Squire's Tale, the earliest manuscript of the work is in Arabic and dates from the mid-fourteenth century; there is unlikely, therefore, ever to be definitive proof that Chaucer was familiar with the frame story, nor is it likely that we will ever be able to identify precisely what version he might have known. The first surviving European translation was not made until between 1703 and 1713, when Antoine Galland produced a version in French. It is clear, however, that the frame story was known in Europe well before that date; Ariosto uses a version of the frame story, for example, in canto 28 of his *Orlando Furioso*, an epic first published in 1516, little more than one hundred years after Chaucer's death and two hundred years before Galland's French translation.

Indeed, the frame story, and along with it a version of the title, had long been attached to the *Thousand and One Nights* collection, as we can see from two tenth-century summaries, contained in the *Muruj adh-dhahab* of Mas'udi and the *Fihrist* of Ibn al-Nadim.[11] As Ibn al-Nadim claims, "I have seen it in complete form a number of times."[12] One can easily imagine that within the next four hundred years the stories would be told and retold, traveling beyond the Middle East to Europe as trade routes opened and other sorts of learning made their way west. In fact, there are good reasons to believe that the *Thousand and One Nights* was primarily known during the Middle Ages in oral rather than written versions. David Pinault has analyzed the oral and performance dimensions of the collection, including formulaic language and explicit allusions in the texts to the conditions of oral performance.[13] Like the Canterbury tales, these narratives are imagined as tales shared among travelers, merchants, and pilgrims; and their far-flung origins—Arabic, Indian, Persian, Egyptian—bear invisible witness to their passage as stories from one hearer to another.[14]

Granted that the stories in the *Nights* were popular tales told as part of an oral tradition, this still does not explain why they do not also survive in European manuscripts. One possible answer lies in the literary culture of the Arabic Middle Ages. Not only does the Koran display hostility to poets and the Muslim tradition in general denigrate storytelling unless for specifically didactic purposes;[15] early evidence suggests that medieval Muslim scholars considered the *Thousand and One Nights* specifically to be literary smut: the tenth-century *Fihrist*, for example, describes it as "truly a coarse book."[16] In truth, the *Nights* does appeal to a prurient interest, and there can be little doubt that its frank, even insistent, sensualism is responsible for its popularity with later Western translators, who could claim the excuse of Orientalist scholarship while indulging their taste for the exotic. Thus, although the ultimate survival of the *Nights* testifies to the continuing popularity of the collection, it would have seemed an unsuitable subject for medieval scholarship or translation, unlike medical and philosophical treatises, which circulated widely in written form, or even a collection of didactic fables like the *Kalilah wa-Dimnah*, which was rendered from Arabic into Spanish by a school of translators in thirteenth-century Toledo.[17]

An absence of translations, then, is no reason for concluding that either the tales or the associated frame narrative, well known in the East, would have been unknown to Western travelers and writers. Indeed, it seems somewhat perverse to suppose that such compelling and enchanting stories would not have been among the shipmen's tales that cram the packs of the travelers Chaucer describes in the *House of Fame* (lines 2121–24) or the Man of Law's Tale (lines 129–33). For just as Chaucer clearly knew the collection of Eastern tales in Petrus Alphonsi's *Disciplina clericalis* (see the Tale of Melibee lines 1053, 1189, etc.), so he seems to have known some of the tales traditionally included in the *Nights* collection.[18] It is worth considering, therefore, that he was acquainted with the even more widely disseminated frame narrative that brought the *Thousand and One Nights* together. As I will argue below, when Dorigen in the Franklin's Tale offers "[m]o than a thousand stories" (line 1412) as a gambit to delay her own death, Chaucer may be self-consciously casting her as a native Shahrazad, a latter-day British version of

the East Indian queen whose wit and long-winded invention won her a
reprieve from the sentence of death.

In the story of Shahrazad, the frame narrative of the *Thousand and One
Nights*, King Shahzaman of Samarkand is on the point of setting off to visit
his older brother, the powerful Shahrayar, king of India and Indochina, when
he discovers his wife "lying in the arms of one of the kitchen boys."[19] He
concludes that "[w]omen are not to be trusted" (p. 4), executes his wife and
her lover on the spot, throws their bodies into a trench outside the palace, and
proceeds to the court of his brother. There he witnesses his brother's wife
performing the act of darkness in circumstances even more lascivious than
those of his own wife's deception and is forced to reveal the queen's infidelity to King Shahrayar. The two brothers set off at once on a quest to find
another "whose misfortune is greater than ours" (p. 8). They do not need to
travel far before achieving their goal. A great (phallic) pillar rises from the
sea, carrying a small chest that contains a woman. The pillar, who turns out to
be a demon, falls asleep under the very tree in which the brothers are hiding,
and, while he sleeps, the woman forces them to have sex with her, revealing
as she exacts rings from them that she has collected one hundred rings as
tribute from the men with whom she has cuckolded the demon. This experience confirms the brothers' distrust of women: "There is not a single chaste
woman anywhere on the entire face of the earth," announces Shahrayar (p.
10), who then demonstrates an even more extreme response to female
betrayal than Shahzaman: he not only executes his offending wife but
decides as well to take his revenge on all womanhood, disproving the maxim
"can't live with 'em, can't live without 'em" by effectively doing both.

Each night Shahrayar marries a new bride, and each morning he kills her
off, thereby satisfying his manhood without running the risk that he will be
betrayed by what he sees as universal female unchastity. This state of affairs
continues "until all the girls perished, their mothers mourned, and there arose
a clamor among the fathers and mothers, who called a plague upon his
head . . ." (p.11). There is not one maiden left in his kingdom except the two
daughters of his vizier, one of whom is the resourceful Shahrazad, "intelligent, knowledgeable, wise, and refined" (p. 11). Against her father's wishes
Shahrazad volunteers to become Shahrayar's bride, for she has formed a
plan. After they go to bed but before the dawn breaks she will call her
younger sister Dinarzad to their bedside, and Dinarzad will beg her to relate
to them one of her enchanting and suspenseful stories, a story of course
designed to take longer than one night in the telling. In turn, Shahrayar will
postpone her execution so that he can hear the story's conclusion the following night, when she will again begin a new tale without finishing it, and so on
and on. The framework is open-ended, in the earliest surviving manuscript
breaking off after only 271 nights, but Shahrazad's plan is clearly succeeding. As the work progresses, even when there is no suspense and a given story

ends at dawn, the king willingly puts off the execution. Tradition has it that during the years she entertains him by night Shahrazad bears King Shahrayar three children and is ultimately pardoned by him.

I cite the frame story so extensively because I want to emphasize the way that this work conceives of storytelling in gendered terms, especially as a form of feminine resistance to masculine power. Shahrazad's tale telling works a kind of magic on her fierce husband, civilizing his sexual and aggressive impulses, creating space for a new relationship with his wife, different from any he has known before. Her stories operate by rules different from those that govern the masculine narrative with which the *Thousand and One Nights* opens. Shahzaman and Shahrayar make judgments about women that are swift, sweeping, and irrevocable. In their enforcement of the law they allow nothing for context and are inattentive to detail (for example, the detail that the demon abducted and imprisoned his lady before her acts of infidelity). The brothers leap to interpretation when confronted with the display of their wives' infidelities; from interpretation, they move at once to punishment. Then punishment itself becomes compulsive, repetitive, closed off from the possibility of change and growth. The defloration and immediate destruction of successive wives is an energetic demonstration of masculine power, reducing the woman to the sign of her sexual power and repeatedly silencing her.

In contrast, Shahrazad manages to open up a space for feminine language, a language that is quite different from her husband's. Misbehaving women in her stories are not killed; they are transformed into various animals, their punishments deferred, the possibility of regret and reform acknowledged. When punishment is delivered too swiftly—as, for example, in the "Story of the Three Apples" (pp. 150–57), the tale of a slave whose casual account of where he acquired an apple causes a husband to kill his wife—the point is the damage that can be done by hasty and unjust acts of revenge. After the initial brutal and unjustified slaying, multiple gestures of mercy redeem not only the wife murderer and the slave but also the beleaguered vizier, who is assigned the task of discovering the culprits and who ultimately protects the slave by telling a story more marvelous than that of the "Three Apples" itself. Indeed, echoing Shahrazad's own plight, characters in the stories often use tale telling as a way to delay and, they hope, prevent unjust punishment, as not only in the "Three Apples" but also in the more famous "Story of the Merchant and the Demon" (pp. 17–29), in which three old men redeem a merchant's life with stories. The lesson conveyed by all these moral tales is deferral, delay, avoidance of haste and undue finality.

In short, Shahrazad and her sister model for Shahrayar and his brother ways of speaking, listening, acting, and understanding that attend to context and subvert heavy-handed masculinity. Shahrazad's art is what I think modern French feminist critics, like Hélène Cixous or Luce Irigaray, would recognize as a writing of the feminine: a writing or speaking (*écriture feminine, parler-femme*) that mimes the seductive and polymorphous female body, that draws upon mythic and metonymical strengths rather than traditional analytic or teleological ones, subversive rather than judgmental, a writing that defers rather than states its meaning directly, that is playful, joyful, transformative.[20] Even the most frivolous of Shahrazad's tales, the "Story of the Porter and the Three Ladies" (pp. 66–76), is thus about the contested nature of language in a world where the purposes of men and women are often at odds. In this story about women's struggle to reclaim the language of their sex, and specifically to reclaim it from the humorless commitment of men to straight denotation and referentiality, a porter is seduced by three lovely women, who doff their clothes, bathe in front of him, and then challenge him to reveal the names of their sex organs. "Womb," "vulva," "clitoris," he keeps offering hopefully, only to be playfully slapped and boxed about, until finally the women provide the names: "the basil of the bridges," "the husked sesame," "the Inn of Abu Masrur." In the spirit of the game now, the porter himself strips, bathes, and challenges them with a similar riddle; the answer, of course, is not a nominal like "penis," "stick," or "testicles," but "the smashing mule . . . the one who grazes in the basil of the bridges, eats the husked sesame, and gallops in the Inn of Abu Masrur" (p. 75). Having established that the serious business of language can become a sport played with zest and by women's rules, the party of four fall over with laughter and resume their drinking, carousing, and carrying on. Although the hierarchy of the sexes is no more seriously threatened here than in the work as a whole—Shahrayar retains control over Shahrazad, and the porter's wit triumphs over the ladies'—there has been an important shift in terms of discourse, which move subtly but significantly from masculine to feminine: denotation becomes metaphor, which shades into narrative and dissolves in pleasure. Shahrazad's narrative method becomes her victory; as Mary Jacobus observes, the writing of the feminine may not defeat the masculine order directly, but it can expose it "through an effect of playful rehearsal."[21]

If Shahrazad's art seems a writing of the feminine in modern terms, it is also a characteristic Eastern kind in more traditional ones.[22] Seen through the eyes of the West, the East is notoriously a region of relativism rather than absolute value: one thinks of Mandeville's pygmies, who possess everything to scale (including life expectancies) and who scorn big men, using them as laborers and slaves. But sexual values are especially made relative in the East, with polygamists, hermaphrodites, even incestuous marriage in Mandeville's land of the khan all a matter of mere custom.[23] The kingdom of Marco Polo's Kublai Khan, with his four wives and numberless concubines, is also such a land of sexual excess.[24] And travel itself is conceived of as a dangerous encounter with the feminine in Mandeville's Island of the Poison Damsels, where virgins might conceal snakes in their sex organs, and newly married husbands employ surrogates on their wedding nights to "test out the route before they themselves set out on that adventure."[25]

Closer to home, the Arabic world clearly had a reputation of sexual exoticism; its scientific tradition launched numerous explorations of sexual hygiene in the Middle Ages, including perhaps as many as one hundred "arts of love" written between the ninth and the thirteenth centuries, though there is no proof that any specific title was known in the West.[26] Indeed, most information in the West about the nature of human sexuality and erotic behavior originated in Arabic medicine, as Chaucer's January certainly knows when he consults Constantine the African's *De coitu* for aphrodisiacs (IV.1810–11). Islam was perceived as giving license to sensuality; Muhammad not only as a polygamist but also as a lecher and adulterer; and even Mecca as etymologically linked to the Latin *moecha*, "adulteress."[27] Correspondingly, in the tales of the *Decameron* that involve travel to the Near East, the women are both sexual victims and adventurers. For example, in the seventh story of the second day, Alatiel, the Babylonian sultan's daughter, having been sent to marry the king of El Gharb as a virgin, is repeatedly raped and abducted, not always to her chagrin, until after four years she is finally returned to her original bridegroom. With the help of a trusted servant, she coyly concocts such a plausible story that the king "receives her joyfully; and she, who had lain with eight men perhaps ten thousand times, was put to bed to him for a maid";[28] the couple then lives happily ever after, proving that value received can outweigh value given and manner of speaking the thing spoken. Interestingly, gender trumps geography here, with the Eastern men becoming the guardians and manipulators of the endlessly malleable female "virtue." But underlying the exercise of control is a strong Western suspicion of a land both exoticized and feminized, a land at once dangerous, seductive, and indiscriminate.

This Western positioning and distancing of the male from the East creates the possibility of a kind of judgment that is lacking in the *Thousand and One Nights*, where Shahrazad's narratives are welcomed and ultimately embraced by her husband. The *Nights*, with its intricacy and endless series of embedded narratives, enacts and in the process endorses feminine writing. Shahrazad's resistance to Shahrayar is seen as heroic. This approval seems far from Chaucer's attitude. As we will see, the narrative logic that informs the Squire's Tale—indeed, to a fault—is a logic of the feminine East, morally relativistic, sexually deviant, building to a potentially incestuous conclusion without regard to the unities of time, place, or theme. Narrative improprieties mirror the more essential sexual improprieties that lie just below the surface of the tale. Like many Eastern stories, this one combines several disparate topoi; the magical gifts of flying horse, prophetic mirror, translating ring, and healing sword each promises its own narrative, though it takes the 664 lines of the existent tale merely to set up the story of the ring; the organization is episodic and open-ended, with one narrative arbitrarily giving way to another. The Squire's excesses contravene the poet's attempt to control the rhythms of narrative pleasure, formulated as a maxim near the end of the extant tale:

> The knotte why that every tale is toold,
> If it be taried til that lust be coold
> Of hem that han it after herkned yoore,
> The savour passeth ever lenger the moore.
>
> (LINES 401–4)

By "knot," the narrator seems to mean the story's point, the climax or end toward which it is heading; and, indeed, there is unlikely to be, in retrospect, a "knot," a central action around which the meaning of the Squire's Tale gathers. But this is not the only meaning of "knot" evoked here. Chaucer lets us know that he has not just matched a traditional Asiatic story but raised it one, for not only does the tale have no climax, it has no real plot to bring to a climax. The narrative generates no complication, no "knot" of another sort that must be unraveled as a condition of closure. This second sense is the original meaning of knot, or *gnodus,* in the passage from Horace that Chaucer probably used as a source here, a meaning I think the poet is playing off against the "knot" as climax.[29] The tale neither ravels into a knot nor unravels. I do not want to minimize the rhetorical excesses and infelicities that have been pointed out by numerous readers,[30] but even more centrally the Squire bungles just those elements of the action that would have given his narrative a Horatian knot, a significant complication of plot joining one episode to the next. The Squire's Tale thus becomes even more discontinuous, more open-ended than the Eastern tales that form its closest analogues.

Take, for example, the story of the brass horse. This is a tale that is told both in later versions of the *Thousand and One Nights* and in the medieval French romances *Meliacin* and *Cleomadés.*[31] In this plot a suitor brings the flying horse as a gift to the king in hopes of winning the hand of the princess in marriage; the suitor, in some versions a prince from the East or from Africa, is, unfortunately, ugly and malformed, and so the marriage is opposed by both the princess and her brother, the real hero of the story. To remove the opposition to his match and ostensibly to demonstrate the value of his gift, the ugly suitor suggests that the brother might like to take the horse for a ride, which he does. But either the mechanics of descent are extremely difficult, or the suitor has neglected to inform his bride's brother about the peg or pin that will cause the horse to descend, so for a time the brother is dangerously caught in flight, unable to land the magic horse. In *Cleomadés,* for example, it is this malicious omission that generates the main action of the story, which involves the brother's courtship, marriage, loss, and recovery of a maiden he meets after he discovers by means of trial and error the secret of how to land the horse. In *Meliacin*, in addition, the four pins that direct the horse are themselves very troublesome to manage.

Look what happens to this plot in the Squire's Tale. One of the first items of information the "strange knyght" provides about the horse is that it can promptly be returned to earth by the simple "writhyng of a pyn" (line 127). Later, when the knight offers more precise instructions about the horse's operation, he does so matter of factly and explicitly. The text even suggests that the knight may literally be pointing out the relevant objects to the king as he speaks, since, when he offers advice about how to make the horse vanish, he suggests, "Trille *this* pyn, and he wol vanysshe anoon" (line 328; emphasis added). Nowhere are the instructions particularly hard, and even the two bits of information that the knight at first withholds he promises to supply before flight. In fact, they are both necessary *to* flight, involving the precise location of the ignition pin in the horse's ear (line 317) and advice about how to retrieve the horse from invisibility: it shall be done "In swich a gyse as I shal to yow seyn / Bitwixe yow and me, and that ful soone" (lines 332–33). Secrecy in both these cases makes sense as a way perhaps to prevent theft of the valuable horse. Not only is the information offered relatively complete as regards navigating and landing the horse; the description of the horse's flying functions seems easily understood by the king, who once "[e]nformed," "conceyved in his wit aright / The manere and the forme of al this thyng" (lines 335–37).

Thus, even though precise information about takeoff may await further elaboration, the knight's words are far from being, as Brian S. Lee has recently argued, "the most muddled driving instructions in the history of transport."[32] Instead, they make the horse's operation surprisingly transparent. Lee does not seem familiar with the importance of landing the horse in the analogues, since part of the muddle he perceives in the instructions is unnecessary explicitness about this part of the operation: ". . . we can hardly overlook the absurdity that on arrival it is necessary to bid the horse descend."[33] Chaucer does stress the mechanics of descent ("Bidde hym descende," "And he wol doun descende"). Yet this is precisely the sort of advice that travelers on medieval flying horses most need and most commonly lack. With it, the horse is ready for riding; only the secret of how to start remains to be told—then "Ride whan yow list; ther is namoore to doone" (line 334). Instructions having been provided, the horse mysteriously vanishes, and the narrator concludes brusquely, "ye gete namoore of me" (line 343). Despite unanswered questions, this is, as Susan Crane explains, "less the silence of wonder than of dismissal."[34]

No surprise, then, that Part II must change direction, turning to Canacee and her adventures with the magic ring. The narrative of the flying horse has been so thoroughly explained and rationalized that there is literally nowhere for the plot to go; the horse cannot take the disgruntled brother on his exotic adventures because anyone listening to the strange knight's speech already knows precisely how to land the brass steed. Moreover, Chaucer offers no suggestion that either this strange knight, manly and courteous, or the king of Arabia and India whose emissary he is would appear as anything other than appropriate suitors for Canacee were they to offer themselves in that capacity. Chaucer effectively out-Easts the East here. If the Oriental tale is characterized by a loose and associative linkage of episodes, the Squire, as in the tale of the flying horse, fails to provide even those intriguing and surprising turns of the plot that guarantee a minimal unity. As the Tale of Sir Thopas is to the English metrical romance, so the Squire's Tale becomes to the exotic tale of the East: transformed by exaggeration into a caricature that turns even the strengths of the form against it.

Moreover, if the characteristic Oriental romance can be seen as a kind of writing of the feminine, it may reflect back ambiguously upon its narrator, who, like the hero of Thopas, is portrayed, especially in comparison with his father the "bismotered" Knight, as somewhat effeminized: "He was as fressh as is the month of May" (I.92). The only two characters related by blood, the Squire and Knight play a counterpoint to each other; the son is not just a younger version of his dad. Not only has Theseus, the Knight's alter ego in his tale, "conquered al the regne of Femenye" (I.866), which the Squire seems to see as a kind of literary playground, but the father is the one who has had real experience in wars against the East, having fought in Turkey, Morocco, Alexandria, and Russia, while the son's military exploits have all been in Flanders and northern France. The Knight arguably has had first-hand experience of the land about which the Squire only tells, and moreover he has crusaded against it. The Squire lacks such experience, and he is perhaps dangerously open and sympathetic to the cultural difference of the East, a combination that may help to explain another way in which his rehearsal of an Eastern tale comically misses the mark. While, on the one hand, his rendering exaggerates the defects of a loose and episodic narrative structure, making it more Eastern, in a sense, than the paratactic plots he parodies, he also blunts the foreignness of the genre, and makes it less Eastern, by substituting highly courtly and Western motifs, especially where women and love are concerned. In John Fyler's terms, he begins a process here of "domesticating the exotic."[35] Or, as Charles Muscatine says of the Squire's Tale, "the exotic magic leaks out of it early."[36]

It is not in the splendid opening of the tale that this leakage occurs, in Cambyuskan's birthday celebration or the magical gifts he receives, though the curious folk do pry into these closely. The primary disappointment of the exotic comes in the tale's representation of womanhood in the lyrical, but static, second section, which even enthusiasts have tended to like less than the rest of the tale. Canacee is especially disappointing in comparison with the women of Eastern legend and narrative, who like Shahrazad tend to be more headstrong, resourceful, and libidinous than their Western counterparts. Canacee's story is, as one early-twentieth-century reader puts it, "plainly *not* of Eastern origin, but . . . on the contrary essentially a study in medieval love psychology."[37] It is this shift of focus from West to East, also registered as a shift from masculine to feminine, that gives the Squire's Tale its particular chiasmatic shape. The masculine appears initially as an expectation, but its fulfillment is feminine. For the celebration of Cambyuskan's birthday is substituted gift giving to Canacee; for the Mongol ruler Cambyuskan, the ladies' men Gawain and Lancelot (lines 95, 287); for the horse and sword, the ring and mirror; for action and adventure, description and complaint. Even the talking bird, which ought to seem a strange and exotic thing, becomes comically indistinguishable from any swooning courtly maiden. Complicating this shift is the association of the masculine Cambyuskan with the feminine East and of the feminine Canacee with the masculine West.

This complex vacillation between Western and Eastern modes finally destabilizes both the narrative itself and the gender distinctions that the marriage plot requires. The suggestion of incest in the final lines of the tale— "thilke wikke ensample of Canacee, / That loved hir owene brother synfully" (II.78–79)—is shocking not only in and of itself but also, and more especially, in context. Incestuous love and marriage may seem a normal complication to the romance of Omar an-Nu'man, cited by Dorothee Metlitzki as an analogue to the Squire's Tale, but the circumstances are drastically different.[38] In this tale King Umar's oldest son and legitimate heir Prince Sharkan has been raised separately from his half sister Nuzhat, daughter of one of the king's 360 concubines, so that brother and sister marry and have an infant daughter before they discover their true relationship. Such an outcome is unthinkable in the familiar domestic world of the Squire's Tale, where "my lady Canacee" (line 144) occupies a central and public spot, and where her brother Cambalus, we discover, ultimately mediates on behalf of Canacee's falcon (lines 654–56). This world is so thoroughly Westernized and domesticated that the promised exotic ending is not just a horror; it is ludicrous.

One wonders, therefore, if the Franklin's so-called "interruption" of the Squire's Tale may not be partly a response to the oscillations between East and West, feminine and masculine, that characterize the Squire's contribution. Or perhaps "interruption" is not the right term. To be sure, the Franklin seems to cut the Squire off by praising his tale and announcing his desire that his own son emulate the young Squire's *gentillesse*. But, though an impressive thirty manuscripts (including Ellesmere) place the Squire's Tale directly before the Franklin's Tale, there is considerably less agreement about the link that constitutes this interruption. According to Manly and Rickert, only six manuscripts (including Ellesmere) join the Squire's and the Franklin's Tales with this link.[39] And even if we accept the link and its placement, there is much dispute about its significance: Did Chaucer intend it to be an interruption? Or does it date from an earlier stage of composition when he thought that he would be finishing the Squire's Tale?[40] Even given its authority, what does the link mean? It is commonly held to suggest that the Franklin aspires to the sort of nobility of birth or *gentillesse* that the Squire possesses, a social ambition that may get him into trouble later when he offers his own definition of *gentillesse* in his tale.[41] But a persuasive counterargument has been offered as well, one that defends the probable social status of Chaucer's Franklin as unlikely to excite such a level of satire.[42] The function of the link comes to seem hopelessly problematic.

Quite a different picture of the relationship between the two tales emerges, however, if we cut directly through the link to the Prologue of the Franklin's Tale proper:

> Thise olde gentil Britouns in hir dayes
> Of diverse aventures maden layes,
> Rymeyed in hir firste Briton tonge. . .
> (LINES 709–11)

Once we have bracketed the notion that the Breton lay is the Franklin's ploy to improve his social status, what seems clearest in these lines is Chaucer's emphasis on the ethnic origin of his tale, especially given the convention in medieval historical romance of establishing a national or lineal connection at the beginning of a work. First and foremost, Chaucer wants to establish that the Franklin is telling a *British* tale.

As Kathryn Hume points out in her often cited "Why Chaucer Calls the *Franklin's Tale* a Breton Lay,"[43] none of Chaucer's known sources calls itself a lay, suggesting that the designation carries special significance. But neither also were any of them set in Brittany. Indeed, even among English lays, the Franklin's Tale is one of only two to be set in that region.[44] And among all lays, French and English, the Franklin's Tale is unusual in the specificity of its location, down to notable landmarks like the rocks off Brittany's coast near Penmarch where the newly married Dorigen and Arveragus live (line 801). Finally, as Hume herself acknowledges, there are problems and contradictions in categorizing the Franklin's Tale as a lay: the variety of the genre, the preference in Chaucer for married rather than courtly adulterous love, the use of natural rather than fairy magic.[45] Add the metrical differences from the traditional lay and one quickly reaches the conclusion, as John Beston puts it, that "the Franklin's Tale is in all important ways an anomaly."[46] More probably, Chaucer wanted to stress the *Breton* in Breton lay.[47] In that case he would have adapted his Italian source, a

story from Boccaccio's *Il Filocolo*, to the lay form to ease his more important act of transplanting the story from Naples to Brittany, a change of scene
underscored as well by the first line of the tale itself: "In Armorik, that
called is Britayne" (line 729).

The deliberate archaism here, "Armorica,"[48] anticipates the ancient
British names in the tale—Arveragus, Aurelius, Dorigen—all of which are
used in some form by Geoffrey of Monmouth in his *History of the Kings of
Britain*. It has long been recognized that the Franklin's Tale is related to
Geoffrey's story of Cymbeline's second son Arviragus, whose happy mar-
riage to Claudius's daughter Genuissa is recounted in the *History*, and it is
sometimes argued that Aurelius recalls Geoffrey's Aurelius Ambrosius, who
is responsible for Merlin's bringing the giant rocks from Ireland to Mount
Ambrius.[49] But why did Chaucer turn to Geoffrey of Monmouth in the
Franklin's Tale? Perhaps he did so because Geoffrey provided a respected
British foundation myth, and one that linked British history to the origins of
Western Civilization in the transplanting of East to West, Troy to Rome; in
the *House of Fame* (line 1470), Chaucer mentions Geoffrey of Monmouth
along with Homer, Dares, and Dictys as bearers of the cultural charge of
Troy: "So hevy therof was the fame / That for to bere hyt was no game"
(lines 1473–74). The fourteenth-century Geoffrey has thus taken pains to
locate his Franklin's story in place and tradition, and that location is securely,
even aggressively, native and Western. If the Squire's Tale is exogamous,
marrying East and West, however unhappily, the Franklin's, I will argue, is
endogamous, concerned with protecting the purity of the hearth from invasion from the outside.

There is one character in the Franklin's Tale, however, who even from
the beginning is contaminated, who carries forward from the Squire's Tale
the threat of the exotic, and that is Dorigen. Even Dorigen's name is less pure
than those of the two men in her life, though it is still clearly Celtic in origin.
Dorigen parallels Genuissa, eponymous heroine of Gwent and the Genhwys-
son,[50] but her name, unlike Arveragus's and Aurelius's, is a deviation. As
Peter J. Lucas has recently demonstrated, rather than a variant reading of the
women's name Ohurguen, Dorigen is probably based on a common man's
name—Dorguen or Dorien—"influenced by Geoffrey of Monmouth's
Genuissa."[51] In other words, Dorigen's name is doubly gendered, both masculine and feminine, a fact that seems significant given the amount of power
she initially wields in her marriage with Arveragus. As critics of the marriage
are fond of pointing out, she wears the pants in the family, making her more
like the aggressive, resourceful heroine we might have expected to find in the
Squire's Oriental romance, but did not.

Indeed, Dorigen's role recollects a foundation myth that is sharply
opposed to the one Geoffrey provides of Brutus civilizing Britain. In a
story that was very popular in the fourteenth and fifteenth centuries, Anglo-
Norman and English romancers describe the background to Geoffrey's

account of Brutus's arrival, and in particular tell of Albin[a], the Greek or Syrian princess who, as in the story of Danaus's daughters, joins with her sisters in plotting against their husbands' mastery by killing them in their sleep.[52] The Greek Albina's plans are thwarted by her younger sister's mildness toward her own husband and betrayal of the insurrection to their father. (In the versions where Albina is Syrian, her murderous designs are successful.) Discovery leads to the sisters' exile and their abortive attempt to found the matronymic nation of Albion. Despite their grand schemes, however, the sisters find that they are unable to get along without men, and they surrender themselves to libidinous appetites and the embraces of the devil, who, in various forms, impregnates them with the giants whose progeny Brutus will come to slay and colonize. The addition of the story of Albina thus recasts the matter of Geoffrey's *Historia* not only as a British foundation myth but also as a cautionary tale about the dangers to society of ambitious—and foreign—women who usurp masculine privilege. A society, like a marriage, the story seems to say, must be founded upon the authority of the male, upon the patriarchal law that brings order to the chaos of the land once the "regne of Femenye" (I.866), like enemies from the outside, is cleared away.

In reality, however, Dorigen is far from realizing the full threat of feminine autonomy. Like Albina and her sisters, Dorigen's elevated social standing may give her the upper hand over Arveragus,[53] and he may swear to her at the beginning of their marriage that he "[n]e sholde upon hym take no maistrie / Agayn hir wyl" (lines 747–48). But the most that can be said is that she momentarily flirts with freedom from masculine subjection just as she flirts with the squire Aurelius. The Franklin has reduced both her imaginative and physical scope, to bring her firmly within the circle of male control. Although she is given "so large a reyne" (line 755) at the tale's beginning, as soon as she tries to exercise any liberty, she is restrained and punished. True to her doubly gendered name, she reveals two aspects in her response to Aurelius's proposition, one proper and chaste:

> By thilke God that yaf me soule and lyf,
> Ne shal I nevere been untrewe wyf,
> In word ne werk, as fer as I have wit;
> I wol been his to whom that I am knyt.
> Taak this for fynal answere as of me.
>   (LINES 983–87)

another in an entirely different spirit, playful and seductive:

> But after that in pley thus seyde she . . . .
>   (LINES 988)

Dorigen's offer to love Aurelius after he has cleared the coast of dangerous rocks is, in the terms I laid out earlier, an expression of the feminine. Intricate, playful, unrelated to the purposes of the moment, it defers closure of their relationship; it supplies the Horatian "knot" that the narrative requires if it is to unravel properly. One need only imagine the Franklin's Tale without this jesting promise: it would, of course, be no tale at all.

Accordingly, the promise generates the action that sends Aurelius to Orleans and puts this squire, like the squire who narrates the Squire's Tale, superficially in touch with the exotic forces of natural magic and astrology associated at this time with the East. If the Franklin is seen as offering a tale that brings the wonders of the Orient firmly under Occidental control, it may explain the otherwise anomalous fact that he travels in the company of the Man of Law (I.331), another pilgrim whose story even more explicitly colonizes the exotic East. Interestingly, in the late nineteenth and early twentieth centuries the Franklin's Tale was one of Chaucer's works most commonly held to incorporate a large amount of Oriental material, primarily because of the role of the magician.[54] As I stated earlier, the use of natural, as opposed to fairy, magic distinguishes the Franklin's Tale from the *Filocolo*, where a sorcerer creates a spring garden in the dead of winter using charms mostly drawn from Medea's rejuvenation of Aeson in Ovid. In contrast, Chaucer's clerk turns to the East for the sources of his power. The trip to Orleans takes place because Aurelius's brother remembers "subtile tregetoures" (line 1141), whose pageants include machinery to simulate water, barges, castles, fierce animals, and other spectacles, reminding one of the automated horse and machinery of the Squire's Tale, and later the clerk's show in Orleans includes a skillful rearrangement of the same illusions that Mandeville describes at the Great Khan's feasts.[55] Finally, the "magic" the clerk uses to remove the rocks requires only the sort of knowledge of the tides and the movements of the planets that could be ascertained from the Toledan Tables, first edited by the eleventh-century astronomer Al-Zarqali of Cordova and mentioned by Chaucer in line 1273. Despite their Oriental genealogy, these instances of magic are masculine, "clerical magic," as Susan Crane puts it, closer to science than to the uncanny magic of women in romance. As an attempt to gain access to the female, this magic is not just a means to possession of the woman or a form of discipline but, as Crane observes, "a compensatory exotic," corrupted by contact with the feminine and thus in *need* of discipline itself.[56]

Normally not hostile to astrology, then, Chaucer makes his Franklin surprisingly antagonistic when he describes the clerk's astrological calculations: they are "japes" and "wrecchednesse / Of swich a supersticious cursed-nesse" (lines 1271–72); the clerk's "observaunces" are "illusiouns" and "meschaunces / As hethen folk useden in thilke dayes" (lines 1291–93). In contrast, when Aurelius had returned to Brittany just a few lines earlier, it was to a sturdy, hypermasculine, native hearth, refined to virtue by the bracing hardship of winter, where Janus sits by the fire with two beards and "every lusty man" cries "Nowel" (lines 1250–55). This oscillation from an exotic, morally ambiguous university culture to the moral comfort of a British homeland seems odd in a tale firmly set in pagan times, where the distances traveled are not really very great. But in this tale Orleans to the south comes to represent a world not that far from the Muslim world of the more distant Middle East, a source of relativism and illusion—of "monstre" or "merveille" (line 1344) that can temporarily obscure even the most solid rocks of home.

In contrast to Aurelius, Arveragus travels north, to England proper, to "Engelond, that *cleped was eek Briteyne*, / To seke in armes worshipe and honour" (lines 810–11; emphasis added). Given that his absence leaves Dorigen vulnerable to Aurelius's advances, the journey is not altogether a good thing. But I cannot think that it is altogether a bad one either. It is common, for example, for heroes in Geoffrey of Monmouth to refine their knightly virtue across the Channel. Both Utherpendragon and the original Aurelius go from Britain to Brittany before assuming the throne. The problem is not so much that Arveragus is abandoning his wife as what he is abandoning her to. In the struggle for possession of Dorigen, Arveragus's absence creates a vacuum into which Aurelius can import the contaminating influences of the outside. Dorigen's betrayal, small as it is, shows the consequences of male surrender to the sovereignty of the female and to the mystery of the far away; in this tale the two are inevitably connected.

Dorigen herself registers the difficulty in her own use of language. Once she has felt the consequences of her single moment of playfulness, she is never the same. On one level the tale registers the brute fact that language has consequences, that it can never be pure play. On another level the tale shows how unheroic, even pathetic, language becomes when its chief purpose is, as Shahrazad's had been, merely to avoid death by passing the time. Like the feminine writing of the East, Dorigen's complaint to Fortune for trapping her between two impossible imperatives—death or dishonor—is (dis)organized by association or parataxis: the thirty tyrants who made Phidon's daughters dance naked in their father's blood remind Dorigen of the fifty Spartan maids who gladly chose death over loss of virginity, who in turn remind her of Stymphalides, who died with the image of Diana in her hands, and so on and on to Bilyea's martyrdom by bad breath (line 1544). In this context it is perhaps not surprising that, unlike Shahrayar, who pardons Shahrazad from death after her stories, Arveragus concludes Dorigen's speech with a threat to kill her (line 1481).

In contrast to the *Thousand and One Nights*, Dorigen's legendary is not simply open-ended; it is awkwardly recursive, like a wheel freely spinning in the air, unable to gain traction with any surface. As the increasing inappropriateness of the examples demonstrates, it slows and stops not only because it is halted by something outside, like the return of Arveragus, but also because it has run out of its own power. Rather than giving Dorigen a way to express "her reading of her world . . . to give a voice to her feelings [and] . . . to cope with a situation she finds painful," to quote one recent formulation,[57] the exempla are sterile, mechanical, nothing more than the expanded version of "She moorneth, waketh, wayleth, fasteth, pleyneth" (line 819). Both falcon's and woman's complaints break off because they are going nowhere. Moreover, in the Franklin's Tale female speech is curtailed afterwards and firmly replaced with male speech. As Elaine Hansen astutely notes, Arveragus's command to his wife in lines 1481–83 ("I yow forbede, up peyne of deeth, / That nevere, whil thee lasteth lyf ne breeth, / To no wight telle thou of this aventure") "expressly forbid[s her] to make a story out of her experience, to tell her own tale."[58]

Once Dorigen has confessed her dilemma to her husband and received absolution—" 'Is ther oght elles, Dorigen, but this?' / 'Nay, nay,' quod she, 'God helpe me so as wys! / This is to muche, and it were Goddes will'e" (lines 1469–71)—she speaks again only once, and then just two lines in broken syntax "half as she were mad" (line 1511). From this point on, she is only spoken through by the male characters. Indeed, the piece of information that tips that balance of Aurelius's compassion is not Dorigen's distress—this has been a constant from the moment she learned the rocks were gone—but Arveragus's *gentillesse*, the only new element in the moral equation. And when Aurelius responds, he does so not directly to her but to her as a means to reach Arveragus:

> Madame, seyth to youre lord Arveragus
> That sith I se his grete gentilesse
> To yow, and *eek* I se wel youre distresse,
> . . . .
> I yow relesse. . . .
> (LINES 1526–28, 1533; EMPHASIS ADDED)

A few lines later, he—or perhaps the narrator, depending on the punctuation[59]—cannot resist disciplining Dorigen's speech even further and more explicitly: "But every wyf be war of hire biheeste! / On Dorigen remembreth, atte leeste" (lines 1541–42). Dorigen and Arveragus are quickly consigned to a happy ending—"Of thise two folk ye gete of me namoore" (line 1556)— and the final fifty lines of the tale concern the negotiations between Aurelius and the clerk of Orleans, ending in the famous *demande d'amour*: "Which was the mooste fre, as thynketh yow?" (line 1622).

This closing question may at first seem to open up the tale to discussion, though, unlike in the *Filocolo*, no discussion follows. But a second, closer look suggests that the openness is an illusion no less than the magic. These characters differ from those in the *Filocolo* in that they have not really given up anything to which they had true title.[60] The illusionist from Orleans does not remove the rocks "stoon by stoon" (line 993), as Dorigen had required; he only predicts the tides.[61] Nor does Aurelius really have the money to pay him; despite his cavalier "Fy on a thousand pound!" (line 1227), he has to go to the clerk hat in hand and beg new terms for his debt to avoid selling off all his property (lines 1583–84). And as many a moral critic of the marriage has observed, Arveragus elevates his wife's playful promise above the solemn vow of their wedding, a substitution to which he has no right. Rather than opening up possibilities, then, the question at the end closes them off, since its answer can only be "None of the above." This control and the reduction of outcomes parallel the Franklin's entire narrative method, which is as far from Eastern openness as imaginable; every topic raised is addressed, every problem by the end resolved. Even rhetorical excess is disciplined and tamped down, as in the famed bathos of the Franklin's description of a sunset: "the brighte sonne loste his hewe; / For th'orisonte hath reft the sonne his lyght— / This is as muche to seye as it was nyght—" (lines 1016–18). Although Squire and Franklin resemble each other in disclaiming knowledge of rhetorical colors, the effects they produce are as different as East and West.

In this way the Franklin's Tale actually carries out the process of rationalization that we saw begun in the Squire's Tale, where each member of the audience already knows how to land the brass horse before it even gets into the air and where Canacee and her falcon both become indistinguishable from the pale and virginal heroines of Western romance. Like Canacee's falcon, Dorigen makes a complaint that leads nowhere except back to the male discourse of the husband, the suitor, the clerk, and the Franklin. And yet even this is not the whole story, for, in the delicate back and forth of the *Canterbury Tales*, most modern editors follow the Franklin's Tale with the Physician's Tale.[62] At first glance, the Physician's Tale seems the culmination of the assault on the feminine pleasures of the text begun in the Squire's Tale and continued by the Franklin. Virginia speaks little, and then only to request space to complain her sentence of death, a complaint that in fact she never produces since her request ends almost at once in a swoon (line 245). The death sentence, which Shahrazad and Dorigen had evaded, is quickly carried out on poor Virginia; her unconstrained virtue (line 61) and refusal to indulge in even those innocent pleasures that entrap Dorigen—"feestes, revels, and . . . daunces, / That been occasions of daliaunces" (lines 65–66)—cannot save her from the cruel judgments of men. Apius plays Shahrayar to Virginia's Shahrazad, but the girl's father, who in the *Thousand and One Nights* had valiantly attempted to shield his daughter from the lusts of the king, in Chaucer becomes her sorrowful executioner;[63] the learned virgin never makes it to her marriage bed, and the utter desolation of female pleasure is applauded as a justice superior to the girl's carnal corruption.

In both cases, too, we have a tale that spurns the delights of the flesh told by a character we might have expected to acknowledge the pleasures of the physical body. The hospitable Franklin is a lover of pleasure, "Epicurus owene sone" (I.336). His table is always at the ready; it snows food and drink in his house (I.345–54). Indeed, "[t]o lyven in delit was evere his wone" (I.335). Similarly, the gold-loving Physician is a practitioner of that very "magyk natureel" (I.416) that gets Aurelius and his brother into so much trouble. He knows the medicine not only of the ancient Greeks but also of the doctors of the East, including Haly Abbas, Avicenna, and the infamous Constantine, whose prescriptions in the *De coitu* had enhanced January's sexual performance in the Merchant's Tale. Harry Bailly, too, carnalizes the Physician, recalling in his response to the tale an array of therapies that include urinals and chamber pots and that same "ypocras" that January had used as a love philtre (VI.306). But the similarities between the two tales and their narrators mask an even more important difference. The Franklin's Tale is one of Chaucer's famous successes; the Physician's Tale is generally conceded to be a failure. Brutal and abrupt, at best it explores "ethical complexities"[64] or exposes the superficiality of its narrator.[65] It does not successfully do away with Virginia; her claims on our sympathy and sense of justice continue to rise up, in the suspicious but surprisingly strong people who defeat the corrupt forces of Roman justice; in the Physician's first critic, Harry Bailly, whose tears are only partly comic; and in modern criticism where outrage at Virginia's fate is widespread. If Dorigen's is a tale that warns against incautious flirtations and exotic liberties, Virginia's demonstrates the dangers for both life and fiction of burying too deeply the spirit of play; taken together, they show Chaucer's hesitancy to embrace either the absolutism of the law of the Roman fathers or the chaotic relativism of the barbarous East.

Notes

1. In most manuscripts the Squire's Tale precedes the Franklin's Tale; see below, n. 39.
2. Donald C. Baker, ed., *The Squire's Tale*, Variorum Edition of the Works of Geoffrey Chaucer 2/12 (Norman, OK., 1990), p. 50. For further discussion of the Franklin's concern with *gentillesse* or social status, see below, nn. 41, 42.
3. The question of how to read Chaucer's narrators is, of course, an extremely vexed one, and not one I have the space to discuss fully here. The Franklin's and Squire's Tales have been especially susceptible to dramatic or ironic interpretations, which read narrative infelicities back onto the characters of the narrators. For a summary of objections to such readings, see David Lawton, *Chaucer's Narrators* (Cambridge, England, 1985), esp. the chapter entitled "The Literary History of the Squire's Tale," pp. 106–29. I would like, however, to avoid Lawton's all-or-nothing approach: the rejection of

sustained narrative incompetence does not entail the rejection of *all* narrative incompetence.

4. All citations of Chaucer are from Larry D. Benson, gen. ed., *The Riverside Chaucer,* 3rd ed. (Boston, 1987). Recent scholars have demonstrated the rich combination of fiction and fact that would have characterized Chaucer's knowledge of the Eastern and Mongol worlds; see Marie Cornelia, "Chaucer's Tartarye," *Dalhousie Review* 57 (1977), 81–89; Carmel Jordan, "Soviet Archaeology and the Setting of the Squire's Tale," *The Chaucer Review* 22 (1987), 128–40; and especially Vincent J. DiMarco, "The Histori-cal Basis of Chaucer's Squire's Tale," *Edebiyât* 1/2 (1989), 1–22, who includes as part of a general analysis of the relationship of the Squire's Tale to the political configuration of the Mamluk and Mongol empires an appendix on possible origins of the names (pp. 14–15).

5. See W. A. Clouston, "On the Magical Elements in Chaucer's Squire's Tale, with Analogues," in *John Lane's Continuation of Chaucer's Squire's Tale,* ed. F. J. Furnivall, Chaucer Society, 2nd ser., 23, 26 (London, 1888–90); Baker, *The Squire's Tale,* pp. 4–20; H. S. V. Jones, "The Squire's Tale," in *Sources and Analogues of Chaucer's Canterbury Tales,* ed. W. F. Bryan and Germaine Dempster (Chicago, 1941), pp. 357–76; Dorothee Metlitzki, *The Matter of Araby in Medieval England* (New Haven, CT, 1977), pp. 75–80, 140–60; and Haldeen Braddy, "The Genre of Chaucer's Squire's Tale," *Journal of English and Germanic Philology* 3 (1942), 279–90.

6. "Chaucer's Squire's Tale and the Rise of Chivalry," *Studies in the Age of Chaucer* 5 (1983), 127–36.

7. See Edward Said, *Orientalism* (New York, 1978), pp. 31–110. See also Sheila Delany, "Geographies of Desire: Orientalism in Chaucer's *Legend of Good Women,*" *Chaucer Yearbook* 1 (1992), 2–3; and *The Naked Text: Chaucer's Legend of Good Women* (Berkeley, CA, 1994), pp. 165–66; Susan Crane, *Gender and Romance in Chaucer's Canterbury Tales* (Princeton, NJ, 1994), pp. 142–44. Crane's analysis of the relationship between the Squire's and Franklin's Tales, which parallels my own at some points, reached me only during my final revisions.

8. *Orientalism,* p. 7.

9. See, for example, Said's analysis of Dante, *Orientalism,* pp. 67–71.

10. See Aziz Al-Azmeh, "Barbarians in Arab Eyes," *Past and Present* 134 (1992), 3–18.

11. D. B. Macdonald, "The Earlier History of the Arabian Nights," *Journal of the Royal Asiatic Society* (1924), 362–66; David Pinault, *Story-Telling Techniques in the Arabian Nights* (Leiden, 1992), p. 4. It could alternatively be called sim-ply *The Thousand Nights* (Macdonald, "The Earlier History," pp. 362–63).

12. Ibn al-Nadim, *The Fihrist of al-Nadim: A Tenth-Century Survey of Muslim Culture,* trans. Bayard Dodge, 2 vols. (New York, 1970), 2: 713.

13. *Story-Telling Techniques,* pp. 12–16.

14. See Macdonald, "The Earlier History"; Pinault, *Story-Telling Techniques,* pp. 1–12.

15. Hasan El-Shamy, "Oral Traditional Tales and the *Thousand Nights and a Night*: The Demographic Factor," in *The Telling of Stories: Approaches to a*

   Traditional Craft, ed. Morten Nøjgaard, Johan de Mylius, et al. (Odense, 1990) pp. 65–67.

16. Ibn al-Nadim, *Fihrist,* 2: 713.

17. Thomas Ballantine Irving, *Kalilah and Dimnah* (Newark, DE, 1980), p. x. The author of the sexually explicit *Placides et Timeo* claims that esoteric exotica like his should be written "on poor quality parchment that is difficult to read and does not last long" to shield its secrets from the initiated; quoted by Danielle Jacquart and Claude Thomasset, *Sexuality and Medicine in the Middle Ages*, trans. Matthew Adamson (Princeton, NJ, 1988), pp. 127–28.

18. See above, n. 5. Haldeen Braddy, in "The Genre of Chaucer's *Squire's Tale*," argues that Chaucer had a specific Eastern source in mind in the Squire's Tale (pp. 284–85) and that he was particularly drawing on Eastern narrative for the frame, though Braddy considers more closely the frame of the Persian *Thousand and One Days* than the *Thousand and One Nights*. Katharine S. Gittes barely touches on the *Nights* in her *Framing the Canterbury Tales: Chaucer and the Medieval Frame Narrative Tradition* (Westport, CT, 1991) and in "The *Canterbury Tales* and the Arabic Frame Tradition," *PMLA* 98 (1983), 237–51.

19. *The Arabian Nights*, trans. Husain Haddawy, 2nd ed. (New York, 1992), p. 3. Future references from the *Thousand and One Nights* will be taken from this translation and cited in the body of my text. Haddawy's is the first English translation to be based on the fourteenth-century Syrian manuscript, itself only recently edited; see *The Thousand and One Nights (Alf Layla wa-Layla) from the Earliest Known Sources*, ed. Muhsin Mahdi, 2 vols. (Leiden, 1984).

20. See, for example, Luce Irigaray, "When Our Lips Speak Together," in *This Sex Which Is Not One*, trans. Catherine Porter with Carolyn Burke (Ithaca, NY, 1985), pp. 205–18. This writing of the feminine is both a central and contested area for contemporary French feminist criticism. Because the idea of a specifically feminine mode of being and speaking seems complicit in the very patriarchal essentialism and biological determinism that it is designed to undermine, it has come recently under sharp attack; see, for example, the essays and bibliography in *Revaluing French Feminism: Critical Essays on Difference, Agency, and Culture*, ed. Nancy Fraser and Sandra Lee Bartky (Bloomington, IN, 1992). I am not taking sides here as to whether it is strategically or epistemologically sound to posit a woman's essence (see Diana J. Fuss, " 'Essentially Speaking': Luce Irigaray's Language of Essence," in Fraser and Bartky, pp. 94–112). The point is that the *Thousand and One Nights* seems to posit such an essence.

21. *Reading Woman: Essays in Feminist Criticism* (New York, 1986), p. 66.

22. This connection is not, perhaps, surprising. As the site of the Other, the Orient has traditionally been associated with maternal power and the mysterious feminine, even by modern feminist critics who ought to be more critical of such exoticism; see Julia Kristeva, *About Chinese Women*, trans. Anita Barrows (New York, 1977). The weaknesses of this approach illustrate one danger of the kind of essentialism addressed above, n. 20.

23. See *The Travels of Sir John Mandeville*, trans. C. W. R. D. Moseley (New York, 1983), pp. 136–60.

24. See *The Travels of Marco Polo*, trans. Ronald Latham (New York, 1958), pp. 113–62. This is not, however, to suggest that the Western attitude is simply or universally judgemental; for Marco Polo's admiration of the opulence and the luxury of the khan's court, and for Mandeville's "naturalization" of the East, see Mary B. Campell, *The Witness and the Other World: Exotic European Travel Writing, 400–1600* (Ithaca, NY, 1988), pp. 106–12, 122–61.

25. Mandeville, p. 175.

26. See Jacquart and Thomasset, *Sexuality and Medicine in the Middle Ages*, pp. 122–30.

27. See Delany, *The Naked Text*, p. 179.

28. Giovanni Boccaccio, *Decameron*, trans. John Payne, rev. Charles S. Singleton (Berkeley, CA, 1982), p. 153.

29. Horace, *Ars poetica*, in *Satires, Epistles and Ars Poetica*, trans. H. Rushton Fairclough, Loeb Classical Library (Cambridge, MA, 1978), line 191. See also Robert S. Haller, "Chaucer's 'Squire's Tale' and the Uses of Rhetoric," *Modern Philology* 62 (1965), 291.

30. For example, Gardiner Stillwell, "Chaucer in Tartary," *Review of English Studies* 24 (1948), 177–88; D. A. Pearsall, "The Squire as Story Teller," *University of Toronto Quarterly* 34 (1964), 82–92 (but see Pearsall's retraction of this interpretation, in *The Canterbury Tales* [London, 1985], p. 140); Haller, cited above; John P. McCall, "The Squire in Wonderland," *The Chaucer Review* 1 (1966), 103–9; and Robert P. Miller, "Chaucer's Rhetorical Rendition of Mind: The Squire's Tale," in *Chaucer and the Craft of Fiction*, ed. Leigh A. Arrathoon (Rochester, MI, 1986), pp. 219–40. Although these and other critics note the digressive structure of the tale, their emphasis is nearly always on local, rhetorical effects.

31. Girart d'Amiens, *Meliacin ou Le Cheval de Fust*, ed. Antoinette Saly (Aix-en-Provence, 1990); Adenet li Roi, *Cleomadés,* ed. Albert Henry (Brussels, 1971).

32. "The Question of Closure in Fragment V of *The Canterbury Tales*," *Yearbook of English Studies* 22 (1992), 194.

33. "The Question of Closure," p. 195.

34. Crane, *Gender and Romance*, p. 140.

35. John M. Fyler, "Domesticating the Exotic in the Squire's Tale," *English Literary History* 55 (1988), 1–26.

36. *Poetry and Crisis in the Age of Chaucer* (Notre Dame, IN, 1972), p. 128.

37. Lillian Winstanley, ed., *The Clerkes Tale and the Squieres Tale* (Cambridge, England, 1908), p. ci.

38. See *The Matter of Araby in Medieval England*, pp. 140–44, 152–53; another medieval Arabic tale that explores the consequences of brother/sister incest is the "First Dervish's Tale," in the *Thousand and One Nights*, in Haddawy, pp. 86–92.

39. John M. Manly and Edith Rickert, *The Text of the Canterbury Tales, Studied on the Basis of All Known Manuscripts*, 8 vols. (Chicago, 1940), 2: 298.

40. David Seaman neatly summarizes debate about this issue in " 'The Wordes of the Frankeleyn to the Squier': An Interruption?" *English Language Notes* 24 (1986), 13, n. 1. N. F. Blake goes so far as to argue that the link is entirely spurious. See his *The Canterbury Tales: Edited from the Hengwrt Manuscript* (London, 1980), p. 8.

41. Such interpretations are widespread and persistent; see, for example, R.M. Lumiansky, *Of Sondry Folk: The Dramatic Principle in the Canterbury Tales* (Austin, TX, 1955), pp. 180–93; Alan T. Gaylord, "The Promises in the Franklin's Tale," *English Literary History* 31 (1964), 331–65; D. W. Robertson, Jr., "Chaucer's Franklin and His Tale," *Costerus* 1 (1974), 1–26; Nigel Saul, "The Social Status of Chaucer's Franklin: A Reconsideration," *Medium Aevum* 52 (1983), 10–26; and Angela and Peter J. Lucas, "The Presentation of Marriage and Love in Chaucer's 'Franklin's Tale,' " *English Studies* 6 (1991), 501–12.

42. Argued most strongly by Henrik Specht, *Chaucer's Franklin in the Canterbury Tales: The Social and Literary Background of a Character* (Copenhagen, 1981); see also Roy J. Pearcy, "Chaucer's Franklin and the Literary Vavasour," *The Chaucer Review* 8 (1973), 33–59, where Pearcy acknowledges both the weaknesses and strengths of the literary vavasour's bourgeois mentality, while P. R. Coss, "Literature and Social Terminology: The Vavasour in England," in *Social Relations and Ideas: Essays in Honor of R. H. Hilton*, ed. T. H. Aston et al. (Cambridge, Eng., 1983), pp. 109–50, shows that little can be concluded about the Franklin's social status from the term "vavasour."

43. *Philological Quarterly* 51 (1972), 365–79.

44. John B. Beston, "How Much Was Known of the Breton Lai in Fourteenth-Century England?" in *The Learned and the Lewed: Studies in Chaucer and Medieval Literature*, ed. Larry D. Benson (Cambridge, MA, 1974), p. 330; the other is *Sir Degaré*.

45. "Why Chaucer Calls the *Franklin's Tale* a Breton Lay," pp. 366, 369–70.

46. "How Much Was Known of the Breton Lai?" p. 320.

47. Indeed, as Emily K. Yoder argues, the term "Breton" in Chaucer normally means "British" as in springing from "the main island of Britain"; see "Chaucer and the 'Breton' Lay," *The Chaucer Review* 12 (1977), 77.

48. See Peter J. Lucas, "The Setting in Brittany of Chaucer's *Franklin's Tale*," *Poetica* 33 (1991), 26; Lucas also demonstrates that Kayrrud, Arveragus's specific dwelling place, is an archaic form (pp. 24–26).

49. In its original form, as argued by William Henry Schofield, "Chaucer's Franklin's Tale," *PMLA* 16 (1901), 405–49, the argument is for a lost Celtic original lying behind both Chaucer's and Geoffrey's stories. The argument was modified by J. S. P. Tatlock in "The Scene of the Franklin's Tale Visited," *Chaucer Society,* 2nd ser., 51 (1914), 55–77. Both Tatlock here and later Tatlock and Germaine Dempster (in Bryan and Dempster, *Sources and Analogues*, p. 383) find the lost original unnecessary and argue for Chaucer's direct use of Geoffrey. For a return to Schofield's position on different grounds, however, see Jerome W. Archer, "On Chaucer's Source for 'Arveragus' in the Franklin's Tale," *PMLA* 65 (1950), 318–23.

50. Schofield, "Chaucer's Franklin's Tale," pp. 414–16.

51. "Chaucer's Franklin's *Dorigen*: Her Name," *Notes and Queries* 37 (1990), 399. Ohurguen, meaning "golden pure (one)" or "golden girl" was the wife of Alain I, duke of Brittany (888–907); a parallel with her name was first noted by Thomas Tyrwhitt.

52. See *The Brut or The Chronicles of England*, ed. Friedrich W. D. Brie, EETS OS 131 (London, 1906), pp. 1–4; *An Anonymous Short English Metrical Chronicle*, ed. Ewald Zettl, EETS OS 196 (London, 1935), pp. 46–54. I am grateful to Jeffrey Jerome Cohen for calling my attention to this story.

53. In the *Brut* Albina and her sisters specifically scorn their husbands because they are not "of so hye parage comen as here fadyr" (p. 36). Similarly, John Fyler has argued that the phrase "for shame of his degree" (line 752) signifies Arveragus's inferior social status; "Love and Degree in the *Franklin's Tale*," *The Chaucer Review* 21 (1987), 321–23.

54. See, for example, Hugo Lange, "Chaucer und Mandeville's Travels," *Archiv für das Studium der Neueren Sprachen und Literaturen* 74 (1938), 79–81; Walter W. Skeat's notes to the Franklin's Tale, in *The Complete Works of Geoffrey Chaucer*, 6 vols. (Oxford, 1894), 5: 387–400, e.g., note to line 1141. It is clear that Schofield, "Chaucer's Franklin's Tale," is resisting this trend in contemporary scholarship; even he, however, is compelled to acknowledge the probability "that the magician is an importation from the foreign tale" (p. 443).

55. The note to line 1141 in the *Riverside Chaucer* (p. 899) summarizes the traditional explanations for this magic show, ranging from group hallucination to the more commonly accepted theory that such illusions could be created using mechanical devices. The illusions described at lines 1189–1208 are very closely paralleled in Mandeville's *Travels* (trans. Moseley, p. 152).

56. Crane, *Gender and Romance*, p. 146.

57. Mary R. Bowman, " 'Half as She Were Mad': Dorigen in the Male World of the Franklin's Tale," *The Chaucer Review* 27 (1993), 248.

58. *Chaucer and the Fictions of Gender*, p. 280.

59. See the *Riverside* note to lines 1541–44, p. 901.

60. Gaylord makes this point very forcefully, in "The Promises in 'The Franklin's Tale,' " pp. 348–50.

61. Chauncey Wood, *Chaucer and the Country of the Stars: Poetic Uses of Astrological Imagery* (Princeton, NJ, 1970), pp. 245–72, although Wood acknowledges that the high tide's duration of a week or two (line 1295) introduces an "ambiguity" (p. 259).

62. This is the Ellesmere order, followed also by three other base-ten manuscripts; see Helen Storm Corsa, ed., *The Physician's Tale*, Variorum Edition of the Works of Geoffrey Chaucer 2/17 (Norman, OK, 1987), pp. 53–61. A number of critics, usually focusing on plot, have discussed the parallels between the two tales, including Donald R. Howard, "The Conclusion of the Marriage Group: Chaucer and the Human Condition," *Modern Philology* 58 (1960), 227–28, 232; Peter G. Beidler, "The Pairing of the Franklin's Tale and the Physician's Tale," *The Chaucer Review* 3 (1969), 275–79; and Brian

S. Lee, "The Position and Purpose of the *Physician's Tale*," *The Chaucer Review* 22 (1987), 149–51.

63. It is worth considering that Chaucer intended this contrast. The relatively elaborate exchange between the father and daughter is in addition to Chaucer's sources in Livy and the *Romance of the Rose*; see Edgar F. Shannon, "The Physician's Tale," in Bryan and Dempster, *Sources and Analogues*, pp. 398–407.

64. Anne Middleton, "The *Physician's Tale* and Love's Martyrs: 'Ensamples Mo than Ten' as a Method in the *Canterbury Tales*," *The Chaucer Review* 8 (1973), 14; also, Lee C. Ramsey, " 'The Sentence of It Sooth Is': Chaucer's *Physician's Tale*," *The Chaucer Review* 6 (1972), 185–97.

65. This is a frequently made argument; see, for example, Richard L. Hoffman, "Jephthah's Daughter and Chaucer's Virginia," *The Chaucer Review* 2 (1967), 20–31. Even critics who praise the tale admit that it is inferior both to the tale that precedes it and the one that follows; see Lee, "The Position and Purpose of the *Physician's Tale*," pp. 149–51.

Orientation and Nation in Chaucer's *Canterbury Tales*

SUZANNE CONKLIN AKBARI

It is becoming commonplace for modern readers of medieval literature to refer to Chaucer's "Orientalism."[1] There are reasons, however, why one might hesitate to do so. To begin with, Said posits a twofold timeline for the rise of Orientalism, with one starting point in the late eighteenth century and another at the dawn of time.[2] Since only the latter, far less specific form of Orientalism could be found in medieval texts, the term may be too vague to be useful.[3] There is, moreover, another obstacle in the path of the effort to speak of medieval Orientalism, located in Said's description of Orientalism as a "discourse," a formulation he presents as crucial: "without examining Orientalism as a discourse one cannot possibly understand the enormously systematic discipline by which European culture was able to manage—and even produce—the Orient."[4] Said goes on to draw upon Foucault's theory of discourse (especially as articulated in *The Order of Things*) not only to define Orientalism but also to identify paradigmatic manifestations of it in the writings of nineteenth-century British colonial administrators, some of whom were also self-identified academic "Orientalists."[5] Said himself specifies, at least initially, that a "discourse," in the Foucauldian sense, is a specifically post-Enlightenment phenomenon. His subsequent use of the term, however, is less scrupulous; for example, Said refers to the "discourse" of Orientalism in Dante's portrait of Muhammad in the *Inferno*.[6] It is unsurprising, then, that those who employ Said's theory use the term *discourse* with comparable vagueness.

Can we speak of a "discourse" existing in medieval culture, let alone a "discourse of Orientalism"? Foucault would say, absolutely not. Discourses, in his formulation, only begin to appear in the seventeenth and eighteenth centuries, with the decline of the *ancien regime*. The rationalism of the Enlightenment provided the philosophical underpinning necessary to the constitution of discourses, while technical and scientific advances provided the mechanisms necessary to construct and to exercise the power embodied in those discourses. Nonetheless, medievalists persist in referring to "discourse," in spite of the fact that they themselves signal an awareness that there must be some disjunction between the Foucauldian sense of the term and their own, more generic use of it. This appears, for example, in the reference to "a discourse of Orientalism" (as if there were many varieties of a single discourse to choose from—a most un-Foucauldian sentiment!), or in the identification of a "Chaucerian Orientalism" that "partakes ... of a patristic and popular Orientalism."[7] To determine, then, whether medieval Orientalism exists, one must first consider whether medieval discourses exist. Any medievalist familiar with the elaborate ordering systems ubiquitous in medieval natural philosophy (astronomy, physics, medicine, meteorology) will agree that the imposition of categories and the development of systems of knowledge in order to regulate behavior were standard practice during the Middle Ages.[8] But are such categories and systems constitutive of "discourses" in the same way that post-Enlightenment categories and systems are? And, if so, can we identify a particular discourse—such as the discourse of Orientalism—in major literary works of the Middle Ages?[9] In the following pages, I outline the ways in which Chaucer orders the world in the *Canterbury Tales*: that is, how he describes the shape of the world and the place of people in it. The former is seen both on the level of the frame (in the form of the pilgrimage) and on the level of the tale (in the descriptions of different parts of the world found in the tales); the latter is also seen both on the level of the frame and on the level of the tale, and in each case is articulated through terms such as "nacioun," "estaat," and "degree." I go on to argue that this twofold system for imposing order upon the world partakes of a discourse that, in spite of its geographic component, is less the discourse of Orientalism than the discourse of nation.

To consider how the world is ordered in Chaucer's *Canterbury Tales* is to invite comparison of that collection of tales with the great compilations of the Middle Ages, for in some important respects, the *Canterbury Tales* is an encyclopedic work. It differs, of course, from the encyclopedias of Isidore of Seville, Bartholomaeus Anglicus, and Vincent of Beauvais; perhaps the most apparent difference is that the *Canterbury Tales* cannot be used by a reader in the way that these encyclopedias can. Its contents are ordered neither alphabetically, as in Bartholomaeus's *De proprietatibus rerum*, nor according to the norms of cosmography, as in Isidore's *Etymologiae*. What the *Canterbury Tales* shares with these works, instead, is capaciousness and the claim to present a representative, yet comprehensive, view of the world. Capaciousness is, of course, not unique to the encyclopedias; it is a feature of frame-tale narratives in general, which expand to contain the wealth of stories that accrue to the collection.[10] The comprehensive view of the world offered by medieval encyclopedias is evident in their most common titles, which sum up the encyclopedia's role as an all-encompassing view of everything, an "image" or "mirror" of the "world" or, simply, of "things."[11] The comprehensive view of the world offered in the *Canterbury Tales* is, by contrast, representative: Although the whole population of the world is not represented, its diversity is mirrored in small in the microcosm of the pilgrim company, so different from the homogeneous *brigata* of Boccaccio's *Decameron*. The encyclopedic nature of the *Canterbury Tales* has been described by Alastair Minnis, who argues that, in the General Prologue, Chaucer disavows responsibility for the tales that follow much in the way that medieval encyclopedists did, claiming to be simply a reporter of others' words: "demeth nat that I seye / Of yvel entente, but for that I moot reherce / Hir tales alle, be they bettre or werse, / Or elles falsen som of my mateere" (I.3172–75; cf. I.725–38).[12] Minnis compares Chaucer's technique to that of Vincent of Beauvais, who in his *Speculum maius* "was content to 'repeat' or 'report' " the words of his sources, "leaving the reader to judge for himself." Chaucer thus drew from the encyclopedias not just on the level of content, but on the level of form.[13] This aspect of the *Canterbury Tales* was not lost on one of the scribes of the Ellesmere manuscript, who wrote in his Explicit, "Heere is ended the book of the tales of Caunterbury compiled by Geffrey Chaucer." Other aspects of the manuscript layout also reflect the scribe's understanding of the work as an example of *compilatio*.[14]

Chaucer takes from the encyclopedic tradition both the role of author as compiler and some of the hierarchical ordering principles found in the medieval encyclopedia. The wide world anatomized in the compilations devoted to world geography and the linguistic groupings of people also appear in Chaucer's work, both on the level of the frame and within the tales themselves. The text is geographically ordered in two ways: both in the distribution of people from ancient and contemporary civilizations spread across the continents of Europe and Asia, and in the voyage to Canterbury made by the pilgrim company. Moreover, the voyage similarly has a twofold destination: the earthly shrine at Canterbury, which is itself a reflection of the Heavenly Jerusalem; and home, back where it all started, at the Tabard Inn. In such a world, where does the center lie? Are there multiple centers— religious, geographic, civic, national—or is the very notion of centrality shown to be an illusory goal?

In the first section of this essay, I show how, in the *Canterbury Tales*, central, fixed locations are repeatedly shown to be stable only provisionally or contingently, with each location being counterbalanced and subsequently replaced by another. In the second section, I show how the category of "nation" functions in a similarly contingent way. Together, the two sections comprise an argument that in the *Canterbury Tales* the world is ordered on two levels, geographic and national: the geographic is illustrated with reference to the Knight's Tale and the Squire's Tale, the national with reference to the Man of Law's Tale and the Wife of Bath's Tale. In the final section of the essay, having outlined the ordering of the world as it appears in the tales, I briefly describe the ordering of the world on the level of the frame, considering how "degree" and "estaat" are used to establish an apparently "natural" hierarchy in the little world of English society that mirrors in small the geographical hierarchies of the great world it inhabits. While the categories of "degree" and "estaat" function in some tales as fixed markers of individual identity, in others these categories appear to be unstable and unreliable—as variable as the shifting centers of the Canterbury pilgrimage itself.

Ordering the World: Geography

As a pilgrimage narrative, the *Canterbury Tales* presupposes a certain model of the world: that of the *mappamundi*, in which Jerusalem appears as the geographical center of the round earth, its pride of place based on its being the site of Christ's crucifixion and, consequently, of mankind's spiritual rebirth.[15] The earthly Jerusalem was a typological prefiguration of the heavenly Jerusalem, so that the pilgrimage there was a physical manifestation of the spiritual journey taken by every Christian soul.[16] Every other pilgrimage, made to more local shrines, was a smaller scale model (as it were) of the great pilgrimage to Jerusalem.[17] In the *Canterbury Tales*, however, the one-way trajectory of the pilgrimage is almost immediately called into question when the Host proposes a game in which each pilgrim will tell two stories on the way to Canterbury, and two on the way back (I.790–95). What he proposes, in effect, is a new center: The final goal is not the shrine at Canterbury but rather the journey's starting point in Southwark, so that the destination is "heere in this place, sittynge by this post" at the Tabard Inn (I.800). In place of the spiritual home of the shrine, the Host substitutes the physical (and, for him, personal) home of the inn.

These two competing models of the journey (the one-way trip to the shrine and the round-trip to the Tabard Inn) remain in tandem throughout the *Canterbury Tales*, with the alternative centers of Canterbury and Southwark competing as rivals for the attention of the *companye* of pilgrim tale-tellers. Canterbury stands in as a more domestic representative of Jerusalem, just as Southwark stands in as a less carefully controlled and therefore more dynamic substitute for the great urban center of London.[18] This double journey (as it were) to Canterbury and Southwark is rendered still more complex by the fact that the form of the pilgrimage is not simply linear: The experience of the journey is almost as important as its culmination at the shrine, as the pilgrim reenacts the struggle and the suffering experienced long ago by Jesus Christ and his saints. The nonlinear nature of pilgrimage is aptly symbolized in the labyrinth found in some medieval cathedrals, which could be used by those unable to make the journey to Jerusalem.[19] This observation led Donald Howard to argue persuasively that the structure of the *Canterbury Tales* is itself that of a labyrinth, with the nodes of linked tales recapitulating the twists and turns of the maze design.[20] Building on Howard's work, Lee Patterson has suggested that the pilgrimage model is merely one of several "foundational moments," which Chaucer retracts almost immediately after he proposes it, so that "the linear purposiveness of pilgrimage is undone by a persistent retracing of previous patterns."[21] It follows naturally that, in Patterson's reading, the Knight's Tale would function as perhaps the strongest of these "foundational moments," a scene in which the struggle to impose order on a chaotic world is carried out successfully—if only for a moment.[22]

Responding to Charles Muscatine's influential reading of the Knight's Tale as a contest between "noble designs" and chaos, Robert Hanning has presented a reading of the Knight's Tale in the context of its sources (Statius's *Thebaid* and Boccaccio's *Teseida*) that sharply illuminates some of the crucial differences in the version of the Theseus story found in the Knight's Tale, and brings out the extent to which the struggle to impose order on a chaotic world is governed, in the Knight's narration, by the mentality of the "professional warrior."[23] Hanning accords particular significance to Chaucer's description of the amphitheatre built by Theseus to serve as a suitable setting for the battle between Palamon and Arcite to determine which man will win the prize: Emelye, the sister of Theseus's wife. While in Boccaccio's text the tournament lists already exist before the conflict between the men develops, in Chaucer's version the arena is built by Theseus specifically for the occasion; in the *Teseida*, the altars dedicated to the gods are located in the forest, while in the Knight's Tale, the "oratorie" for each god is placed in the amphitheatre itself. The form of the amphitheatre is consistent in both texts: In each case, a geometrically perfect circle is surrounded by multiple "giri," tiers or "degrees."[24] Yet Chaucer, unlike Boccaccio, draws a correlation between the physical structure of the edifice and the social structure of the people who inhabit it: When the time comes for the audience to be seated, they enter "oon and oother, after hir degree" until Emelye and Ypolita are surrounded by "othere ladys in degrees aboute" (I.2573, 2579). Chaucer's amphitheatre thus serves as a kind of "*theatrum mundi*" or "image of the universe,"[25] in which all "degrees" (I.1890) of humanity are arrayed neatly around the central spectacle. The human ruler Theseus presides over the competition, with his temporal authority in turn surmounted by the divine authority of the gods Mars, Venus, and Diana, whose temples are located in the amphitheatre aligned with the cardinal points of the compass (I.1903–13).[26]

The amphitheatre of the Knight's Tale is a powerful symbol, one that refers not only to the direct literary tradition lying behind the Knight's Tale (Statius's *Thebaid* and Boccaccio's *Teseida*) but also to other literary antecedents such as Dante's *Divine Comedy* and Boccaccio's *Decameron*.[27] The tiered structure of the amphitheatre is similar to an important location in

Boccaccio's *Decameron*, the "Valle delle Donne" (Valley of Ladies), visited by the members of the *brigata* on the seventh day of their travels. Like the amphitheatre, the Valley of Ladies is arranged about a central arena; the spectacle here, however, is not made up of bloodied men on the field of battle but rather of the "chaste white bodies" of the unclothed ladies who swim in the cool waters of the pool located at the Valley's center, catching fish in their smooth hands.[28] Boccaccio's Valley, in turn, refers back to the literary antecedent of Dante's *Divine Comedy;*[29] the difficulty lies in determining whether Boccaccio's tiered Valley refers back to the tiered rose of the blessed in Paradise, or to the concentric circles of the Inferno.[30] The answer, without a doubt, is both: The exquisite enjoyment of the spectacle must echo the ethereal joys of heaven, even as the luxurious pleasures offered by the women's bodies must open up a door into hell. If the resemblance of the topography of the Valley of the Ladies to the landscape of Dante's inferno were not sufficiently evident, the connection would surely be reinforced by the story, told earlier in the *Decameron*, of the young girl Alibech who is taught by the corrupt hermit Rustico how to play the game of "putting the devil back in Hell."[31] Boccaccio's Valley of Ladies thus functions as a material manifestation of a larger cosmology: It represents, in small, the ordered structure of the universe, be it paradise or the inferno. It does so, moreover, in geographical terms, establishing a terrestrial center that grounds the narrative of the *Decameron* about a spectacle that offers the potential for sexual license and consequent social chaos, but that delivers instead sexual restraint and the reassertion of social order—for the ladies of the *brigata* bathe in the pond in the afternoon, the gentlemen in the evening.[32] The reaffirmation of order at the Valley of Ladies sets the stage for the return of the *brigata* to Florence at the end of the tenth day, and their subsequent efforts to restore Florence to what it had been before the devastation of plague and consequent breakdown of society.[33]

Like the Valley of Ladies, the amphitheatre of the Knight's Tale is both a material manifestation of a larger cosmology and the stage on which the effort to impose order is played out. Readers have long been sensitive to this aspect of the amphitheatre; for example, Douglas Brooks and Alastair Fowler have proposed that the "round construction" of the tournament lists must represent the "cosmic model" of the zodiac.[34] Still more apt, perhaps, is Sylvia Tomasch's suggestion that the cosmological referent in Theseus' amphitheatre is the terrestrial world, with the circular amphitheatre (different in many respects from that in Boccaccio's *Teseida*) being based on the circular shape of the *mappamundi*: "what Theseus commands to be built is not just a tournament round but the world in miniature."[35] The construction of the amphitheatre is powerful testimony to the incapacity of man to bend the unfolding of events to his own will. Despite "using every available means" of control, "including the cartographic," Theseus's efforts prove futile: "what the tale most clearly illustrates for us is not his successful control but his failure."[36] The structure of the amphitheatre also reveals, according to Tomasch, what crucial element of the *mappamundi* is left out, the very basis of Theseus's inability to bend events to his own will: "Theseus' amphitheatre fails to correspond with T-O maps precisely where correspondence is most needed: there is no center here; this map has no Jerusalem."[37] This lack of a central point, both spatial and spiritual, accounts for Theseus's failure, and dramatically illustrates the limitations of the pre-Christian world of the tale.

While this identification of what one might call the "missing center" of the microcosm of the Knight's Tale is certainly striking, another significant omission appears as well. Tomasch rightly states that we must "take careful note of what Chaucer leaves out of his description as well as what he so carefully puts in";[38] what, then, to make of the other, curious omission in the geographical format of the amphitheatre, the assignation of only three of the four cardinal points to the divine patrons of the participants? In Boccaccio's *Teseida*, the amphitheatre is designed in decidedly binary terms: It has two entrances, one in the direction of "il sol nascente," one toward "l'occidente"; the audience members partial to Palamon enter through the east gate, those partial to Arcite through the west gate; Arcite enters "through the portal where Eurus blows," Palamon "from the other side."[39] Boccaccio uses the cardinal directions, identified by celestial bodies and the winds, to construct a stage on which the eternal struggle of Venus and Mars will be played out once more. In Chaucer's adaptation, the binary opposition is maintained and even intensified, but is also made more complex. The east gate has attached to it a shrine dedicated to Venus, patron of Palamon, while the west gate has one dedicated to Mars, patron of Arcite. In addition, a third shrine is added at the northern point of the amphitheatre, dedicated to the chaste goddess of the hunt, Diana. This shrine is perched up in a "touret" (I.1909), away from the central action, which is appropriate to the position of Diana's supplicant, Emelye, who is not a competitor but rather the prize to be awarded at the conclusion of the contest. The northern orientation of Diana's "oratorie" is appropriate as well, for the chill of the north suits the goddess's frigid disposition. As Andreas Capellanus notes in his *De arte honeste amandi*, at the castle of Amors, those ladies who congregate near the northern door are the most unreceptive to the pangs of love.[40] The northern orientation is, in addition, especially appropriate to Emelye who, along with her sister Ypolita, came originally from the land of the Amazons (I.866–71; cf. I.2304–11), which is located at the extreme reaches of the north on medieval *mappaemundi*.

Curiously, the frigidity of the north also finds its way into the west gate under the domination of Mars: The opening of the shrine itself is oriented in that direction, so that "the northren lyght in at the dores shoon" (I.1987). This aspect is appropriate to the god, whose "grete temple" is located in "Trace, / In thilke colde, frosty regioun / Ther as Mars hath his sovereyn mansioun" (I.1972–74). One might expect, in view of the binary opposition of Mars and

Venus developed in the *Teseida* and enhanced in the Knight's Tale, that the goddess would correspondingly be associated with the warm quality of the south. Instead, however, she is characterized in terms of moderation, as Boccaccio takes pains to emphasize in the glosses he provides to the *Teseida*: The temple of Venus is located in "a temperate region as regards the heat and the cold" in order to represent the "bodily temperance" that is necessary for a man to successfully execute "venereal acts."[41] For Arcite, the western location of Mars' gate is an ominous harbinger of the defeat he will suffer: The sun will set on his hopes just as surely as it does daily in "l'occidente." Moreover, the northern orientation of the shrine prefigures the darkness and cold with which, for him, the contest will end: His body is "overcome" by "the coold of deeth," while "dusked his eyen two" (I.2800, 2806). From the outset, it seems, the final results of the contest were already built into the design of the little world of the amphitheatre. Yet the asymmetry of that design is striking, comprised as it is of only three cardinal directions, lacking both a fixed point located in the south and a southern influence on the eastern gate to correspond to the northern influence on the western gate.

The solution lies, unsurprisingly, in the Knight's Tale's fundamental preoccupation with the imposition of order on a chaotic world. On medieval maps, the direction of the south connotes heat and light, as does the east; yet the heat of the south is not the regenerative, nutritive heat of the more temperate regions, but the oppressive, overwhelming heat that destroys life. This made exploration virtually impossible, so that several maps label the southern reaches "Unknown to us due to the heat of the sun."[42] The only creatures that can survive in the torrid climates are monstrous, their natural form affected by the excessive heat. The region of the south, then, represents danger to the rigidly ordered world that Theseus constantly struggles to maintain: It is unpredictable and unknowable, deformed and threatening. These qualities are unacceptable, and are therefore excluded by Theseus from the little world of the amphitheatre. In spite of his best efforts, however, the disorder that Theseus had sought to contain erupts in the midst of his carefully controlled microcosm. This *theatrum mundi* (to borrow Hanning's phrase) contains in its midst not Jerusalem, but the gaping maw of hell: "Out of the ground a furie infernal sterte, / From Pluto" (I.2684–85). The forces of chaos have erupted into the midst of order; catastrophe has occurred—or so it seems. The interruption has been instigated by a fourth divine entity, one who ranks above Mars, Venus, and Diana and who causes destruction to rain down upon mankind: Saturn declares "Myn is the stranglyng and hangyng by the throte, / The murmure and the cherles rebellyng, / The groynynge, and the pryvee empoysonyng" (I.2458–60). These apparent calamities, paradoxically, are precisely that: only apparent. Saturn concludes, "I do vengeance and pleyn correccioun" (I.2461).[43] Chaos, it seems, may actually work in the service of order.

This "Boethian" solution, as Kolve calls it,[44] is explicitly articulated in the Squire's Tale, a tale that is linked in several significant ways to the tale told by the Squire's father. For our purposes here, the significant correspondence concerns geography, for it is in the Squire's Tale that the conspicuous omission of the Knight's Tale—that is, the dangerous heat of the south—appears in all its seductive glory. Near the end of the Squire's Tale, the hapless falcon mourns the loss of her mate, a tercelet who proved to be full of "doublenesse," who abandoned her and fled into the depths of the woods. The falcon comforts herself with Boethian wisdom:

> I trowe he hadde thilke text in mynde,
> That 'alle thyng, repeirynge to his kynde,
> Gladeth hymself'; thus seyn men, as I gesse.
> Men loven of propre kynde newefangelnesse,
> As briddes doon that men in cages fede.
> For though thou nyght and day take of hem hede,
> And strawe hir cage faire and softe as silk,
> And yeve hem sugre, hony, breed and milk,
> Yet right anon as that his dore is uppe
> He with his feet wol spurne adoun his cuppe,
> And to the wode he wole and wormes ete;
> So newefangel been they of hire mete,
> And loven novelries of propre kynde. (V.607–19)

She paraphrases Boethius's *Consolation of Philosophy*, a text whose oft-repeated lesson is that the apparent manifestation of chaos, in the reckless spin of Fortune's wheel, is actually evidence of the orderly workings of Nature's law. Even the yearning for disorder is built carefully into the very fibre of nature: for example, if a domesticated bird "skippynge out of hir streyte cage seith the agreables schadwes of the wodes, sche defouleth with hir feet hir metes ischad, and seketh mornynge oonly the wode, and twytereth desyrynge the wode with hir swete voys" (*Boece* 3.m2.27–31).[45] The Boethian pun, of course, is that what the bird wants is "silva," which means both "woods" and "chaos";[46] paradoxically, chaos is "natural," or, as Chaucer puts it, "of proper kynde" (V.611, 619). This is the case whether the chaotic impulse appears in the form of the bird's desire to break away and lose itself in the woods, or in the form of a "furie infernal" (I.2684) that bursts forth from the earth. Even the luxurious "wode" that Theseus relentlessly hacks down in order to construct Arcite's elaborately wrought funeral pyre (I.2913–40) will inevitably grow back again to mock man's effort to hold back the forces of disorder.[47]

It is appropriate that the acknowledgment of the omnipresence of chaos appears in the Squire's Tale, for the tale is pervaded by the southern aspect conspicuously absent from the orderly microcosm of the amphitheatre in the

Knight's Tale. Chaucer draws attention to the omission of a fixed point to the south in the amphitheatre, and induces anticipation of its ultimate appearance, by altering the order in which Palamon, Emelye, and Arcite visit the temples of their divine patrons. While in the *Teseida* the order is Arcite–Palamon–Emelye, in the Knight's Tale the order is Palamon–Emelye–Arcite. The change, I would argue, is motivated not by the characters who make the visits, but rather by the locations of those visits: first to the east, second to the north, third to the west. This is the counterclockwise order, beginning with the east, in which the *mappaemundi* were conventionally read, exactly the same sequence found in the geographical sections of the encyclopedias of Isidore of Seville and Vincent of Beauvais. What is left over, that which has not yet appeared, is the region of the south, dominated by excessive warmth that depletes the vital spirits of its inhabitants and gives rise to monstrosity in both man and beast. This southern region makes its belated appearance in the Squire's Tale, in spite of the fact that the Squire's Tale is conventionally identified as an "oriental" tale, based on its setting in "Tartarye" and the unconventional structure of the plot, which has been compared to stories found in Arabic and Persian frame tale narratives. The setting of the Squire's Tale is certainly "oriental" in the most basic sense: that is, the region is dominated by the effects of the sun, the celestial body that gives the "orient" its name. Yet this region experiences less the positive effects of the sun than the negative: not radiant illumination, but luxurious warmth. The steamy "vapour" that rises from the earth seemingly magnifies the sun, causing it "to seme rody and brood" (V.393–94). Shining "ful joly and cleer," the hot sun produces "lusty . . . weder," which inflames the passions of the people who live near it (V.48, 52), so that "now dauncen lusty Venus children deere" (V.272). The Squire's Tale serves two functions in the cultural geography of the *Canterbury Tales*: first, it acts as a supplement to the Knight's Tale, providing a space for the appearance of the chaotic, southern aspect omitted (yet only deferred) in the earlier tale. Second, the Squire's Tale provides the basis for an additional geographical relationship in the *Tales*, this one of a distinctively binary nature—the torrid, emotional climate of the Squire's Tale finds its counterpart in the cool, rational climate of the Franklin's Tale.[48] The Squire's Tale thus begins by filling in the missing gap in the Knight's Tale, then goes on to provide an inchoate, dangerous basis for the upright social order celebrated in the Franklin's Tale.

Ordering the World: Nations

In the *Canterbury Tales*, the world is divided in an orderly way, as are the peoples who inhabit it: the land is ordered geographically, while the people are ordered in terms of national identity. It may seem anachronistic to consider the categorization of people in medieval texts in terms of national identity; after all, the "nation" and "nationalism" have come to be popular topics in medieval literary studies only in the wake of substantial work on nationalism in modern history, sociology, and political science.[49] Nonetheless, historical studies have appeared, some focused on England, some on continental Europe, that contend that a phenomenon similar to (although not identical with) modern nationalism appeared during the Middle Ages.[50] Modern nationalism is defined as a post-Enlightenment phenomenon, made possible only after the decline of religious modes of thought and exercised only with the first stirrings of revolutionary fervor in the late eighteenth century.[51] In addition, Benedict Anderson argues that modern nationalism emerged first in the colonies of North and South America rather than in their European parent countries, which implies that nationalism could not exist in a precolonial culture.[52] Surely, then, it is only with caution that we may speak of medieval nationalism, in spite of the frequent use of terms in Middle English such as "nacioun" and "natife." Those who write about the English nation in medieval literature often note, as a caveat, the disparity between the theory of modern nationalism and the manifestation of medieval nationalism. They go on to state, however, that certain medieval texts fully participate in "the discourse of the nation" or, more flatly, that "discourses of the nation are visible and can be read with ease in medieval England."[53] The gap between medieval and modern modes of thought is elided by the apparent continuity of the "discourse," in these accounts of medieval nationalism as in accounts of the "discourse" of Orientalism in the Middle Ages. These readers consider neither whether it is possible at all to speak of a "discourse" in premodern culture, nor (if it is possible) in what terms the discourse of nation might be constituted in medieval culture. The most articulate and well-supported argument for the existence of an idea of the English nation appears in the work of Thorlac Turville-Petre, who argues that certain texts of the late thirteenth and early fourteenth centuries evince what can be identified as English "nationalism," albeit of a primarily linguistic kind.[54] The increasing use of English both in literary texts and in official documents, as well as pointed references to "Ingland the nacion" in texts such as the *Cursor Mundi* or Robert Mannyng's *Chronicle*, suggest that medieval writers wrote in English with great self-consciousness and a vigorous awareness of the significance of their action.

Derek Pearsall has addressed the question of whether Chaucer's role as "the poet of Englishness" is based on the presence of nascent English nationalism in his writings, or simply on the romantic idealization of later ages. He concludes that Chaucer's decision to write in English was far from being an assertion of English nationalism; instead, he suggests, following Elizabeth Salter, that Chaucer's "use of English is a triumph of internationalism," for by writing in English Chaucer was merely following the example of other great poets, French and Italian, who had chosen to write in the "illustrious vernacular." What Chaucer displays, according to Pearsall, is not nationalism but "xenophobia": "there is no English poet who is *less* interested in England as a nation."[55] Interestingly, however, nationalism is sometimes defined precisely as xenophobia, the identification and exclusion of strangers in order to constitute the "imagined community" of the nation. As Eric Hobsbawm asks, "How do men and women know that they belong to this community? Because they can define the others who do not belong, who should not belong, who never can belong. In other words, by xenophobia."[56] Yet this definition of the nation, based on the anthropological (rather than political) study of cultures,[57] is too general to afford much insight into Chaucer's use of the term "nacioun," much less his attitude toward English nationalism. I therefore take a different approach: in the remainder of this section I illustrate how "nacioun" functions in Chaucer's writings, viewing it in the context of John Trevisa's use of the term in his late fourteenth-century translations of Bartholomaeus Anglicus's *De proprietatibus rerum* and Ranulph Higden's *Polychronicon*, and comparing it with certain episodes in fourteenth-century Middle English romances in which the category of one's nation (that is, one's state of being at the time of birth) is shown to be mutable. I will suggest that nation is indeed a viable category for late medieval English writers, that it is the cornerstone of a discourse (that is, a system of language that participates in the exercise of power) that is used both to reinforce social boundaries and, on occasion, to accommodate movement between "national" identities.

In the *House of Fame*, Chaucer explicitly identifies the nation as being founded on biological essentialism, that is, on blood: The narrator calls on the Trojans' enemy, Juno, who has always hated "Al the Troianyssche blood," and finally causes the destruction "of al the Troian nacion" (201, 207). In the General Prologue to the *Canterbury Tales*, "nacioun" appears as a category that provides social order: The Knight displays his superiority when he takes his place "aboven alle nacions" (I.53) as he and his international counterparts gather at the dinner table in a foreign land. Each knight metonymically represents his nation, so that the Knight's eminence also connotes England's pride of place. Just as the first of the *Canterbury Tales* provides a geographical basis for the ordering of the world (in the microcosm of the amphitheatre constructed by Theseus), so the first of the portraits in the General Prologue provides the category of "nacioun" to designate those who populate that world. Subsequently, in the Man of Law's Tale, Chaucer uses the term "nacioun" twice to refer to the people of Syria, the foreign land to which Custance is sent as wife of the Sultan and emissary of God, while in the Wife of Bath's Tale, the term reappears in a peculiarly personal context. For these instances, the fourteenth-century analogues to be described later in this chapter are invaluable.

Before turning to Trevisa's Middle English translations of the compendium of Bartholomaeus Anglicus and the universal history of Ranulph Higden, we might note how nation functions generally as an ordering principle in medieval encyclopedias, for they display an increasing tendency to integrate geographic and national identity. In encyclopedic texts, the world is always divided up in two ways: geography and nation. We see this most clearly in Isidore's *Etymologies*, where the ninth book is devoted to the languages and traits of the disparate nations of the world, and the fourteenth to its geographical regions. Similar categories appear in Bartholomaeus Anglicus's mid-thirteenth-century *De proprietatibus rerum*, although there we find the materials of Isidore's books nine and fourteen conflated into a single book, organized according to the most objective and arbitrary principle imaginable: the alphabet.[58] In Vincent of Beauvais' *Speculum maius*, we again find materials from Isidore redistributed in a different form, with a brief geographical overview of the world (in the *Speculum naturale*) followed by a detailed historical chronicle (the *Speculum historiale*), which includes within it salient details about the geographical properties of each land and the national character of its people. In each of these encyclopedic texts, language and geography are the two formative elements in the definition of the nation. The people are defined by the language they speak, but they are shaped by the quality of the terrain they inhabit: As Isidore puts it, "The diversity of face, color, body size, and temperament in human beings is determined by the diversity of the skies above. Therefore the Romans are serious, the Greeks shallow, the Africans fickle, the Gauls naturally ferocious but also of sharper mind, because of the nature of their climate."[59] Bartholomaeus's emphasis on the relationship of people and terrain builds on the basic correspondence noted by Isidore,[60] but develops the relationship far more richly. "Nacioun" (in the words of Trevisa's Middle English translation) always refers to the people who inhabit a territory, "contree" to the land itself; nonetheless, the attributes of a "nacioun" frequently correspond to those of the "contree" its members inhabit.[61] For example, the diversity of the land of Ethiopia, which includes mountains, deserts, and gravel, is reflected in the variety of its "many naciouns, with dyuers faces, wonderful and horribleche yshape." Ethiopia's "blacke ryuere" corresponds to "the colour of men" there, which "sheweth the strengthe of the sterre." Similarly, India is not only "the moost" (that is, the largest), but also "most ryche, moste mighty, moste ful of people." Its size is mirrored by its "huge beestes," "grete houndes," "highe treen," and, of course, "men of grete stature, passynge fyue cubites highe."[62]

In spite of the apparent discrepancies between modern and premodern nationalism, it is nonetheless true that some of the elements commonly seen by historians as basic to modern manifestations of nationalism are present in European culture from a very early date. As early as the ninth century, certain manuscripts of Isidore's *History of the Goths* include interpolations, entitled "De proprietatibus gentium," enumerating the qualities of each national group. Later versions of these interpolations, dating from the eleventh century, even put these attributes in tabular form, eloquent testimony to the human instinct to categorize other human beings in terms of their national origins: The Saxons are foolish, but earnest; the Franks are ferocious, but valorous; the Irish are lewd but faithful; and so on.[63] The categorization of nations could serve an abstract function, as in these interpolations in the *History of the Goths*, or a pragmatic one. Dividing up students based on their national origin was the usual practice at the universities from the early thirteenth century: At the University of Paris, students were organized into "nations," depending upon where each student came from. This was done not to facilitate communication (since all students, of course, spoke Latin at the university) but rather as a matter of political expediency, designed to keep order.[64] In England, where the student population was geographically much less diverse, students came primarily from England; nonetheless, they continued to be split up into nations, the "northern nation" and the "southern nation," with the former composed of those from above the River Trent, the latter of those from below.[65] At the same time, however, the linguistic gap between northern and southern speakers of English did not prevent both groups from identifying themselves as "English," for both the northern and the southern versions of the *Cursor Mundi* include verses on the need to write in "inglis tong" for "inglis men."[66] By the early fifteenth century, the use of English had become an integral part of an attempt to consolidate and advance the position of England within the European community. It was actively promoted by Henry IV as he endeavored to distinguish the Lancastrian dynasty he had founded from the (supposedly) degenerate, pro-French regime of Richard II. His son Henry V continued to promote the use of English, both domestically and internationally: At home, he played an important role in the development of Chancery English, while abroad he urged the English delegates to the Council of Constance to use their native tongue as a partial basis of their nation's claim to parity with the long-established nations of Italy, Germany, France, and Spain.[67]

The special place of England, and the special role of the English language, is evident in the early fourteenth-century Latin text of Higden's *Polychronicon*.[68] The geographical survey of the world that opens the first book concludes, appropriately, with an elaborately detailed description of "Britannia," because this place is "specialissimam"—in the words of Higden's anonymous fifteenth-century translator, "a specialite moste specialle."[69] Higden devotes thirty-one of the sixty chapters that make up the first book of the *Polychronicon* to England, including a geographical survey of the territory, a history of its colonization by various peoples, and a summary of the national character of the English. Higden follows Isidore (*Etym.* 9.2.105) in stating that the nature of people is determined by the nature of their territory: "Ysidre, Eth., libro nono, seith that dyuersite of contrayes vnder heuene is dyuersite of face in man in strengthe, in colour, and in witt."[70] He goes on, however, to accord special importance to the role of language in defining the people of a nation. Although "fyue naciouns" live in "Brytayne" (Scots in the north, Britons and Flemings in Wales, Normans and "Englischemen" all over), they do not remain fully distinct, due to the changeable nature of language. The Welsh and the Scots "beeth nought i-medled with other naciouns" and therefore "holdeth wel nyh hir firste longage and speche," but everywhere else, language appears to be in a state of flux: The Flemings in the western part of Wales "haueth i-left her straunge speche and speketh Saxonliche i-now," while "Englische men" have seen their language change "by comyxtioun and mellynge first with Danes and afterward with Normans." Higden explains the variability of language in terms of climate, presumably following the correlation of climate and bodily traits found in Isidore: The "Saxon tonge" is "i-deled athre," so that "men of the est with men of the west, as it were vndir the same partie of heuene, acordeth more in sownynge of speche than men of the north with men of the south." The linguistic gap that separates those from the north from those in the south (which corresponds to the division into northern and southern "nations" at Oxford and Cambridge) places those in the midlands in the position of mediators: "Mercii, that beeth men of myddel Engelond, as it were parteners of the endes, vnderstondeth bettre the side langages, northerne and southerne, than northerne and southerne vnderstondeth either other."[71]

By the last decades of the fourteenth century, when John Trevisa was writing his Middle English translation of Higden's early fourteenth-century text, the use of English had changed considerably. Higden had stated that "children in scole ayenst the vsage and manere of alle othere naciouns beeth compelled for to leue hire owne langage, and for to construe hir lessouns and here thynges in Frensche," while "gentil men children beeth i-taught to speke Frensche from the tyme that they beeth i-rokked in here cradel." Trevisa interrupts to note how much things had altered during the fifty-odd years since the *Polychronicon* was written: The teaching of language "is siththe sumdel i-chaunged . . . so that now . . . in alle the gramere scoles of Engelond, children leueth Frensche and construeth and lerneth an Englische."[72] Trevisa also occasionally breaks into Higden's text in order to explain how the diversity of languages in Britain, far from suggesting that its people are not fully unified, actually bears witness to their similarity to the longestablished nations of the Continent. When Higden, for example, refers to the French people as a homogeneous group ("Franci, that is fre men so for to mene"), Trevisa intervenes to note their heterogeneity: "But how er they come to that name, Franci beeth Frensche men, and hatte bothe Sicambri and Galli. And so it is alle oon peple, Sicambri, Galli, and Franci, and Frensche men."[73] Higden is puzzled as to why English "is so dyuerse of sown in this oon ilond," while the French spoken in England "hath oon manere soun among alle men that speketh hit aright in Engelond." Trevisa immediately jumps in to correct the notion that English is unusual in being spoken in several different dialects: "Neuertheles there is as many dyuers manere Frensche in the reem of Fraunce as is dyuers manere Englische in the reem of Engelond."[74]

Trevisa also supplements Higden's narrative in more subtle ways. For example, where Higden simply states that English came to be "corrupta" by the presence of Danes and Normans, Trevisa brings out the fertility of the living language: "in meny the contray longage is apayred, and som vseth straunge wlafferynge, chiterynge, harrynge, and garrynge grisbayting." The vitality of English is also emphasized when Trevisa translates Higden's word "nativa" explicitly in terms of birth: Where the anonymous fifteenth-century translator renders Higden's words literally ("the corrupcion of that natife langage"), Trevisa refers to the "apayrynge of the burthe of the tunge." Similarly, a few lines later, he renders Higden's "nativa et propria Anglorum lingua" as "Englische, that is the burthe tonge of Englisshe men."[75] In part, this is simply evidence of Trevisa's habit, in all of his translations, to provide English cognates for Latin terms that might be unfamiliar to his readers.[76] In part, however, seen in the light of Trevisa's many rejoinders to Higden regarding the relationship of people to their vernacular, these references to "the burthe tonge" reinforce the reader's sense of the organic, dynamic nature of English. As the diverse peoples living in Britannia become "i-medled" ("permixtum"), their languages similarly undergo "comyxtioun and mellynge." The result is "the medled peple of Engelond"; the Flemings, for example, "beeth now by torned as though they were Englische by cause of companye with Englische men."[77] While regional differences may remain (men of the south are "more mylde," men of the north "more cruel"), they make up a unified community—namely, "the Englische men that woneth in Engelond, that beeth i-medled in the ilond."[78]

In Higden's *Polychronicon*, together with Trevisa's supplementary comments, we find an idea of English national identity in which language plays a crucial role, for its mutability is precisely what enables the unified community to come into being. Language, according to Trevisa, is never completely consistent and homogeneous, for other influences continually come to bear upon it. Yet, far from compromising the unity of the group, these influences nourish it. The text witnesses to the presence of a strong sense of national identity in medieval English culture, even though this sense certainly differs significantly from modern manifestations of nationalism. One way in which it differs pertains to the political ideology of nationhood, a phenomenon we cannot expect to find in premodern texts. Another way in which it differs pertains to the function of religious identity. As Anderson puts it, the idea of the nation comes into being precisely to fill the void left by "the ebbing of religious belief," so that the rise of the imagined community coincides with "the dusk of religious modes of thought."[79] In medieval texts, however, national identity is often intricately intertwined with religious identity. The author of *Mandeville's Travels*, for example, states that the old Roman port of Famagosta still serves as the port of entry to the Holy Land for "Cristene men and Sarazynes and men of alle nacyons."[80] Here, the category of nation does not differentiate between what a modern reader would identify as national identity (French, German, English) and religious identity (Christian, Muslim). This blurring of the line between (modern) national and religious identity is maintained in the narrator's meeting with the Sultan of Babylon, in which the Saracen leader reveals his intimate knowledge of "the state of Cristene men" and "the manere of euery contree amonges Cristene men." The Sultan's knowledge comes from the Saracen lords he sends out disguised as merchants, who tell the English narrator "of my contree and of manye other Cristene contrees, als wel as thei had ben of the same contree."[81] As in Trevisa's translation of Higden's *Polychronicon*, "contree" and "nacioun" are distinct entities, where the former refers to the land itself and the latter to the people who inhabit it. Nonetheless, the land and its people do correspond to one another, for a land inhabited by "Cristene men" is a "Cristene contree." This correspondence, however, proves to be volatile, since it turns out that the Saracen lords who were disguised as merchants know as much about the "Cristene contrees" as if they were "of the same contree": that is, as though they had been natives. Religion, taken in medieval culture as the very foundation of identity, proves to be the easiest of all to disguise.[82]

The alignment of religion and nation is just one of the ways in which the medieval use of the term *nacioun* differs from the modern paradigm; another difference concerns the alignment of race and nation. Although some historians of medieval culture simply equate these two terms,[83] doing so obscures the complex history of the development of the discourse of race in the eighteenth and nineteenth centuries.[84] The medieval alignment of race and nation can be seen in Middle English romances that feature the conversion of a Muslim to Christianity, such as the various versions of the *Ferumbras* romance and *The King of Tars*. In the former, the Saracen prince Firumbras undergoes the symbolic rebirth of baptism, and is christened with a new name, "Floreyne." In ordinary practice, a convert uses his new name; this can be seen, for example, in the conversion of the Saracen queen Bramimonde, who becomes "Juliana" in the closing stanzas of the *Song of Roland*, or in Orable, who becomes "Guiborc" in *The Conquest of Orange* in the Guillaume d'Orange cycle. Curiously, however, Firumbras is exempt: "than was cristned sir Firumbras, a man of gret deffens; / ys name ther y-chaunged was and was ihote Florens, / ac thogh me tornde thar ys name, as the manere was, / Euere yet after a baar the same and men cliped him Firumbras."[85] Although his name is "tornde" in a reflection of the spiritual movement of "conversion," Firumbras remains essentially unchanged, retaining his monstrous stature of "fifteuene fet" and his former name (significant in a philosophically realist world, where the word corresponds to the thing it names).[86] The difference that remains is "nation," in its etymological sense: the circumstances of birth that cannot be changed, as language and religion can be. The case of Firumbras suggests that nation is written on the body, and cannot be erased; an exception to this rule appears, however, in *The King of Tars*, in which the marriage of a Christian princess and a Saracen sultan produces a shapeless lump of "flesche." Following Christian baptism, the "flesche" is miraculously transformed into a perfectly shaped baby boy. When the Sultan learns of the miracle, he agrees to be baptized as well. When he emerges from the font, his skin, formerly "blac and lothely," becomes "al white." Like Ferumbras, the Sultan retains certain aspects of his origin: In battle, he continues to be "wode"—mad with furor and passion.[87] Yet, unlike Ferumbras, the Sultan's baptism is more than a symbolic rebirth: It is a literal rebirth, which alters the physical marks of his original "nation." In *The King of Tars*, the Sultan's color tells the reader who he is, both spiritually and culturally, for his spiritual cleanliness is made manifest by his white skin.

The visible conversion of the Sultan brings us to Chaucer's Man of Law's Tale, for it has been plausibly suggested that *The King of Tars*, which appears in the Auchinleck manuscript tentatively linked to Chaucer, is the source of certain elements in that Tale.[88] Both texts center on the theme of conversion and the transmission of Christianity by means of the marriage of a Christian woman to a pagan ruler. They share minor themes as well, including religious hypocrisy: In *The King of Tars*, the Christian princess pretends to worship the pagan gods of her husband, while in the Man of Law's Tale, the Sultan's mother and her followers allow themselves to be baptized even though they do not believe in Christ.[89] It is not surprising that the theme of religious hypocrisy is transferred from Custance to her mother-in-law, for it is crucial that there be no discrepancy between Custance's inner character and outward appearance. Unlike the falsified messages that circulate during the latter part of the Tale and bring about her exile from Northumberland, Custance is a perfect mediator.[90] Lauded by the merchants of the Tale's opening as a "mirour of alle curteisye" and a "chambre of hoolynesse" (II.166–67), the very look of Custance turns people toward her: "alle hir loven that looken in hir face" (II.532). It is clear that Chaucer wishes to emphasize Custance's (as it were) legibility. In the Anglo-Norman chronicle of Nicholas Trevet, which is the main source of the Tale, Custance converts people in part through her unusual command of languages; in the Man of Law's Tale, Custance converts people through her look alone, speaking only in "a maner Latyn corrupt" (II.519).

Perhaps the most significant correspondence between *The King of Tars* and the Man of Law's Tale concerns the way in which the presence of the monstrous, strange, or unnatural serves to mediate between binary oppositions. In *The King of Tars*, the deformed "flesche" born to the pagan Sultan and the Christian princess is the focus of the contest between right and wrong, expressed in the dichotomies of "hethen lawe" and "cristen lawe," a "blac and lothely" Sultan and a princess who is "as white as fether of swan."[91] The "flesche" is at the center of the poem over an extended period, first in the pagan temple where the Sultan begs in vain for a miracle while the "flesche lay as stille as ston," and second in the princess' chamber where the "flesche" is baptized and becomes a "child . . . with limes al hole and fere."[92] The Man of Law's Tale is similarly based on the binary opposition of pagan and Christian, yet while it resembles *The King of Tars* in presenting the opposition in terms of the conflict of "Makometes lawe" (II.336) and "Cristes lawe deere" (II.237),[93] it differs in playing out that conflict not between husband and wife, but between mother-in-law and daughter.[94] The disturbingly alien Sultan, dark-skinned and "wode" with fury and passion, is replaced first by the Sowdanesse, whose status as an unnatural, "feyned womman" makes her a fitting representative of the "strange nacioun" of Syria (II.362, 268), and second by Donegild, whose "feendlych spirit" makes her seem "mannysh" (II.782–83). The deformed "flesche" born to the princess in *The King of Tars* appears in the Man of Law's Tale not as the actual baby born to Custance, but as the false message *about* the baby sent to the father by Donegild, which states that Custance had given birth to a "horrible . . . feendly creature" (II.751). The "strange" nature of both monstrous mothers-in-law is projected not just onto the baby, but onto Custance herself, as Donegild marvels that her son would marry "so strange a creature" (II.700).[95] The fear that Custance feels at the outset of the Tale is produced precisely by strangeness: "what wonder is it thogh she wepte / That shal be sent to strange nacioun" (II.267–68). The narrator comments that her tears are perfectly natural, for she will "be bounden under subjeccioun / Of oon, she knoweth nat his condicioun" (II.270–71). Ironically, Custance's plight is due precisely to the fact that she is already under the subjection of a man: her father. She goes on to register her acceptance of her position, acknowledging that "Wommen are born to thraldom and penance, / And to been under mannes governance" (II.285–86). Clearly, the problem in being sent to Syria is not that one will be subject to a man's authority. The problem is that the man to whom she will be subject is unknown: "she knoweth nat his condicioun." The Sultan is an enigma to Custance, a fitting representative of his "strange nacioun."

How are we to understand this "strange nacioun"? The phrase is familiar from other medieval texts: for example, the Saracens in the *Song of Roland* are called (among other things) the "gent estrange."[96] Trevisa's translations, of both the *Polychronicon* and the *De proprietatibus rerum*, provide a particularly useful context. In the Man of Law's Tale, Chaucer uses the term *nacioun* twice, both times in reference to pagan Syria: He calls it first the "strange nacioun" (II.268), then the "Barbre nacioun" (II.281). The two adjectives are synonyms, as we can see in the Middle English translations of Higden's *Polychronicon*: Where the anonymous fifteenth-century translator renders "barbarie" as "the speche of barbre," Trevisa reads "straunge speche."[97] We find even more apposite examples in Trevisa's rendering of

Bartholomaeus Anglicus's encyclopedia, where the phrase "barbaras gentes" appears several times. Interestingly, Trevisa renders this sometimes as "straunge naciouns," sometimes as "stronge naciouns."[98] One might attribute this simply to scribal error if it were not for the fact that, for Trevisa, strength and strangeness are regularly linked together.[99] Of the people of Sambra, for example, Trevisa states that "Amonge other strange naciouns the men ben semeliche of body, bolde of hert, and passen other naciouns aboute with crafte and crafty worching."[100] Even more explicit is his description of the Palestinians, whom he identifies with the biblical Philistines, people of great "myght and strength," whose name reveals their true nature: "And thei were fyrst ycleped Alophili that is to menynge 'aliens and straungers'; for alweye they were straunge to the children of Israel."[101] These children of Israel are, of course, the Jews, themselves the frequent object of exclusion and attack during the Middle Ages. Estrangement (or, as it is more often put, "Othering") is thus local, contingent on immediate circumstances and subject to change, with the focus of exclusion repeatedly being shifted elsewhere. This takes place not only universally but also specifically within the narrative of the Man of Law's Tale, where the "strange" nature of the pagan world is projected back upon Custance herself. The two locations in which the Tale is set—Syria and Northumberland—highlight the variable nature of strangeness. On the one hand, both lands are strange because both are pagan; on the other hand, Northumberland goes on to become not only a Christian country but part of England itself. It is both strange (then) and familiar (now). Yet even after its assimilation into England, Northumberland retains a flavor of strangeness, which Trevisa emphasizes in his expanded translation of Higden's text: "Al the longage of the Northumbres, and specialliche at York, is so scharp, slitting, and frotynge and unschape, that we southerne men may that longage vnnethe vnderstonde. I trowe that that is bycause that they beeth nyh to straunge men and naciouns that speketh strongliche."[102]

We have seen, then, that "nation" functions as a category in two ways. It is used to divide people in an orderly fashion, sometimes in order to hierarchize them, as seen (for example) in the university system of dividing students by "nation" and in lists of peoples together with their characteristic attributes found in some manuscripts of Isidore's *History of the Goths*. In addition, "nation" can be used to actually accomplish the act of estrangement, that is, to define a border separating one group from another. In the *Canterbury Tales*, the former usage appears in the General Prologue portrait of the Knight, who sits "aboven alle nacions in Pruce" (I.53), while the latter appears in the Man of Law's Tale. In the Wife of Bath's Tale, however, the term *nacioun* appears in a rather different context. Once again, it functions as a category, but as one that is explicitly shown to be mutable—in fact, its mutability provides the climax of the tale. When the young knight rejects the old hag, he laments that any "of my nacioun / Sholde evere so foule disparaged be" (III.1068–69). To be disparaged, literally, is to be paired wrongly, mated with a person who is not one's peer: the hag is simply of too "lough a kynde" (III.1101). The knight's "nacioun" is different from the hag's "nacioun"; here, the term *nacioun* is used to describe something like our modern category of class. (A comparable use of "natural" order in the service of the class system can be found in *The Parliament of Fowls*.) The interchangeability of nation and class seen here is mirrored in the words of the Clerk at the conclusion of his tale, when he praises the Wife of Bath "Whos lyf and al hire secte God mayntene / In heigh maistrie" (IV.1170–71). The unusual use of "secte" in this context shows how readily categories such as religion, race, ethnicity, and class could be conflated.[103] This is indicative not of the primitive, undeveloped nature of the discourse of nation during the Middle Ages, but rather of the consistent, ubiquitous tendency to use one category of difference in order to construct another. For example, as Kenan Malik has shown, in the immediate post-Enlightenment period categories of race were used to construct a model of "natural" social order within a given culture (that is, class); subsequently, during the Victorian period, race was used first to characterize class distinctions, then redefined to refer specifically to skin color.[104] If the discourse of nation is to be described as "emergent" during the Middle Ages, then it is chronically emergent.

The "Companye" as Social Microcosm

The two ways of ordering the world—through geography and through nation—are integrated in accounts of the repopulation of the world by the sons of Noah after the great deluge. Gower, for example, writes that through "the Sones of Noe," "the world of mannes nacion / Into multiplicacion / Was tho restored newe ayein." They produced many offspring, "of naciouns seventy and tuo / In sondri place."[105] According to the medieval encyclopedists, the diversity of the offspring of Shem, Ham, and Japheth, together with the linguistic diversity caused after the construction of the Tower of Babel, accounts for the heterogeneous nature of the world's people, while the effects of climate serve to enhance inborn differences.[106] Some encyclopedias, however, use the framework of the sons of Noah to account not just for ethnic difference, but for social class: Honorius of Autun states that free men are descended from Shem, knights from Japheth, and serfs from Ham.[107] This genealogy is reiterated in the *Cursor Mundi*: "Knyght and thral and fre man / Of these thre britheren bigan: / Of Sem fre mon, of Iapheth knyght, / Thral of Cam."[108] Lee Patterson has argued that this deterministic paradigm is relevant to the social interactions of the "companye" of pilgrims in the *Canterbury Tales*, both with regard to the Miller's telling of a "cherles tale" (I.3169) and in the Summoner's account of what constitutes a "cherles dede" (III.2206; cf. 2218–42). Patterson notes that the subjugation of the serfs is grounded not just in the genealogical descent from the sons of Ham, but in a kind of spiritual genealogy that derives from Cain.[109] In the *Cursor Mundi*, these two modes of descent—bodily and spiritual—are conflated in terms of "nacioun": Ham is rebuked by his father Noah, who declares "thou hast the kynde of that natioun / Of caym, curside moost of othere, / that with tresoun sloughe his brothere."[110] Here, "nacioun" is used, paradoxically, to describe a genealogical descent that is not true literally, but spiritually: Ham is not the bodily offspring of Cain, but his spiritual progeny.

Although Chaucer uses the term only a few times in his works, the categorization of society that can be expressed using the term *nacioun* (as in the *Cursor Mundi*) appears in the *Canterbury Tales* under a term that he uses very frequently indeed: *degree*. Chaucer uses the word both to identify the social status of characters within the Tales and to describe the pilgrim tale-tellers themselves—most famously in the General Prologue, where he apologizes for having "nat set folk in hir degree" (I.744), that is, having failed to observe the proper order of estates.[111] In an influential article, Derek Brewer suggests that "degree," in Chaucer's writings, functions like "the rungs of a ladder," on which individuals can travel up and down. He distinguishes between three modes of social division: the ladder-like "pragmatic" division of society, a "binary system" that separates "gentils" from "cherles," and a three-part system of "estates."[112] Brewer's framework, while useful in some respects, leaves out the crucial function of performance both in the maintenance of social status and in the movement from one state to another. As Howard Kaminsky has shown, medieval texts such as the *Songe du Vergier* emphasize the role of "l'opynion du peuple" in the effort to move from one estate to another: Public opinion could be swayed by conspicuous (but not too conspicuous!) display of wealth, generous hospitality, more ornate attire, and so on.[113] Members of the "companye" such as the Franklin, whose hospitality makes him known as "Seint Julian . . . in his contree" (I.340), participate in just this kind of social performance, seeking social advancement for the family if not for the individual person.[114]

While the possibility of upward mobility might be presented in a positive light, it could also be seen as dangerous to the maintenance of a stable society. Higden addresses this problem in the last lines of the first book of his *Polychronicon*, describing how men are discontent with their own "estate" and try to appear as though they belonged to another:

> These men despiseth hir owne, and preiseth other menis, and vnnethe beeth apaide with hir owne estate; what byfalleth and semeth other men, they wolleth gladlyche take to hem self; therfor hit is that a yeman arraieth hym as a squyer, a squyer as a knyght, a knight as a duke, and a duke as a kyng. Yit som gooth a boute to alle manere staate and beeth in noon astaat, for they that wole take eueriche degree beeth of non degre. . . .[A]mong alle

> Englische i-medled to giders is so grete chaungynge and diuersite of
> clothinge and of array and so many manere and dyuerse shapes, that wel
> nyghe is there ony man knowen by his clothynge and his arraye of what
> degre he is. . . . [T]he world schal be so vnstable and so dyuers and variable
> that the vnstabilnesse of thoughtes schal be bytokened by many manere
> dyuersite of clothinge.[115]

This chaotic state of affairs is precisely what Theseus struggles against, in the
Knight's Tale, when he repeatedly works to maintain all things in their proper
"degree": Guests who come to participate in the contest are lodged "everich
at his degree" (I.2192), while Palamon and Arcite, who are of equal rank, are
placed together into a single "degree" where Fortune can determine their fate
(I.1841). The rows and rows of the amphitheatre itself are "degrees" that correspond to the social position of those who take their places there as the contest begins. Such stability, however, is transitory, and can only be maintained
by a ruler who is prepared to observe the law and to enforce it, as Chaucer
urges his own king to do in "Lak of Steadfastness": "Suffre nothing that may
be reprevable / To thyn estat don in thy regioun. / Shew forth thy swerd of
castigacioun, / Dred God, do law" (24–27). The sword must be used to preserve order even though, paradoxically, it also presents a threat to him that
uses it.[116]

The system of language constructed around the term *nacioun* in the *Canterbury Tales* is vitally concerned with the expression of power through the
construction of categories. Since power and knowledge are intertwined in
this way, we are surely justified in referring to the "discourse of nation" in
late fourteenth-century English literature, a discourse in which Chaucer participates. Can we then also speak of the "discourse of Orientalism"? It has
been suggested that modern and medieval manifestations of Orientalism are
quite similar, both featuring an "exotic alterity" in which the Orient is figured
as "monstrous, mysterious, exotic, sensual, sexually deviant."[117] I would
argue instead that the discourse of Orientalism emerged only with the exploration of the New World, made possible by the formation of a crucial paradigm: namely, the opposition of a torrid, passionate East to a cool, rational
West.[118] The discourse of nation, on the other hand, was already in good
working order.

Notes

An earlier version of part two of this essay was presented at the biennial
meeting of the New Chaucer Society, 17–20 July 1998. Thanks are due to
audience members there, and to Kathryn Lynch and David Klausner, who
read and commented on the complete essay.

1. Sheila Delany, "Geographies of Desire: Orientalism in Chaucer's *Legend of
   Good Women*," *Chaucer Yearbook* 1 (1992): 1–32, and cf. *The Naked Text:
   Chaucer's* Legend of Good Women (Berkeley: University of California

Press, 1994), 183–86, 230; Kathryn L. Lynch, "East Meets West in Chaucer's Squire's and Franklin's Tales," *Speculum* 70 (1995): 530–51; Susan Schibanoff, "Worlds Apart: Orientalism, Antifeminism, and Heresy in Chaucer's *Man of Law's Tale*," *Exemplaria* 8 (1996): 59–96; Kathryn L. Lynch, "Storytelling, Exchange, and Constancy: East and West in Chaucer's *Man of Law's Tale*," *Chaucer Review* 33 (1999): 409–22.

2. Edward W. Said, *Orientalism* (1978. New York: Random House, 1994), 2–4. In the Afterword to the 1994 edition (333), he identifies 1798 as the foundational moment.

3. On the dichotomy of East and West so crucial to the theory of Orientalism, and its unsuitability to medieval depictions to Islam and the Orient, see Suzanne Conklin Akbari, "From Due East to True North: Orientalism and Orientation," *The Postcolonial Middle Ages*, ed. Jeffrey Jerome Cohen (New York: St. Martins, 2000), 19–34, esp. 19–20 and 31.

4. Said, 3.

5. Ibid., 119.

6. Said initially stipulates that "Orientalism as a discourse" is seen "during the post-Enlightenment period" (3); but "Orientalist discourse" appears "whenever the Orient is spoken or written about" (71). On Said's slippery use of Foucault, see James Clifford, "On Orientalism," in *The Predicament of Culture: Twentieth-Century Ethnography, Literature, and Art* (Cambridge, MA: Harvard University Press, 1988), 255–76; Aijaz Ahmad, *In Theory: Classes, Nations, Literatures* (London: Verso, 1992), 164–67.

7. For "a discourse of Orientalism," see Schibanoff, 59; on other weaknesses in Schibanoff's argument, see Lynch, "Storytelling," 409–10 and 420 n.1. On "Chaucerian Orientalism," see Delany, *Naked Text*, 186.

8. See, for example, the account of the intersection of medicine, astrology, and physics in Raymond Klibansky, Erwin Panofsky, and Fritz Saxl, *Saturn and Melancholy: Studies in the History of Natural Philosophy, Religion, and Art* (London: Nelson, 1964), 90–123.

9. This requires that we agree with Said's argument that canonical texts are constitutive of a discourse in the special case of Orientalism, in spite of Foucault's assertion that no discourse can be defined on the basis of master-texts (Said, 23; cf. Ahmad, 167).

10. On the capacious nature of the frame-tale form, see Derek Pearsall, *The Canterbury Tales* (London and Boston: Allen and Unwin, 1985), 34–40; on the relationship of the *Canterbury Tales* to other frame-tale narratives, see Katherine S. Gittes, "The *Canterbury Tales* and the Arabic Frame Tradition," *PMLA* 98 (1983): 237–51, and *Framing* The Canterbury Tales: *Chaucer and the Medieval Frame Narrative Tradition* (New York: Greenwood, 1991). On the form and dissemination of Petrus Alfonsi's *Disciplina clericalis*, see John V. Tolan, *Petrus Alfonsi and His Medieval Readers* (Gainesville: University of Florida Press, 1993). The model of Boccaccio's *Decameron* is an exception to the usual "capacious" nature of frame-tale narratives, since its "capacity" is deliberately limited to one hundred tales.

11. Honorius of Autun, *De imagine mundi* (early 12th c.); Isidore of Seville and Alexander Neckam, *De naturis rerum* (late 7th c. and late 12th c.);

Bartholomaeus Anglicus, *De proprietatibus rerum* (ca. 1245); Vincent of Beauvais, *Speculum maius* (ca. 1264); Roger Bacon, *Opus maius* (ca. 1260).

12. All citations are from *The Riverside Chaucer*, 3rd ed., ed. Larry D. Benson (Boston: Houghton Mifflin, 1987).

13. Alastair J. Minnis, *Medieval Theory of Authorship: Scholastic Literary Attitudes in the Later Middle Ages*, 2nd ed. (Aldershot: Wildwood, 1988), 158, 191. On Chaucer's use of Vincent of Beauvais in terms of content (rather than form), see Pauline Aiken's series of articles: "Vincent of Beauvais and Dame Pertelote's Knowledge of Medicine," *Speculum* 10 (1935): 281–87; "Arcite's Illness and Vincent of Beauvais," *PMLA* 51 (1936): 361–69; "Vincent of Beauvais and Chaucer's Knowledge of Alchemy," *Studies in Philology* 41 (1944): 371–89; "Vincent of Beauvais and the 'Houres' of Chaucer's Physician," *Studies in Philology* 53 (1956): 22–24.

14. "The *ordinatio* of the Ellesmere manuscript interprets the *Canterbury Tales* as a *compilatio*" (190). On other *Canterbury Tales* manuscripts that refer to the work as a compilation, see 191 n. 61 in A. I. Doyle and M. B. Parkes, "The Production of Copies of the *Canterbury Tales* and the *Confessio Amantis* in the Early Fifteenth Century," *Medieval Scribes, Manuscripts, and Libraries: Essays Presented to N.R. Ker*, ed. M. B. Parkes and Andrew G. Watson (London: Scolar, 1978), 163–210.

15. Mandeville identifies a circle on the floor of the Church of the Holy Sepulchre as "the myddes of the world," while Matthew Paris simply lists, in his terse itinerary of the holy places, "Templum Domini. Templum Salomonis. E la est le mitlui du mund. Sepulchrum." *Mandeville's Travels*, ed. M. C. Seymour (Oxford: Clarendon, 1967), 58 (ch. 10); Matthew Paris, "Iter de Londinio in Terram Sanctam," in Konrad Miller, *Mappae Mundi: Die Ältesten Weltkarten*, vol. 2 (1895), 84–93, rpt. in Renato Stopani, *Le Vie di pellegrinaggio del Medioevo: Gli itinerari per Roma, Gerusalemme, Compostela* (Florence: Lettere, 1991), 92–96. On the central position of Jerusalem on medieval maps, see David Woodward, "Medieval *Mappaemundi*," *The History of Cartography*, vol. 1, ed. J. B. Harley and David Woodward (Chicago: University of Chicago Press, 1987), 341–42.

16. A useful survey of the literature of pilgrimage can be found in Donald R. Howard, *Writers and Pilgrims: Medieval Pilgrimage Narratives and Their Posterity* (Berkeley: University of California Press, 1980), 11–52; for a survey of the practice, see Suzanne M. Yeager, "Remembering the Passion: Spiritual and Practical Aspects of Medieval Pilgrimage," in *Medieval Travel Writing 1096–1492: A Multi-Disciplinary Introduction*, ed. Joan Curbet (Frankfurt and New York: Peter Lang, 2002 [in press]). On the history of pilgrimage more generally, see Jonathan Sumption, *Pilgrimage: An Image of Mediaeval Religion* (Totowa, NJ: Rowman and Littlefield, 1975).

17. This is true even of the great pilgrimages to Rome and Santiago; on the fluctuations of the popularity of the pilgrimage to Rome depending on access to the Holy Land, see Debra J. Birch, *Pilgrimage to Rome in the Middle Ages: Continuity and Change*, Studies in the History of Medieval Religion 13 (Woodbridge: Boydell, 1998), 173–86, 199–202, and 23–24 (on the patterning

of the pilgrimage to Rome on the pilgrimage to Jerusalem). On the frequency of pilgrimage to Santiago among the English, see Constance Storrs, *Jacobean Pilgrims from England from the Early Twelfth to the Late Fifteenth Century* (Santiago de Compostela: Xunta de Galicia, 1994) and, more generally, Maryjane Dunn and Linda Kay Davidson, eds., *The Pilgrimage to Compostela in the Middle Ages*, Garland Medieval Casebooks 17 (New York: Garland, 1996).

18. On the significance of Chaucer's choice of Southwark rather than the City of London as the point of origin of the pilgrimage, see David Wallace, "Chaucer and the Absent City," in *Chaucer's England: Literature in Historical Context*, ed. Barbara A. Hanawalt, Medieval Studies at Minnesota 4 (Minneapolis: University of Minnesota Press, 1992), 59–90.

19. Howard, *Writers*, 7–8, 12.

20. Donald R. Howard, *The Idea of the* Canterbury Tales (Berkeley: University of California Press, 1976), 326–32.

21. Lee Patterson, *Chaucer and the Subject of History* (Madison: University of Wisconsin Press, 1991), 19–20.

22. "[T]he *Knight's Tale* serves the *Canterbury Tales* as that which it must summon up and then reject in order to be itself." Patterson, *Subject*, 236.

23. Robert W. Hanning, "'The Struggle between Noble Designs and Chaos': The Literary Tradition of Chaucer's Knight's Tale," *The Literary Review* 23 (1980): 519–41. Patterson has refined this formulation somewhat, proposing that "the central issue of the *Tale* [is] not the idea of order per se but the *chivalric* idea of order" (*Subject*, 168).

24. "In the middle there was a plain as round as a compass [ritondo al sesta]. . . . Circular terraces [scale in cerchio] rose up from it in more than five hundred tiers [giri]" (*Teseida* 7.109–10). Compare Chaucer's Knight's Tale: "Round was the shap, in manere of compas, / Ful of degrees, the heighte of sixty pas" (I.1887–90). Giovanni Boccaccio, *Opere Minori in volgare*, ed. Mario Marti (Milan: Rizzoli, 1970), 2: 481; trans. Bernadette Marie McCoy, *The Book of Theseus* (New York: Medieval Text Association, 1974), 187.

25. Hanning, 533.

26. See also V. A. Kolve's detailed analysis of how the amphitheatre serves as an emblem of Theseus's efforts to impose order on a chaotic world in *Chaucer and the Imagery of Narrative: The First Five* Canterbury Tales (Stanford, CA: Stanford University Press, 1984), 105–32.

27. The debate regarding whether Chaucer knew Boccaccio's *Decameron* or not shows no signs of abating: while there is no direct textual evidence that he did, the broader correspondences make it "hard to believe that the *Decameron* did not provide a germ of growth or even a direct source of inspiration for the *Canterbury Tales*" (Pearsall, *Canterbury Tales*, 37). For a summary of the parallels and the debate, see Helen Cooper, "Sources and Analogues of Chaucer's *Canterbury Tales*: Reviewing the Work," *Studies in the Age of Chaucer* 19 (1997): 183–210, esp. 192–99; see also the summary of evidence in Peter G. Beidler, "Just Say Yes, Chaucer Knew the *Decameron*: Or, Bringing the *Shipman's Tale* Out of Limbo,"

The Decameron *and the* Canterbury Tales: *New Essays on an Old Question,*
ed. Leonard Michael Koff and Brenda Deen Schildgen (Madison, NJ: Fair-
leigh Dickinson University Press, 2000), 25–46. For a forceful argument
that Chaucer knew Boccaccio's version of the Griselda story (*Decameron*
10.10), see John Finlayson, "Petrarch, Boccaccio, and Chaucer's Clerk's
Tale," *Studies in Philology* 97 (2000): 255–75.

28. "[T]he floor of the valley was perfectly circular in shape, for all the world as
if it had been made with compasses. . . . The sides of the hills ranged down-
wards in a regular series of terraces, concentrically arranged like the tiers of
an amphitheatre, their circles gradually diminishing in size from the top-
most terrace to the lowest." Giovanni Boccaccio, *The Decameron*, trans.
G. H. McWilliam (1972; rpt. Harmondsworth: Penguin, 1995), 480–81
(Conclusion of Day Six); *Decameron*, ed. Vittore Branca, Tutte le opere di
Giovanni Boccaccio 4 (Milan: Mondadori, 1976), 577–78.

29. On the interrelation of Boccaccio's Valley of Ladies and Dante's celestial
rose, see Thomas C. Stillinger, "The Language of Gardens: Boccaccio's
'Valle delle Donne,'" *Traditio* 39 (1983): 301–21.

30. Dante Alighieri, *The Divine Comedy*, ed. Giorgio Petrocchi, trans. Charles
S. Singleton, Bollingen Series 80, 3 vols., 1970–75 (Princeton, NJ: Princeton University Press, 1980), *Paradiso* 30: 109–14 and cantos 31–32, *passim.*

31. Boccaccio, *Decameron*, trans. McWilliam, 276 (Day Three, Story Ten); ed.
Branca 335.

32. The Valley of Ladies is, as Millicent Marcus puts it, an emblem of "human
order imposed on the natural world" (168): "An Allegory of Two Gardens:
The Tale of Madonna Dianora (*Decameron* X, 5)," *Forum Italicum* 14
(1980): 162–74.

33. "In the face of so much affliction and misery, all respect for the laws of God
and man had virtually broken down and been extinguished in our city. For like
everybody else, those ministers and executors of the laws who were not either
dead or ill were left with so few subordinates that they were unable to dis-
charge any of their duties. Hence everyone was free to behave as he pleased."
Boccaccio, *Decameron*, trans. McWilliam, 7–8 (Introduction); ed. Branca 13.

34. Douglas Brooks and Alastair Fowler, "The Meaning of Chaucer's *Knight's
Tale*," *Medium Aevum* 39 (1970): 123–46; quotation from 128.

35. Sylvia Tomasch, "*Mappae Mundi* and 'The Knight's Tale': The Geography
of Power, the Technology of Control," in *Literature and Technology*, ed.
Mark Greenberg and Lance Schachterle (Bethlehem, PA: Lehigh University
Press, 1992), 66–98; quotation from 83. As Tomasch notes, Chaucer indi-
cates his knowledge of the form and function of the *mappamundi* in his lyric
"To Rosemounde" (97 n. 59).

36. Ibid., 86, 82.

37. Ibid., 87.

38. Ibid.

39. *Teseida*, 7.108–9, 112, 114, 118; ed. Marti, 481–84; trans. McCoy, 187–89.

40. "[T]hose who have the watch in the north and always keep their doors
closed are those women who never open to anybody who knocks, but deny
to everyone an entrance into Love's palace. . . . Those of the north are those

who refuse to love, although they may be loved by many." Andreas Capel-lanus, *The Art of Courtly Love*, trans. John Jay Parry (New York: Columbia University Press, 1990), 73–74.

41. *Teseida*, gloss to 7.50; ed. Marti, 714; trans. McCoy, 199–200.

42. Anna-Dorothee von den Brincken, *Fines Terrae: Die Enden der Erde und der vierte Kontinent auf mittelalterlichen Weltkarten*, MGH, Schriften 36 (Hannover: Hansche, 1992), 158, 171, 57.

43. On the astrological significance of this part of the Knight's Tale, see J. D. North, "'Kalenderes Enlumyned ben They': Some Astronomical Themes in Chaucer," *Review of English Studies* n.s. 20 (1969): 129–54, esp. 149–51; Chauncey Wood, *Chaucer and the Country of the Stars: Poetic Uses of Astro-logical Imagery* (Princeton, NJ: Princeton University Press, 1970), 70–76.

44. "In a Boethian paradox, the planet most disorderly becomes the efficient cause of order within the poem's larger action" (Kolve, 125–26).

45. "Yet if she sees, hopping in her narrow cage, / The beloved shade of trees, / She scatters her food beneath her feet/And all she wants is her woods [*silva*], / Sings sadly, softly, sweetly of her woods." Boethius, *The Consola-tion of Philosophy*, trans. S.J. Tester, Loeb Classical Library (Cambridge, MA: Harvard University Press, 1973), 238–39 (3.m2.23–26).

46. More precisely, *silva* denotes primordial matter awaiting the imposition of form, especially in neoplatonic philosophy. See Calcidius's Latin translation of Plato's *Timaeus* 51A; *Commentarius in Timaeum Platonis*, ed. J. H. Waszink (London: Warburg, 1962), 235. See also the elaborate personifica-tion of Silva in Bernardus Silvestris, *Cosmographia*, ed. Peter Dronke (Lei-den: Brill, 1978), 97–104 (1.1–2).

47. As Kolve notes, the site of Arcite's pyre is the site of the amphitheatre itself, since both are explicitly said to be placed on the site of the competitors' original, ungoverned combat. (On the apparent contradiction, see Kolve 130–31.) The destruction of the forest and construction of the bier thus reen-act Theseus's effort to impose order upon chaos in the construction of the amphitheatre.

48. See Lynch, "East Meets West," 546–50; Akbari, "Due East," 29–30.

49. Benedict Anderson's *Imagined Communities: Reflections on the Origin and Spread of Nationalism*, rev. ed. (London: Verso, 1991) has been taken as authoritative in this respect, at least in literary studies. See the useful cri-tiques of Anderson's work found in Gopal Balakrishnan, ed., *Mapping the Nation* (London and New York: Verso, 1996).

50. See the seminal article by G. G. Coulton, "Nationalism in the Middle Ages," *Cambridge Historical Journal* 5 (1935–37): 15–40; also Bernard Guenée, *States and Rulers in Later Medieval Europe*, trans. Juliet Vale (Oxford: Blackwell, 1985). On English nationalism, see Richard Southern, "Eng-land's First Entry into Europe," *Medieval Humanism and Other Studies* (Oxford, 1970), 135–57.

51. See Anderson, *Imagined Communities*, 11–12, 67–82; Eric J. Hobsbawm, *Nations and Nationalism since 1780: Programme, Myth, Reality*, 2nd ed. (Cambridge: Cambridge University Press, 1992), and "Ethnicity and Nationalism in Europe Today," in Balakrishnan, 255–66.

52. Anderson, *Imagined Communities*, 47–65.

53. Diane Speed, "The Construction of the Nation in Middle English Romance," *Readings in Middle English Romance*, ed. Carol M. Meale (Cambridge: D.S. Brewer, 1994), 135–57; quotation from 146. Geraldine Heng, "The Romance of England: *Richard Coer de Lyon*, Saracens, Jews, and the Politics of Race and Nation," *The Postcolonial Middle Ages*, ed. Jeffrey Jerome Cohen (New York: St. Martins, 2000), 135–71; quotation from 151. See also Alan S. Ambrisco's excavation of *Richard Coer de Lyon*'s "national discourse" (522) in "Cannibalism and Cultural Encounters in *Richard Coeur de Lion*," *Journal of Medieval and Early Modern Studies* 29 (1999): 499–528.

54. Thorlac Turville-Petre, *England the Nation: Language, Literature, and National Identity, 1290–1340* (Oxford: Clarendon, 1996).

55. Derek Pearsall, "Chaucer and Englishness," *1998 Lectures and Memoirs. Proceedings of the British Academy* 101 (1999): 77–99; quotations from 86, 85, and 99. Elizabeth Salter, "Chaucer and Internationalism," *Studies in the Age of Chaucer* 2 (1980): 71–79, quotation from 79; noted in Pearsall, "Englishness," 90.

56. Hobsbawm, "Ethnicity and Nationalism," 265.

57. Anderson presents his famous definition of nation as imagined community "in an anthropological spirit" (*Imagined Communities*, 5–6). On the limitations of this approach, see Gopal Balakrishnan, "The National Imagination," in Balakrishnan 198–213, esp. 203–8.

58. For stimulating remarks on the relationship of alphabetization and cartography, see Kathleen Biddick, "The ABC of Ptolemy: Mapping the World with the Alphabet," *Text and Territory: Geographical Imagination in the European Middle Ages*, ed. Sylvia Tomasch and Sealy Gilles (Philadelphia: University of Pennsylvania Press, 1998), 268–93, esp. 279–87.

59. "Secundum diversitatem enim caeli et facies hominum et colores et corporum quantitates et animorum diversitates existunt. Inde Romanos graves, Graecos leves, Afros versipelles, Gallos natura feroces atque acriores ingenio pervidemus, quod natura climatum facit." Isidore, *Etymologiae sive Originum*, ed. W. M. Lindsay, 2 vols. (Oxford: Clarendon, 1911), 9.2.105.

60. The passage from Isidore quoted in the previous note (*Etym.* 9.2.105) appears verbatim in the *De proprietatibus rerum*, 15.67.

61. On the correspondence of climate and body type in the encyclopedias, see Akbari, "Due East," 24–27.

62. Bartholomaeus Anglicus, *De proprietatibus rerum*, 15.52, 15.75; *On the Properties of Things: John Trevisa's Translation of Bartholomaeus Anglicus, "De proprietatibus rerum,"* ed. M.C. Seymour et al., 3 vols. (Oxford: Clarendon, 1975–78), 2: 754, 770.

63. Paul Meyvaert, "'Rainaldus est malus scriptor Francigenus'—Voicing National Antipathy in the Middle Ages," *Speculum* 66 (1991): 743–63, esp. 747–49.

64. Hilde de Ridder-Symoens, *A History of the University in Europe. Vol. 1: Universities in the Middle Ages* (Cambridge: Cambridge University Press, 1992), 114–16; see also Gray Cowan Boyce, *The English-German Nation in the University of Paris during the Middle Ages* (Bruges: St. Catherine, 1927).

65. De Ridder-Symoens 115. "[F]rom probably its earliest days . . . the University took very careful note of one fundamental division, that between the northern and southern nations" (21): T. H. Aston, "Oxford's Medieval Alumni," *Past and Present* 74 (1977): 3–40. See also T. H. Aston, G. D. Duncan, and T. A. R. Evans, "The Medieval Alumni of the University of Cambridge," *Past and Present* 86 (1980): 9–86.

66. "This ilk bok i[t] es translate / In to Inglis tong to rede / For the loue of Inglis lede, / Inglis lede of Ingland. . . . Of Ingland the nacion, / Es Inglis man thar in commun." *Cursor Mundi*, ed. Richard Morris, EETS OS 57, 59, 62, 66, 68, 99, 101, 4 vols. (Oxford: Oxford University Press, 1874–93), lines 232–35, 241–42 (Cotton MS); compare *The Southern Version of* Cursor Mundi, ed. Sarah M. Horrall, vol. 1 (Ottawa: University of Ottawa Press, 1978), 40–41.

67. John H. Fisher, "Chancery and the Emergence of Standard Written English in the Fifteenth Century," *Speculum* 52 (1977): 870–99; John H. Fisher, "A Language Policy for Lancastrian England," *PMLA* 107 (1992): 1168–80; J.-P. Genet, "English Nationalism: Thomas Polton at the Council of Constance," *Nottingham Medieval Studies* 28 (1984): 60–78. On Lancastrian "state-generated linguistic nationalism" (82), see Lee Patterson, "Making Identities in Fifteenth-Century England: Henry V and John Lydgate," *New Historical Literary Study: Essays on Reproducing Texts, Representing History*, ed. Jeffrey N. Cox and Larry Reynolds (Princeton, NJ: Princeton University Press, 1993), 69–107.

68. On the *Polychronicon*, see John Taylor, *The Universal Chronicle of Ranulf Higden* (Oxford: Clarendon, 1966), esp. 48 (on Higden's encyclopedic method) and 82–83 (on his use of Isidore and Bartholomaeus Anglicus).

69. *Polychronicon*, 1.3; in *Polychronicon Ranulphi Higden monachi cestrensis*, ed. Churchill Babington (vols. 1–2) and Joseph Rawson Lumby (vols. 3–9), Rerum Britannicarum Medii Aevi Scriptores 41, 9 vols., 1865–86 (Nendeln, Liechtenstein: Kraus Rpt., 1975), 1: 26–27.

70. "Secundum Isidorum, Etymologiarum libro nono, secundum diversitatem coeli facies hominum, colores corporum, qualitates animorum existunt." *Polychronicon* 1.28, ed. Babington, 1: 294–95.

71. *Polychronicon*, 1.58, ed. Babington, 2: 152–63.

72. *Polychronicon*, 1.59, ed. Babington, 2: 158–61. On this passage, see David C. Fowler, *The Life and Times of John Trevisa, Medieval Scholar* (Seattle: University of Washington Press, 1995), 183–84.

73. *Polychronicon*, 1.25, ed. Babington, 1: 274–77.

74. *Polychronicon*, 1.59, ed. Babington, 2: 160–61.

75. *Polychronicon*, 1.59, ed. Babington, 2: 158–61.

76. Traugott Lawler, "On the Properties of John Trevisa's Major Translations," *Viator* 14 (1983): 267–88.

77. *Polychronicon*, 1.58, ed. Babington, 2: 154–55; 1.59, 2: 156–57, 158–59; 1.60, 2: 164–65.

78. *Polychronicon*, 1.60, ed. Babington, 2: 164–67.

79. Anderson, *Imagined Communities*, 11. This opposition of religion and nation has met with objections in the modern postcolonial context as well:

see Partha Chatterjee, "Communities and the Nation," *The Nation and Its Fragments* (Princeton, NJ: Princeton University Press, 1993), 220–61.

80. *Mandeville's Travels*, 20 (ch. 5).

81. Ibid., 101 (ch. 15).

82. On the scene in the Sultan's chamber, see Iain Macleod Higgins, *Writing East: The "Travels" of Sir John Mandeville* (Philadelphia: University of Pennsylvania Press, 1997), 110–23. For a reading of religious identity in *Mandeville's Travels* in the context of modern postcolonial theory (Abdul JanMohamed's theory of the "Manichean allegory" of race), see Andrew Fleck, "Here, There, and In Between: Representing Difference in the *Travels* of Sir John Mandeville," *Studies in Philology* 97 (2000): 379–400.

83. Nation "is a group of men of common origin, bound together by ties of blood. In the Middle Ages it simply meant race." Guenée, 52.

84. Enlightenment writings on "national character" describe what a modern reader understands as race; see, for example, excerpts from Hume's essays "Of the Populousness of Ancient Nations" and "Of National Character" in *Race and the Enlightenment*, ed. Emmanuel Chukwadi Eze (Oxford: Blackwell, 1997), 29–33. On the intersection of categories of race and nation, see Brian K. Taylor, ed., *Race, Nation, Ethnos and Class* (Brighton: Pennington Beach, 1996), 7–12; Kenan Malik, *The Meaning of Race: Race, History and Culture in Western Society* (London: Macmillan, 1996), 128–48.

85. *Sir Ferumbras*, ed. Sidney J. Herrtage, EETS ES 34 (London: EETS/Trübner, 1879), lines 1086–89.

86. For a provocative analysis of race in Middle English romance, see Jeffrey Jerome Cohen, "On Saracen Enjoyment: Some Fantasies of Race in Late Medieval France and England," *JMEMS* 31 (2001): 113–46. On conversion and race, see Steven F. Kruger, "Conversion and Medieval Sexual, Religious, and Racial Categories," in *Constructing Medieval Sexuality*, ed. Karma Lochrie, Peggy McCracken, and James A. Schultz, Medieval Cultures 11 (Minneapolis: University of Minnesota Press, 1997), 158–79.

87. *The King of Tars*, ed. Judith Perryman (Heidelberg: Carl Winter, 1980), lines 577–85, 772–78, 928–30, 1153–70.

88. On Chaucer and the Auchinleck MS, see Derek Pearsall and I. C. Cunningham, "Introduction," in *The Auchinleck Manuscript: National Library of Scotland Advocates' MS. 19.2.1* (London: Scolar, 1977), vii–xvii, esp. xi, and the essays by Loomis cited there. On *The King of Tars* and the Man of Law's Tale, see Perryman, 53–56.

89. *King of Tars*, lines 481–504; Man of Law's Tale, II.351–85.

90. Robert W. Hanning, "Custance and Ciappelletto in the Middle of It All: Problems of Mediation in *The Man of Law's Tale* and *Decameron* 1.1," in Koff and Schildgen, pp. 177–211, esp. 194–98.

91. *King of Tars*, lines 188, 212; 928, 12.

92. Ibid., 639, 704–5.

93. On "the conflict of opposing religious 'laws'" as a manifestation of "the binary quality of the Man of Law's thinking" (410), see Lynch, "Storytelling," 417–18.

94. On the idealization of Custance, see Sheila Delany, "Womanliness," *Chaucer Review* 9 (1974): 63–72; David Raybin, "Custance and History: Woman as Outsider in Chaucer's *Man of Law's Tale*," *Studies in the Age of Chaucer* 12 (1990): 65–84.

95. On this passage, see Lynch, "Storytelling," 418; Derek Pearsall, "Strangers in Late-Fourteenth-Century London," in *The Stranger in Medieval Society*, ed. F. R. P. Akehurst and Stephanie Cain Van D'Elden, Medieval Cultures 12 (Minneapolis: University of Minnesota Press, 1997), 46–62, esp. 46–48.

96. *Song of Roland*, line 1086; they are also called the "gent criminel" (2456), the "gent averse" (2630), and the "gent paienor" (2639, 2694). *The Song of Roland*, ed. Gerard J. Brault, 2 vols. (University Park: Pennsylvania State University Press, 1978).

97. *Polychronicon* 1.59, ed. Babington, 2: 158–59; another example at 162–63.

98. *De proprietatibus rerum* 15.118, ed. Seymour, 796 ("straunge naciouns"); 15.50, ed. Seymour, 752 ("stronge naciouns"); 15.133, ed. Seymour, 803 ("strange naciouns" in the base MS, "stronge naciouns" in six other MSS).

99. Note the similar conflation of strength and strangeness at the conclusion of the Merchant's Tale, when Januarie cries out, "O straunge lady stoore" (IV.2367).

100. *De proprietatibus rerum*, 15.133, ed. Seymour, 803.

101. *De proprietatibus rerum*, 15.113, ed. Seymour, 792–93.

102. "Tota lingua Northimbrorum, maxime in Eboraco, ita stridet incondita, quod nos australes eam vix intelligere possumus; quod puto propter viciniam barbarorum contigisse." *Polychronicon*, 1.59, ed. Babington, 2: 162–63.

103. See Kruger, 160–62.

104. Malik, 79–84, 91–100.

105. *Confessio Amantis*, 8.84–87, 91–92, in *The English Works of John Gower*, ed. G. C. Macaulay, EETS ES 81–82, 2 vols. (1901; rpt. Oxford: Oxford University Press, 1957), 2: 388.

106. On the sons of Noah and world geography, see Akbari, "Due East," 22–23.

107. "Huius tempore divisum est genus humanum in tria: in liberos, milites, servos. Liberi de Sem, milites de Japhet, servi de Cham." Honorius of Autun, "De imagine mundi," ed. J.-P. Migne, *Patrologia Cursus Completus, Series Latina*, 172: 115–88; quotation from col. 166B.

108. *Cursor Mundi*, 2133–36, ed. Horrall, 102–3.

109. Lee Patterson, "'No man his reson herde': Peasant Consciousness, Chaucer's Miller, and the Structure of the *Canterbury Tales*," *South Atlantic Quarterly* 86 (1987): 457–95, esp. 472–78, 487–88.

110. *Cursor Mundi*, 2070–72, ed. Horrall, 100.

111. See Jill Mann, *Chaucer and Medieval Estates Satire: The Literature of Social Classes and the General Prologue to the* Canterbury Tales (Cambridge: Cambridge University Press, 1973).

112. D. S. Brewer, "Class Distinction in Chaucer," *Speculum* 43 (1968): 290–305, esp. 292–93, 297.

113. He quotes a text from 1408, which contains responses concerning what one must do to be thought noble; among the answers are "prandere bene et

nobiliter" and "tenere hospitium appertum" (701). Howard Kaminsky, "Estate, Nobility, and the Exhibition of Estate in the Later Middle Ages," *Speculum* 68 (1993): 684–709, esp. 695–99.

114.   On the Franklin's social status, see Anne Middleton, "Chaucer's 'New Men' and the Good of Literature in the *Canterbury Tales*," in *Literature and Society*, ed. Edward W. Said (Baltimore, MD: Johns Hopkins University Press, 1980), 15–56; Paul Strohm, "Chaucer's Audience," *Literature and History* 5 (1977): 26–41. Carl Lindahl points out that "fully two thirds of the pilgrims" fall in the middle range of the social strata, showing Chaucer's interest in issues of social mobility: *Earnest Games: Folkloric Patterns in the* Canterbury Tales (Bloomington: Indiana University Press, 1987), 3, 22–23.

115.   *Polychronicon*, 1.60, ed. Babington, 2: 168–75.

116.   See the "sharpe swerd" of Damocles hanging in the temple of Mars (I.2027–30), a sign that "the central source of stability in the world conceived by chivalry is himself permanently at risk" (Patterson, *Chaucer*, 227).

117.   Lynch, "East Meets West," 531–32.

118.   Akbari, "Due East," 28–31.

Scientific Imagery in Chaucer
[The Canon's Yeoman's Tale]

DOROTHEE METLITZKI

Chaucer's knowledge of medieval science and philosophy is deeply embedded in his literary work. It is an integral and inseparable part of his poetic vision and expression. Chaucer's "star-wisdom" is crucial to his profound, humorous, and compassionate understanding of the human predicament on "this litel spot of erthe." His use of the contemporary sciences in presenting the physical and spiritual condition of man, medieval and universal, reflects the observations, ideas, and methodology of great Arabian masters whose names occur throughout the body of Chaucer's works: Alkabucius, Alocen, Arsechiel, Averrois, Avycen, Haly, Razis. So do the names of the two most important medieval transmitters: Constantyn (Constantinus Africanus), the earliest translator of medical treatises from the Arabic, and Piers Alfonce (Petrus Alfonsi), the pioneer of Arabic studies on English soil whose interests and gifts, like Chaucer's, encompassed the intellectual discipline of the scientist, the imaginative sweep of the poet, the moral insight of the philosopher, and the accumulated wisdom of folklore. Chaucer's mastery of the medieval sciences, astronomy, astrology, dream-lore, medicine, is a commonplace of Chaucerian scholarship. But the precision with which scientific imagery is used in his works is still a surprising, not fully comprehended factor. The precision is an important aspect of Chaucer's poetic genius and technique. It can only be probed within the rigorous framework of Arabic learning.

. . . .

The tradition that Chaucer was a master of alchemy as well as astronomy and astrology, was reiterated in 1652 when Elias Ashmole included the Canon's Yeoman's Tale in his compendium of English alchemical treatises

These pages first appeared in *The Matter of Araby in Medieval England* (New Haven: Yale University Press, 1977), 73–74, 80–92, 273–77. Reprinted by permission.

called *Theatrum Chemicum Britannicum*. Ashmole describes Chaucer as ranking "among the Hermetick Philosophers" and adds that "he that Reads the latter part of the *Canon's Yeoman's Tale*, will easily perceive him to be a Judicious Philosopher, and one that fully knew the *Mistery*."[1] We know that "in portraying the yeoman-narrator, the alchemist-canon, and the canon and priest of *Secunda Pars*, Chaucer made significant use of the alchemical treatises and other writings about alchemy available to him at the end of the fourteenth century."[2]

The use of allegory by medieval alchemists as a strictly defined intellectual system of implicit secrecy is best illustrated in a "code of secrecy" which entered medieval Europe from Arabic sources. Its application reveals itself in two features characteristic of Arabic alchemical literature: the use of "code words" and the "topic" of "secret of secrets."

In the lines that bring the Canon's Yeoman's Tale (CYT) to an end Chaucer cites some of the source material of his alchemical knowledge: the *Rosarium* of Arnold of Villa Nova (1240–1311) and the "book Senior."

> Lo, thus seith Arnold of the Newe Toun,
> As his Rosarie maketh mencioun;
> He seith right thus, withouten any lye:
> "Ther may no man mercurie mortifie
> But it be with his brother knowlechyng."
> How be that he which that first seyde this thyng
> Of philosophres fader was, Hermes—
> He seith how that the dragon, doutelees,
> Ne dyeth nat, but if that he be slayn
> With his brother; and that is for to sayn,
> By the dragon, Mercurie, and noon oother
> He understood, and brymstoon by his brother,
> That out of Sol and Luna were ydrawe.
> "And therefore," seyde he,—taak heede to my sawe—
> "Lat no man bisye him this art for to seche,
> But if that he th'entencioun and speche
> Of philosophres understonde kan;
> And if he do, he is a lewed man.
> For this science and this konnyng," quod he,
> "Is of the secree of secrees, pardee."
> Also ther was a disciple of Plato,
> That on a tyme seyde his maister to,
> As his book Senior wol bere witnesse,
> And this was his demande in soothfastnesse:
> "Telle me the name of the privee stoon?"

And Plato answerde unto hym anoon,
"Take the stoon that Titanos men name."
"Which is that?" quod he. "Magnasia is the same,"
Seyde Plato. "Ye, sire, and is it thus?
This is *ignotum per ignocius*.
What is Magnasia, good sire, I yow preye?"
"It is a water that is maad, I seye,
Of elementes foure," quod Plato.
"Telle me the roote, good sire," quod he tho,
"Of that water, if it be youre wil."
"Nay, nay," quod Plato, "certein, that I nyl.
The philosophres sworn were everychoon
That they sholden discovere it unto noon
Ne in no book it write in no manere."[3]

[ll. 1428–66]

The alchemical teaching which the Canon's Yeoman cites from "Arnold of the Newe Toun" is a classical hermetic passage whose substance, in a variety of open and hidden forms, is a basic concept of medieval alchemical literature. The core of the matter is an instruction for making the philosopher's stone "Elixer clept" from a compound of mercury and sulphur. In the works of Arnold of Villa Nova, Chaucer's formulation of the alchemical core—"the dragon and his brother"—has been traced to *De lapide philosophorum* and, most recently, to a treatise called *De secretis naturae*: "The discipulus asked: Why have philosophers said that mercury does not die unless it is slain with its brother? The magister replied: The first who said this was Hermes, who said that the dragon never dies unless with his brother it be killed. He means to say that Mercury never dies . . . except with his brother. . . ."[4]

The allegory of alchemy in the works of Latin writers that we have in the above passage reveals their dependence on Arabic treatises in the most direct and dramatic way. The key to an understanding of the mythological symbolism in Chaucer's quotation is the terminology of code words—"Decknamen," Arabic *rumūz* (hints)—in which the secret of alchemical knowledge was transmitted to the initiates of medieval Islam. The symbolic designations (dragon for mercury, the dragon's brother for "brymstoon" [CYT ll. 1438–39], sol and luna for gold and silver [CYT l. 826]) clearly reveal the astrological pattern which underlies the hermetic tradition of alchemy.[5] Though there is considerable diversity in the attachment of certain "cover-names" to certain metals and minerals, the study of Arabic alchemical works by Ruska, Holmyard, and, most recently, Siggel, has found an essential uniformity of designation, reflected in the alchemical treatises of the Latin West.[6]

The Canon's Yeoman's display of learning which brings his tale to a close represents the most rudimentary elements of alchemical knowledge. Its formulation is properly ascribed to Hermes "that first seyde this thyng." Like Roger Bacon before him, the Canon's Yeoman calls Hermes "the father of philosophers."[7] The authentic touch in using the authority of "the father of alchemy" to teach the properties of mercury may have escaped the Canon's Yeoman's audience if they did not remember that Mercury was the name by which Hermes himself was also known. In its synonymous association with Hermes Mercurius, mercury is therefore the root of alchemical wisdom.

The importance of sulphur in a variety of allied and related forms is also basic in Arabic alchemical writings. Throughout the Middle Ages mercury and sulphur were considered as the primary components in all metals and, at times, as the elixir par excellence.[8] The experimentation to make the elixir was based on a theory of transmutation which derived from the premise that a mixture of mercury and sulphur in various proportions had led to the formation of metals and minerals under planetary influence in the womb of the earth.[9]

The symbolic designation of mercury as "dragon" in Chaucer is only one of over sixty code words for quicksilver by which it was known to Arabic alchemical writers.[10] Many Arabic writers compiled lists of allegorical terms for the benefit of future initiates—e.g., the anonymous author of "The Book of Treasure on the Solution of the Symbol," in which mercury is designated as "serpent-dragon."[11] While the oldest Arabic treatises based themselves on Hellenistic nomenclature, the code names which entered the Latin West are mostly translations of Persian and Arabic designations. They often expressed a quality in the metal or mineral that seemed most apparent. Thus, many code words for mercury express its property of elusiveness or winged flight, e.g., "white bird" (*ṭair abyad*), "white eagle" (*uqāb abyad*), "demon" (*ghūl*), "the fleeing one" (*al-farr*), by the side of such images as "foam of the sea" (*raghwrat al-baḥr*), "spittle of the moon" (*lu 'āb al-qamar*), "moist pearl" (*lu'lu' raṭib*).[12] The term "dragon" (*at-tinnīn*) for mercury is found in an anonymous "Epistle on the Science of Chemistry" which lists twenty-four code words for each substance.[13] "Draco autem est aqua divina," explains the Latin translator in Chaucer's "book Senior," where its original Arabic author, Muhammad ibn Umail, wrote only the Arabic word for dragon—*tinnīn*.[14] The classification of the substances into "bodies" and "spirits" is also as we find it in Chaucer. Mercury is cited as both "body" and "spirit," though its code names are given among "bodies."

> As to quicksilver, we have enumerated its names with the metals. As to its being mentioned among the metals, this is necessary because it is the first of them and the others are derived from it and descend from it. As to its being mentioned among the "spirits," this is because it flees from fire and

does not resist it, and thus it is also counted among the "spirits." Accordingly the "bodies" are those which melt in fire and do not flee from it, while the "spirits" flee from fire and cannot bear it.[15]

The "spirits" are mercury, sal ammoniac, realgar, orpiment, "yellow sulphur," "red sulphur," and "white sulphur." The great importance of sulphureous substances is easily apparent to the lay eye in the incipits of medieval Latin alchemical treatises and the chapter headings in Geber's *Summa perfectionis*.[16] Chaucer lists the alchemical trinity: "Arsenyk, sal armonyak, and Brymstoon" (CYT l. 799).

The variety of code words for sulphur extends to the designations for *zarnīkh*, termed "arsenicum" in the Latin treatises, which is both realgar and orpiment.[17] Sulphur is most commonly named "scorpion" (*al-ʿaqrab*), a designation which, for some reason, is not found in the Latin texts.[18] It is also "the winged" (*dhū al-jināḥain*), "the golden" (*adh-dhahabī*), and "son of the sun" (*ibn ash-shams*). It is *zarnīkh* which is referred to as "brother" (*akh*) or, to comprise realgar and orpiment as one, "the two brothers" (*al-akhwān*) or "the two friends" (*al-khalīlān*).[19] The sibling relationship which, in Chaucer's passage, links mercury and "brymstoon" is a basic principle of medieval alchemical allegory.

The symbolism of life and death in the transmutation of alchemical substances is explained as follows by a thirteenth-century writer, Abu al-Qasim al-Iraqi:

> By "death" and "life" they [the alchemists] refer to a substance from which it is possible by suitable treatment to remove its lightness, and do away with its movement in the fire, so much so that when it is placed therein it shows no movement. . . . By "life" they mean the opposite of this. . . .[20]

The metaphysical poignancy of the technical term *mortificare* (cf. "this quyksilver I wol mortifye"—CYT l. 1126) in its application to quicksilver was fully realized by Arab alchemical writers. Argentum vivum is the "living" ("quick") silver. Its Arabic designation, *zibāq*, is a Persian form which preserves the "living" element of the substance in the Indo-European root, *jiv*.[21] The metaphorical impact in the "killing" of mercury by sulphur, his "brother," which permeates the Chaucerian passage with biblical force, is fully brought home in the opening words of an ordinary instruction contained in al-Razi's alchemical "Book of the Secret of Secrets": "take living quicksilver and kill it."[22]

How closely all alchemists, including Arnold of the Newe Toun and Chaucer, followed conventional Arabic usage in their phrasing of alchemical thought is also clear from the *Turba Philosophorum*, an alchemical classic of the twelfth century which depicts a general debate of philosophers and is a compilation translated from Arabic sources: "Item notificio vobis," says the speaker to the crowd of philosophers, "quod Draco nunquam moritur."[23] An interpolated passage toward the end of the *Turba*, the *Visio Arislei*, is a dream vision of the marriage of sulphur and mercury which explains the "multiplying" family relationships in the idiom of alchemy—"Thogh that he multiplie terme of his lyve" (CYT 1. 1479)—within a typical allegory of love. The names of the romantic couple are Cabritis, the Arabic word for sulphur (*kibrīt*), and Beua, a corruption of Beida, the Arabic *al-baiḍa* (the white one). The allegorical marriage is incestuous, for Beua is the sister of Cabritis. This immorality, however, is countered by citing the example of Adam, who married his sons to his daughters in order to have them "multiply." The setting in which the marriage takes place is the dream in which Arisleus and his alchemist companions arrive in a region of the sea at the end of the world where nothing "multiplies." They offer the inhabitants and their king to teach them their secret. "If there were a philosopher among you," says Arisleus to the assembled strangers, "your sons could multiply, your trees would not die but your seed would grow and your good things would increase and you would be kings prevailing over your foes."

Arisleus then proceeds to teach the king the facts of life by which a union of male to male, which the natives practice, cannot be fruitful. Nature requires a union of male to female. It is under these circumstances that sulphur and mercury, son and daughter of the king, are to be united in marriage, and the objection of the father—"Heu tibi: Numquid vir suam ducit sororem?"—is overruled on biblical authority. Moreover, the marriage of sister to brother will improve the brother "eo quod ex ipso est." However, at the moment of union, sulphur, Cabritis, "dies." The enraged king puts the alchemists in jail, accusing them of murdering his children. The philosophers promise to resuscitate the son through the daughter if the daughter, quicksilver, is allowed to stay with them in jail for eighty days. At the end of the period, "in the shadows of the waves, the intense heat of summer and the turbulence of the sea," they joyfully announce that the king's son has been resurrected.[24]

The allegorical siblings, sulphur and mercury, change their sex in Arabic alchemical treatises. Sulphur may be mercury's "brother" or "sister," and mercury may be a feminine or masculine "body" allied to sulphur of the opposite sex. Thus we have the following pronouncement by Mercury in an allegorical debate between mercury and gold in a Latin work, *De aluminibus et salibus*, ascribed to Razi by Vincent de Beauvais:[25] "And if anyone unites me with my brother or sister, he will live and rejoice, and I shall be sufficient unto him in all eternity, were he to live a thousand times thousand years."[26]

The descent of mercury and sulphur from the "sun" and the "moon" ("That out of Sol and Luna were ydrawe, " CYT 1. 1440) is explained in a "Tractatulus Avicennae" in a chapter of "De Natura Corporum: id est, Solis & Lunae, & eorum Sulphure."[27] After pointing out that gold (sol) is the most perfect body, lord and king of all substances, the author states that it has much of the virtue of sulphur and little of its substance, while, conversely, containing much of the substance of mercury and little of its virtue. Silver (luna), on the other hand, has much of the substance of sulphur and little of its virtue, while containing little of the substance of mercury and much of its virtue. Moreover, silver is a feminine body so that the extraction of mercury and sulphur in their perfect relationship and form implies the marriage of Sol and Luna. An Arabic writer explains the allegorical coupling:

> They also use the term "marriage" meaning thereby a substance to which this name is necessarily appropriate, since it will join with a substance female in relation to itself, and its lightness is transferred to it as sperm is transferred from the male to the female; they therefore describe it by this characteristic of it. From this thou mayest judge of the rest of the analogies and allegories of the Sages.[28]

The part of the "Tractatulus Avicennae" which deals with Sol and Luna is an excerpt from *De aluminibus et salibus* ascribed to Razi.[29] There is no Arabic original of the treatise among the works of Razi, but a fragmentary Arabic text originating in Spain has been found for parts of the Latin,[30] an illustration of the complex interdependence of Latin tracts and their relation to original Arabic treatises.[31]

The text of the "book Senior" in Chaucer presents no obscure problem of origins. As Ruska was the first to point out,[32] the passage is found in an Arabic alchemical treatise of the tenth century by "Sheikh" Muhammad ibn Umail at-Tamimi as-Sadiq, known to the West as "Senior Zadith filius Hamuel." The work, poetically entitled "The Book of the Silvery Water and the Starry Earth," is a compendium of quotations from ancient philosophers who practiced alchemy. Ibn Umail wrote it as a commentary on an alchemical poem of sixty-seven stanzas, entitled "A Letter from the Sun to the Moon" (*risālah ash-shams ila al-hilāl*). The Latin versions of Ibn Umail's treatise, which constitute the "book Senior," contain large portions of the commentary and part of the risālah under the title "Epistola solis ad lunam crescentem."[33] The Latin "book Senior" and the "Epistola solis ad lunam crescentem" are therefore frequently titles of an identical work.[34]

The learned dialogue between two alchemists with which the Canon's Yeoman impresses the Canterbury pilgrims has the following form in the Arabic original of Ibn Umail:

> Qālīmūs said: "Take a stone called Titānūs. And it is a stone, white, red, yellow, black, which has many names and diverse colours, and they are a single spiritual nature hidden in the sand, describe it in its colours which appear from it when it is treated." And Rūnūs said: "Describe it to me, oh sage," he said, "it is the body of the noble magnesia which all philosophers praise." And he said: "And what is magnesia?" He said: "It is congealed

composite water which endures the killing through the fire. It is the wide large good sea, whose excellence Hermes described, and he considered as magnesia here the spirit and the soul, and its body is the ashes which are in the core of the ashes." And Plato said: "Everyone is one because every man has a soul."[35]

The teacher Qalimus and his interrogator, Runus, are transformed into Solomon and a sage (sapiens) in the Latin text.[36] In view of Solomon's place in the "wisdom literature" of Jews, Christians, and Muslims, the transformation seems natural. It may, however, have been due to a misreading of the Arabic lettering,[37] one of the most common phenomena in Arabic–Latin translation. The names, transformed from the Greek, are still obscure.[38]

Chaucer's substitution of Plato for Solomon in the dialogue as reported by the Canon's Yeoman may be explained from Ibn Umail's text in which the discussion of magnesia is followed by "and Plato said," both in Arabic and Latin. The association of alchemical teaching with Plato is a common feature of alchemical literature. It is found, in its most representative form, in the *Kitāb muṣaḥḥaḥāt Aflāṭūn* (The Book of Rectifications of Plato) of Jabir, "a very curious compilation" in which Plato initiates his disciple Timaeus into the secrets of alchemy.[39]

In Ibn Umail's text, Plato continues the dialogue on magnesia by affirming the doctrine of the World Soul as One and discussing man's soul in its interdependence with the animate and inanimate world of created beings. He then transfers the Platonic principle of the encompassing soul to the alchemical relation of gold to copper, and of mercury to sulphur and magnesium. The passage ends with the elixir:

> . . . and if they called it a stone, it is one kind which has no equal to it among the stones and no match, and if he collected it, [and] indeed it is the Name, and if it was called water, it is not particles of waters and it has no match, and if he collected it, [and] indeed it is one Name, it is uncompounded, not perfected except from itself and in itself, [and a greeting of peace] and verily this is the secret which is in it and there is none in any outside it.[40]

The Latin "book Senior" has a gloss to replace "the Name" in the Arabic text: "tamen est spiritus, & habet nomen spiritus. Et si dicatur aqua, non est sicut caeterae aquae, nec habet intellectum distinctum."[41] In the Chaucerian version the dialogue ends as follows:

> "What is Magnasia, good sire, I yow preye?"
> "It is a water that is maad, I seye,
> Of elementes foure," quod Plato.
> "Telle me the roote, good sire," quod he tho,

> "Of that water, if it be youre wil."
> "Nay, nay," quod Plato, "certein, that I nyl.
> The philosophres sworn were everychoon
> That they sholden discovere it unto noon,
> Ne in no book it write in no manere.
> For unto Crist it is so lief and deere
> That he wol nat that it discovered bee,
> But where it liketh to his deitee
> Men for t'enspire, and eek for to deffende
> Whom that hym liketh; lo, this is the ende."
> [ll. 1458–71]

The refusal, in the alchemical Platonic dialogue, to reveal the secret of "the Name," or the "spirit," which is reflected in Chaucer, shows the connection between the idiom of alchemy and the idiom of religious mysticism as transmitted to the Latins from Arabic sources. An additional feature in Chaucer is the elaboration of "the secret" in a Christian admonition about the spiritual hazards of alchemy. In this, as E. H. Duncan has shown, Chaucer was using the "book Senior" as well. He was, in fact, using the literal translation of an Islamic invocation to Allah.

The lines of direct translation are apparent in another passage in Ibn Umail:

And this is the secret about which they swore that they would not put it into a book and not one of them would reveal it and they referred the matter concerning it to Allah who is great and mighty. His name inspires him whom He wishes to inspire and hinders him whom He wishes to hinder for He is the root without which the art does not avail anyone ever except through Him, and what they concealed is the management of this thing until it becomes firm through the fire so that it becomes a great matter and verily such powers appear from it . . . and if they do not learn it they will not have . . . these powers which this deed makes and Muhammad ibn Umail praises Allah, may His name be sanctified, for what He bestowed on him and that He made him excel in it and inspired him to it with knowledge of this hidden secret and this after the long search and long-lasting wakefulness, and he disclosed what was obscure in their expressions with such praise through which he could attain His pleasure and according to his merits and deserts.[42]

The substitution of Deus for Allah presented no problem to the Latin translator who turned Arabic into Latin for the benefit of his fellow Christians in the West. One of the Latin Geber tracts, composed in the form of a dialogue between Demogorgon and Geber, is opened by hailing Geber as the wisest descendant of "the great Muhammad."[43] The tendency to "translate" from the Arabic whatever ideas presented themselves is an important component in the Christian attitude to alchemy, as it is in the attitude to astrology. The religious view of Islam on the secret art had entered the West as an integral part of the scientific material.

. . . .

In its immediate context Chaucer's "secree of secrees" expresses the ritual injunction to secrecy from master to pupil and author to reader that characterizes all Arabic alchemical treatises. "Labour not to expose our secret more than we have exposed it unto thee, or thy exposure thereof will expose thyself," says the thirteenth-century Abu'l Qasim al-Iraqi in concluding his "Book of Knowledge Acquired Concerning the Cultivation of Gold."44 We find the same admonition at the end of Arnold's Rosarium, the Canon's Yeoman's acknowledged source: "Et qui habes istum librum in sinu tuo reconde nullique ipsum revelles nec manibus impiorum offeras: quia secretum secretorum onmium philosophorum plenarie comprehendit."45 Chaucer's own version in the Canon's Yeoman's Tale—" 'For this science and this konnyng,' quod he, 'Is of the secree of secrees, pardee' "—is more closely related to a passage in the Arnoldian De lapide philosophorum and De secretis naturae.46 However, the medieval rendering of "secretum secretorum" is the usual translation of a common Semitic superlative, the Arabic sirr al-asr¥r, a key designation, widely known in the West, in the literary convention of hermetic writing. It appears in the title of al-Razi's alchemical work "The Book of the Secret of Secrets"47 and in the pseudo-Aristotelian Secret of Secrets whose extraordinary popularity in Western medieval literature in the thirteenth century version of Philip of Tripoli is attested by 207 Latin manuscripts.48

The historical origins of "the secret of secrets" as a figure of speech in the idiom of alchemy take us to the secret fraternities and mystic sects of medieval Islam which were known as the movement of the Isma'iliya and gave rise to the Assassins, the Sufi poets, and the Ikhwan as-Safā (the "Brethren of Purity").[49] The core of their teaching is the belief that the series of revealed prophets who followed Muhammad would stop with the seventh Imam, Isma'il, "the hidden prophet," an incarnation of the divinity. The role of man is to express the need that the universal soul feels to attain perfect knowledge. In the corpus of Jabir ibn Hayyan, the Geber of the Latins, that perfect knowledge is alchemy—the mystic doctrine of "art" by definition.[50]

The authorship of the tenth-century alchemical writings, attributed to the eighth-century mystic Jabir, is one of the most fascinating problems in the history of medieval thought. Jabir was the most famous alchemical authority among the Arabs; Geber was celebrated among the Latins as the author of a Latin alchemical compendium, the "Summa perfectionis," the earliest manuscripts of which date from the thirteenth century. In Arabic, the works of Jabir are a "vast body of literature which comprises all the sciences of the ancients which passed to Islam,"[51] in which, however, alchemy is the science of sciences. The writings cannot be the work of a single author; the scientific terminology, "without exception," is that introduced at the end of the ninth century by Hunain ibn Ishaq, the first translator of "Greek into Arabic."

The Latin Geber tracts have been shown to incorporate Latin translations of al-Razi's *Book of the Secret of Secrets*.[52] According to Ruska, the influence of Razi is most apparent in the methodical classification, for Razi divested alchemy of its superstitions and gave it a strict scientific form.[53] Nevertheless, the title of his alchemical book respects the strict tradition of the "elvysshe craft" in which gold is "the greatest secret" (*sirr a'zam*); sulphur, "the divine secret" (*sirr ilāhī*); and mercury, "the revealed secret" (*sirr makshūf*).[54]

The reason for the preeminence of alchemy in the writings of Jabir has been explained by Paul Kraus[55]: the empirical "worldly" sciences rank below the religious and metaphysical ones and, in fact, owe their existence to the latter. Alchemy is the most important worldly science, the other sciences having mainly an auxiliary function. Alchemy is the only worldly science to be pursued for its own sake. It is the perfection of empirical knowledge. Its task is the making of the elixir, the completely harmonious substance in which all components are balanced to perfection. This elixir is a third cosmos, linking microcosm and macrocosm. In this way the material sciences are united with the spiritual ones of which they were originally a part, and alchemy is the science which unites them. What is important in the making of the elixir is not the process of transmutation to gold for the sake of its material value but the achievement of perfect religious knowledge, the penetration into the most sublime secret of mystical truth: the hidden Imam.

On the practical level, the injunction to secrecy in the transmission of alchemy may be regarded as the need to guard professional knowledge from outsiders.[56] This "trade" element is discernible in the alchemical portions of the pseudo-Aristotelian *Secret of Secrets*, which gave the term *the secret of secrets* wide currency in the West:

> And know, O Alexander, that I am going to impart to thee a secret of divine knowledge which has been strictly guarded and preserved, and regarding the secrecy and inviolability of which sages and philosophers have taken mutual promises and oaths, in order that it may not fall into the hands of a weaver, horse-doctor, blacksmith, and carpenter who may cause corruption in the earth, and destroy agriculture and procreation.[57]

The concluding discourse on talismans, astrology, and the virtues of stones is specifically addressed to the practitioners of the "special sciences":

> And know that those who are endowed with clear intellect and good memory for acquiring knowledge, and who can find out the hidden through

that which is apparent to them, having reached to hidden truths of this deep and mysterious science, they observed extreme caution and miserliness in communicating it to others, although it is of such a universal benefit. They did so from the fear that they may come to share this knowledge with those who did not possess sufficient understanding for it, and because God's wisdom has decreed that His gifts should not be equally divided among His creatures. But, thanks to God, thou art not one of those who are debarred from knowing these mysteries, but thou art fully worthy of it.[58]

The importance which Western writers on alchemy attached to the *Secretum Secretorum* is clearly expressed by Petrus Bonus, a "physicus" of Ferrara who in 1330 wrote the alchemical work *Margarita Pretiosa*. He refers to the significance which the Old Philosopher (Aristotle) attributed to the "art": "Et idem scripsit eam Alexand. Regi discipulo suo in lib. de Secretis secretorum, cap. de lapidibus preciosis eodem more, quo antiqui Philosophi alii scripserunt scilicet occulto, figurato, velato sermone. Imo totus ille liber est mysticus, & est de hac arte, sicut de principali proposito."[59] There is also some indication that the *Secretum Secretorum* was regarded as a guide to spiritual mystic knowledge in Europe when the Latin text was translated into the vernacular by a German Cistercian nun.[60] In the works of Jabir, however, the association of alchemy, the dominant subject, with the doctrines of a religious fraternity, the Isma'iliya, is so close as to give the alchemical exposition the character of Isma'ilitic teaching: "For these books, oh brother, are miracles of my master, and nobody—and the Great One may prove it true—may take possession of what is in them of the sciences except our brother."[61]

The Isma'ili content is equally pronounced in the treatises of the "Brethren of Purity" to which the writings of Jabir are closely related.[62] This secret fraternity of Basra, which flourished in the tenth century, produced a compendium of knowledge in the form of fifty-two treatises *rasā'il* ("epistles") addressed to the "faithful brother." The compendium contains the story of the *Magian and the Jew*, which reached Gower from the *Secret of Secrets* and is an analogue of the *Secretum Secretorum* both in content and form.[63] The "secret" is conveyed by the Brethren of Purity in a conventional frame of direct instruction and concealed in the names and actions of a literary plot.[64] "And I think that in this there is an allegory of the allegories and a secret of the secrets," says a king to the head philosopher of the "jinn" in a discourse on the nature of man and beast. "So make known to me what the truth of these sayings is and the allusion of these allegories."[65]

It is the essence of this tradition that is preserved in its original formulation in the writings of the Latin alchemists. Strange as it may seem, Chaucer's Canon's Yeoman thus expounds the terminology of Isma'ili doctrine in which the outward form (*zāhir*) serves to hide and protect the inward esoteric core (*bāṭin*). The pseudo-Aristotelian *Secret of Secrets* had done most to spread this information among the international elite of learned medieval men:

> The secret means is one peculiar to the saints and sages whom God has chosen from amongst His creatures and endowed with His own knowledge. And I shall impart to thee this secret as well as others in certain chapters of this book, which is outwardly a treasure of wisdom and golden rules, and inwardly the cherished object itself. So when you have studied its contents and understood its secrets you will thereby achieve your highest desires and fulfil your loftiest expectations. Rejoice in it therefore, and may God help you attain this knowledge and to honour the masters thereof.[66]

Notes

1. Elias Ashmole, *Theatrum Chemicum Britannicum* (London, 1652), p. 470. See Gareth W. Dunleavy, "The Chaucer Ascription in Trinity College, Dublin, MS. D.2.8." *Ambix* 13 (1965), 12.

2. Edgar H. Duncan, "The Literature of Alchemy and Chaucer's Canon's Yeoman's Tale': Framework, Theme, and Characters," *Speculum* 43 (October, 1968), 633.

3. *The Works of Geoffrey Chaucer*, ed. F. N. Robinson, 2nd ed. (Boston, 1957), p. 222.

4. J. L. Lowes, "The Dragon and his Brother," *Modern Language Notes* 28 (1913), 229; Duncan, p. 652.

5. The scheme originated in a theory of correspondence between the properties and colors of metallic substances and the planetary system (cf. CYT ll. 826–29) which was developed by the star-worshipping Sabeans of early medieval Harran; it reached the scholars of the Muslim world in the guise of Babylonian and Greek learning, and the Latin Middle Ages in the Arabic writings of Muslim mystics and alchemists. Cf. D. Chwolsohn, *Die Ssabier und der Ssabismus* (St. Petersburg, 1856), I, 196.

6. J. Ruska and E. Wiedemann, "Alchemistische Decknamen," *Sitzungsberichte der Physikalisch-medizinischen Sozietaet in Erlangen* 56 (1924), 17–36; E. J. Holmyard, "Abu' l-Qāsim al-Irāqi," *Isis* 8 (1926), 402–24; Alfred Siggel, *Decknamen in der arabischen alchemistischen Literatur* (Berlin, 1951).

7. *Opus Minus* (*Opera quaedam hactemus inedita II*), ed. J. S. Brewer (London, 1859), p. 313: "sicut dicit Hermes Mercurius, pater philosophorum."

8. Siggel, p. 32, citing al-Jildaki (d. 1342), Arabic MS. Gotha 1291, 73b, 10. On Aidamur ibn Ali al-Jildaki, see Fuat Sezgin, *Geschichte des arabischen Schrifttums*, I, 643–44.

9. Paul Kraus, *Jābir ibn Ḥayyān II* (Cairo, 1942), p. 1. Cf. F. Dieterici, *Die Naturanschauung und Naturphilosophie der Araber im zehnten Jahrhundert* (Posen, 1864), p. 97. The scientific analysis of the seven metals of the Sabean system, corresponding to the seven planets, proceeded on the principle of the

balance of the four elements within them. See Paul Kraus, "Studien zu Jābir ibn Hayyān," *Isis* 15 (1931), 17.

10. CYT 1. 1438. See list of "Decknamen" in Ruska and Wiedemann, pp. 28–32, "dragon," p. 32. Cf. Siggel, "Alphabetisches Verzeichnis der Decknamen," *Decknamen*, pp. 33–54, "tinnīn," p. 36.

11. *Kitāb al-kanz fīfakk ar-ramz*, Arabic MS. Berlin 4191 in Siggel, *Katalog der arabischen alchemistischen Handschriften Deutschlands* (Berlin, 1949), pp. 93–95; Siggel lists "serpent-dragon" in *Decknamen*, p. 36.

12. See Siggel, "Alphabetisches Verzeichnis," *Decknamen*, passim.

13. "Risālah fi'Ilm al-Kimiyah" (Arabic MS. Dresden 210) in Ruska and Wiedemann, pp. 19, 31–32. "A list so similar as to point to a common origin" was found by Holmyard in an Arabic manuscript in the British Museum (MS. Add. 25724, ff. 15v–17r). The code words for mercury "show perfect agreement," E. J. Holmyard, "Alchemistische Decknamen," *Nature* 117 (January, 1926), 155–56.

14. *Three Arabic Treatises on Alchemy by Muhammad ibn Umail (10th Century A.D.)*, ed. M. Turāb 'Ali, with Excursus, and *Edition of the Latin Rendering of the Mā' al-Waraqī* by E. Stapleton and M. Hidāyat Husain (Calcutta, 1933), pp. 1–213; "tinnīn," p. 46; "draco," p. 191.

15. Ruska and Wiedemann, p. 32.

16. See Lynn Thorndike and P. Kibre, *A Catalogue of Incipits of Mediaeval Scientific Writings in Latin*, Index, column 1917; *Gebri Regis Arabum Philosophi Perspicacissimi Summa Perfectionis* in J. J. Manget, *Bibliotheca Chemica Curiosa* (Geneva, 1702), I, 519–57; German translation by E. Darmstaedter, *Die Alchemie des Geber* (Berlin, 1922).

17. J. Ruska, *Al-Rāzi's Buch Geheimnis der Geheimnisse* in *Quellen und Studien zur Geschichte der Naturwissenschaften und der Medizin* 6 (Berlin, 1937), p. 40.

18. J. Ruska, *Das Buch der Alaune und Salze* (Berlin, 1935), p. 23.

19. Ruska and Wiedemann, pp. 34–35; Siggel, *Decknamen*, pp. 34, 39.

20. Abū'l-Qāsim Muḥammad ibn Aḥmad al-Irāqi, *Kitāb al-'Ilm al-Muktasab fi Zirā 'at adh-Dhahab (Book of Knowledge Acquired concerning the Cultivation of Gold)*, ed. and trans. E. J. Holmyard (Paris, 1923), p. 56.

21. J. Ruska, *Al-Rāzi's Buch Geheimnis der Geheimnisse*, p. 37.

22. Ibid., p. 105.

23. J. Ruska, *Turba Philosophorum* (Berlin, 1931), p. 162.

24. Ibid., pp. 324–28. The dream of Arisleus is also mentioned by Petrus Bonus, *Margarita Pretiosa* in J. J. Manget, *Bibliotheca Chemica Curiosa* (Geneva, 1702), II, 29.

25. *Speculum Doctrinale*, liber XI, cap. 127; *Speculum Naturale*, liber VII, cap. 26. On ascription to Razi, see J. Ruska, *Das Buch der Alaune und Salze*, pp. 13 ff.; *Uebersetzung und Bearbeitungen von al-Rāzīs Buch Geheimnis der Geheimnisse* in *Quellen und Studien zur Geschichte der Naturwissenschaften und der Medizin* 4 (Berlin, 1935), p. 4.

26. Ruska, *Das Buch der Alaune und Salze*, pp. 59, 92. For a similar debate between mercury and gold in Jabir's "Book of Seventy," see M. Berthelot, *Archéologie et histoire des sciences* (Paris, 1906), p. 351.

27. Printed in Manget, I, 626–33, cap. II, pp. 627–28.

28. Abū'l-Qāsim al-Irāqi, *Kitāb al 'Ilm al-Muktasab*, ed. and trans. E. J. Holm-yard, p. 57.

29. J. Ruska, "Die Alchemie des Avicenna," *Isis* 21 (1934), 48.

30. Ruska, *Das Buch der Alaune und Salze*, pp. 18, 12; *Uebersetzung und Bear-beitungen von al-Rāzis Buch Geheimnis der Geheimnisse*, p. 85.

31. The claim of Latin treatises to be translations from the Arabic when there is no Arabic original in the exact form is often substantiated by passages of direct translation, as in Robert of Ketton's *De compositione alchymiae*; see E. J. Holmyard, "Abū'l-Qāsim al-Irāqī," *Isis* 8 (1926), 424–25.

32. J. Ruska, "Chaucer und das Buch Senior," *Anglia* 61 (1937), 136–37; "Senior Zadith—Ibn Umail," *Orientalistische Literaturzeitung* 31 (1928), 665–66; "Muhammad ibn Umail al-Tamīmī's 'Kitāb al-mā' al-waraqī wa'l-arḍ an-najmiyya,'" *Orientalistische Literaturzeitung* 37 (1934), 593–96.

33. J. Ruska, "Studien zu Muhammad Ibn Umail al-Tamīmī's 'Kitāb al-Mā' al-Waraqī wa'l-Arḍ an-Najmīyah,' " *Isis* 24 (1936), 311–42; Stapleton and Husain, *Three Arabic Treatises on Alchemy by Muhammad ibn Umail*, "Excursus," p. 117. E. H. Duncan discusses passages from a Vienna manuscript of the "Epistola" in *"The Literature of Alchemy,"* pp. 653–54. The attribution of the *Epistola* to "Senior Calid filius Hahmil," which is found in medieval manuscripts, is a confusion of Ibn Umail with Khalid ibn Yazid, who, in the Latin text of the "book Senior," is quoted as "Calid filius Seid," or, more correctly, as "Calid filius Isid" (*Three Arabic Treatises*, pp. 153, 191). Khalid ibn Yazid, the first alchemist of Arab tradition, is said to have studied the science with a hermit, Maryanus, with whom he is associated in the "Book of the Monk" by Jabir ibn Hayyan, "king of medieval alchemy" (Ruska, *Arabische Alchemisten 1. Chalid ibn Jazīd ibn Mu'ā wija* [Heidelberg, 1924], pp. 48–49; Paul Kraus, *Jābir ibn Ḥayyān I* [Cairo, 1935], Arabic text, p. 569, line 14; Studien zu Jābir ibn Ḥayyān," *Isis* 15 [1931], 8; Ibn Khaldūn, *Muqaddimah*, trans. F. Rosenthal (Princeton, 1958), III, 229–30). The legendary association is clearly expressed in the title of an early alchemical treatise by Robert of Ketton: "Liber de compositione alchemiae, quem edidit Morienus Romanus, Calid Regi Aegyptiorum: quem Robertus Castrensis de Arabico in Latinum transtulit." Printed in Manget, I, 509–19; F. Wuestenfeld, "Die Uebersetzungen arabischer Werke in das Lateinische seit dem XI. Jahrhundert," *Abhandlungen der Koeniglichen Gesellschaft der Wissenschaften zu Goettingen* 20 (1877), 47.

34. For printed Latin text, see Stapleton and Husain in *Three Arabic Treatises on Alchemy by Muhammad ibn Umail*, pp. 147–97. The "book Senior" itself is attributed to Plato in one English fourteenth-century manuscript, Cambridge, Trinity College 1122, f. 35r, in which a hand contemporary with the handwriting of the manuscript has written above the second word of the *incipit* "Dixit senior: *i.e.* Plato" (Duncan, p. 653). Whatever the relationship of this superstition to Chaucerian usage, Ibn Umail's "book Senior" was to alchemy what Ptolemy's *Almagest* was to astrology. The disciple's reference to "his book Senior," which implies the authorship of Plato, is probably nothing more than an expression of thorough familiarity with a basic alchemical textbook, i.e., the disciple's alchemical "Bible."

35. *Three Arabic Treatises*, p. 39. Professor Joel Kraemer has helped me to clarify the neoplatonic meaning of this passage.
36. Ibid., p. 180.
37. The Arabic for Solomon is "Sulaimān." My suggestion is that Qālīmūs may have been mistakenly read as "Sālīmūn."
38. J. Ruska, "Chaucer und das Buch *Senior*," *Anglia* 61 (1937), 136–37.
39. Paul Kraus, *Jābir ibn Ḥayyān, II*, p. 48 and in *Mémoires de l'Institut d'Egypte* 44 (Cairo, 1943), pp. 64–66.
40. *Three Arabic Treatises*, p. 39.
41. Ibid., p. 181.
42. Ibid., p. 41; Latin text, pp. 183–84.
43. Manget, I, 567.
44. *Kitāb al'Ilm al-Muktasab*, ed. E. J. Holmyard, p. 57.
45. *Opera Arnaldi de Villanuova* (Venice, 1505), p. 351.
46. K. Young, "The 'Secree of Secrees' of Chaucer's Canon's Yeoman," *MLN* 58 (1943), 98–105; Duncan, p. 653.
47. J. Ruska, *Al-Rāzi's Buch Geheimnis der Geheimnisse* in *Quellen und Studien z. Geschichte der Naturwissenschaften und der Medizen* 6 (1937), xii–240. Peter Bonus also mentions "Haly in suo. lib. de Secretis secretorum," *Margarita Pretiosa* in Manget, II, 80.
48. R. Foerster, "Handschriften und Ausgaben des pseudoaristotelischen 'Secretum Secretorum,'" *Centralblatt fuer Bibliothekswesen* 6 (Leipzig, 1889), pp. 3–10.
49. Paul Kraus, "Dschābir ibn Hajjān und die Ismāʿīlījja," *Dritter Jahresbericht, Forschungs-Institut fuer Geschichte der Naturwissenschaften* (Berlin, 1930), pp. 23–42, especially pp. 30–32, 41; Bernard Lewis, *The Origins of Ismāʿilism* (Cambridge, 1940) and *The Assassins* (New York, 1968); G. S. Hodgson, *The Order of the Assassins* (The Hague, 1955). On the Ikhwān aṣ-Ṣafāʾ, see F. Dieterici, *Die Philosophie der Araber in IX. und X. Jahrhundert* (Berlin, 1865), III; (1868), IV; (1883), XI. For general information, see Stanley Lane-Poole, *Studies in a Mosque* (London, 1883), pp. 186–207; E. G. Browne, *A Literary History of Persia* (Cambridge, 1928), I, 292–93. For recent work on the tracts of the brotherhood, see M. Stern "The Authorship of the Epistles of Ikhwān aṣ-Ṣafā," *Islamic Culture* 20 (1946), 367–72; A. L. Tibawi, "Ikhwān aṣ-Ṣafā and their Rasāʾil, a Critical Review of a Century and a Half of Research," *Islamic Quarterly* 2 (1955), 28–46.
50. Kraus, "Dschābir Ibn Hajjān und die Ismāʾilijja," p. 35.
51. "Jābir ibn Ḥayyān" by M. Plessner in *Encyclopaedia of Islam*, new edition, II, 357.
52. Ruska, *Uebersetzung und Bearbeitungen von al-Rāzīs Buch Geheimnis der Geheimnisse*, pp. 85–87.
53. Ruska, *Al-Rāzī's Buch Geheimnis der Geheimnisse*, p. 13.
54. Siggel, *Decknamen*, p. 41.
55. "Studien zu Jābir ibn Ḥayyān," *Isis* 15 (1931), 7–30, 11–13.
56. Siggel, *Decknamen*, p. 9.
57. Arabic text translated by A. S. Fulton in *Opera hactenus inedita Rogeri Baconi Fasc. V (Secretum Secretorum)*, ed. R. Steele (Oxford, 1920), p. 258.

58. Ibid., p. 254.

59. Manget, II, 80; in Venice, 1546 edition, p. 84.

60. G. Kriesten, *Ueber eine deutsche Uebersetzung des pseudo-aristotelischen "Secretum Secretorum" aus dem 13. Jahrhundert* (Berlin, 1907), p. 63; Hiltgart von Huernheim, *Mittelhochdeutsche Prosauebersetzung des "Secretum Secretorum,"* ed. R. Moeller (Berlin, 1963).

61. Arabic text of "The Book of the Ancient" in Kraus, *Jābir ibn Ḥayyān I*, p. 546, lines 9–10.

62. Kraus, *Jābir ibn Ḥayyān, II*, p. 316.

63. M. Steinschneider, *Die hebraeischen Uebersetzungen des Mittelalters* (Berlin, 1893), I, 251; F. Dieterici, *Die Logik und Psychologie der Araber* (Leipzig, 1868), pp. 113–16 contains a translated version of the tale from the "Rasā'il" of the "Brethren of Purity." Cf. John Gower, *Confessio Amantis*, liber VII, "Tale of the Jew and the Pagan," lines 3207–329; "The Story of the Jew and the Philosopher" in *Three Prose Versions of the Secretum Secretorum*, ed. R. Steele (London, 1898), pp. 165–67.

64. Ignaz Goldziher, "Ueber die Bennenung der Ichwān al-ṣafa," *Der Islam* 1 (1910), 22–26; G. von Grunebaum, *Medieval Islam* (Chicago, 1946), p. 42, n. 50.

65. Arabic text in F. Dieterici, *Thier und Mensch* (Leipzig, 1881), p. 104.

66. Robert Steele, *Secretum Secretorum . . . Fratris Rogeri* (Oxford, 1920), p. 179.

The *Canterbury Tales* and the Arabic Frame Tradition

KATHARINE SLATER GITTES

According to T. S. Eliot's well-known formulation, any literary work is a product of the author's individual talent and an underlying tradition. Although the scope of the individual talent evident in the *Canterbury Tales* has received ample attention, critics trying to define the precise organizing principle behind the work have given insufficient weight to the frame-narrative tradition in which Chaucer was writing. To be sure, scholars have adequately examined other traditions. For instance, George L. Kittredge (155–56) and R. M. Lumiansky (3–12), among others, have invoked the tradition of the drama, asserting that the General Prologue forms the first act of a dramatic structure and that a dramatic focus gives coherence to the whole. Ralph Baldwin (98–99) and Paul G. Ruggiers (3–8) explain the form of the *Canterbury Tales* by relating Chaucer's pilgrimage to the tradition of the celestial journey. Recently, Donald R. Howard, invoking elements of Gothic architectural tradition, has argued that the General Prologue and the Parson's Tale function together as organizing focuses, analogous to the rose window and the maze in Chartres Cathedral. Because the General Prologue portrays everyday life and ordinary persons and the Parson's Tale mirrors society's values and morality, Howard says, "From either end we see the whole reflected from the viewpoint of the individual or the society and then see it reflected again in reverse" (217). Robert M. Jordan refers to the Gothic tradition in another way, calling Chaucer's organization "inorganic," in accord with "the Gothic principle of juxtaposition," and suggesting that seams similar to "exposed beams" of a Gothic cathedral join apparently unconnected tales and portions of tales (130, 237–38).[1]

All these traditions—dramatic, celestial journey, and Gothic—are Greek or Western in origin. The frame narrative, however, of which the *Canterbury Tales* is the culmination, incorporates a tradition that originated and developed in Arabia.[2] To put the idea most simply, the structure of the *Canterbury*

This essay first appeared in *PMLA* 98 (1983): 237–51. Reprinted by permission of the Modern Language Association of America.

Tales can be most appropriately compared not with the cathedral but with the mosque. In this essay, I trace the development of the frame narrative, showing its Arabic roots and character, and suggest that the organizing principles and many of the features of the *Canterbury Tales* derive from this tradition.

I

The earliest frame narrative of significance is the *Panchatantra*, an eighth-century Indian–Arabic work that played a large role in shaping the frame narrative in medieval Europe. (My comments on the *Panchatantra* are all based on Ryder's edition.) The stories in the *Panchatantra* originated in India, many going back to the second century B.C. (Chaitanya 361). The original Sanskrit version of this work is lost, but the *Panchatantra* escaped extinction because the Arabs translated it into Arabic during the eighth century. A subsequent translation from the Arabic back into Sanskrit forms the basis of all the existing Sanskrit texts. Although the stories in the *Panchatantra* originated in India, the frame evidently did not. B. E. Perry, contrary to received scholarly opinion, has demonstrated that the Arabs, not the Indians, first enclosed this collection within a frame (54). Thus the *Panchatantra*, once merely a collection of stories, assumed the frame-narrative form by passing through Arabic hands. Further, as we shall see, all European frame narratives represent a continuation, in one way or another, of a genre invented by the Arabs.

The brief outer framing story that appears in the introduction to the *Panchatantra* tells of a mighty king whose three doltish sons refuse to be educated. A wise man promises to instruct the princes in worldly and political wisdom by telling them stories; the princes accept the instruction and in six months learn all that the wise man has told them. The rest of the work comprises five books, each focusing on one aspect of statecraft or knowledge: the losing of friends, the winning of friends, war and peace, loss of gains, and hasty action. This loose grouping of stories according to theme forms the basic organization of the work. The *Panchatantra* exemplifies a kind of secular-wisdom literature prevalent throughout the East, stressing intelligence and everyday knowledge rather than religious morality (Keith 243). The many moral verses that appear throughout the work and the resolutions of the stories' plots usually focus on a secular justice according to which rogues are punished and honest men vindicated.

Besides the Arabic outer framing story, each book of the *Panchatantra* has an Indian boxing tale of its own. The outer framing story (level A) encloses the entire work; the boxing tale of each individual book (level B) encloses tales (level C) that can enclose still other tales (level D). This insertion of tales within tales, a characteristic of Indian collections (Keith 244), sometimes continues until a number of tales are boxed, with three or more levels of narration operating simultaneously. The outer framing story of the wise man and the princes appears briefly at the start of each new book, taking up fewer than a dozen lines, and has no apparent ending; book 5, the last book, comes to a close without returning to the outer framing story. The absence of a final reminder that the wise man accomplished his mission leaves the form of the *Panchatantra* imperfect and unfinished. In contrast, the Indian boxing tales of the individual books and the short boxed tales within the books are finished and conclusive, with tightly resolved plots. The Arabic outer framing story does not interfere with the collections of tales, and each of the five books of the *Panchatantra* can exist as a complete narrative. The central point here is that the Arabic elements are open-ended and unfinished, the Indian elements closed and complete. The inconclusive plot of the Arabic framing story has allowed redactors to expand the *Panchatantra* or to subtract from it. Arthur Ryder has remarked that in some of its early versions, the last two books are so short that they are almost nonexistent and, in fact, may have been later additions (11).

The division of the *Panchatantra* into five separate books, each with a clearly stated topic, and the sense of completeness that the tightly plotted boxing tales provide imply that the *Panchatantra* has a fixed overall plan of organization. But many of the tales—some of the erotic ones, for instance—could go anywhere, for they have no clear connection with any of the books' themes: a book's boxing tale does not determine the nature of the stories it encloses. The arrangement of the books within the frame is also arbitrary, for the placement of the book on losing friends at the start or of the book on hasty actions at the end has no particular rationale, nor does the order in which the books appear affect their power to entertain or to instruct. The only exception to this random order occurs in the occasional balancing of themes, like the theme of book 1's boxing tale, the losing of friends, and the theme of book 2's boxing tale, the winning of friends. More than any other thematic or structural feature, the theme of wisdom organizes the *Panchatantra*, for it loosely links many of the stories to one another and to the frame, while never interfering with the stories' structures or plots.

Considering that the outer story takes up so little space and that the *Panchatantra* had existed for centuries without a frame, it is curious that the Arabs bothered to enclose the work at all. Similar collections of tales, like Aesop's *Fables*, existed in other cultures besides India, and their writers had not framed them. The Greeks and Romans did not develop the frame narrative, although some of their longer narratives frame short, complete tales: the tales Odysseus tells at Alcinous' court (*Odyssey* 7–12), the stories the daughters of Minyas tell in the *Metamorphoses* (4.1–415), the adventures Aeneas relates at Dido's court (*Aeneid* 2–3), and the tales the guests recount at Trimalchio's dinner in the *Satyricon* (9–16). As Robert Pratt and Karl Young point out, the larger framing stories existed for reasons other than the inserted tales, so that the tales do not justify the frames (9).

II

Even though we cannot define the Arabic outlook—in Leff's sense of the word (2–6)—any more than we can the outlook of any other cultural group, certain patterns of thought do seem to be peculiar to Arabic literature, art, music, and mathematics. These structural patterns determine Arabic principles of organization, which in turn explain the Arabic practice of enclosing tales within a framework. Typical of the medieval Arabic approach to organizing material is the way the Arabs developed and modified mathematical principles originating in Babylonia, in contrast to the way the Greek mathematicians dealt with those principles. The ancient Babylonians worked out by observation and experiment a system of mathematics that they used as a tool of trade and commerce. But because Babylonians had not devised zero as a place holder, they could not write numbers like 1,230 without ambiguity and could not develop modern methods of addition. They handled computation by using tables similar to our multiplication tables, which they arrived at by trial and error (Kramer 1: 35–36).

In the sixth century B.C., Pythagoras studied Babylonian mathematics and rejected observation and experiment, the practical side of Babylonian computational mathematics. He dwelt instead on mathematical theory and insisted that mathematical proof be accomplished by deductive reasoning, a method that starts with a whole and deduces relations within that whole (Kramer 1: 46). His approach led to a concept of unity in which the whole has greater importance and the parts are subordinate. Irrational numbers baffled the Pythagoreans, who found a number like the square root of 2 an impossible concept. The Babylonians had used a number approximating the square root of 2 and left it at that, but the Greeks, bothered by the lack of precision, wrote irrational numbers (and all numbers) geometrically. To represent the square root of 2, the Greeks drew a line equaling the hypotenuse of a right triangle whose sides were one measure long, thereby eliminating Babylonian ambiguities. But their system of working with irrational numbers always remained geometric: they never became accustomed to dealing with irrational numbers numerically as we do or as the medieval Arabs did (Kline 32–33, 48–50, 173).

Pythagoras, voicing what had been implied in Greek thought before his time, stated emphatically that the universe is harmonious because all its parts are related to one another mathematically. Pythagorean mathematics sees underlying order in the mysterious, arbitrary, and chaotic workings of nature (Kline 147–49). Following Pythagoras, other Greek mathematicians and philosophers dealt with the theoretical, scorning the practical and utilitarian.

Plato recommended the study of calculation, not for trade and utilitarian purposes, but for the sake of knowledge and truth. He thought that the study of mathematics compels the soul to a loftier region, where number theory is related to the idea of the good; that numbers should not be attached to objects in the sensible world; and that a unit should always appear as a unit and not as a group of small pieces (*Republic* 6.510, 7.525A–26D; see also Kline 42–46). Like Pythagoras, Plato held that the order of the world is modeled on an ideal and completed whole; that the universe is perfect, finite, and one; and that it is wrong to speak of the plurality or infinity of the universe, since all things in the universe form a part of the perfect whole and their combined sum equals this whole (*Timaeus* 30–31). The whole ranks foremost, and the parts of the whole are subordinate to it.

The same set of concepts underlies Aristotle's poetic theory, which says that tragedy should imitate a whole, complete action; that wholeness means having a beginning, a middle, and an end; and that the unity of a work should be easily comprehended. To unify a plot, an artist must select actions that revolve around one central theme. Each part of a good tragedy or epic (and, by implication, of any well-constructed literary work) contributes to the entire work so that the displacement or removal of that part disrupts the unity of the whole; any section that can be added to or subtracted from the work at random cannot truly qualify as part of the whole. Literary works with episodic plots connected by loose transitions or not at all are the worst kind, for they lack continuity (*Poetics* 7–9). Aristotle carries on the Platonic belief that unity in art requires the well-proportioned and harmonious balance of parts. The model for this Greek concept of unity is geometric, for geometry deals with enclosed space; it stresses the whole, the complete, and the finite and disregards the limitless and the infinite. Like the Pythagoreans, who had connected the limited with good and the unlimited with evil, Aristotle downplays the notion of infinity because he finds it imperfect and incomplete (*Physics* 3–4; see also Kline 175).

The concept of unity manifested in Greek mathematics and in Aristotle's *Poetics* also appears in Horace's *Ars Poetica*, which praises a kind of oneness where all the parts are appropriate to the whole. Horace likens disunity in a work of art to a man's head joined onto a horse's neck or to the top half of a beautiful woman set on the body of an ugly fish (lines 1–40). Like the Greeks, Horace believes that unity should consist in completeness and in the orderly relations of parts to one another and to the whole. This insistence on the harmonious subordination of parts to the whole, a theory rooted in Pythagorean mathematics, underlies not only the literature of the Greeks and Romans but also their art, their architecture, and their view of the cosmos. Medieval Europe inherited these classical Greco-Roman views, incorporating their emphasis on otherworldliness, on ideality, and on the harmony of the universe into Neoplatonism and Christian theology.

The medieval Arabs, unconstrained by an intellectual tradition that insisted on strong structural unity, developed a conception of organization different from the Greeks'. In mathematics, for example, where the Greeks stressed the theoretical, the Arabs emphasized the pragmatic, the inductive, and the empirical. Prompted by practical concerns, the Arabs made particularly significant advances in algebra and in computation. They needed precise computational and algebraic skills to find the correct position of Mecca, to determine the exact moments of sunrise and moonrise so that they could observe their fasts, to measure land so that they could divide estates according to Koranic law, and to calculate accurately for their mercantile affairs and trade (Landau 166; see also Hitti 107). The Arabs' finest achievement in computation was their development of zero as a place holder. No longer did the Arabs need to rely on cumbersome Babylonian multiplication tables or deal with the ambiguity of numbers containing zeros. The use of zero gave the Arabs speed and accuracy in their computations.

Irrational numbers like the square root of 2 did not trouble the Arabs as they had troubled the Greeks. Whereas the Greeks had used geometry to express the irrational, the Arabs wrote irrationals as numbers (Kline 173, 197). The Greek method of writing the square root of 2 as a line makes the irrational appear integral; the Arab method of using a number suggests that the Arabs felt more comfortable than the Greeks with infinite series and limitless chains. Moreover, when Arabs read a number, they may have a keener sense of boundlessness. Because Arabs read numbers as they do texts, from right to left, in reading a large number like 1,034, they read the smallest number (4) first and the largest number (1,000) last. Westerners read the largest number (1,000) first and the smallest (4) last. The Arab must first grasp the units, the parts, before moving on to the whole. A Westerner does the reverse, comprehending first the thousands before moving to the smallest part, the unit. Arabs, then, tend to view a number as an expanding entity; with the smallest part comprehended first, the progression moves toward the limitless. In the Western approach, the number contracts; the progression is limited. Furthermore, when faced with a large number like 2,331, a Westerner tends to ignore the 1 and the 30 and to round it off to 2,300, unless circumstances dictate attention to the tens and units. These two approaches to reading numbers illustrate the Western inclination to focus on the largest number at the expense of smaller numbers and the Arabic tendency to consider all numbers, large and small, as significant.

In concentrating on arithmetic and algebra, not on geometry as the Greeks did (Kline 199), the Arabs, again characteristically, showed a sharper awareness of the concept of boundlessness and infinity. Rom Landau says that al-Khwarizmi, the ninth-century founder of modern algebra, viewed numbers as finite parts of an infinite series of potential processes. The use of symbols for numbers enhances the sense of limitlessness inherent in algebra, for an x in an unsolved problem represents a limitless number of possible answers (169). Whereas Greek mathematicians saw the whole as foremost in importance and as a finite balance of parts, the Arabs saw the whole as less confining, and less structured, unlimited in its potential and neither more nor less important than the part. In mathematics, science, and medicine, the Arabs' outlook drew them toward inductive reasoning, experiment, and observation, all of which center on details and facts in preference to theories.

Arabic prose and poetry reveal similar thought processes. The literature stresses, on the one hand, limitlessness and boundlessness and, on the other, the part and the individual unit. These predilections explain why the Arabs framed the *Panchatantra* and much of their own literature. The earliest known Arabic literature, the pre-Islamic ode (or *qasida*), comes close to the frame narrative in its formal structure. Most pre-Islamic qasidas were written down during the century before Islam, though they had been composed and transmitted orally for hundreds of years before that (Nicholson xxii). These wholly secular odes glorify the Bedouin life, the life of the wanderer. Many have a tripartite structure. In the prelude, the speaker often tells of a ruined campsite that had once been the setting for a love affair. In the second part, the speaker, typically male, usually describes his camel, his wanderings, or the individuals he meets as he travels; and in the last part, he satirizes an enemy, glorifies a tribe, teaches wisdom, or describes a chase, a celebration, or a thunderstorm. Shifts in theme appear in all qasidas: the topics discussed (women, tents, camels) are rarely, if ever, linked to one another. Some qasidas have only one or two of the usual three sections, and some sections consist of one verse or one word, perhaps a place name. Portions of the qasida can even be shifted in position, the basic tripartite structure of the qasida allowing for a multitude of modifications (Lyall xix–xx, Nicholson 78).

The most significant characteristic of the qasida is its mode of organization. Unlike the odes of Pindar or Horace or the English Romantics, the qasida has no central unifying theme that penetrates each line; instead, it presents a series of pictures or episodes, loosely connected to one another or not connected at all. Each line represents a complete thought, almost all lines can stand independently, and their arrangement appears arbitrary. As G. E. von Grunebaum has observed, the emphasis in a qasida rests on the "perfection of the individual verse rather than of the composition of the whole" (*Islam* 19).

The lack of an overall principle of organization like that in Western odes has caused concern among critics. Reynold Nicholson says, "The structure of the qasida, its disconnectedness and want of logical cohesion, favored the omission and transposition of whole passages or single verses" (134). Although Nicholson rightly believes that each verse is complete insofar as it is expendable or transposable and that the verses do not reflect a central theme, he ignores the pivotal role played by the speaker. The qasida is organized around the speaker because all the lines involve him: the various unlinked elements in his life (his women, his tribe, his animals, the desert landscape and wildlife) all belong to his world. In a sense, the speaker represents a frame to the ode, for by recounting his experiences and impressions he links the three sections and the separate verses.

In a qasida, usually written in the first person, the speaker claims that he has either witnessed or actually experienced everything he describes. He often heightens the authenticity of his accounts by using names of real places and persons and depicting small details, like tent awnings or ropes. Furthermore, a qasida always contains elements of travel, of change, and of motion. Significantly, the word *qasida* comes from the verb *qasada*, which means "to have a purpose" or "to go towards something, to endeavor to reach an end" (Goldziher 10). It is easy to see why a nomadic people developed such poetry, with its emphasis on travel and discontinuity; for the Bedouins wandered from one grazing land to another, taking part in unconnected episodes at separate camping grounds, each far away and isolated from the next. The nomadic life and the poetry it generated accurately reflect each other.

Like algebra and the use of zero, the qasida contains a sense of boundlessness. The inconclusiveness produced by the breaking off of portions of the qasida and by the arbitrary arrangement of the lines indicates that the structure of the ode is not closed but loose, open-ended, even limitless. The organizational forces in the qasida—the speaker, his eyewitness reports, and the travel motif—act externally rather than internally. Travel and eyewitness reporting and similar externally organizing features appear in Arabic literature of a later date and in both Arabic and non-Arabic frame narratives. The qasida, the prevailing literary mode before the rise of Islam, constitutes the standard by which all later Arabic literature is measured (E. Marmura 61).

In the first centuries after Islam, Arabic literature continues to exhibit the traits seen in the pre-Islamic odes. The Koran (A.D. 651) has an arrangement that Nicholson, expressing the view of many Western critics, calls "chaotic" (143). The fragmentary and nonchronological contents, which the Prophet received at different dates, include every imaginable sort of writing from legislative pieces to biblical commentary, and the title of each sura has nothing or little to do with the contents. Not surprisingly, critics who impose Western standards on the work find it lacking in unity. But in the Koran, as in the qasida, the speaker unifies the work. All thoughts and experiences described are purportedly the Prophet's own. The principles reflected in this arrangement parallel Arabic mathematical principles, for the whole is no less and no more important than the part and each sura in the Koran can stand alone. Similarly the companion piece to the Koran, the *Tradition*, which relates various deeds and sayings of the Prophet, resembles the qasida in its dependence on eyewitness accounts. The recounter follows such patterns as "I was informed by A, who was told by B, who heard it from C, that the Prophet said thus and so" (Nicholson 144). The use of eyewitnesses to corroborate facts gives the work a sense of accuracy and authenticity, operating much like the details and place names in the qasida. The speaker in the qasida and the Prophet in the Koran and in the *Tradition* constitute framing devices, organizational instruments for these collections.

Most medieval Arabic histories, travel books, and biographies also feature eyewitness reporting in a loosely structured format. The histories—collections of unrelated and even contradictory pieces of information—do not analyze, interpret, or describe the development of a society; they simply provide data. Arab historians often trace an event back through a continuous chain of reporters to one person who witnessed it, fulfilling their roles as impartial providers of authenticated facts. It remains for the reader to analyze, to reconcile contradictions, and to provide conclusions. The episodes in travel literature, which take place all over the Middle East, are linked not by theme or by location but by a single point of view—that of the speaker who describes them. (For a good example of travel literature, see Shahriyar.) Biographies contain collections of details, often nonchronological, relating to the life of one man or a group of men (Nicholson 351–54; Grunebaum, *Medieval Islam* 277–87; see also Gerhardt 378–79). Grunebaum says of one Arabic biographer that he packs into his frame, without artistic arrangement, "a farrago of stories, verse, and extraneous matter conjured up by association' " (*Medieval Islam* 278).

In Arabic picaresques of the tenth and eleventh centuries, the typical hero is a vagabond or rogue who travels to different towns, often playing different roles (teacher, lawyer, doctor) in adventures described by a friend. These works, which feature eyewitness reporting and travel commentary, contain serious and humorous sections, maxims, religious verses, puzzles, and jokes, all of which are independent entities connected only by the continuing presence of the narrator and the hero (Goldziher 86–88, Nicholson 328–36). The diverse roles allow the picaro to display an encyclopedic type of knowledge called *adab*, much admired by medieval Arabs. Books on *adab* contain a mixed compilation of general information or fragments from wisdom literature, with no internal system of organization (Goldziher 81–83; for a fine example of *adab*, see *Life and Works of Jahiz*).

In all Arabic literature, the experiences of a single man, a group of men, or events in one part of the world act as connectives or, in a loose sense, frames. All the works emphasize each fragment of the whole, as well as the whole itself. The Arabs did not demand that knowledge have a focus or that literature have a unified structure in a Greek sense; yet their works exhibit a means of organization, an external one. It is no wonder, then, that the Arabs framed the *Panchatantra* and produced great frame narratives like the *Book of Sindbad* and the *Thousand and One Nights*. These works, because their original versions are lost, are not useful in this study; however, the idiom "thousand and one," meaning a large, indefinite number of nights, is in keeping with the Arabic preference for loose, open frames that do not place limitations on the framed material (Rosenthal 337).

The Arabs developed the frame narrative in lieu of longer, unified narratives. In spite of cultural interchange between the Greek, Byzantine, and Arab worlds, the Arabs never embraced the epic, the novel, or the drama as Western cultures did. Some plots of the tales in the *Thousand and One Nights* (A.D. 900–1500) bear marked similarities to plots of Greek novels (100 B.C. to A.D. 300), but the Arab stories always remain short (Grunebaum, *Medieval Islam* 294, 305–10). Plainly, the Arabs restricted their fictive literature to the frame structure because they chose to, not because they were unacquainted with longer, internally unified works.

The principles of organization in other Arabic arts resemble those of Arabic literature. Early Islamic architects did not conceive of the mosque as a complete and enclosed unit like the medieval cathedral; they believed that the mosque should have the potential to be made larger or smaller in the event of changes in a city's population. As Oleg Grabar suggests,

> The mosque of early Islamic times tended to be defined in terms of certain social needs and not as a more or less perfect or successful reflection of an ideal composition. . . . To be able to expand or contract, the mosque had to have a flexible and additive system of construction. The early Muslim hypostyle system can be defined as one in which the main internal support consisted of a single element that could be multiplied at will in any needed direction. (*Islamic Art* 114)

The plan of the early mosque was a "diffuse system that lacked architectural focus and direction," and the architecture of later mosques continued to be "primarily functional, with the need for flexible space predominating" (124, 126).[3] In fact, during the first two and a half centuries after the mosque at Medina was founded in A.D. 622, the building underwent fourteen expansions to accommodate the growing population (Jairazbhoy 7–9). In the mosque's structure, as in the frame narrative, flexibility and openness take precedence over a tightly controlled plan of organization. This structural elasticity also existed in palaces like the Alhambra. As Grabar says, "The important point is that the palace was not an aesthetically conceived and aesthetically organized entity, but a series of separate elements" ("Architecture" 259).

The successive bands of black or red and white stone, which appeared first in Arabic structures like the mosque in Córdoba, undoubtedly evolved from the same mode of thinking that produced the mosque itself (Landau 218). The candy-stripe bands of the Córdoban arches seem to Westerners to lack focus, but according to the Arabic aesthetic behind the construction of the mosque, the banded arches form a progressive, horizontal principle of organization in which each solid and isolated block of color, instead of being subordinate to a larger portion of the mosque, retains its individual aesthetic effect. Other architectural ornaments function in the same way. The geometric arabesques on the mosque—which, like the stories in a frame narrative, often appear in arbitrary positions—display a balance and geometric harmony in themselves; the architectural structure does not determine their composition and placement in the way that the form and structure of a medieval cathedral determine the size and contours of windows and alcoves. Observing that the random placement of these ornaments expresses the Islamic principle of "arbitrariness," Grabar says, "The most consistent characteristic of most Islamic ornament is that neither its size nor its internal forms are dictated by anything but itself" (*Islamic Art* 200).

Arabic developments in music, especially in mensural notation, embody similar artistic principles. In the medieval West, the long whole note, which took an entire measure, ranked above all shorter notes because the shorter ones could be included within it. Arab musical theoreticians, however, viewed mensural notation and composition differently, tending to work upward from the note with the smallest value to the one with the largest, a process that does not deemphasize the shorter notes' significance. Unlike the medieval Europeans, who, by the tenth century, viewed harmony as vertical, as closed and limited, like a chord, Arabs thought of harmony as horizontal, as a series of notes played in succession, a progression (Wright 494; Farmer, "Music of Islam" 471, "Music" 1175–76).

The stress on the individual part in Arabic literature, architecture, and music results in a loose, malleable overall frame or structure that has an organizing rather than a governing function. If the frame carried no significance at all, the Arabs would not have bothered to frame the *Panchatantra*. The crucial point is that the individual tale or anecdote or the separate architectural detail carries considerable weight also.

No one has satisfactorily explained the Arabs' tendency to focus in their various arts on details and isolated, loosely connected episodes. Some critics, like von Grunebaum, link the Arab emphasis on the small part to the atomistic world view held by the Asharites, a tenth-century school of Islam, who saw time as a disconnected series of indivisible atomic moments. Believing that God created the world anew in each small atom of time, destroyed it at the end of the atom of time, only to recreate it again in the next atom, the Asharites viewed human beings as a collection of atoms and accidents (Grunebaum, *Islam* 98; Grabar, *Islamic Art* 203; M. E. Marmura 47–48). Many medieval Islamic philosophers, however, opposed the atomistic Asharite view, so that it cannot be said to typify medieval Arabic thought in this period (M. E. Marmura 46–49).

Whatever the reasons behind Arabic aesthetic principles, the concept of organization evident in most Arabic literature, beginning with the qasida, emphasizes the individual unit and does not allow the open-ended and inconclusive overall framing structure to determine the nature or construction of a work's parts. This artistic perspective enabled the Arabs to develop the frame structure, to refine it, and to explore its possibilities. Ultimately, the Arabic conquest brought the frame narrative model, including the popular *Panchatantra* (renamed *Kalilah and Dimnah* in Arabic), to Europe, where it became a device widely used by medieval storytellers.

III

In Spain, which was the most important bridgehead for the dissemination of Arabic culture (Gabrieli 65–80), *Kalilah and Dimnah* served as a model for Petrus Alfonsi's twelfth-century *Disciplina Clericalis*. The first European frame narrative of importance, it ranks above all other works in bridging Eastern and Western narrative traditions and in funneling Arabic content and structure to medieval European vernacular writers (Metlitzki 18–19, 95–106). Petrus Alfonsi was a rabbi, an Islamic scholar, and a physician who converted to Catholicism. He traveled to England in 1110, where he became royal physician to Henry I. He wrote the *Disciplina Clericalis* in Arabic, then translated it into a simple Latin. Spanish Jews held a special position as middlemen between Arabic and Christian cultures, upholding a moral outlook similar to that of the Christians and a scholarly, artistic outlook akin to that of the Moslems. Thus men like Petrus Alfonsi played a central role in transmitting Islamic cultural ideas to Christian Spain and to Europe.[4] The *Disciplina Clericalis* became a model for other medieval Spanish writers, including Don Juan Manuel and Juan Ruiz, as well as for Boccaccio and for Chaucer, who refers to Petrus Alfonsi and his work five times in the *Canterbury Tales* (Robinson 7.1053, 1189, 1218, 1309, 1566; see also Metlitzki 18). Dorothee Metlitzki calls the *Disciplina Clericalis* "the first link in a Western chain that leads to Chaucer's narrative art" (96).

The *Disciplina Clericalis* contains many (though not all) of the external organizing features of earlier Arabic framed material, among them the use of a chain of eyewitness reporters, which, in this work, introduces the plot of the framing story. Petrus Alfonsi identifies himself in the prologue as the narrator of the work (level A), whose purpose he declares is didactic. He goes on to quote various sayings of philosophers. One of these, Balaam (level B), an Old Testament figure from the Book of Numbers, introduces the main framing story of the dying Arab (level C), who imparts wisdom to his son in the form of a series of proverbs and stories containing moral lessons. Because both the narrator of the entire work (Petrus Alfonsi) and the introducer of the framing story (Balaam) seem to be persons who actually lived, the framing story has an air of authenticity. As in the *Panchatantra* and in Arabic literature, the contemporary settings (e.g., Egypt and Baghdad), the small details (like those of a doctor's examination), and the many direct quotations enhance the sense of accuracy and verisimilitude. And also as in the *Panchatantra*, most of the material in the *Disciplina Clericalis* stresses a secular, earthly wisdom that can help a man to select his friends, to identify his enemies, to outwit rogues, to win riches, to understand the world's transitory nature, and even to learn about heaven and hell.

Although the *Disciplina Clericalis* as a whole is organized around the wisdom theme, secondary themes link some groups of tales. One group deals with friendship; a second focuses on the wiles of women; a third centers roughly on death. Instead of forming independent, isolated chapters, however, each of these groups thoroughly explores its topic, carefully weighing all sides of the issue. As in the *Panchatantra*, several erotic stories appear to be included solely on their merit as entertainment. At the ends of many stories, the Arab and his son discuss the stories' morals in dialogues that, like similar transitional material in the *Panchatantra*, form transitions between tales. As Eberhard Hermes has noted, these dialogues provide evidence that Petrus Alfonsi used the *Panchatantra* as a model for the *Disciplina Clericalis* (183, n. 70). The dialogues also serve to characterize father and son; and because the framing story of the *Disciplina Clericalis* is treated in greater depth and at greater length than the *Panchatantra*'s framing story, the characterization of the Arab father and son is richer than the *Panchatantra*'s characterization of the wise man and the princes. But even though the *Disciplina Clericalis'* framing story is more pervasive than that of the *Panchatantra*, the individual stories remain independent entities.

The resemblance between the encyclopedic variety of material in the *Disciplina Clericalis* and that in Arabic books on *adab*, along with similarities in transitional material, furnishes strong evidence that Petrus Alfonsi understood and drew on Arabic artistic concepts of content, structure, and form. As in most Arabic literature, the arrangement of stories in the *Disciplina Clericalis* appears to be arbitrary. Each story is complete, its plot tightly resolved. But the different lengths of the many medieval versions of the *Disciplina Clericalis* indicate that the frame had proved flexible and adaptable. Moreover, the framing story, like that of the *Panchatantra*, is incomplete, for the Arab father never dies, the son never clearly shows that he has gained wisdom, and the framing story disappears before the work ends.

Eberhard Hermes partially explains Petrus Alfonsi's choice of the frame-structure form by suggesting that principles of Arabic experimental medicine influenced this literary physician in his writings. The teaching of wisdom through a series of tales resembles the medieval Arabic scientific method: studying evidence inductively, depending on collections of observations and facts, and avoiding general abstract theories (72–75, 89–90). Hermes' theory seems valid; however, the Arabic scientific approach forms only one aspect of a larger Arabic methodology that handles all material, scientific or artistic, in more or less the same way, namely, by assembling information sequentially without centering it on one narrow theme.

Among other pre-Chaucerian frame narratives, Boccaccio's *Decameron* retains many external organizing forces akin to those used by Petrus Alfonsi and earlier Arabic writers: the authorial voice, the travel theme in the Florentines' journey, and the wisdom theme, with all the stories teaching secular knowledge (Scaglione 51, Ferrante 212–14). At first, Boccaccio seems to deviate from the open-ended pattern established in earlier frame narratives. The stated plan is that each Florentine will preside over the storytelling for one day and that ten stories on a certain theme will be told on every day but the first and ninth. Significantly, this rigid plan breaks down on occasion. At the end of the first day, Dioneo asks to be excused from telling stories on the assigned topics, thus breaking the arrangement that all tellers will keep to one theme. Again, in the introduction to the fourth day, Boccaccio, not one of the tellers, tells a tale and thereby disrupts the plan that the Florentines alone will tell the stories. Boccaccio's failure to finish his tale also upsets the implicit plan that all tales will be complete. And at the end of the last day, the king's suggestion that the group choose another king for the next day and continue the storytelling implies that the stories might continue indefinitely. Clearly the strict structural plan can be overthrown, and if it can be overthrown once, it can presumably be overthrown any number of times. Boccaccio's obvious need to keep structural boundaries open indicates that he was probably under the influence of Spanish and ultimately Arabic models.

The same sort of process appears in Gower's *Confessio Amantis*, which uses the frame structure for an allegorical purpose. Since books 1 through 6 deal with six of the seven deadly sins, one would naturally expect book 7 to discuss lechery. But instead Gower devotes this book to the education of a prince, postponing the discussion of lechery until book 8. G. C. Macaulay calls this deviation a "deliberate" disruption of the pattern established by the first six books (2: xix). As in the *Decameron*, this refusal to meet expectations produces the sense of boundlessness typical of the frame narrative.

IV

The *Canterbury Tales* continues the Arabic plan of the frame narrative, despite having a design far more elaborate than that of an uncomplicated, simply organized work like the *Disciplina Clericalis*. And even though many Western medieval characteristics are present in the *Canterbury Tales*, so too are most of the Arabic organizing features: the open-endedness, the grouping and balancing of tales and topics, the wisdom theme, the eyewitness narration. Chaucer develops these features, however, in ways never previously attempted.

The most striking Arabic feature of the *Canterbury Tales* is the work's

open-endedness: the pilgrims never reach Canterbury; twenty-nine are said
to be in the group at the inn (1.24), but the mention of three priests (1.164)
brings the total to thirty-one; the Host asserts that each pilgrim will tell two
tales coming and two going (1.792–94), but the Franklin's Prologue states
that each pilgrim will tell "a tale or two" (5.698); and the Parson's Prologue
declares that only one tale is lacking (10.16), though only twenty-two pilgrims have told tales. Moreover, the surprise arrival of the Canon and his
Yeoman upsets the limitations on the number of pilgrims and tale-tellers
established in the General Prologue. Just as in the *Decameron* and the *Confessio*, disrupted expectations of order and symmetry in the *Canterbury Tales*
put to rest any notion that the scope of the work is foreseeably contained.

Donald R. Howard, in describing the way Chaucer's work changes from
a closed to an open structure, says, "The narrator's recitation might go on
indefinitely, producing more people and from them more tales" (171).
Howard says that the inconsistencies and the shifts in the stated number of
tales make the work "unfinished but complete" (1, 27–28, 79, 122). Perhaps
a better description of the *Canterbury Tales* would be "finished but incomplete," for it is in the nature of frame narratives to leave structural boundaries
loose; this open-endedness permitted later authors to extend and alter
Chaucer's plan, in works like the *Tale of Beryn* or Lydgate's *Siege of Thebes*.
That the Cook, the Squire, the Monk, and Chaucer the pilgrim, like Boccaccio, do not finish their tales provides further evidence that incompleteness is
an almost inevitable element in a frame narrative. The Squire and the Monk
leave unfinished a series of tales (frame and near-frame narratives within a
frame narrative); the Cook and Chaucer the pilgrim leave individual tales
unfinished.[5]

Loose connections and groupings of tales further contribute to the
work's open-endedness. As in the *Panchatantra* and the *Disciplina Clericalis*, the balancing and grouping of stories or themes in the *Canterbury
Tales* act as occasional connective devices that provide some organization
without imposing any demands on the content or arrangement of the tales.
Just as in the *Disciplina Clericalis*, groups of Chaucer's tales focus on certain
topics. Kittredge finds a marriage group, which begins with the Wife of
Bath's Prologue and ends with the Franklin's Tale (185–210). Other groups
of tales appear: the tales of the Reeve, Friar, Summoner, Pardoner, and
Canon's Yeoman center on greed, and the tales of the Miller, Reeve, Cook,
Friar, Summoner, Merchant, and Shipman are fabliaux. Examples of the balancing of tales include the Friar's Tale, about a summoner, and the Summoner's Tale, about a friar; the Miller's Tale and its rebuttal, the Reeve's; the
Knight's Tale and its parody, the Miller's; the Knight's Tale and his son's, the
Squire's. Howard says that the balancing of tales forces the reader to look
back to their tellers in the General Prologue, to see them as tightly linked
members of a common society; he adds that the result suggests limitlessness,

for "a finite number of tellers and tales gives us the possibility of an almost infinite number of associations" (199).

Some tales contain subtle and imaginative linking devices. The word "sweat" that the Canon's Yeoman uses in his prologue to describe the men and horses (8.560, 563, 578, 579–81) who have ridden rapidly from the Inn connects his prologue to his tale, which describes a sweating priest leaning over a crucible (8.1186), and to the previous tale, the Second Nun's, which describes St. Cecilia in the boiling bath: "It made hire nat a drope for to sweete" (8.522). Since the Canon's Yeoman joins the group after the Second Nun has told her story and cannot have heard about the martyrdom of St. Cecilia, the link between his tale and hers is inexplicable and unexpected, part of a web of apparently accidental and capricious motifs that suggest Arabic organizational principles. Such subtle connections typify the complexity of the *Canterbury Tales'* design.

Parallels between the tales of the Second Nun and the Canon's Yeoman exemplify the unusual way in which the poet connects two diverse elements, the secular and the religious. The scene of St. Cecilia, martyred in the bath, is narrated by the Second Nun in hagiographic language, and the scene of the priest, leaning over a crucible—an object with religious associations—is narrated by the Canon's Yeoman in the language of alchemy. The pilgrims are innocent purveyors of Chaucer's sophisticated design, a design that can link the elevated courtly love triangle in the Knight's Tale to the vulgar, promiscuous ménage à trois in the Miller's Tale and that can also link the loftily presented idea of nobility in the Knight's Tale to the dampeningly, degenerately treated idea of nobility in the Reeve's Tale, in which the miller deplores the sexual activity of his women and of the two students because it insults and threatens his own rustic, most ignoble ideas of lineage. Similar groupings and balancings exist in the *Disciplina Clericalis*, but in Chaucer's work such groups overlap, forming an elaborate interlacing of themes and relations that does not exist in earlier frame narratives. Like the order in the Arabic frame narrative, the order in the *Canterbury Tales* is an arbitrary matter, somewhat modified by linked tales and unfinished motifs. No one has yet demonstrated that the tales follow a necessary design; however, Chaucer plays with disorder, giving the impression that the arrangement is more arbitrary than it really is.[6]

Initially, the drawing of lots to pick the first tale-teller suggests that chance will decide the order of the stories. The Host disrupts this plan by nominating the Monk as the second teller, thereby introducing a second plan: the Host will decide the order. The Miller's drunken insistence that he tell the second tale violates the expectation that the Monk will tell a tale and constitutes a breakdown in order, momentarily imposing the idea that the sequence of tellers will be arbitrary and random. Innovative and sophisticated as Chaucer's design may be in arranging the tales, their arbitrary order, both real and apparent, still clearly shows the influence of Arabic notions of organization.

External forces help to organize the *Canterbury Tales* as they do Arabic works. One such force is the wisdom theme; for just as the *Panchatantra*'s moral verses and the *Disciplina Clericalis*' dialogues between father and son reinforce the moral themes of the tales, so do the pilgrims' comments provide morals to the stories, underlining the work's didacticism. The Host acts as a guide to the moral interpretation of the Merchant's Tale, pointing out to the group that the tale illustrates the wiles of women (4.2419–23); the Host also compares the Tale of Melibee to his own marriage and his hot-tempered nagging wife (7.1891–922); the Clerk says that his own tale teaches women to be constant (4.1145–47); the Pardoner tells the Wife of Bath that her prologue has taught him something about marriage, making him reconsider taking a wife (3.166–68, 186–87); the Merchant contrasts the Clerk's Griselda to his own wife (4.1223–25); the pilgrims decide that the Knight's Tale is a "noble storie" (1.3111), indicating that it is meant to edify; and the laughter prompted by the Miller's Tale suggests that his is sheer ribaldry. These comments of the pilgrims provide evidence that the *Canterbury Tales* aimed to teach a form of wisdom that one can learn from the experiences of others, a central concern in both the *Panchatantra* and in the *Disciplina Clericalis*.

One cannot say that the travel motif comes from the Arabic tradition, despite its prominence in qasidas and other Arabic genres. Some pre-Chaucerian frame narratives lack the travel element, and, besides, Chaucer had many Western predecessors in travel and pilgrimage literature. But Chaucer's travel-pilgrimage theme corresponds to the wisdom theme in suggesting spiritual growth. Ralph Baldwin sees the pilgrimage as an organizing motif that connects the spiritual journey to the literal one, citing as evidence the Parson's lines "Of thilke parfit glorious pilgrymage / That highte Jerusalem celestial" (10.50–51; Baldwin 96–99). Moreover, by Chaucer's time a pilgrimage represented not only a spiritual journey but also a way of satisfying *curiositas*, a simple human urge to know more about the secular world (Zacher 88–92, Howard 168–69). The quest for spiritual and secular wisdom associated with the travel-pilgrimage theme, then, provides another external mode of organization. Even during the storytelling, the author keeps the reader aware, by various subtle devices, that the pilgrimage forever progresses. Such devices strengthen and extend the travel theme and the framing story—the pilgrimage—which constitutes only one sixth of the work. Enhancing the sense of movement implicit in the pilgrimage, the Prologue sketches the pilgrims as they ride on their journey, not as they appear to Chaucer at the inn, though they have not yet started on the trip. Such a disruption in chronology—in a sense speeding up the clock—forces the reader to envision the pilgrims as embarked on their travels from the very outset of the work.

The Prologue's account of the special equestrian skills or the extensive travels of some pilgrims (the Knight, 1.47–66; the Squire, 1.85; the Monk, 1.166; the Parson, 1.491–95; and the Wife of Bath, 1.463–67) accentuates the travel-pilgrimage theme. Chaucer also exploits the device *occupatio* so that, besides playing its traditional role, it adds an aura of haste and expeditiousness. Five times (1.875–90, 985, 1000, 1190, 1201) the Knight interrupts his story to remind the pilgrims that he will keep his tale short to leave time for the others to tell theirs. The Host's admonitions to the pilgrims to hurry up and get on with the storytelling (1.3905, 2.19–21, 10.70), also alert the reader to time's passing and to the group's brisk movement.

The arrival of the Canon and his Yeoman, after their long, hard ride to join the pilgrimage, further intensifies the sense of speed and of travel. That the men and their horses are sweating heavily (8.560, 563, 578, 579–81) underlines the distance that the pilgrims have traveled better than a mere statement of the miles covered. The word *sweat* thus plays a double organizational role, heightening the travel theme as well as connecting the Canon's Yeoman's Prologue with his tale and with the Second Nun's. The Host's announcements of the time of day and the towns through which the pilgrims pass serve as additional reminders of their progress: they arrive at Deptford (1.3906) at seven-thirty in the morning, the Man of Law starts his tale at ten o'clock (2.1–3), and the Parson begins his tale at four in the afternoon (10.5).

Chaucer uses the travel-pilgrimage theme as an external organizing device in much the same way that earlier medieval writers of framed literature used similar devices, but other themes help to organize his work as well. Chaucer's role as pilgrim and eyewitness in the *Canterbury Tales*, like the role of the narrator in Arabic literature, acts as a unifying force to some extent, authenticating the framing story and making the pilgrimage appear actual. Chaucer, however, alters the narrator's traditional eyewitness role; for, as E. Talbot Donaldson points out, the difference between the *Canterbury Tales* and similar works lies in the irony that Chaucer, the character he creates as a pilgrim, does not understand the significance of what he sees (929). Standing behind Chaucer the reporter is Chaucer the poet, a figure who, unlike Petrus Alfonsi, is a manipulator of irony, of details, of structure—the fabricator of a design whose features are so inextricable that only some are clearly visible while others are merely sensed. But Chaucer's alteration of the traditional eyewitness role does not weaken its organizational effectiveness.

The eyewitness reporting method, the use of the authorial "I," also functions transitionally (Eliason 144–45). An example occurs at the start of the Prologue, directly before Chaucer's description of the pilgrims:

> But nathelees, whil I have tyme and space,
> Er that I ferther in this tale pace,
> Me thynketh it acordaunt to resoun
> To telle yow al the condicioun
> Of ech of hem. . . .
>
> (1.35–39)

Such transitional passages strengthen the organizing role of Chaucer as pilgrim and eyewitness, for the more pervasive the authorial presence, the better that presence organizes the work. The appearance of two tales told by Chaucer, the only pilgrim who tells more than one, doubles the authenticating effect that one tale alone would have had.

The use of actual place names, like the Tabard Inn (1.20) and the watering place of St. Thomas (1.826), increases the sense of unity and authenticity, as do the contemporary settings of some of the stories, the Miller's Tale taking place in Oxford, the Reeve's in Cambridge. Furthermore, some evidence exists that Chaucer modeled certain of the pilgrims on actual people (Manly). The details and the contemporary settings operate much as these features do in the *Disciplina Clericalis* and in Arabic prose and odes.

The search, never truly successful, for internal organizing elements in the *Canterbury Tales* stems from medieval European philosophical concepts of wholeness and coherence. Such notions have produced theories like that of G. L. Kittredge, who sees the work as organized by its dramatic focus. He says, "The Pilgrims do not exist for the sake of the stories, but *vice versa*"; the tales, like the soliloquies of Hamlet, Iago, or Macbeth, reveal depths of the tellers' characters and function as conversation because they are directed toward the other pilgrims (155). Robert Jordan, who challenges the dramatic theory on several grounds, contends that a drama requires a better internal organization than the *Canterbury Tales* has, that many tales cannot be connected with their tellers, and that the dramatic theory fits "our prescription, but not . . . Chaucer's" (114–17). In addition, the dramatic theory reduces the emphasis on the individual pilgrim, subordinating the individual to the group and to the drama. Chaucer's characterization of each pilgrim, instead of making a unified drama of the work, heightens the importance of the part, the individual tale. In this focus on the unit, Chaucer follows Arabic principles of organization.

Jordan adds that the seemingly unconnected elements in the *Canterbury Tales* are connected a priori because medieval society considered existence "finite and comprehensible" and that the work reflects "the medieval presupposition that wholeness exists and is apprehensible, whether the object of contemplation is the cosmos itself or any element or concept within it. The idea of finitude is essential to Chaucer's aesthetic practice" (237–38). Jordan's theory, which involves comparing the *Canterbury Tales* to the Gothic cathedral, does not take into account the frame-narrative tradition that influenced Chaucer in designing the *Canterbury Tales*, for the inconclusive quality of the frame structure connects the work more to the infinite than to finitude. Because the progression is linear and the organization horizontal, it is more fitting to compare the *Canterbury Tales* to the mosque, for the mosque, like Chaucer's work, contains a sense of boundlessness not in keeping with the Western tendency to finish things.

Statements that the *Canterbury Tales* is poorly organized or not organized at all result from the insistence that all good art be unified internally. Such thinking ignores less obtrusive horizontal and external organizing devices: the travel theme, the framing story itself, the authorial "I" of Chaucer the pilgrim and eyewitness reporter, and motifs like secular wisdom. Coherence in the *Canterbury Tales* differs from that in much other Western medieval literature, for Chaucer's organizing principles set down no limitations on form; content; length of framing story; numbers of pilgrims, tale-tellers, or tales; or even the journey to Canterbury, which never ends. This release from limits puts the emphasis on the individual pilgrims, on the tales they tell, and not on their roles in some larger drama. Although the framing story remains important, each teller and each tale exist as a significant individual unit, to be viewed independently. Perhaps the most unusual feature of the medieval frame narrative is its limitlessness, for the plots of most framing stories are open-ended. For Western readers of a frame narrative, the idea that the structure is boundless represents the highest hurdle, for their training leads them to believe that literature should be organized from within and confined in an enclosing structure.

The Arabs invented and developed the frame narrative, but it remained for Chaucer to bring the genre to its fullest flowering. The consideration of the *Canterbury Tales* within the context of an Arabic tradition is not meant to deny Chaucer's debt to Western culture or to downplay his peculiarly English talent. But the fact remains that the genre in which he was working played a part in the form and design of the *Canterbury Tales*. Seeing this, one will avoid imposing on the *Canterbury Tales* qualities of form and design that are alien to its tradition, a tradition that originated not in European villages but at distant Bedouin campsites.

Notes

1. For a more general treatment of the medieval concept of unity, see Moore.
2. I use the word "Arabic" in a broad sense to include the work of Persians and others writing in Arabic under the aegis of the caliphs.
3. For the opposing concept of unity in Gothic cathedrals, whose architects began with a preconceived notion of the whole, see Simson 35, 125, 133, 214, et passim.
4. For Petrus Alfonsi's biographical connection with Arabic material, see Hermes 35–43. For the likelihood that Petrus Alfonsi translated his own Arabic into Latin, see Vossler 129. For the function of Jews as intermediaries between the Arabic and Western cultures, see Jackson 102–8.
5. I subscribe to the interpretation of the Squire's Tale as being an aborted frame narrative, as in Howard 264 and Braddy 282–90.
6. The line of interpretation in this and the preceding paragraph will be developed by David K. Crowne, University of California, San Diego, in a forthcoming book. Discussions with him were helpful in formulating the thesis of this article.

Works Cited

Baldwin, Ralph. *The Unity of the* Canterbury Tales. Anglistica, 5. Copenhagen: Rosenkilde and Bagger, 1955.

Braddy, Haldeen. "The Genre of Chaucer's Squire's Tale." *Journal of English and Germanic Philology* 41 (1942): 279–90.

Chaitanya, Krishna. *A New History of Sanskrit Literature*. London: Asia Publishing House, 1962.

Donaldson, E. Talbot. "Chaucer the Pilgrim." *PMLA* 69 (1954): 928–36.

Eliason, Norman E. *The Language of Chaucer's Poetry*. Anglistica, 17. Copenhagen: Rosenkilde and Bagger, 1972.

Farmer, Henry George. "Music." In *A History of Muslim Philosophy*. Ed. M. M. Sharif. Wiesbaden: Otto Harrassowitz, 1966, 2: 1124–78.

———. "The Music of Islam." In *Ancient and Oriental Music*. Ed. Egon Wellesz. London: Oxford University Press, 1957, 421–77.

Ferrante, Joan M. "The Frame Characters of the *Decameron*: A Progression of Virtues." *Romance Philology* 19 (1965): 212–26.

Gabrieli, Francesco. "Islam in the Mediterranean World." In *The Legacy of Islam*. Ed. Joseph Schacht and C. E. Bosworth. 2nd ed. Oxford: Clarendon, 1974, 63–104.

Gerhardt, Mia I. *The Art of Storytelling*. Leiden: E. J. Brill, 1963.

Goldziher, Ignace. *A Short History of Classical Arabic Literature*. Trans., rev., and enl. by Joseph Desomogyi. Hildesheim: Olms, 1966.

Grabar, Oleg. "Architecture." In *The Legacy of Islam*. Ed. Joseph Schacht and C. E. Bosworth. 2nd ed. Oxford: Clarendon, 1974, 244–73.

———. *Formation of Islamic Art*. New Haven: Yale University Press, 1973.

Grunebaum, G. E. von. *Islam*. New York: Barnes and Noble, 1961.

———. *Medieval Islam*. 2nd ed. Chicago: University of Chicago Press, 1953.

Hermes, Eberhard. Introd. Trans. P. R. Quarrie. In *The Disciplina Clericalis of Petrus Alfonsi*. London: Routledge, 1977.

Hitti, Philip K. *Islam: A Way of Life*. Minneapolis: University of Minnesota Press, 1970.

Howard, Donald R. *The Idea of the* Canterbury Tales. Berkeley: University of California Press, 1978.

Jackson, Gabriel. *The Making of Medieval Spain*. New York: Harcourt, 1972.

Jairazbhoy, R. A. *An Outline of Islamic Architecture*. Bombay: Asia Publishing House, 1972.

Jordan, Robert M. *Chaucer and the Shape of Creation*. Cambridge: Harvard University Press, 1967.

Keith, A. Berriedale. *A History of Sanskrit Literature*. Oxford: Oxford University Press, 1920.

Kittredge, George Lyman. *Chaucer and His Poetry*. Cambridge: Harvard University Press, 1915.

Kline, Morris. *Mathematical Thought from Ancient to Modern Times*. New York: Oxford University Press, 1972.

Kramer, Edna E. *The Nature and Growth of Modern Mathematics*. Greenwich, CT: Fawcett, 1974.

Landau, Rom. *Islam and the Arabs*. New York: Macmillan, 1959.

Leff, Gordon. *The Dissolution of the Medieval Outlook*. New York: Harper, 1976.

The Life and Works of Jahiz. Trans. into French Charles Pellat. Trans. from the French D. M. Hawke. Berkeley: University of California Press, 1969.

Lumiansky, R. M. *Of Sondry Folk: The Dramatic Principle in the* Canterbury Tales. Austin: University of Texas Press, 1955.

Lyall, Charles James, ed. *Translations of Ancient Arabic Poetry*. New York: Columbia University Press, 1930.

Macaulay, G. C., ed. *Complete Works of John Gower*. 1901; rpt. Grosse Pointe, MI: Scholarly, 1968.

Manly, John Matthews. *Some New Light on Chaucer*. 1926; rpt. Gloucester, MA: Peter Smith, 1959.

Marmura, Ella. "Arabic Literature: A Living Heritage." In *Introduction to Islamic Civilisation*. Ed. R. M. Savory. Cambridge: Cambridge University Press, 1976, 61–70.

Marmura, Michael E. "God and His Creation: Two Medieval Islamic Views." In *Introduction to Islamic Civilisation*. Ed. R. M. Savory. Cambridge: Cambridge University Press, 1976, 46–53.

Metlitzki, Dorothee. *The Matter of Araby in Medieval England*. New Haven, CT: Yale University Press, 1977.

Moore, Arthur K. "Medieval English Literature and the Question of Unity." *Modern Philology* 65 (1968): 285–300.

Nicholson, Reynold A. *A Literary History of the Arabs*. 1907; rpt. Cambridge: Cambridge University Press, 1953.

Perry, B. E. *The Origin of the* Book of Sindbad. Berlin: Walter de Gruyter, 1960.

Pratt, Robert A., and Karl Young. "The Literary Framework of the *Canterbury Tales*." In *Sources and Analogues of Chaucer's* Canterbury Tales. Ed. W. F. Bryan and Germaine Dempster. 1941; rpt. Atlantic Highlands, NJ: Humanities, 1958, 1–81.

Robinson, F. N., ed. *The Works of Geoffrey Chaucer*. 2nd ed. Boston: Houghton, 1957.

Rosenthal, Franz. "Literature." In *The Legacy of Islam*. Ed. Joseph Schacht and C. E. Bosworth. 2nd ed. Oxford: Clarendon, 1974, 321–49.

Ruggiers, Paul G. *The Art of the* Canterbury Tales. Madison: University of Wisconsin Press, 1965.

Ryder, Arthur W., trans. *The Panchatantra*. Chicago: University of Chicago Press, 1925.

Scaglione, Aldo D. *Nature and Love in the Late Middle Ages*. Berkeley: University of California Press, 1963.

Shahriyar, Buzurg Ibn. *The Book of the Marvels of India*. Trans. Peter Quennell. London: Routledge, 1928.

Simson, Otto von. *The Gothic Cathedral*. New York: Harper, 1964.

Vossler, Carlos. *España y Europa*. Madrid: Instituto de Estudios Políticos, 1951.

Wright, O. "Music." In *The Legacy of Islam*. Ed. Joseph Schacht and C. E. Bosworth. 2nd ed. Oxford: Clarendon, 1974, 489–505.

Zacher, Christian K. *Curiosity and Pilgrimage*. Baltimore, MD: Johns Hopkins University Press, 1976.

Criticism, Anti-Semitism, and the Prioress's Tale

LOUISE O. FRADENBURG

Let us turn, now, to what the Prioress's Tale can tell us about the many critical questions that criticism on the tale has left unaddressed.

The Prioress's Prologue begins as follows:

> O Lord, oure Lord, thy name how merveillous
> Is in this large world ysprad—quod she—
> For noght oonly thy laude precious
> Parfourned is by men of dignitee,
> But by the mouth of children thy bountee
> Parfourned is, for on the brest soukynge
> Somtyme shewen they thyn heriynge.[1]

From the very beginning of the Prioress's Tale divinity is linked with the concept of the marvelous, specifically with the marvelous capacity of the disembodied name of the Lord to spread throughout the "large world," to achieve fully creative extension. (In Psalm 8 the Lord's magnificence is "elevated above the heavens"; the Prioress's leveling figure brings the disembodied and distant magnificence of the Lord down into the sphere of worldly production and reproduction, where the Lord's "name" [rather than, as in Psalm 8, his magnificence] will be substantiated.[2]) The Lord's name achieves this extension through the performing of his "laude precious" by "men of dignitee" and the "mouth of children," but this dependence of the Lord's name for its marvelous fertility upon the voices of men and children is elided, first by displacing the voice with the image of the "mouth" performing the "bountee" of the Lord (so that the childish singer is somehow embodied through his singing)

These pages first appeared as section 4 in the essay of this name, in *Exemplaria* 1 (1989): 90–108, 114–15. Reprinted by permission of Pegasus Press, University of North Carolina, Asheville, NC 28804 and then by the displacement, in turn, of that image with the more precisely visualized "on the brest soukynge / Somtyme shewen they thyn heriynge." By this time, the syntax of the stanza has become so ambiguous that it is not even possible to say whether the infant's "heriynge" is a form of speech, an exercise of the human voice, or consists simply of sucking at the "bountee" of the Lord through the medium of the (partially represented) mother's body; thus at stake in this passage is also the appropriation of woman's role in reproduction by God's making, a situation of which we are reminded when the "bountee" of the Virgin Mary is mentioned twice in the next three stanzas.

Praise is itself a linguistic surrendering of the interior to belief, an attempt at guiltless or "innocent" speech, at having in one's mouth only the words of the Lord, no filth, no rival creation, no presumptuous attempt to disembody the human by and through voice. And though [Sherman] Hawkins stresses that the "infants and sucklings [of Psalm 8] represent the beginner, who must be nourished on the historical faith of Scripture that he may grow up . . . to an understanding of eternal things,"[3] the Prioress actually collapses the maturational narrative understanding proposed in Augustine's commentary, by *paralleling* the "mouth of children" with "men of dignitee." Leveling in this instance becomes a way of collapsing even the speech of powerful men into the "soukynge" of the "mouth of children," of collapsing vocal distance from the body back into the relation of the mouth to the breast; it thus becomes a way of collapsing ends into beginnings, of representing the space of human narrativity, of human life, as instantly overcome through "heriynge." In the first stanza of the Prioress's Prologue, easy passage ("spreading") through the "large world" is accomplished not by the travels of Oedipus but by the miracle of praise. Thus also the fourth stanza of the Prologue, in which the Virgin's virtues cannot be "expressed" in learned discourse by any "tonge," so that the borderline quality of the tongue, its positioning between the body and language, is reduced to the body, at the same time that prayer is revealed as always belated with respect to the priority, the going-before, of the Virgin:

> Lady, thy bountee, thy magnificence,
> Thy vertu and thy grete humylitee,
> Ther may no tonge expresse in no science;
> For somtyme, Lady, er men praye to thee,
> Thou goost biforn of thy benyngnytee,
> And getest us the lyght, of thy preyere,
> To gyden us unto thy Sone so deere.
> (VII.474–80)

The Virgin is the "open door," the mediator, the easy passage; the collapse of prayer's fledgling narrativity, its trajectory of desire, into the foregone

conclusion of the Virgin's "benyngnytee," is imaged through the silence of
the human "tonge" which cannot, but need not, speak. The miraculous
going-before of the Virgin, her mediation, her guiding of souls and of the
Prioress's own song (VII.487) are of course in stark contrast to the
obstructed passages of the Jewish ghetto and the cut throat of the little clergeon, which together constitute the very narrow space allotted by the tale to
human aspiration and change and growth. The miraculous going-before of
the Virgin, and the language which describes her as both origin and guide
(though never end) thus figures at once her ubiquity and her unobstructive
surpassability in a narrative whose end is the "Sone." This is perhaps the
simplest instance of how her own (re)productive powers circle round (to
the son she "bar," who is her own Creator) rather than extending themselves outward.

The conflation of voice with sucking in the first stanza of the Prologue
makes it safe for the Prioress to introduce herself as a speaking subject,
though in the first line of the next stanza she must precede that introduction
with a further evocation of the idea of "laude," and must throughout the rest
of the stanza articulate what it means to speak as a creature rather than as a
creator:

> Wherfore in laude, as I best kan or may,
> Of thee and of the white lylye flour
> Which that the bar, and is a mayde alway,
> To telle a storie I wol do my labour;
> Nat that I may encressen hir honour,
> For she hirself is honour and the roote
> Of bountee, next hir Sone, and soules boote.
>
> (VII.460–66)

The Prioress's story-telling "labour" has in fact no capacity to *produce*
("encressen") the honor of the Virgin, for honor itself (the disembodied,
abstract quality) *is* the Virgin; likewise she is the "roote," the origin, of
whatever "bountee" the Prioress's own creativity might produce. The dis-
carnational poetics of these lines extends into the following stanza, wherein
we find the miraculous paradoxes of the Virgin's body ("O mooder Mayde!
o mayde Mooder free!" [VII.467]), expressed not only through her con-
founding of the ordinary human transformations attendant on the loss of
virginity, but also through the image of the "bussh unbrent, brennynge in
Moyses sighte," wherein the identity of the entity remains miraculously
unchanged; paradoxes expressed, moreover, through the stanza's intricacies of gender, which seem to assert the Virgin's status as the very icon of
belief (and hence perhaps inscribe belief as a feminization of the body),
insofar as she fully surrenders her interior to God,[4] and hence becomes, in

the coincidence of interior with exterior, almost indistinguishable from the object of her belief:

> O bussh unbrent, brennynge in Moyses sighte,
> That ravyshedest doun fro the Deitee,
> Thurgh thyn humblesse, the Goost that in th'alighte,
> Of whos vertu, whan he thyn herte lighte,
> Conceyved was the Fadres sapience,
> Help me to telle it in thy reverence!
>
> (VII.468–73)

The request for help, however, which follows upon the constitution of the Virgin's body as an icon of belief, has already been anticipated by her going-before. The Prologue (ironically, given the narrativity incipient in the term "prologue") makes only so much progress in the flowering of the human voice as is required to reassure the speaking subject that she will not be punished for articulating the sufficiency of silence to fulfill desires scarcely sprung, scarcely separable from the weight of magical possession and unending generosity: "bountee," "boote," "magnificence," "benyngnytee," "worthynesse." The "weighte" of the gift that cannot be reciprocated is not in fact sustained by the final stanza. Accordingly, we learn in it that the speaking subject is scarcely a speaking subject at all, has been forced, as it were, by the weight of "benyngnytee" back to the beginnings of life and language:

> My konnyng is so wayk, O blisful Queene,
> For to declare thy grete worthynesse
> That I ne may the weighte nat susteene;
> But as a child of twelf month oold, or lesse,
> That kan unnethes any word expresse,
> Right so fare I, and therfore I yow preye,
> Gydeth my song that I shal of yow seye.
>
> (VII.481–87)

The tale is thus in some sense established as itself a miracle, a song given easy passage by the mediation of the Virgin just as she gives it to the little clergeon in the tale. As miracle, it replaces human production with divine intervention. What the language of the Prioress's Prologue, then, tells us about itself is that it is language that can barely make any space or articulate any distance that would allow the play of presence and absence that constitutes meaning. The paradox is that the very fullness of these stanzas attests to their narrative emptiness and ideational repetition.[5]

The emptiness, repetition, circularity of the Prologue in turn, however, throw into a kind of relief the intricacies of the Prioress's rhetoric. If praise "increases" nothing, if praise cannot supplement an inviolate fullness, it nonetheless fills the mouth. The desire of the Prioress's Tale is for a language that erases the difference between word and thing, for a language that, in effect, escapes the differences of symbolicity. Childish language, in the Prioress's Tale, doesn't have to mean anything; it just is, and so it represents for the Prioress a pure signifier, a sign coinciding completely with itself, not defined by its difference from whatever it's trying to signify. Repetition of the pure signifier tries to barricade language against abjection by insisting on its fullness, self-presence, circularity; what's produced is literally a fascinating style, a style in whose very fascination lies its meaninglessness. Hence the Prioress's love of alliteration, and the coincidence of idyll and near-stasis in a stanza like the following, which actually says—if one reads carefully and is not mesmerized—very little.

> A litel scole of Cristen folk ther stood
> Doun at the ferther ende, in which ther were
> Children an heep, ycomen of Cristen blood,
> That lerned in that scole yeer by yere
> Swich manere doctrine as men used there,
> This is to seyn, to syngen and to rede,
> As smale children doon in hire childhede.
>
> (VII.495–501)

In this stanza, the time marker, "yeer by yere," establishes that nothing changes; and the information we are given—that Christian children come of Christian blood, that children do what children do, that they learn the kind of learning that they learn in that school—establishes that there is nothing really new to learn. Like the spool of thread in *Beyond the Pleasure Principle*, thrown out and reeled in by a little boy as a way of regulating the presence and absence of his mother,[6] the language of the Prioress's Tale differs, folds, alters just enough to show us that we have not really gone anywhere and nothing has really happened to us (in the last line, for example, "smale" disrupts, however diminutively, the circularity of the line; the morphophonemic alteration, too, between "children" and "childhede" actually allows the line not to say "as children do when they are children"). Learning, in the Prioress's Tale, is itself an object of phobia; it is figured as a terrifying alteration of innerness by the outside world or outside events. Learning and speaking by rote—being spoken through—is thus counterphobic: it allows the Prioress to defend against change, against the advent of meaning or narrative event. The circularity of the Prologue is, in and through the tale, constantly being opposed to temporal and linguistic difference, in the form either of alteration or significance. Thus the fascination of form is linked with the trajectory of return: the carnal mother will be lost, but the ideal mother will be re-found.

> Through the mouth that I fill with words instead of my mother whom I miss
> from now on more than ever, I elaborate that want, and the aggressivity that
> accompanies it, by *saying*.[7]

As we noted earlier, the formal intricacy of phobic language expresses the
desire for dissolution, for merger; hence the terror and terrorism of its
response to anything that reminds the subject of otherness, separation, difference. Few aspects of the Prioress's Tale have been so consistently mishan-
dled, in short, as its artistry.

Matthew Arnold illustrates the evanescence and delicacy and "power of
liquidness and fluidity" of Chaucer's verse with lines like "My throte is kut
unto my nekke boon" (VII.649); pain disappears into formality.[8] And somewhat more recently [Albert] Friedman makes, via the defile of the Prioress's
"fluency" and of a "*tone*" (my emphasis) of prayerful seriousness, an easy
passage from the Prioress's artistry to meaning. This kind of easy passage
from artistry to meaning, which we could perhaps also describe as a merging
of signifier with signified, no doubt produces precisely "the edifying effect
[the Prioress] . . . intended":

> The *Prioress's Tale* and the pious invocation that introduces it would seem
> on first, or even tenth reading to require little interpretative assistance. The
> shimmeringly eloquent rime royal stanzas move with unimpeded fluency,
> the tone of prayerful seriousness is uniformly maintained. . . . When the
> Prioress is done a hush of sobriety falls over the company—precisely the
> edifying effect she had intended, and a response which the tale, considering
> the immediate audience, thoroughly deserves.
>
>   The response of many Chaucerians is quite different.[9]

It's interesting to note that Friedman's opening mirrors the opening of
the Prioress's Tale itself: captation by shimmering eloquence is unpleasantly
broken off, in the tale by a narrative about perfidy and homicide, in Friedman by the appearance of the critic—of "many Chaucerians." But part of the
point of the tale is that perfidy and homicide merely serve to perfect the
identity of the entity; the cruelty and pain of the middle, in fact essential to
the perfection of praise, are elided and engulfed by the weighty emptiness of
the tale's beginning and end. This, too, Friedman mirrors; he links the tale's
hypnotic power to its beginning and end. The middle, where all the anti-
semitism and cruelty happen, only shows up after the critics have broken
into the garden. And since Friedman believes that "the whole critical enterprise directed toward explaining away Chaucer's bigotry is misconceived
and unnecessary,"[10] it is difficult to see how the goal of his essay can be anything other than the pacification of the critic—the return of the critic to his
initial state of wonder. If Friedman as critic must go through an arc of interpretation to arrive at his goal, it is clear that the essay wants to return from
whence it came, for the "hush of sobriety" that falls upon the pilgrims is,

after all, "a response which the tale, considering the immediate audience"—
the good audience, versus "many Chaucerians"—"thoroughly deserves."[11]
So pain, and narrative, and criticism are elided.

That the Prioress's Tale seems at first to "require little interpretative
assistance" seems to be related, for Friedman, to the hypnotic power of the
tale's artistry; the Prioress's Tale solicits not criticism but a "hush of sobriety." In the last lines of the Prioress's performance,

> Whan seyd was al this miracle, every man
> As sobre was that wondre was to se,
> Til that oure Hooste japen tho bigan,
>   (VII.691–93)

the Prioress's narration of a miracle of the Virgin is seen to work its own
miracle in the "wondre" of the pilgrims' unwonted sobriety and unanimity,
one mood for "every man." Between this miraculous tale and its miraculous audition, no gap opens, no possibility of misinterpretation because no
possibility or need for interpretation; if meaning is an issue at all, it is possessed magically, not striven for through dialectic or debate, not negoti-
ated between differences within the community. The pilgrims simply form
a devotional tableau, strike a certain attitude; their sobriety suggests something like a meaning, something like edification, but in this case edification has neither substance nor history. The alliteration of "miracle" and
"man," of "sobre was . . . to se" further heightens the effect of repetition,
of unanimity.

Thus the power of the "wondre" that is supposed to have occurred must
be set against the perfunctory and indeed almost dismissive quality of these
lines: the pilgrims are sobered for all of two lines of what is in fact utterly
banal verse. There is, again, nothing very much *in* these lines; they try so
hard to go nowhere, to coincide utterly with themselves, that the speed with
which the narrative leaves them behind is hardly even noticeable. So we have
the casting of a miraculous literary spell that's broken as soon as the incanta-
tion is finished. Defensive repetition—what Freud would name the death
drive, the desire of the organism to return to its beginnings in its own way[12]—
issues not so much in devotional fervor as in the vapidity which affective
piety was meant to combat in the first place. The empty formality, then, of
the Prioress's poetic effects (by which I do not mean that they have no power,
for they have the power, precisely, of emptiness) itself demonstrates the
dependence of a miraculous poetics upon conscripted substance and narrative and on suspension of disbelief: the Prioress's Tale does not seem, to
Friedman, to require much in the way of interpretation because—unlike, let
us say, the Nun's Priest's Tale—its imaginative work is not "self-announc-
ing."[13] Its fictionality—its status as verbal artifact—tries to lose itself in

superreality. Criticism is to Friedman's essay as the Jew is to the Prioress's Tale: a difference which makes abjection appear.

The absence of criticism at the end of the Prioress's Tale—the absence of the kind of debate and critical opinion which follows some of the other tales—likewise marks a refusal of the artificed nature of the objects which lay claim to human belief. The Prioress's Tale registers its anxieties and desires—its fear of internal differences, its desire for union—through a phobic narrative about the threat posed by the "outside" (learning, criticism, Jews) to the "inside." It is a story about how terrifying it is to lose one's children to the outside world and to the future. In the Prioress's Tale, the realm of the sacred narrows the space of human life, of narrative, of open-ended creativity, indeed of generational change and conflict, to a pinpoint.

The movement from the Prioress's Prologue into the tale is thus an (abortive) move into the world, into the possibility of change and futurity.

> Ther was in Asye, in a greet citee,
> Amonges Cristene folk a Jewerye,
> Sustened by a lord of that contree
> For foule usure and lucre of vileynye,
> Hateful to Crist and to his compaignye;
> And thurgh the strete men myghte ride or wende,
> For it was free and open at eyther ende.
>
> (VII.488–94)

Narrative begins, in the Prioress's Tale, with a world whose "outsideness" is marked by its distance, its exoticism, its urbanity. Immediately, the tale attempts to fix location, to map a terrain with an inside and an outside, with entrances and exits. The goal of this cartography is in part the location, even the detection, of the Jewry; from its embedded position, the tale will uncover it, bring it to light, make its inwardness available to view. The Jewry is "in Asye, in a greet citee, / Amonges Cristene folk"; we move from the outsideness of "Asye" to the "greet," probably polyglot, "citee," to "Cristene folk," and then to the *Jewerye*—a movement which attempts to fix, in the midst of an unfamiliar and urban scene, the bounds of an opposition based on belief. That is, the setting is one of an artificed and artificing city, its strangeness marked by its placement in "Asye"; the opposition between Christian and Jew, the opposition used in the tale to substantiate belief, is used to relocate the city not as a site of human making but as a site of miracle.[14] The emptiness of the Prioress's characterization of urban "Asye" is, precisely, an emptying-out of the city for the purposes of the staging of belief. The opposition between Christian and Jew thus displaces the struggle of belief itself against the recognition of human artifice, though the opening map of the tale may be said to reveal the very dependence of belief on artifice: the drama of belief makes the city disappear, but it is staged within it—necessarily so, because the city is the site of economic activity, represented in the tale only in the form of Jewish money-lending, and associated with filth and evil: "For foule usure and lucre of vileynye, / Hateful to Crist and to his compaignye." The embedding and uncovering of "Cristene folk" within the space of Asye and then within that of the "greet citee" makes possible the distinguishing of "Cristene folk" from the economy of the city and its involvement with Jews. The tale's (mis)recognition of the temporal power's responsibility for the presence of the Jewry ("Sustened by a lord of that contree"[15]) likewise prepares for the movement into a drama of belief, which is, precisely, a movement away from the temporal world towards the superreality of "Crist" and "his compaignye."

The hope is, of course, that the movement will be easy, that transition will be painless and will not disfigure the identity of the entity. But the text of the Prioress's Tale everywhere registers the dependence of miraculous passage on the substance of the obstacle. The opening lines of the tale put the Jew on the borderline, by trying to define a space that resists definition: a space whose margins aren't firm, a space that's open to penetration, but yet, still, a *different* space—a "Jewerye." The fragility of boundaries, of entrances and exits, generates the poem's sense both of danger and safety. The poem's anxiety about openness includes the body as well as the body politic: the fascination with dangerous passages, with comings to and fro, is reflected not only in the geography of the ghetto ("For it was free and open at eyther ende") but also in the strangely physiological description of the little clergeon's singing, and in the wound to his throat—a wound that mutilates the linings, the borderlines, of a bodily passageway. So the *Alma redemptoris* "Twies a day . . . passed thurgh his throte, / To scoleward and homward whan he wente" (VII.548–9). Both movement through space and movement of illicit song through the throat are fraught with danger in the Prioress's Tale; miracle is figured as the capacity to move without danger, to transcend obstacle, so that narrative can come to rest ultimately in silence and in the image of the devivified body.[16] The boy becomes

> This gemme of chastite, this emeraude,
> And eek of martirdom the ruby bright,
> Ther he with throte ykorven lay upright
> (VII.609–11)

—where the pain and horror of the boy's wound is both elided and appropriated by the vision that transforms him into a lapidary statement of the opposition of miracle to the vulnerability of human life. And at the end of the poem is the body's entombment, its enclosure in marble—an image of final immobility and inviolacy:

> And in a tombe of marbul stones cleere
> Enclosen they his litel body sweete.
> Ther he is now, God leve us for to meete!
>   (VII.681–83)

The wish for an ease of movement that becomes a kind of immobility is itself encoded in the rapid movement inward, and the corresponding intensity of focus, that characterize the opening of the poem—so that we go from "Asye" to the "wydwes sone" (VII.502) in the space of two stanzas. The narrative movement inward thus encodes not only a wish for easy passage but specifically a wish that the adult world of the city and its artifices and idolatries can be quickly left behind, so that we can enter the space of childhood, which is a space not of rapid change but of pure repetition and of the ideal facility of the movement of identity:

> Among thise children was a wydwes sone,
> A litel clergeon, seven yeer of age,
> That day by day to scole was his wone,
> And eek also, where as he saugh th'ymage
> Of Cristes mooder, hadde he in usage,
> As hym was taught, to knele adoun and seye
> His *Ave Marie*, as he goth by the weye.
>   (VII.502–8)

Change and extension are present in these lines in the phrase "day by day," which avoids a near-purity of repetition (thus enabling miracle to stage itself *against* the temporal dimension of human life) through the preposition "by": something happens, we are in the presence of duration, of expansiveness even—yet what happens is always the "same." Too, the "wone" of the boy, his habit of going to school day by day, is punctuated, but by ritual gestures of belief—by kneeling down and saying, not words that depart from his world, but what he has been taught to say by his mother, the matrix from which he sprang ("Thus hath this wydwe hir litel sone ytaught" [VII.509]). Distraction or errancy proves to be neither; alteration in movement is a circling back, through the language of praise, to origins. Thus identity tries to prove its very sameness through recurrence or through departures that signify return; in doing so, identity both risks and appropriates difference from itself.

The risk is marked by the little clergeon's difference, so to speak, from himself. Hawkins, working from Carleton Brown and Marie Hamilton, has emphasized the significance of Chaucer's "reduction of the boy's age to seven. As Marie Hamilton notes, this places the 'litel clergeon' on the 'threshold of accountability' "; "he is on the verge of a debatable land, but he has left behind the secure boundaries of infancy. He is growing."[17] Hawkins finds in the tale a symbolism of emancipation from the carnality of the old law and of the passage of the soul from spiritual infancy to maturity; but what he fails to see is the use to which this symbolism is being put. For the Prioress's Tale is at once a horrifying warning against "growth" and an appropriation of it—an incitement, that is, *so that* a distinction can be made between significant difference, on the one hand, and difference that can be reappropriated by identity on the other. At the crisis of the "'threshold of accountability,' " at the moment that "concupiscence"[18] enters the boy's life, his body is re-made for belief by sacrifice, its pain transformed into testimony of that which is beyond pain; the double sacrifice which involves the pain of the Jews and the pain of the clergeon, and the difference between the two (the difference between imposed pain, or torture, and *imitatio Christi*), exemplify the poem's drive toward a sanctified innerness in which difference becomes nothing but the play of devotion.

In one way, then, we could say that the attempt of the Prioress's Tale to leave behind adulthood, urbanity, making, fictionality, and change is unsuccessful; the tale itself inscribes the impossibility of a pure repetition, or of a perfect repression. In another way, we could say that the Prioress's Tale needs all of these things—needs danger to the body—in order to substantiate miracle. We would, though, be meaning the same thing. As Mary Douglas points out—and as the Prioress's Tale demonstrates through the fate of the little clergeon enclosed in his marble tomb—a pure culture is a dead one.[19] The problem faced by a culture (or a poetic) committed to purity *and* aliveness is one of resources—how to make use of that which is terrifying, how to bring back "in" that which has been expelled. If, then, we can speed past "Asye" and the "greet citee" to get to the heart of the matter, we will find that which we have left behind facing us once again, but in an altered form: the Jews, who "stand for" that which has been left behind— the "Old Law," in Hawkins's reading; and the pathetic scene of ambition, not found in Chaucer's sources, in which the older "felawe" *"prively"* teaches the clergeon the "Alma redemptoris," a song made, the "felawe" explains,

> ". . . of our blisful Lady free,
> Hire to salue, and eek hire for to preye
> To been oure help and socour whan we deye."
> (VII.532–34)

At this moment of the clergeon's vulnerability—this moment of his surpassal of the kind of worship taught him by his mother (VII.509 ff.), and of his transgression against the restrictions placed on learning by his culture—the power of the Virgin to "help" us through our most vulnerable moment of all, our most critical passage, our death, is invoked. (Later on, when the clergeon's transgressive voice has been remade by miracle—" 'by wey of kynde, / I sholde have dyed, ye, longe tyme agon' " [VII.650–51]—the power of the Virgin to transcend the limits of human embodiment is again stressed; she says to the clergeon, " 'Be nat agast, I wol thee nat forsake' " [VII.669].)

As Hawkins points out, the clergeon "breaks the rules of his little world," rules which include the obligation of public, choral, rote learning of permitted knowledge, of what the culture "already" knows:

> "Though that I for my prymer shal be shent
> And shal be beten thries in an houre,
> I wol it konne Oure Lady for to honoure!"
> (VII.541–43)

Hawkins comments: "The penalty is more grim than he expects, and he is 'shent' indeed." But while it is true that the boy "violates the letter of the law, and the law condemns him,"[20] the law cannot be treated as an external agent or as a past to be overcome, however much the patristic material on the question tries to do so. The Prioress's Tale, and Hawkins's reading of it, are complicit with a New Testament and patristic analysis of the relation between Judaism and Christianity which attempts to equate the former with literalism, death, carnality—with the experience of imposed limits—while equating the latter with emancipation, transcendence, freedom through the sanctification of interiority. That the law is at work in the clergeon's life nonetheless makes clear that the Christian's struggle with sin and the law must be a *continuing* one. Though Paul tries to split off Judaism from Christianity—the Old Law from the New, the letter from the spirit (Romans 2–3)—his account of his own interiority suggests that the difference between Judaism and Christianity is also a difference within the entity that is Paul himself:

> For I am delighted with the law of God, according to the inward man; but I
> see another law in my members, fighting against the law of my mind and
> captivating me in the law of sin that is in my members. Unhappy man that I
> am, who shall deliver me from the body of this death? (Romans 7:22–24)

That the law is thus at work within the life and body of the (concupiscent) Christian makes clear too, then, the continuing dependence of the Christian sanctification of interiority on bodily abjection, deprivation, and suffering.

As we noted earlier, Kristeva, writing on Céline, argues that antisemitism is itself a kind of rage against the symbolic order (of law and authorized language), of which Jewish monotheism is taken to be the "foundation" and "forebear." Anti-semitism becomes an attempt to substitute "*another*

Law for the constraining and frustrating symbolic one, a law that would be absolute, full, and reassuring":

> It is impossible not to hear the liberating truth of such a call to rhythm and joy, beyond the crippling constraints of a society ruled by monotheistic symbolism and its political and legal repercussions.[21]

A number of writers speak of anti-semitism as a parody of revolution, a "nostalgia for periods of crisis";[22] anti-semitism wants to throw off the law, it indeed does throw off the law by its indulgence in brutality and hysteria and fusion; but it does so, always and finally, *in the service of* the law,[23] and this is where the celebratory quality of Kristeva's remarks requires severe modification.

The "rhythm and joy" of which Kristeva speaks can indeed be heard in the lines which describe the boy's singing of the *Alma redemptoris*:

> As I have seyd, thurghout the Juerie,
> This litel child, as he cam to and fro,
> Ful murily than wolde he synge and crie
> *O Alma redemptoris* everemo.
> The swetnesse his herte perced so
> Of Cristes mooder that, to hire to preye,
> He kan nat stynte of syngyng by the weye.
> (VII.551–57)

But the joy is imagined as one of possession of the interior by the sacred, a possession so deep that it is piercing; and "rhythm," which in Kristeva's thinking is associated with the mother, becomes an expression of the magical possession of belief: in these lines, rhythm gives a new urgency, the urgency and vitality of crisis, to the Prioress's repetitious poetics. The phrase "As I have seyd" records a repetition, but by its slightly abrupt placement at the beginning of the stanza, by its tone, and by the suspenseful delay in the communication of what has been repeated, we are being told that the quality of repetition has changed: there is a new sense, again, of energy, even of compulsion: "He kan nat stynte of syngyng by the weye." Repetition, in this last line of the stanza, becomes almost furious; that is, it becomes the inability to stop doing something. Intervals collapse; "fusion" is achieved; crisis is upon us. The energy of these lines spills over into the next stanzas; when "joy" and "rhythm" threaten to disrupt repetition altogether, "Oure firste foo, the serpent Sathanas, / That hath in Jues herte his waspes nest," swells up—"Up swal" (VII.558–60). Interior crisis, the threat of intimate violence, of dissolution—which becomes the threat of self-extension, of flooding out into the world (expressed through the clergeon's exposure in the Jewry, his loud and provocative singing)—is given to the Jew through Satan.

But so is the law: says Satan to the Jews,

> "Is this to yow a thyng that is honest,
> That swich a boy shal walken as hym lest
> In youre despit, and synge of swich sentence,
> Which is agayn youre lawes reverence?"
>
> (VII.561–64)

The law is thus projected onto the Jew at the very same time as crisis, "fusion," excitement. And though the stanzas that follow try to separate the criminal legalistic violence of the Jew from the "song al newe" (VII.584) of the virgins and martyrs, the tale later recovers the law for Christian culture through the sentence passed on the Jews by the "provost":

> "Yvele shal have that yvele wol deserve";
> Therfore with wilde hors he dide hem drawe,
> And after that he heng hem by the lawe.
>
> (VII.632–34)

The language of this sentence, restrained *and* violent, bespeaks the extent to which the pogrom is an authorized madness, a madness in the service of authority.

Thus Hawkins's desire to move quickly past, indeed almost to ignore, the boy's fear of being beaten by his teachers, also requires severe modification. Hawkins's statement implies that there is a real shift in levels of cruelty from the kind of violence feared by the clergeon and the kind of violence to which he is subjected by the Jews. Of course, on one level, he is right: there is a difference between being beaten by Christian teachers and having one's throat cut by scary Jews. But what is being skipped over once again is that the violence imagined and feared by the boy as being *within* his own culture, the world of his little Christian school, is being projected by the tale onto the *outside*, onto the Jews, onto the Old Law. In short, the violence done to children of "Cristen blood" by "Cristen folk" is being attributed to the Jewish scapegoat, just as, in the doctrine of the New Law versus the Old, the repressive authoritarianism of Christianity is being attributed to Judaism so that new icons of belief—Mary, for example, who is herself a libidinal threat to "monotheism" and a champion of the abject—can be instituted with all the fervor of what Bataille calls "affective effervescence."[24] We might put the question this simply: if the Jews were not responsible for those dead Christian children, who was?

The clergeon's fear of being beaten reminds us that violence was done to Christian children by Christians, not only in the extreme form of murder, but in everyday ways (familial violence was not uncommon) and in public ways. The tale's association of violence with the school reminds us, too, of the extent to which the control of knowledge in the service of belief was backed up, in the Middle Ages, by force.[25] Thus the tale projects both the disorder of violence *and* the violence of order onto the Jews. It does so because the tale fears not only change, but the incapacity for change—death in all of its forms. The degree to which the kind of *culture* represented by the clergeon's "scole" (and by convents) threatens to fall in on itself, to devour itself in acts of pure repetition, and the degree to which this kind of culture forbids the creation and acquisition of knowledge that is not "already" known are assigned to the Jews, in their role as punishers of transgression—a slippage recorded in the movement from the "felawe's" communication of forbidden knowledge "prively," to the "privy" in which the clergeon's still-singing body, on its way to becoming an icon of belief, is secretly cast. The secret of secret and unauthorized knowledge, of incipient creativity, is transformed into the secret of the identity of the criminal, which is really no secret at all: "Mordre wol out, certeyn, it wol nat faille" (VII.576).

Detection thus substantiates projection; this murder, the Prioress's uncreating "creation," is transformed into something that can and will be found out, so that even the boy's will to knowledge returns in alienated and authorized form. It is authorized by the fact that, as the mother searches for the son (who, in his own very small way, had tried to go beyond what she knew and what she had taught him), the Virgin "already" knows, already has the knowledge the mother wants:

> With moodres pitee in hir brest enclosed,
> She gooth, as she were half out of hir mynde,
> To every place where she hath supposed
> By liklihede hir litel child to fynde;
> And evere on Cristes mooder meeke and kynde
> She cride, and atte laste thus she wroghte:
> Among the cursed Jues she hym soghte.
>   (VII.593–99)

What is at issue, finally, in this detection is the recovery of the interiority of the son by the knowledge of the mother, which in the Prioress's Tale is identified with the knowledge of the culture. The culture's own will to knowledge and to power, to territorial and economic expansion, and to making, is, in the Prioress's Tale, given release, but in the alienated form of seeing into the hearts of its children, remaking those hearts for belief in its icons, and thereby remaking the "alterity" of the future by colonizing its interior. The tale's concern with the space of the body leads us inexorably within, into "Asye," the city, the school, finally to the boy, to his heart pierced by the sweetness of the Virgin; through the opening made by the wound in the boy's body—a wound which the Prioress wants us to believe is inflicted by Jews rather than by the anxieties of "Cristen folk"—to the inside of the "wardrobe . . . / Where as thise Jewes purgen hire entraille" (VII.572–73); to the inside of the Jew's heart, where

Satan has "his waspes nest." The appearance of the body's insides marks the continuing collapse, in the Prioress's Tale, of the border between inside and outside, and of the attempt to give that border shape. The inward movement into ghetto, heart, privy—the desire to see, to master chaos by vision—indicates a desire to occupy, indeed to colonize, the borderline.

The desire to master abjection by seeing within is linked to the tale's narrative urgency, to its desire for the crisis that will bring about the end of change. Once transgression has occurred and the Jew has appeared, narrative rapidity is brought on and then stopped short by apocalyptic spectacle. Vision, in the Prioress's Tale, attempts to articulate space once-and-for-all, to preserve the body intact. The narration of the clergeon's murder is extremely rapid:

> And as the child gan forby for to pace,
> This cursed Jew him hente, and heeld hym faste,
> And kitte his throte, and in a pit hym caste.
>
> (VII.569–71)

There follow two stanzas that stop the rush of narrative by introducing rhetorical apostrophe and apocalyptic iconography: first, the vision of the infernal pit, "where as thise Jewes purgen hire entraille," and the apostrophe against the "cursed folk of Herodes al newe" (VII.573–74); then, the apostrophe to the "martir, sowded to virginitee," and the vision of the "white Lamb celestial" with the company of virgins, "That nevere, flesshly, wommen they ne knewe" (VII.579–585).

The Prioress repeats this anticipation of the end of narrative when, after describing the widow's desperate search for her child, she moves on to the apostrophe "O grete God, that parfournest thy laude / By mouth of innocentz, lo, heere thy myght" (VII.607–8), in which the human voice, as in the Prioress's Prologue, becomes the vehicle for God's creative self-extension, and then to the vision of the

> . . . gemme of chastite, this emeraude,
> And eek of martirdom the ruby bright,
> Ther he with throte ykorven lay upright.
>
> (VII.609–11)

Here, a single stanza asks us simultaneously to visualize both the lapidary body, the body without flaw or cut, entrance or exit; and the abject body, cut through, immured not within a chaste marble tomb but within human wastes. The apocalyptic borderline finally makes all too visible the dependence of clean, proper, self-coincident space, upon abjection; and so the Prioress's Tale is forced to work through repeated attempts to shape abjection. The stanza which records

the "honour of greet processioun" (VII.623) with which the clergeon is carried
to the abbey gives way, through an abrupt transition, to the stanza which records
the torture and execution of the Jews; this stanza, in turn, gives way, again
through an abrupt transition, to a vision of the "innocent" lying on his bier "whil
the masse laste," still compulsively singing. The child's singing is here converted into an unbroken continuity against which the violence of the Jew's execution erupts. The very effort to end time becomes perpetual.

Narrative in the Prioress's Tale is, then, structured as a series of abrupt
breaks, of breakings-in on eternity; alternatively, the brief space of human narrative and time is perpetually being collapsed through anticipation of the
apocalyptic moment and hence its own repetition within the narrative. The
Prioress's Tale is a narrative in which all change can only be imagined as crisis. To celebrate this view of change is to defend against our culture's deepest
fears of its own capacity for, and vulnerability to, change and creativity. To
understand this view of change is to try to recover, for ourselves, our power to
imagine and make the new; it is to reveal to ourselves that our power to produce the world goes hand in hand with the fragility, the openness to change, of
our institutions and beliefs. This is why "criticism," or the movements of difference—generational, gendered, ethnic—must displace the silent sobriety of
the pilgrims' response to the Prioress's Tale. And it is why we must give full
weight to the difference that modern "theory" makes to the ways in which
poems like the Prioress's Tale have previously been read, because to fail to do
so is actually to refuse the historicity of our own being. "True madness," write
Horkheimer and Adorno, "lies . . . in immutability."[26]

Notes

Thanks to Brenda Silver, Matthew Rowlinson, Ivy Schweitzer, Thomas
Luxon, and Peter Travis for reading and commenting on a draft of this essay.
Thanks above all to Richard Corum, whose writings on "oppositional criticism" and whose patient reading of this essay have helped me beyond measure.

1. All citations of the Prioress's Tale are taken from *The Riverside Chaucer*,
   gen. ed., Larry D. Benson (Boston: Houghton Mifflin, 1987). The present
   passage is VII.453–59.

2. Sherman Hawkins, "Chaucer's Prioress and the Sacrifice of Praise," *JEGP* 63
   (1964), notes that the Introit of the Mass of Holy Innocents is from the opening of Psalm 8 (605).

3. Hawkins, 605.

4. Elaine Scarry, *The Body in Pain: The Making and Unmaking of the World*
   (Oxford: Oxford University Press, 1985), 204–5.

5. Alfred David discusses repetition in prayer[; see] "An ABC to the Style of the
   Prioress," in *Acts of Interpretation: The Text in its Contexts 700–1600: Essays
   on Medieval and Renaissance Literature in Honor of E. Talbot Donaldson*,

ed. Mary J. Carruthers and Elizabeth D. Kirk (Norman, OK: Pilgrim Books, 1982), 150.

6. Sigmund Freud, *Beyond the Pleasure Principle* (New York: W. W. Norton, 1961), 8–10.

7. Julia Kristeva, *Powers of Horror: An Essay on Abjection*, trans. Leon S. Roudiez (New York: Columbia University Press, 1982), 41.

8. Derek S. Brewer, ed. *Chaucer: The Critical Heritage*, 2 vols. (London: Routledge and Kegan Paul, 1978), 2: 218.

9. Albert Friedman, "The *Prioress's Tale* and Chaucer's Anti-Semitism," *Chaucer Review* 9 (1974), 118.

10. Friedman, 119.

11. Friedman, 118.

12. Freud, *Beyond the Pleasure Principle*, 56–58.

13. Scarry, 314.

14. Scarry, *The Body in Pain*, notes the "unequivocally negative consequences to city-dwelling" (Babel, Sodom and Gomorrah, the destruction of Jericho) in her analysis of the Old Testament's prohibition of "Human acts of building, making, creating, working" (221). One New Testament example is the story of the prodigal son.

15. Cf. Max Horkheimer and Theodor W. Adorno on "the hatred felt by the led," *Dialectic of Enlightenment*, trans. John Cumming (New York: Continuum, 1972), 171.

16. Klaus Theweleit, in *Male Fantasies, Volume 1: Women Floods Bodies History* (Minneapolis: University of Minnesota Press), speaks of "deanimation" and "devivification" as central features of fascist narrative and desire (106–7).

17. Hawkins, 607–8. He cites Carleton Brown, *A Study of the Miracle of Our Lady Told by Chaucer's Prioress*, Chaucer Society, 2nd Series, No. 45 (London, 1910), 112[;] . . . see also . . . Marie P. Hamilton, "Echoes of Childermas in the Tale of the Prioress," in *Chaucer: Modern Essays in Criticism*, ed. Edward Wagenknecht (New York: Oxford University Press, 1959), 89.

18. Hawkins, 611.

19. Mary Douglas, *Purity and Danger: An Analysis of the Concepts of Pollution and Taboo* (1984; reprint London: Ark Paperbacks, 1985): "It is part of our condition that the purity for which we strive and sacrifice so much turns out to be dead as a stone when we get it" (161).

20. Hawkins, 610.

21. Kristeva, *Powers of Horror*, 178–79.

22. See Jean-Paul Sartre, *Anti-Semite and Jew*, trans. Geeorge J. Beckner (New York: Schocken Books, 1948), on the anti-semite's "nostalgia for periods of crisis in which the primitive community will suddenly reappear and attain its temperature of fusion" (30).

23. Cf. Horkheimer and Adorno: "Anti-Semites gather together to celebrate the moment when authority permits what is usually forbidden, and become a collective only in that common purpose" (*Dialectic of Enlightenment*, 184).

24. Georges Bataille, "The Psychological Structure of Fascism," in *Visions of Excess: Selected Writings, 1927–39*, ed. Allan Stoekl, trans. Allan Stoekl,

with Carl R. Lovitt and Donald M. Leslie, Jr. (Minneapolis: University of Minnesota Press, 1985), 143.

25. Philippe Ariès, in *Centuries of Childhood: A Social History of Family Life,* trans. Robert Baldick (New York: Vintage Books, 1962) notes that "In the allegorical iconography of the fifteenth century, grammar is depicted with younger children than are the other arts, and is armed with a whip or a birch" (159). We should think also, at this juncture, of the violent repression of heresy in the Middle Ages. See Edward Peters, ed. and trans., *Heresy and Authority in Medieval Europe: Documents in Translation* (Philadelphia: University of Pennsylvania Press, 1980).

26. Horkheimer and Adorno, *Dialectic of Enlightenment,* 194.

Mappae Mundi and "The Knight's Tale": The Geography of Power, the Technology of Control

SYLVIA TOMASCH

Like other technological systems, cartography is also strongly and inevitably ideological: it involves not merely the drawing of maps but the making of worlds.[1] Maps are not just colorings in of preset outlines or simple depictions of portions of the physical universe. Maps present entire world views, with all that that phrase implies in terms of philosophical or scientific outlook, theological import, political influence, aesthetic perspective, and artistic choice. The multifarious worlds cartographers draw are far more than merely passive reflectors of particular cultural circumstances or idiosyncratic renderings of some otherwise objective reality; rather, maps are among the most powerful statements of belief in the worlds that they help to create. They are tools, to be sure, but they are inscriptive tools that allow as well as necessitate perspective; they are tools without which we cannot read and without which we cannot see.

Until very recently, maps have been treated by historians of cartography as transparent objects, mediums for the transmission of information, texts needing interpretation but in themselves innocent of creative function. Perhaps it is this assumption of transparency that explains the many unsuccessful attempts to classify maps, medievals maps in particular.[2] For example, Arthur H. Robinson posits "three general functions" of maps: "1. as a record of the location and identity of geographical features[;] 2. As a guide for the traveler[;] 3. As a vehicle for the figurative expression of abstract, hypothetical, or religious concepts."[3] And David Woodward draws upon Geoffrey LaPage's distinction between three types of scientific illustration: descriptive, interpretive, and imaginative.[4] Both Robinson and Woodward confine medieval *mappae mundi* to their third categories. According to Woodward, descriptive maps "depict as accurately as possible what the scientist sees," and "the interpretive may leave out details that are not necessary for the immediate purpose of the illustration and involves some subjective

This essay first appeared in *Literature and Technology*, ed. Mark Greenberg and Lance Schachterle (Bethlehem, PA: Lehigh University Press, 1992), 66–98. Reprinted by permission of the Associated University Presses.

judgement by the scientist"; naturally, then, a medieval map must be imaginative, for it is used to "interpret . . . ideas, hypotheses, and speculations rather than the structure or functions of the subject."[5] Both geographers present thoughtful considerations of maps that supersede earlier, superficial views that the history of cartography could be divided into two distinct phases, "a decorative phase, in which geographical information was usually portrayed inaccurately, and a scientific phase, in which decoration gave way to scientific accuracy."[6] Neither, however, acknowledges the complexity of maps as ideological constructs. To suggest that a map as a "guide for a traveler" must concern itself solely with physical matters and cannot partake of the "figurative" mode, or to oppose and privilege "structure or functions" over "hypotheses and speculations" is to ignore the inherent biases of any map from any place at any time. Juergen Schulz presents the two poles of the dilemma clearly: "[E]ven in Renaissance Italy," he says, "a map was not always a map. Often it was the vehicle for elaborate non-geographical ideas."[7] This is precisely the point: a map *is* a map even when (or perhaps because) it includes functions other than geographical positioning. In fact, it is the incorporation of such information that makes maps so important and that makes mapping, as graphic and textual recreations of the world, so problematical.[8]

The specific uses to which medieval maps were put were very different from those of modern maps and reflect an understanding of the universe as a unified and orderly creation.[9] That alien vision is reflected in striking differences of form and content between medieval and modern instances, so striking that it is tempting to see modern maps as accurate, objective depictions of the earth and medieval maps as merely metaphorical representations. However, a careful reading of the early maps as well as of the geographical treatises in which many were originally embedded reveals that these maps were understood first as being literally true.[10] All maps, medieval as well as our own, are a means of cultural inscription; maps are declarations that the universe *as presented* is just what and as we say it is. Because they do not simply reflect reality but create it by informing our vision of what the world "really" looks like, maps can be used as instruments to implement, to impose, or to exploit that vision.[11] They serve as tools of conquest and as technologies of control.[12] The use of maps as tools to further the aims of particular individuals or societies is neither natural (i.e., inevitable) nor unnatural (i.e., necessarily deplorable), but in the making of maps we actively read and revise the world. A vision of a better world—or, in the case of medieval maps, of a divine one—is also part of the cartographic process.

In this essay I suggest that a conception of mapmaking as a process of world-creating was as important in the Middle Ages as it is in our own,[13] and I analyze the uses to which one fourteenth-century English writer, Geoffrey Chaucer, put the discourse of medieval cartography.[14] In the following pages

I show that not only does Chaucer draw upon map terminology, map lore, and map form in the imagery of his poems, not only is he familiar enough with geographical representations to reproduce them verbally, but certain of his cartographic references indicate an awareness of some of the problems and consequences of vision, perception, and perspective always implicit in map-production.

I

In the Middle Ages, the predominant geographical vision was based on the Ptolemaic system of orderly creation, with the solid orb of the earth imagined as the centerpiece of a series of crystalline spheres in which were embedded the moon, the sun, the planets, and the fixed stars. These spheres were ultimately empowered by the first mover and locally mobilized by angelic spirits. The sublunary earth, consisting of the three known continents and the ocean sea, was thought of as a post-Edenic world inhabited by the descendants of Noah's three sons.[15] One of the most common medieval cartographic representations of the earth is known as the T-O *mappa mundi*. "T-O" is medieval terminology[16] and refers to the lines (the T) dividing the central land mass (the three known continents, Europe, Africa, and Asia) and the circle of the encompassing ocean (the O) (Figure 1). The Mediterranean Sea comprises the upward column of the T, while the Don (or the Tanais) and the Nile neatly meet to form the crossbar. The standard T-O map is oriented with East at the top and typically includes such details as the Garden of Eden in the upper central (eastern) portion, Alexander's fortification against the hordes of Gog and Magog in the upper left (northeast), and at the very center, the navel of the world, Jerusalem (Figure 2).[17] This form appears as early as the seventh century in illustrations of Isidore of Seville's *Etymologies* and continues to be used through the fifteenth.[18] Important British T-O maps include the rectangular Anglo-Saxon map of the late tenth century, the Psalter map of c. 1225, the Matthew Paris world map of c. 1250 (another rectangle), the Hereford map of c. 1290 (still to be seen today in Hereford Cathedral[19]), and an ovoid T-O illustrating Ranulph Higden's *Polychronicon* (c. 1350), executed in Chaucer's own time.[20]

Possibly conceived in the fifth century B.C. by Ionic philosophers, the T-O idea was adopted by Christian thinkers, and the form was adapted to Christian purposes.[21] In his *Historia adversus paganos*, Orosius follows the authoritative division of all land into three great continents:

> Our elders made a threefold division of the world, which is surrounded on
> its periphery by the Ocean. Its three parts they named Asia, Europe and
> Africa. . . . Asia, surrounded on three sides by the Ocean, stretches across
> the whole East. Towards the West, on its right, it touches the border of

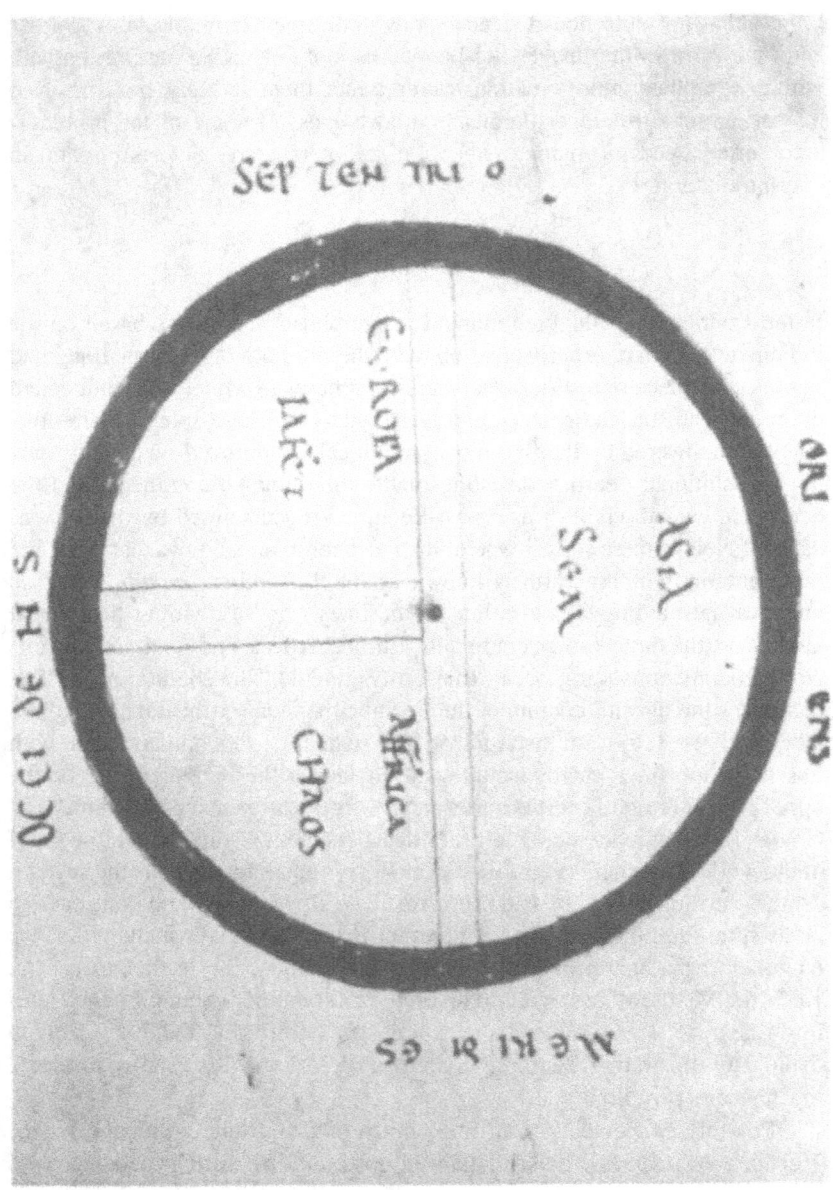

Figure 1. Twelfth-century T-O world map illustrating Isidore of Seville's *Etymologiae.*
Reproduced by permission of the Bibliothèque nationale de France.

Figure 2. Detail from upper portion of thirteenth-century Ebstorf map. Reproduced by permission of the William L. Clements Library, University of Michigan.

Europe near the North Pole, but on its left it extends as far as Africa, except that near Egypt and Syria it is bounded by Mare Nostrum which we commonly call the Great Sea.[22]

Similarly, Isidore states in his *Etymologies*:

The ancients did not divide these three parts of the world equally, for Asia stretches right from the south, through the east to the north, but Europe stretches from the north to the west and thence Africa from the west to the south. From this it is quite evident that the two parts of Europe and Africa occupy half the world and that Asia alone occupies the other half. The former were made into two parts because the Great Sea (called the Mediterranean) enters from the Ocean between them and cuts them apart.[23]

In the *De Universo*, Rabanus Maurus provides the important Christian justification for the tripartite structure:

And most appropriate is this division of the earth into three parts, for it has been endowed with faith in the Holy Trinity and instructed by the Gospels, where we read the words of the Saviour that the world is like unto leaven which the women took and hid in three measures of meal until the whole was leavened.[24]

Rabanus also uses the alternate names for the continents when he states that the earth "has been peopled by the three sons of Noah,"[25] Ham for Africa, Shem for Asia, and Japheth for Europe. This tradition of double naming persists well into the fifteenth century (Figure 3). These illustrations and statements reveal a theologically rationalized presentation of the earth that was in no small part also politically based. As Lee Patterson has shown, although the tripartite physical conformation was explained as stemming from divine causation rather than from any human agency, social control was often the aim.[26]

Although our modern American reliance upon empirical data makes it difficult for us to acknowledge how ideologically based our own maps are,[27] we can easily recognize that medieval maps are products of older cultural values analogously manifested in other visual arts as well.[28] For instance, it is commonly recognized that one hallmark of medieval art is the determination of size of persons or objects by allegorical or political importance rather than by any objective physical reality. Such flattening of perspective,[29] along with "the selective magnification of cartographic signs,"[30] suggests a hierarchizing of value apparent also in literary descriptions of the physical world. For instance, when Geffrey, in Chaucer's *House of Fame (HF)*[31] is carried aloft in the eagle's claws, he describes his bird's eye view:

> . . . y adoun gan loken thoo,
> And beheld feldes and playnes,
> And now hilles, and now mountaynes,
> Now valeyes, now forestes,
> And now unnethes grete bestes,
> Now ryveres, now citees,
> Now tounes, and now grete trees,
> Now shippes seyllynge in the see.

(*HF* 896–903)

Although he sees them in passing, Geffrey views animals, mountains, forests, trees, ships, and rivers all from the same lofty vantage point. This unitary view is that of medieval maps and paintings as well; they too show a similar imbalance of perspective. On the Catalan Atlas of 1375, for example, the caravan travelers appear far larger than the castles along their route to China (Figure 4). Foregrounding these figures (rather than natural features or national boundaries) emphasizes their importance as well as the fact of their journey. Obviously the opposite emphasis could have easily been the case, depending upon the purposes of those who requisition or make any particular map. As the rectangular *mappae mundi* make clear, medieval cartographers rarely hesitated to distort size or shape of land mass for reasons of space, as if the T-O form were not distortion enough (Figure 5). Political and religious

Figure 3. French manuscript, c. 1455, showing Noah's three sons. Bibliothèque Royale Alber Ier, Bruxelles, MS. 9231, fol. 281. Reproduced by permission.

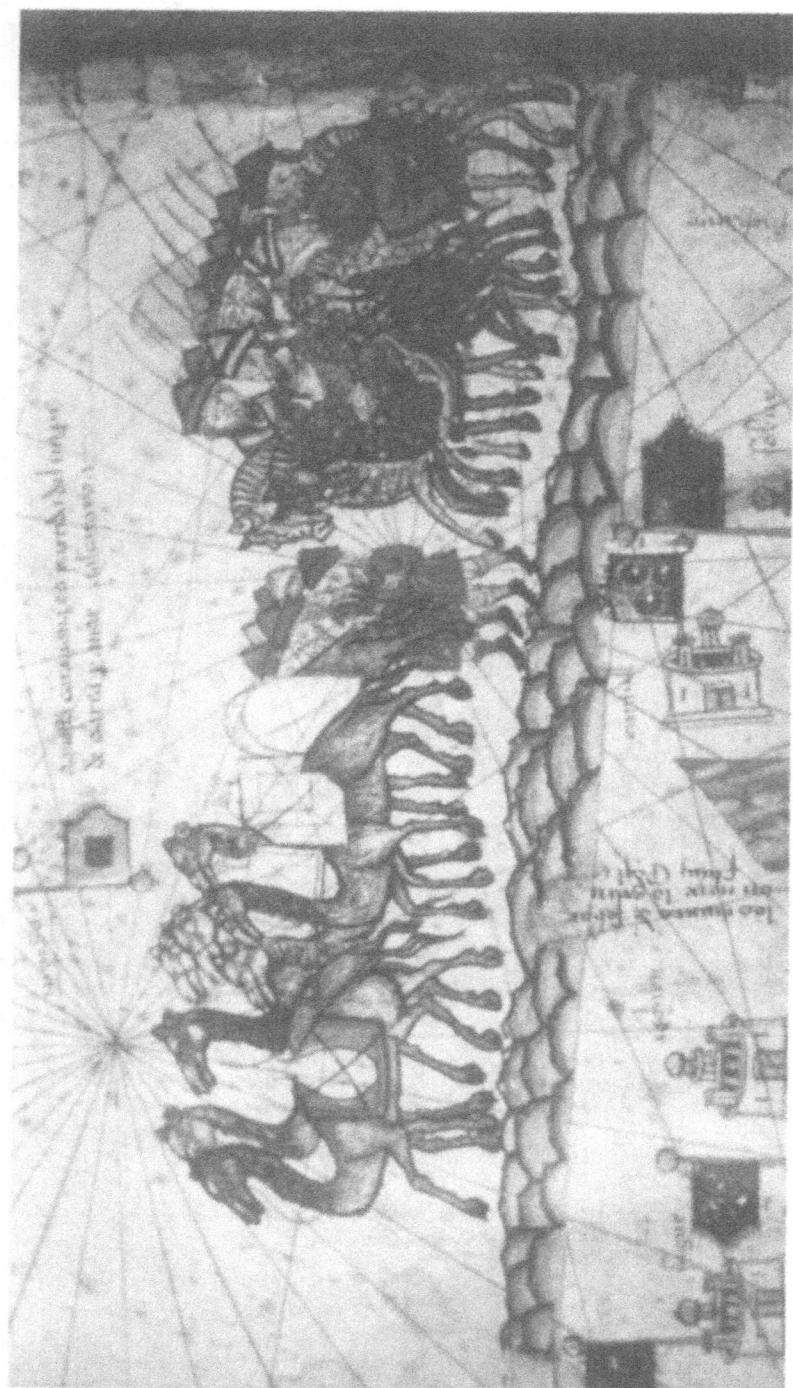

Figure 4. Detail from Catalan Atlas of 1375. MS. Esp. 30. Reproduced by permission of Bibliothèque nationale de France.

Figure 5. Tenth-century "Cottonian" T-O map "squared" to fit the page. British Library MS. Cotton Tiberius B.V., fol. 56v. By permission of The British Library.

beliefs were matters of value that necessarily took precedence over mere accuracy of geographical fact.

Such subjective imbalance becomes significant when we attempt to understand certain images in Chaucer's poems. One previously misunderstood instance of geographical reference occurs in a well-known passage in *Troilus and Criseyde (T&C)*, when at the poem's end Troilus looks down from the eighth sphere to which he has been transported upon his death and sees

> This litel spot of erthe that with the se
> Embraced is . . .

> (*T&C* 5.1815–16)

Concerning these lines, modern commentators, noting parallels with the little earth Cicero and Macrobius mention in connection with the dream of Scipio, assert that the whole world appears small simply by virtue of Troilus's great distance.[32] Yet if the desired effect had been merely to emphasize the hero's physical removal from the earth and his simultaneous understanding of its insignificance, Chaucer could have had Troilus say, as Geffrey does in the *House of Fame*,

> . . . fro the grounde so hye
> That al the world, as to myn ye,
> No more semed than a prikke . . .

> (*HF* 905–7)

In the *Troilus*, however, Chaucer seems to be more deliberately pictorial, presenting a large, foregrounded Troilus and a small, distanced earth—an important variation on the usual hierarchical imbalance. Troilus is no longer on the earth and hence can see it whole. What he sees accords with standard medieval cartographical practice: this earth has a central core surrounded ("embraced") by water; the three massed continents are ringed by the circumfluent ocean. These verse-lines thus constitute a verbal description of the circular T-O *mappa mundi*. This depiction does not accord with modern visualizations of a bright blue marble, but it is a striking example of Chaucer's very different geographical imagination.

Another important aspect of the medieval geographical imagination is the different understanding of the extent of the world. In the Pardoner's Tale, we read of the glutton's chase for dainty bits through "est and west and north and south, / In erthe, in eir, in water" (PardT 518–19).[33] Similarly, the Monk states about Nero: "This wyde world hadde [he] in subjeccion, / Bothe est and west, [south] and septemptrioun" (MkT 2466–67, editor's addition).

According to the Wife of Bath, the world ranges "from Denmark unto Ynde" (WBPro 824), "[b]itwix this and the mount of Kaukasous" (WBT 1140), and "bitwixe the est and eke the west" (WBT 1247). More than just poetic synonyms for the ends of the earth, these phrases refer to the recognized boundaries of the *oikoumene*.[34] The ecumene may be defined as "the inhabited world" or "the habitable world." To the orthodox in the Middle Ages, these were thought to be the same. Although there were continual rumors of the Antipodes, authorities such as Lactantius and Augustine denied the possibility of its human habitation.[35] Based on Scripture (Acts 17: 26), the reasoning ran thusly: God created all nations of one blood; Christ died for all men; therefore no man can exist except for those here, in this *oikoumene*. The alternative theory of Crates of Mallos (second century B.C.) that there were four ecumenes "symmetrically distributed over the four quarters of the globe"[36] had its adherents, among them Macrobius in his commentary on the dream of Scipio.[37] More usual, however, was the view that the Antipodes, if they existed, could not hold human life, simply because nothing, including the news of Christ, could pass through the intervening torrid zone (Figure 6). Therefore, Christ would have had to die four times or he would have failed to redeem all men. Because both of these options are clearly impossible, there is only one *oikoumene*.[38]

Chaucer presents the limits of this ecumene even more specifically in the description of the Knight in the General Prologue to the *Canterbury Tales*. In listing thirteen separate battles in fifteen lines, Chaucer uses these placenames not only to delineate the world of medieval military campaigning but also to delimit the bounds of the known world, which is, in medieval terms, the only world that matters. In traveling from Alisaundre, Pruce, Lettow and Ruce, through Gernade, Algezir, Belmarye, Lyeys, and Satalye, to the Grete See, Tramyssene, Palatys, and Turkeye (GP 51–66), the Knight touches far and wide in Europe, Africa, and Asia. These references serve as an economical presentation of the *oikoumene*, as an idealized listing that symbolizes the extent of knighthood's range rather than as a reporting of any individual chivalric career.[39] To be sure, Franciscan missionaries, Norse outlaws, and Italian merchants journeyed further (not to mention armchair travelers like Mandeville), but the known world, the habitable world, the Christian world (not the lands of griffins and *sciapodes*), these are the referents of the Knight's travels, these are in the realm of possibility.[40]

Like the maps that attempt to portray it, the Christian *oikoumene* is an incorporative and recuperative model of reality. Understanding it as such helps explain the many urgent attempts to pin down the location of such figures as Prester John and such places as the Terrestrial Paradise and the Fortunate Isles, figures and places whose location kept shifting throughout the Middle Ages and well into the Renaissance. Indeed, they had to keep shifting, not merely because explorations pushed the limits of the *oikoumene* out-

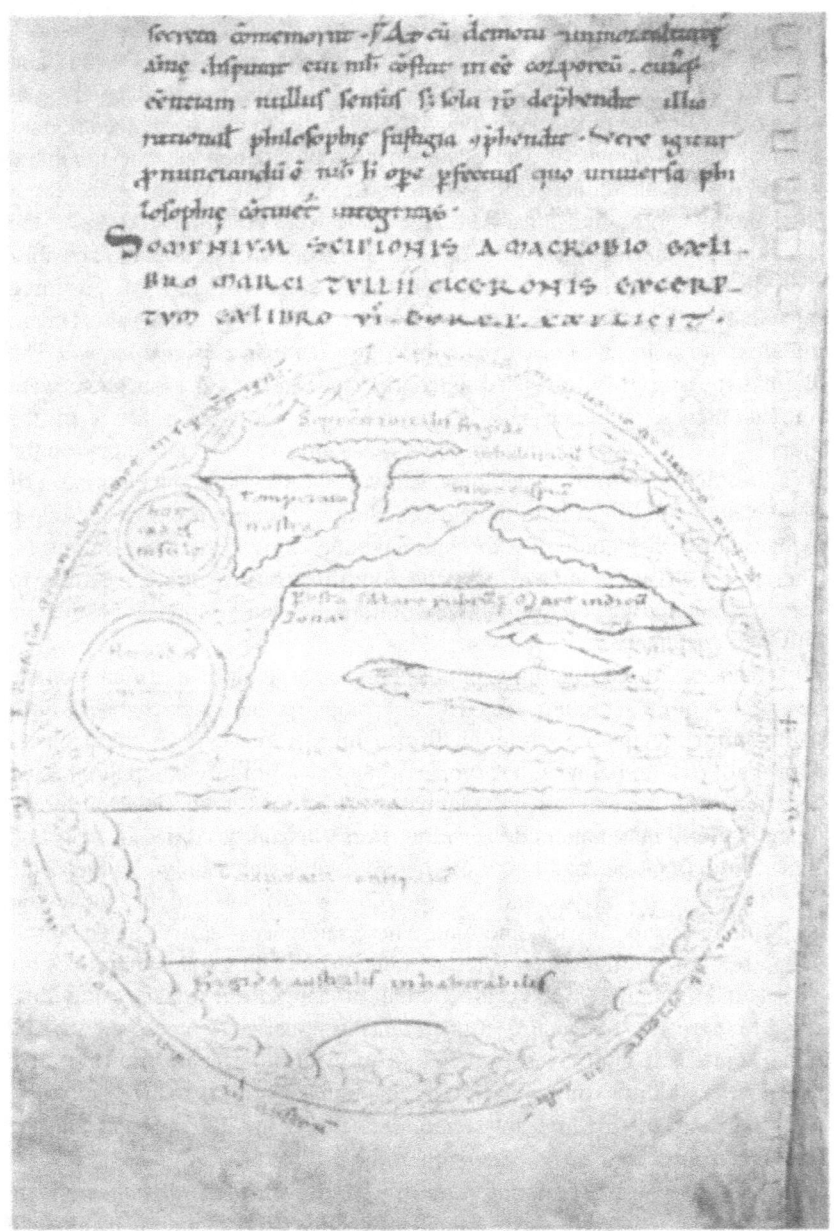

Figure 6. Twelfth-century hemispheric-zonal world illustrating Macrobius's commentary on geography. The Walters Art Gallery, Baltimore, MS. W. 22, fol. 64v. Reproduced by permission.

ward but because such shifts ensured that the boundaries of the *oikoumene* kept expanding, that anywhere a European traveled would not be outside the limits of the real and the known, and that wayfarers would not find themselves in the dangerous wilderness of truly alien lands. Mapmakers have two choices when faced with undelimited spaces: either dismiss them as unknown (and probably unknowable) bits of *terra incognita*, or incorporate them as territories not yet known but still definable in their potentiality by inclusion through graphic visualization. In this second way, Orosius's phrase "*Mare Nostrum*" serves, if only on paper, to conquer the Mediterranean. So maps become, in William Boelhower's phrase, "performative scripture."[41] Exclusion and incorporation work simultaneously, though of course neither strategy can ever rest entirely secure. However, in the totalizing system of medieval Christianity, as there were no limits to God's power there could be no rightful bounds to Christendom's geographical sway on the divinely created earth. Ultimately, this is the message of the *mappae mundi*. This is the lesson of the Ebstorf map as well (Figure 7).

Cartographic recuperation works temporally as well as spatially; like other contemporary texts, medieval maps are frequently, and deliberately,

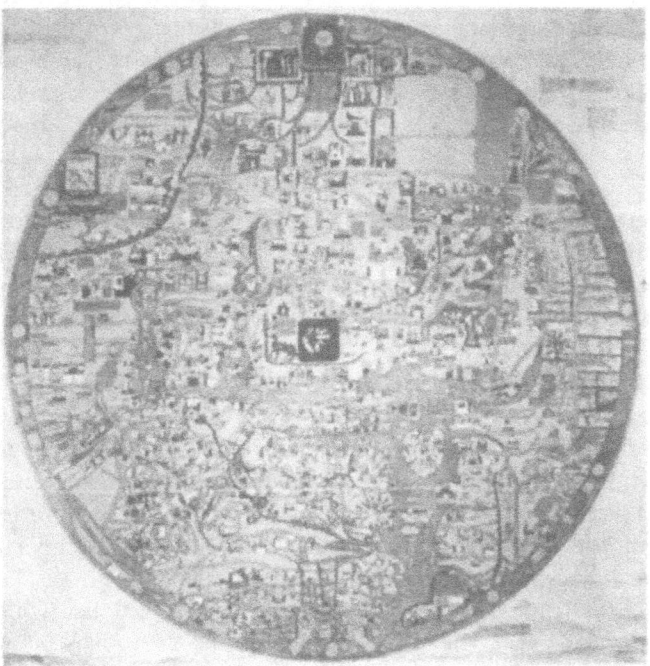

Figure 7. Thirteenth-century Ebstorf map. Reproduced by permission of the William L. Clements Library, University of Michigan.

anachronistic. In the same simultaneous and ahistorical way, Chaucer also
presents places from three distinct eras, classical, contemporary, and biblical.[42] From classical sources come Atthenes, Thebes, and Troye (KnT 861,
933, 2833), Trace, Parnaso, and Rome (*HF* 391, 521, 1930), and Cartage,
Macidonye, and Grece (FranT 1400, 1435, 1444), just to mention a few.
These places are all commonly found on *mappae mundi*, as is the Strait of
Gibraltar, mentioned in these lines from the Monk's Tale that describe Hercules's extraordinary strength: "At bothe the worldes endes . . . / In stide of
boundes he a pileer sette" (MkT 2117–18). Not infrequently, as in Figure 5,
medieval maps portray a pair of pillars just outside Gibraltar, or, as the
Man of Law says, "thurghout the narwe mouth / Of Jubaltare and Septe"
(MLT 946–47).

From contemporary sources come the actual English towns on the road
from London to Canterbury, the places named in the Knight's campaigns,
and other locations on the continent, such as Ytaille (ClT 57) and Lumbardye
(MerT 1245). Chaucer mentions the three continents as a trio in the *House of
Fame* ("Auffrike, Europe, and Asye," *HF* 1339), as well as that significant
body of water, the Mediterranean. Instead of employing that term, however,
he uses, in the General Prologue (GP 59), in the *Romaunt of the Rose* (*RR*
2748), and in the *Book of the Duchess* (*BD* 140) the words "the Grete See,"
the same terminology employed by Orosius and Isidore. As we have seen, the
phrase "Grete See" implies more than just size; aside from the obvious political, economic, religious, and cultural importance of the Mediterranean in the
later Middle Ages, this sea was special navigationally as well. It was safe in a
way that even the North Sea, much closer to Chaucer's own England, was
not. It was not free from pirates or pagans, but very early on it was charted, it
was mapped, it was known. Perhaps most importantly from a cartographic
perspective, on eastward-oriented *mappae mundi* the Mediterranean serves
as the vertical column of the T, rising straight from the surrounding ocean to
point like an arrow to the very center of the Christian world: the city of
Jerusalem.[43] In Chaucer's works, as on many medieval maps, Jerusalem is
also used in three different, and achronic, ways.[44] In the General Prologue
(GP 463), it refers to the contemporary city to which the Wife of Bath went
on a previous pilgrimage. In the Monk's Tale (MkT 2147, 2196), it describes
the ancient city of biblical times. In the *Romaunt of the Rose*, it is used gener-
ically, as part of a phrase to describe extremes of distance: "Fro Jerusalem
unto Burgoyne" (*RR* 554). Each use recalls the other in a literary conflation
of time and space, a move typical of map illustration as well.

From the Bible comes not only Jerusalem but Babilan (MLPro 63),
Nynyvee (MLT 487), the Cane of Galilee (WBPro 11), mount Oreb
(SumT 1891), and Gazan and Chaldeye (MkT 2047, 2157). After
Jerusalem perhaps the most significant place is the one that exemplifies
the unflinching amalgamation of both real and unreal locations on the
same surface of the earth: the Terrestrial Paradise (Figure 2).[45] If we fol-

low the arrow of the Mediterranean upward (that is, eastward), continuing through Jerusalem, we arrive at that most favored spot on earth. Isidore explains that Asia "contains many provinces and districts," of which Paradise is one:

> Paradise is a place lying in the eastern parts. . . . It is planted with every kind of wood and fruitbearing tree, having also the tree of life. There is neither cold nor heat there but a continual spring temperature. In the middle of the Garden, a spring gushes forth to water the whole grove and, dividing up, it provides the sources of four rivers. Approach to this place was barred to man after his sin, for now it is hedged about on all sides by a sword-like flame . . . , that is to say it is surrounded by a wall of fire that reaches almost to the sky.[46]

Most of the aspects Isidore describes, the tree, the rivers, the walls of flames, were typical features of *mappae mundi*. Usually, as in the detail from the Ebstorf map, Adam, Eve, and the serpent were portrayed as well (Figure 2). While Chaucer does not enumerate these features, he does appear to acknowledge the actual existence of this place. Twice he briefly tells the story of the expulsion, in the Summoner's and in the Pardoner's tales, the latter explicitly mentioning Adam and the tree (SumT 1915–17 and PardT 505–11, respectively), and he has the Merchant compare (ironically, I believe) marriage to the "paradys terrestre" (MerT 1332).

Given his propensity for irony, it is certainly possible that in making these references Chaucer is using the tradition to toy with his audience, not always intending his instances of cartographical visualization to be taken entirely seriously. For example, in the *House of Fame* Geffrey learns of the palace that stands "[r]yght even in myddes of the weye / Betwixen hevene and erthe and see" (*HF* 713–15). By proposing such an obvious geographical impossibility, perhaps Chaucer is playing on the credulity of an audience that accepted anything or any place as long as it was located cartographically. Well into the fifteenth century, St. Brendan's Island, the Fortunate Isles, Ultima Thule, and Prester John would be found on maps.[47] While I do not necessarily credit Chaucer with any greater skepticism than his contemporaries, there were those, like the Polos and the Franciscan missionaries, who looked for themselves and reported only what they actually saw.[48] When the eagle carries Geffrey aloft, he tells his unwilling passenger that he is now more than twice as high as "Daun Scipio" (916), who saw in his "drem, at point devys, / Helle and erthye and paradys" (917–18). While some medieval maps did in fact show hell on the map, more usual is the representation of the terrestrial paradise. Like Mandeville, Chaucer carefully does not say he saw this place with his own eyes,[49] but, like Mandeville again, his belief in its earthly existence comes through clearly enough.

II

It is in the Knight's Tale, in the description of the actions of Theseus, that we have the strongest evidence of Chaucer's awareness of some of the implications of medieval geographical theory and practice. In the first two sections of the poem, Theseus is seen as a fierce warrior, a compassionate conqueror, and a righteous ruler. His actions in the third and fourth parts continue and complement his earlier roles; he appears as a builder for and of generations, an architect of edifices, a maker of marriages. These actions reveal his understanding of the importance of consolidation of power and reestablishment of order when the just rule of the realm is threatened by the chaos of private vengeance. It is significant that this consolidation and reestablishment take cartographic form.

In commanding the building of the amphitheater for the tournament between the two suitors of his wife's sister, the Duke of Thebes exercises his pragmatic understanding of the need to control his subjects and their actions as well as the best means for doing so. In having every artisan in his domain concentrate all their skills on the erection of this structure, Theseus illustrates his dominance over men and materials. In shaping this edifice as he so particularly does, he reveals his belief in his own far-reaching and infallible power and declares his faith in technological display and geographical control. However, contrary to Theseus's expectations and intent, what the tale most clearly illustrates for us is not his successful control but his ultimate failure. The Knight's Tale discloses the deficiency that Theseus continually tries to conceal: despite his noble will, no merely human agent can ever truly take the measure of the earth or make the earth his own. Although, as Kenneth J. Knoespel says, "technology is not a spectacle that momentarily diverts our attention but a medium through which a culture defines itself,"[50] sometimes, as here, such technological definition simply does not work.

The crux of the problem of the amphitheater is its shape: Why is this structure round, when the contemporary pattern for tournament lists was rectangular? Chaucer's source has long been debated. V. A. Kolve, for example, proposes the Roman colisseum as a possible prototype for the circular shape, a form for which there is as yet no evidence earlier than the fifteenth century.[51] I suggest instead that the T-O *mappa mundi* is a far better model; as described by the narrator, the amphitheater matches the typical T-O form in most important respects, from location to configuration to orientation:

> I trowe men wolde deme it necligence
> If I foryete to tellen the dispence
> Of Theseus, that gooth so bisily
> To maken up the lystes roially,
> That swich a noble theatre as it was

I dar wel seyen in this world ther nas.
The circuit a myle was aboute,
Walled of stoon, and dyched al withoute.
Round was the shap, in manere of compas,
Ful of degrees, the heighte of sixty pas,
That whan a man was set on o degree,
He letted nat his felawe for to see.
    Estward ther stood a gate of marbul whit,
Westward right swich another in the opposit.
And shortly to concluden, swich a place
Was noon in erthe, as in so litel space;
For in the lond ther was no crafty man
That geometrie or ars-metrike kan,
Ne portreyour, ne kervere of ymages,
That Theseus ne yaf him mete and wages
The theatre for to maken and devyse.

(KnT 1881–1901)

This amphitheater is wide ("a myle . . . aboute"), round ("in manere of compas"), encompassed by a "wall [. . .] of stoon," with the emphasis on the east–west axis: the very image, in earth and stone, of the "O" of the typical *mappa mundi*. In effect, then, what Theseus commands to be built is not just a tournament round but a world in miniature.

In the creation of this *imago mundi*, Theseus would seem to be following Mircea Eliade's dictum that "to organize a space is to repeat the paradigmatic work of the gods."[52] And because he organizes a space and creates a world, he naturally expects his creation to follow his rules. Such control may ultimately be illusory, but technological fiat, especially on a grand scale, impels a movement from resistance to complicity; spectators become participants and participants become believers. Thus, in the Knight's Tale, it is Theseus's own subjects who not only build the structure but make its meaning as well (just as we, the reading subjects of the Knight's Tale, are also active participants in the making of the meaning of Chaucer's work). In various ways, all under the Theban lord are subject to the power of this colossal theater, whether laboring during its construction, painting the decorative images, fighting in the tournament, cheering on the contestants, or marrying the winner. But what does the power of Theseus's structure amount to in the end? Countering his (and his subjects') efforts and best intentions are the deeds of the pagan gods, who have their own agenda—and the gods themselves are shown to be overpowered by forces greater than their own. (We learn of Emily's unwilling participation as well as Diana's own inability to undertake independent action; they make an appropriate pair.) The tale continually insists that all such endeavors toward order by this pagan prince—by all pagans—must ultimately be in vain.[53]

Two couplets of the description of the amphitheater become particularly significant in this regard:

> That swich a noble theatre as it was
> I dar wel seyen *in this world ther nas.*
>
> And shortly to concluden, swich a place
> *Was noon in erthe,* as in so litel space.

(KnT 1885–86, 1895–96; MY EMPHASIS)

In the midst of his elaborate description, the narrator emphasizes the impossibility of the earthly existence of this structure. At the very least, these lines imply the failure built into its very conception (though, as explained below, I believe they do more than this as well). However much Theseus would position himself as a builder of worlds (the epitome of the "crafty man" [KnT 1897]), in the terms of this tale, manifested concretely in this amphitheater, he cannot succeed. He may call upon the gods, he may identify himself with them and even imitate them, but he is only a man, and a pagan at that. He gets the lists built, he sets the rules of the contest, he concentrates all the energy of all the members of his society (and of many outsiders as well) on fulfilling his goals. As we learn, however, it is neither the actions nor wishes of lovers, nor those of kings, nor even those of the pagan deities to whom they pray, which finally conquer; rather it is fate in the form of "a furie infernal" (KnT 2584) that triumphs in the end.[54]

According to the rules Theseus sets for the tournament, when a contestant is unhorsed he loses the contest, even though, like Palamon (the first of Emily's two suitors), he goes down fighting. If the narrative had ended with Palamon's defeat, it would indeed have served to support Theseus's own view that his judgments result in natural, necessary, and foreseeable consequences—in this case, the enforcement of his rules. But the poem continues, and actions the narrator describes as "a myracle" (KnT 2675) lead us, though not Theseus, to the opposite view. Arcite, the second suitor and the momentary winner, is suddenly, unexpectedly, fatally thrown from *his* horse; despite all healing attempts, he dies. The narrator himself despairs:

> Nature hath now no dominacioun.
> And certeinly, ther Nature wol nat wirche,
> Far wel phisik! Go ber the man to chirche!
> This al and som, that Arcita moot dye.

(KnT 2758–61)

Readers must now ask, what kind of world is it where nature, elsewhere the vicar of God, has no domination? The inevitable answer is that this is a pagan world, under false gods, where only nature exists. Theseus's father, Egeus, states the lesson:

> This world nys but a thurghfare ful of wo,
> And we been pilgrymes, passynge to and fro.
> Deeth is an ende of every worldly soore.

> (KnT 2847–49)

Perhaps because this lesson appears to be accepted by his subjects (just as they, in their earlier participation in the building of the theater, accepted his previous interpretative efforts), Theseus has some justification for his continuing attempts at controlling an unruly world. If there is no higher power, only an end in death, then why not? So we read of still further reorderings of the natural landscape:

> Duc Theseus, with al his bisy cure,
> Caste now wher that the sepulture
> Of goode Arcite may best ymaked be.
> And eek moost honurable in his degree.
> And at the laste he took conclusioun
> That ther as first Arcite and Palamoun
> Hadden for love the bataille hem bitwene,
> That in that selve grove, swoote and grene,
> Ther as he hadde his amorouse desires,
> His compleynte, and for love his hoote fires,
> He wolde make a fyr in which the office
> Funeral he myghte al accomplice.
> And let comande anon. . . .

> (KnT 2853–65)

Where once he attempted topographical interference on the grandest scale, Theseus now commands sepulchers and funeral pyres. In one of Chaucer's neatest puns, Arcite is returned to the site of his "hoote fires," but this is not now the location of lamenting desire nor the triumphant locale of a better love. Now there is only a return to the forest, the undefeated domain of unrulable passion, the place of death.

The Theban duke believes in an original orderly creation of the world by a first mover.[55] But what does this belief add up to in terms of human existence?

> "What maketh this but Juppiter, the kyng,
> That is prince and cause of alle thyng,
> Convertynge al unto his propre welle
> From which it is dirryved, sooth to telle?
> And heer-agayns no creature on lyve,
> Of no degree, availleth for to stryve,
>   "Thanne is it wysdom, as it thynketh me,
> To maken vertu of necessitee. . . ."

(KnT 3035–42)

In raising the amphitheater, Theseus tries to reconstruct the world according to a better, more orderly model, tries to create civilization out of natural wilderness, tries to impose rules of combat on raging passions, tries to change bestial fighters into chivalric heroes. To the best of his ability, using every available means including the cartographic,[56] he indeed tries to turn necessity to virtue. Command as he will, however, in this famous speech he is forced to rationalize his evident powerlessness. Although he identifies himself with Jupiter the omnipotent, the narration serves instead to illustrate Jupiter's impotence as well as Theseus's own.

In addition to the couplets stating the impossibility of the earthly existence of the amphitheater, some of the remaining lines of the description reveal why such such failure is fundamental. In reading this part of the description, we need to be aware that what is omitted, what is so seriously missing, may be of even greater significance than what is included. Although exclusion may sometimes be more difficult to document than inclusion, for that among other reasons it may also be a particularly subtle and powerful force.[57] On maps, modern as well as medieval, omission is frequently as important a strategy as depiction, for, as J. B. Harley says, "silences on maps . . . c[o]me to enshrine self-fulfilling prophecies about the geography of power."[58] We know that Chaucer was familiar with medieval *mappae mundi*, since he referred to them by name in his lyric "To Rosemunde."[59] We know that Chaucer was well acquainted with Macrobius's *Commentary on the Dream of Scipio*, the manuscripts of which contain some of the oldest and most important medieval maps of the world.[60] We should therefore take careful note of what Chaucer leaves out of his description as well as what he so carefully puts in:

> And for to doon his ryte and sacrifise,
> He estward hath, upon the gate above,
> In worshipe of Venus, goddesse of love,
> Doon make an auter and an oratorie;
> And on the gate westward, in memorie

> Of Mars, he maked hath right swich another,
> That coste largely of gold a fother.
> And northward, in a touret on the wal,
> Of alabastre whit and reed coral,
> An oratorie, riche for to see,
> In worshipe of Dyane of chastitee,
> Hath Theseus doon wroght in noble wyse.

(KnT 1902–13)

Placing the three temples at the primary compass points around the perimeter emphasizes the structure's circularity and encourages an ongoing visualization of the "O" portion of the T-O form. But this placement also emphasizes omission: in all the many words of the description (204 lines altogether, including lengthy elaborations on the ornamentation of each temple), there is no "T," no intersection of vertical and horizontal lines.[61] As a man-made edifice, Theseus's amphitheater fails to correspond with T-O maps precisely where correspondence is most needed: there is no center here; this map has no Jerusalem.

When listening to a tale told by the Knight, an experienced crusader, a late medieval Christian audience would not be likely to forget Jerusalem. As the most significant spot in mundane creation, Jerusalem was placed, especially in the later Middle Ages, at the midpoint of the circular world-map, a location befitting its position as the focal point of the Christian religion, as the meeting-place of the three continents, and as the center of the entire *oikoumene*. In this, medieval *mappae mundi* illustrate "a universal feature of early world maps, . . . the way they have been persistently centred on the 'navel of the world.' "[62] The "*omphalos syndrome*," as Samuel Y. Edgerton, Jr., calls this tendency,[63] is well illustrated in the Ebstorf map, which not only centers the world on Jerusalem but implies a further correspondence of that city with the navel of Christ, making the map of the world a literal representation of Christ's body (Figure 7).[64] In contrast, Theseus's cartographic recreation has three altars but none where it would count the most; on this map, the center is empty. This pagan world embodies the truth of Yeats's lines, but here it is not so much that "things fall apart; the center cannot hold"[65] as that without a center, things *must* fall apart. According to the narrative, everything ordered by humans goes awry, even the best-laid plans of the lovers, of Theseus, and of the gods themselves. When some greater geography of power is at work, human technology is doomed.

Like the teller of the tale, and like the author of the poem, Theseus tries to force his will upon the world in his attempts to impose artificial order upon natural disorder. However, not being and not recognizing a perfect creator, Theseus's grand attempts come to little; he builds an amphitheater but does not succeed in reordering the world. By imitating the greater world, he thinks he has conquered it, but in fact, to borrow Alfred Korzybski's phrase, he confuses the map with the territory.[66] According to Judith Ferster, "the First Mover speech is not an attempt to describe the design *of* the world but an indication of Theseus's design *on* the world. ... Theseus is seeking not to describe or imitate reality, but to control it" [her emphases].[67] I would suggest that Theseus's imitation of the design of the world stands not in contradistinction to domination but is itself a powerful first move in that direction. *Inscription* is a word for the search for permanence, for the immortality of the text, for an ultimate form of control. Inscription is what Theseus tries, and fails, to do.

III

The inscriptive impulse need not be entirely explicit; individual characters need not be as self-conscious as their author. But if some at least did not make the "mistake" of confusing fiction and reality, we would not have the Friar's and Summoner's tales angrily juxtaposed, nor would we have the Parson's rejection of rhymed fictions in favor of a truthful treatise in prose. The rhetorical "japes" Chaucer continually plays remind us of his awareness of the duality of the inscriptive process. Stories have no meaning unless we accept the rules of the storytelling game; but while these rules allow us to see the created worlds, they also remind us that these worlds are creations of the rules themselves. Maps are similarly rule-bound fictions through which we read the worlds they present. Symbol becomes fact, ideology becomes axiom, and maps not only define the landscape but become their own visible interpreters. When the Miller "quytes" the Knight, when in turn the Reeve "quytes" the Miller, and so on throughout the pilgrimage, their tales come to be seen not merely as stories told to pass the time but as cartographic endeavors, contesting visions of reality, individual versions of the greater universe through which they ride. Like medieval maps, the *Canterbury Tales* offers many partial views at once, chorographies as it were, refusing to choose between them, pretending to present them all on the same level of reality. Like a T-O *mappa mundi*, however, it can fashion this seemingly egalitarian display, because in its self-definition as a Christian pilgrimage, ultimate choices have already been made.

The process of alternation of vision culminates not in the long-awaited arrival in Canterbury but in an unforeseen presentation that nonetheless imputes finality. The "Retraction" is the unexpected termination of the *Canterbury Tales*[68] that both warns us of the superfluity of writing and informs us that the world is indeed susceptible to our imaginings. It reminds us that although within the *Tales* the martyr's shrine is never reached, Canterbury, as a type of Jerusalem, nonetheless provides the meaning for the pilgrimage. As sacred space, Canterbury has value within the Christian hierarchy far greater than that of Southwerk or Rochester, those merely temporary stopping places; it thus comes to stand for that for which the pilgrimage—and ultimately the pilgrims—exists. If knowledge of this proper end is either unknown (the pagan's problem) or ignored (the heretic's dilemma), movement in any direction is worthless or, worse, damnable.

Throughout his poetry, Chaucer presents the futility of any human activity (including his own writing) not founded on the proper, preordained order. In the palinode to *Troilus and Criseyde*, Chaucer repudiates the love poem he has just written in favor of a better depiction of the world and suggests that his readers do the same. Note, however, that neither the palinode nor the "Retraction" is an admission of futility. Rather, each is a repudiation of that which is only and entirely human. Like the Ebstorf map (Figure 7), the verses that help close the *Troilus* invite a similar move from the dependent earth to the cruciform body of Christ:

> O yonge, fresshe folkes, he or she,
> In whiche that love up groweth with youre age,
> Repeyreth hom fro worldly vanyte,
> And of youre herte up casteth the visage
> To thilke God that after his ymage
> Yow made, and thynketh al nys but a faire,
> This world that passeth soone as floures faire.
>
> And loveth hym the which that right for love
> Upon a crois, oure soules for to beye,
> First starf, and roos, and sit in hevene above;
> For he nyl falsen no wight, dar I seye,
> That wol his herte al holly on hym leye.
> And syn he best to love is, and most meke,
> What nedeth feynede loves for to seke?

> (*T&C* 1835–48)

Both the graphic and the verbal texts simultaneously connect and distinguish the created world and its creator. In each case the lesson is traditional: while it is right and important to recognize and acknowledge the creator in his works, do not place trust in mundane things. Most importantly, do not mistake the map for the territory, not even the T-O *mappa mundi* imaged during these final moments.[69] These lines make explicit what the creation of the Theban amphitheater (by Theseus, by the Knight, by the pilgrim-narrator, by Chaucer) leaves only implicit: that writing and mapmaking are both strategies for inscribing a world, giving their audiences no choice but to accept the truth of that inscription. Like Theseus, we today attempt to impose our view of the world on the world by means of maps and globes; from a medieval perspective, however, we can never succeed. We are doomed to mere description. We are limited by our beliefs to imperfect imitation.

Questions of power and human creation are very much at issue here. It is not just that the technologies of mapmaking and writing are analogous in that both are means for creating worlds; this, they assuredly do. More importantly, every technology manipulates its audience by presenting fictions of the world that are simultaneously asserted not to be fictions at all but passive reflections of the thing itself. The better the map, the closer to some prior, knowable reality, the more power (i.e., truth) it is felt to contain. The paradox is that neither maps nor stories can function until and unless we recognize them as both true and false at the same time (even though in any individual case the expectations may not be balanced on both sides; belief may be greater than disbelief, or vice-versa). They gain their power from us, and that is their power over us: this is the duality of inscription.

The force behind spatial and temporal manipulation is not, finally, geographical but imaginative, and cartographic systems and symbols arise out of the imaginations not merely of individuals but of cultures. They are of course ideological constructions, and we think, as Theseus does, that we control them when in fact the opposite is equally true. It may be, as Harley argues, that the "ideological arrows" of cartographic power fly in one direction only (i.e., maps are used for protection or aggrandizement by elite groups),[70] and in fact, this unilateralness is illustrated in the Knight's Tale: it is the duke, Theseus, who controls the technologies of building, of mapmaking, of war and peace. But Theseus's ultimate impotence illustrates another, more important fact, one that Chaucer appears to know as well: we are all, to some extent, controlled by our creations when we accept the rules that bind them to us. Like the *Canterbury Tales*, medieval maps are valued for their ornamentation and beauty, for their complexity of rhetoric, for their often confusing illusion of completeness. The competing versions of the many tales are matched in the maps by the inclusion of all possible (and some seemingly impossible) elements of the cosmos in one all-encompassing vision of creation. In their incorporative, arbitrary, and anachronistic aspects they are unlike their modern Western counterparts, which pretend to uniformity and objectivity of perspective and sign. On the contrary, these medieval works celebrate the fullness, range, and contradictions of human existence (as seen from a human perspective).

In one sense *mappae mundi* are like modern road maps: they both lead their users on a journey—but in the former case the end of the journey lies off the map. As allegorical devices important beyond the game of verbal or visual decipherment, maps allude to a greater end and, as far as they are able, bring their audiences to their proper terminus. The *oikoumene* is both transitory and meaningful in its transience—is this not why Troilus laughs on seeing "that litle spot of erthe"? Just so, medieval maps, allusive and inaccurate as they must be, indicate the presence of uncharted eternity. By presenting scenes of the visible world, *mappae mundi* intimate the invisible; in this way, they lead pilgrims to the territory beyond. No technology can work without its users' belief in its ultimate efficacy, but, as Theseus refuses to learn, *correct* beliefs are crucial to the *proper* functioning of any technology. Right recognition is the task for which pilgrimage texts are created; without it, order, eternity, wholeness, salvation are lost. This is the lesson of the Knight's Tale; this is the lesson of the *mappae mundi*.[71]

Notes

1. On the relationship of ideology and technology, see Stanley Aronowitz, *Science as Power: Discourse and Ideology in Modern Society* (Minneapolis: University of Minnesota Press, 1988); and Michael Zimmerman, "Heidegger and Marcuse: Technology as Ideology," *Research in Philosophy & Technology* 2 (1979): 245–61. As to a definition of "technology," despite the attempts of Carl Mitcham (among others), we still lack a thoroughly satisfactory one; see "Types of Technology," *Research in Philosophy & Technology* 1 (1978): 229–94. For my purposes here, I follow the editors of this volume in accepting R. G. Collingwood's suggestion that " *'techne'* signifie[s] both art (literature) and craft (technology)" (Mark Greenberg and Lance Schachterle, "Introduction," *Literature and Technology*, ed. Mark Greenberg and Lance Schachterle [Lehigh, PA: Lehigh University Press, 1992], p. 17).

2. Recent standard cartographical histories and surveys include J. B. Harley and David Woodward, eds., *The History of Cartography: Cartography in Prehistoric, Ancient, and Medieval Europe and the Mediterannean*, vol. 1 (Chicago: University of Chicago Press, 1987), pt. 3; M. J. Blakemore and J. B. Harley, *Concepts in the History of Cartography: A Review and Perspective*, *Cartographica* 17 (1980), Monograph 26; W. W. Ristow, *Guide to the History of Cartography* (Washington, DC: Geography and Map Division, Library of Congress, 1973); R. A. Skelton, *Maps: A Historical Survey of Their Study and Collecting* (Chicago: Univ. of Chicago Press, 1972); and N. J. Thrower, *Maps and Man* (Englewood Cliffs, NJ: Prentice Hall, 1972). In addition, I have not yet been able to see Jorg-Geerd Arentzen, *Imago Mundi Cartographica: Studien zur Bildlichkeit mittelalterlicher Welt- und Okumenikarten unter besonderer Berucksichtigung des Zusammenwirkens von Text und Bild*, Munstersche Mittelalter-Schriften 53 (Munich: Wilhelm Fink, 1984). Woodward argues in favor of retaining a more complex system of classification against Arentzen's suggestions for simplification (*History of Cartography*, 1.296).

3. Robinson, *Early Thematic Mapping in the History of Cartography* (Chicago: University of Chicago Press, 1982), p. 3.

4. LaPage, *Art and the Scientist* (Bristol: Williams & Wilkins, 1961), cited in Woodward, "Introduction," in *Art and Cartography*, ed. David Woodward (Chicago: University of Chicago Press, 1987), p. 7.

5. Woodward, "Introduction," p. 7.

6. Ibid., p. 2.

7. Schulz, "Maps as Metaphors: Mural Map Cycles of the Italian Renaissance," in *Art and Cartography*, p. 122.

8. Recently, some scholars have begun to study early maps as ideological arti-facts that inevitably combine functions and defy easy categorization. For example, Richard Helgerson discusses the ironies of representations of power in Elizabethan maps ("The Land Speaks: Cartography, Chorography, and Subversion in Renaissance England," *Representations* 16 [1986]: 50–85) and J. B. Harley explicitly connects maps and other Tudor cultural forms: "In many contexts maps would have articulated symbolic values as part of the visual languages by which specific interests, doctrines, and even world views were communicated" ("Meaning and Ambiguity in Tudor Cartography," in *English Map-Making, 1500–1800*, ed. Sarah Tyacke [London: British Library, 1983], p. 22). Others are beginning to question the conceptions that rule our understanding of cartography itself. See Denis Wood's review of *Art and Cartography*, "Commentary," *Cartographica* 24 (1987): 76–82; and especially the short essays in the Pompidou Centre exhibition catalog *Cartes et Figures de la Terre* (Paris: Centre Georges Pompidou, 1980).

9. The special character of medieval maps is discussed by David Woodward, "Reality, Symbolism, Time, and Space in Medieval World Maps," *Annals of the Association of American Georgraphers* 75 (1985): 510–21; this article is a preliminary report of research later expanded upon in Harley and Wood-ward, eds., *The History of Cartography*, vol. 1. Although this special charac-ter would seem to be an obvious point, some are still unaware of it. For instance, the recently published *Encyclopedic Dictionary of Semiotics* omits any reference to non-Western or nonmodern maps. See M[artin] K[rampen], "Cartography," *Encyclopedic Dictionary of Semiotics* (Berlin: Mouton de Gruyter, 1986), 1: 98–99.

10. In this way, medieval maps are like other medieval texts in that the literal reading is always primary, the kinds of allegory following; see Hugh of St. Victor, *The Didascalicon*, 1939 ed. C. H. Buttimer, trans. J. Taylor (New York: Columbia University Press, 1961); extracts from books 5 and 6 reprinted in A. J. Minnis and A. B. Scott, eds., *Medieval Literary Theory and Criticism c.1100–c.1375: The Commentary Tradition* (Oxford: Clarendon Press, 1988), pp. 71–86.

11. See J. B. Harley, "Maps, Knowledge, and Power," in *The Iconography of Landscape: Essays on the Symbolic Representation, Design and Use of Past Environments*, ed. Denis Cosgrove and Stephen Daniels (Cambridge, Eng-land: Cambridge University Press, 1988), pp. 277–312.

12. William Boelhower, in *Through a Glass Darkly: Ethnic Semiosis in Ameri-can Literature* (New York: Oxford University Press, 1987), discusses fif-teenth- and sixteenth-century European world maps as powerful instruments of colonization that contrast with the weakness of Native American choro-graphic perspectives; see esp. chap. 2. The bivalent relationship between maps and political and economic power in various periods is discussed in a number of recent works, including Juergen Schulz, "Jacopo de' Barbari's View of Venice: Map Making, City Views, and Moralized Geography Before

the Year 1500," *Art Bulletin* 60 (1978): 425–74; Victor Morgan, "The Cartographic Image of 'The Country' in Early Modern England," *Transactions of the Royal Historical Society*, 5th ser., 29 (1979): 129–54; Chandra Mukedi, *From Graven Images: Patterns of Modern Materialism* (New York: Columbia University Press, 1983), pp. 79–130; and Svetlana Alpers, *The Art of Describing: Dutch Art in the Seventeenth Century* (Chicago: University of Chicago Press, 1983), chap. 3. Such relationships have recently been dramatized in Brian Friel's play, *Translations*, in his *Selected Plays* (Washington, DC: Catholic University of America Press, 1984), pp. 377–451.

13. The contemporary reluctance to view maps within their political contexts is illustrated by those on both sides of the debate over the Peters Projection. For two contrasting views, see Ward L. Kaiser, *A New View of the World: A Handbook to the World Maps: Peters Projection* (New York: Friendship Press, 1987), and Anngret Simms, "Playing Politics with Maps," *The Irish Times*, 15 April 1989 (a review of Arno Peters, *Peters Atlas of the World* [London: Longman, 1989]).

14. This essay is part of a larger study that considers two basic questions that have not hitherto been brought together: (1) What were the medieval conceptions of the physical world? (2) What were the consequences of these conceptions for artistic discourse of the period? On Chaucer's geographical references and sources, see John A. Hertz, "Chapters toward a Study of Chaucer's Knowledge of Geography," DA 19 (1959), 2600–1; for an annotated list of Chaucerian place names, see Francis P. Magoun, Jr., *A Chaucer Gazetteer* (Chicago: University of Chicago Press, 1961).

15. For a brief but excellent overview of "The Image of the World before the Portolan Charts," see Michel Mollat du Jourdin, "Introduction," in Michel Mollat du Jourdin and Monique de la Ronciere, *Sea Charts of the Early Explorers: 13th to 17th Century,* trans. L. le R. Dethan (Fribourg: Thames & Hudson, 1984), pp. 8–11.

16. References to the T-O form occur in Dati's *La Sfera*, Brunetto Latini's *Livre du Tresor*, and Gervase of Tilbury's *Otia Imperialia*, cited in W. L. Bevan and H. W. Phillott, *Mediaeval Geography: An Essay in Illustration of the Hereford Mappa Mundi* (London: E. Stanford, 1873), p. xv. See also the discussion of T-O maps in C. Raymond Beazley, *The Dawn of Modern Geography: A History of Exploration and Geographical Science from the Conversion of the Roman Empire to A.D. 900*, 3 vols. (London: J. Murray, 1897–1906), 2: 576–79, 2: 627–32.

17. There was a strong scriptural tradition for the central placement of Jerusalem: "This city of Jerusalem I have set among the nations, with the other countries round about her" (Ezek. 5:5). On the centrality of Jerusalem, Woodward states that it is only in "the fourteenth and fifteenth centuries [that] the practice of placing Jerusalem at the center became common" (*The History of Cartography*, pp. 341–42), but this is of course the period under scrutiny in this essay.

18. See *History of Cartography*, vol. 1. See also the chronological table of world maps in Leo Bagrow, *History of Cartography*, 1951; 1960 trans. D. L. Paisey, rev. R. A. Skelton (London: Watts, 1964), p. 45.

19. At this writing (August 1989), Richard of Haldingham's map is still owned by Hereford Cathedral, but as it has been advertised for sale that situation may not hold at the time of publication.

20. Bevan lists medieval *mappae mundi* in England (*Mediaeval Geography*, pp. xxxiv–xlvi).

21. Lloyd A. Brown, *The Story of Maps* (Boston: Little, Brown, 1949), p. 96.

22. Trans. George H. T. Kimble, *Geography in the Middle Ages* (New York: Methuen, 1938), p. 20.

23. Ibid., p. 24.

24. Ibid., p. 32.

25. Ibid., p. 32.

26. On the politically repressive connection made in the later Middle Ages between Noah's sons and the three estates, see Lee Patterson " 'No man his reson herde': Peasant Consciousness, Chaucer's Miller, and the Structure of the *Canterbury Tales*," *South Atlantic Quarterly* 86 (1987): 457–95.

27. See Harley's discussion of accuracy as "a new talisman of authority," in "Maps, Knowledge, and Power," p. 300.

28. Woodward notes the "family of spatial representations and ideas found in architecture as well as in cartography" ("Medieval *Mappaemundi*," p. 340.)

29. See Samuel Y. Edgerton, *The Renaissance Rediscovery of Linear Perspective* (New York: Harper & Row, 1975), on the medieval "lack" of perspective.

30. Harley, "Maps, Knowledge, and Power," pp. 292–94.

31. All citations and line references are to *The Riverside Chaucer*, 3d ed., ed. Larry D. Benson (Boston: Houghton Mifflin, 1987).

32. For example, Chauncey Wood, *Chaucer and the Country of the Stars: Poetic Uses of Astrological Imagery* (Princeton, NJ: Princeton University Press, 1970), p. 184. For a recent bibliography of the critical discussion of these lines in context, see the *Riverside Chaucer*, p. 1057.

33. I follow standard usage in abbreviating the titles of Chaucer's works using PardT = Pardoner's Tale, WBPro = Wife of Bath's Prologue, GP = General Prologue, etc. For a complete list of abbreviations, see the *Riverside Chaucer*, p. 779.

34. Boies Penrose discusses classical and medieval conceptions of the *oikoumene* in *Travel and Discovery in the Renaissance 1420–1620* (1952; Cambridge, MA: Harvard University Press, 1963), p. 2.

35. Discussed in Bevan, *Mediaeval Geography*, p. 2.

36. Trans. Bevan, *Mediaeval Geography*, p. xvii. See also the discussion of Crates's theory in John Kirtland Wright, *The Geographical Lore of the Time of the Crusades: A Study in the History of Medieval Science and Tradition in Western Europe* (New York: American Geographical Society, 1925), pp. 18–19.

37. On Macrobius's views, see Kimble, *Geography in the Middle Ages*, pp. 8–9.

38. Pierre d'Ailly discusses the size and composition of the *oikoumene* in *Ymago Mundi*, trans. Edward Grant, in *A Source Book in Medieval Science*, ed. Edward Grant (Cambridge, MA: Harvard University Press, 1974), pp. 636–38. See also Kimble's discussion, *Geography in the Middle Ages*, pp. 209–10.

39. For a bibliography of critical views on the Knight and his campaigns, see the *Riverside Chaucer*, p. 800. In particular, I agree with Maurice Hussey, *Chaucer's World: A Pictorial Companion* (Cambridge: Cambridge University Press, 1967, p. 13) that the "outlying regions [named by Chaucer] are more figures of speech than actual places." For my purposes, recognizing the metaphoric extent of the knight's travels is far more important than identifying any place or actual person who might have served as a model for this character, though numerous readers have attempted to do just that. See William Urban, "When Was Chaucer's Knight in 'Ruce'?" *Chaucer Review* 18 (1984): 347–53, for a typical article of the latter type.

40. Note that the Shipman piloted along the shore, the Merchant traded only across the Channel, the Pardoner had been (he says) to Rome, but only the Wife of Bath journeyed as far as Jerusalem, and that, in terms of travel conditions in the Middle Ages, was far indeed. On travel and literature in the later Middle Ages, see Christian K. Zacher, *Curiosity and Pilgrimage: The Literature of Discovery in Fourteenth-Century England* (Baltimore, MD: Johns Hopkins University Press, 1976). On medieval European travel writing, see Mary B. Campbell, *The Witness and the Other World: Exotic European Travel Writing, 400–1600* (Ithaca, NY: Cornell University Press, 1988).

41. Boelhower, *Through a Glass Darkly*, p. 55.

42. These categories are Bevan's in *Mediaeval Geography*, p. xxiii. He adds "legendary" as a fourth source, but I have not found any such references in Chaucer.

43. As Mollat du Jourdin writes, "Predestined to be the site of the spreading of the Gospel, the Mediterranean serves as the axis of the whole [T-O] structure. Everything stems from there, in a convergence of the knowledge of antiquity and biblical traditions" (*Sea Charts*, p. 8).

44. Magoun, *A Chaucer Gazeteer*, also lists three, though different, types of usage for Jerusalem: the biblical city, the medieval pilgrimage city, and the celestial city (p. 95).

45. Bevan, *Mediaeval Geography*, discusses the understanding of the Terrestrial Paradise as an "existing contemporaneous fact" (p. xx) by Higden, Mandeville, Gervase of Tilbury and others, pp. xx–xxi. Kimble, *Geography of the Middle Ages*, adds John of Hesse and John Marignolli, p. 184.

46. Trans. Kimble, *Geography in the Middle Ages*, p. 24.

47. We might note in this context a representative of the race of apple-sniffers, who subsisted entirely on the odor of apples, seated in the lower right-hand portion of the Ebstorf detail (Figure 2). Nicholas H. Steneck, *Science and Creation in the Middle Ages: Henry of Langenstein (d. 1397) on Genesis* (Notre Dame: University of Notre Dame Press, 1976), notes the persistence of standard medieval geographical beliefs about the composition and inhabitants of the world into and past Chaucer's own time (p. 83).

48. On Asian travels and travelers, see Campbell, *The Witness and the Other World*; also Kimble, *Geography in the Middle Ages*, chap. 6. On pilgrims and missionaries, ninth through thirteenth centuries, see Beazley, *The Dawn of Modern Geography* 2, chaps. 3–6.

49. *Mandeville's Travels*, ed. M. C. Seymour (London: Oxford University Press, 1969): "Of Paradys ne can I speken propurly, for I was not there. It is fer beyonde, and that forthinketh me, and also I was not worthi. But as I haue herd seye of wyse men beyonde, I schalle telle you with gode wille" (p. 220). After this disclaimer, Mandeville goes on to describe the usual components of paradise, the enclosing wall, the four rivers, etc.

50. Kenneth J. Knoespel, "Gazing on Technology: *Theatrum Mechanorum* and the Assimilation of Renaissance Machinery," in *Literature and Technology*, p. 120.

51. V. A. Kolve, *Chaucer and the Imagery of Narrative: The First Five Canterbury Tales* (Stanford: Stanford University Press, 1984), esp. pp. 105–14. As Kolve notes, Robert A. Pratt, "Chaucer's Use of the *Teseida*," *PMLA* 62 (1947): 598–621, first suggested the Colisseum as a possible model for Boccaccio (Chaucer's direct source); Kolve explains the importance of Chaucer's elaborations of this image but overlooks the possibility of a connection with the T-O *mappa mundi*. Kolve lacks appropriately dated source images of tournament rounds, but Steven I. Pederson, *The Tournament Tradition and Staging of The Castle of Perseverance* (Ann Arbor, MI: UMI Research Press, 1987), presents two fifteenth-century illustrations of circular lists (figures 5 and 6, pp. 105–6). Neither list, however, contains any of the features emphasized by Chaucer. Some earlier critics have noted the problematic nature of the amphitheater, but none has suggested any but a purely metaphorical resolution. See Merle Fifield, "The 'Knight's Tale': Incident, Idea, Incorporation," *Chaucer Review* 3 (1968): 95–106; and Joseph Westlund, "The 'Knight's Tale' as an Impetus for Pilgrimage," *Philological Quarterly* 43 (1964): 526–37.

52. Mircea Eliade, *The Sacred and the Profane: The Nature of Religion*, trans. Willard R. Trask (New York: Harcourt, Brace, 1969), p. 33; quoted by Jesse M. Gellrich, *The Idea of the Book in the Middle Ages: Language Theory, Mythology, and Fiction* (Ithaca, NY: Cornell University Press, 1985), p. 68; Gellrich also discusses medieval maps, pp. 62–64.

53. Some recent discussions of the theme of order in the "Knight's Tale" include Thomas H. Luxon, "'Sentence' and 'Solaas': Proverbs and Consolation in the 'Knight's Tale,'" *Chaucer Review* 22 (1987): 94–111; T. McAlindon, "Cosmology, Contrariety and the Knight's Tale," *Medium Aevum* 50 (1986): 41–57; Judith Ferster, *Chaucer on Interpretation* (Cambridge, Eng.: Cambridge University Press, 1985), pp. 23–45; Kolve, *Chaucer and the Imagery of Narrative*, chap. 3; David Aers, *Chaucer, Langland and the Creative Imagination* (London: Routledge & Kegan Paul, 1980), pp. 174–95, 228–31.

54. Jerold C. Frakes, "'Ther Nis Namoore to Seye': Closure in the *Knight's Tale*," *Chaucer Review* 22 (1987): 1–7, suggests "*fortuna* as the controlling *agens* of the events" of this tale (p. 2).

55. Theseus begins by asserting the great chain of being: "with that faire cheyne of love he bond / The fyr, the eyr, the water, and the lond / In certeyn boundes, that they may nat flee" (KnT 2991–93). From this orderly creation he derives the existence of the first mover: "Thanne may men by this ordre wel discerne / That thilke Moevere stable is and eterne" (KnT 3003–4).

56. Thomas H. Luxon asserts the deliberate quality of Theseus's choices, both of action and of language: "Theseus's proverbial utterances serve much the same purpose of his frequent creation of ceremonies throughout the tale. He choreographs ceremonies as a strategy for containing or resolving the apparent disorder in the world. He does not simply pick from the 'catalogue' of ceremonies or proverbs one that can be applied to a type of situation; he creates the ceremony or sentence he needs out of a hard-won perception of underlying (or overarching) order" ("'Sentence' and 'Solaas'," p. 105).

57. Harley, "Maps, Knowledge, and Power," pp. 290–92.

58. Ibid., p. 292.

59. Chaucer's use of this word in "To Rosemounde" is noted by Donald R. Howard, *Chaucer: His Life, His Works, His World* (New York: Dutton, 1987), p. 173. I believe that Chaucer's lines here may refer not only to the roundness of the typical T-O map but also (as in the case of the lines of *Troilus and Criseyde* discussed above) to the "embracing" of the continental core by the circumfluent ocean: "Madame, ye ben of al beaute shryne / As fer as cercled is the mapamounde" ("To Rosemounde" 1–2). See note to these lines in the *Riverside Chaucer*, p. 1082.

60. Although it should be noted that Macrobian maps are of the zonal kind, and not the tripartite T-O, so many contemporary examples of the latter existed that Chaucer's familiarity with both sorts is quite likely. See Woodward, *The History of Cartography*, p. 300.

61. On the significance of the T, see Jonathan T. Lanman, "The Religious Symbolism of the T in T-O Maps," *Cartographica* 18 (1981): 18–22.

62. Harley, "Maps, Knowledge, and Power," p. 290.

63. Edgerton, "From Mental Matrix to *Mappamundi* to Christian Empire: The Heritage of Ptolemaic Cartography in the Renaissance," in *Art and Cartography*, p. 26; cited by Harley, "Maps, Knowledge, and Power," p. 290.

64. On a literary analogue to the Ebstorf map, see John B. Friedman, "Medieval Cartography and 'Inferno' xxxiv: Lucifer's Three Faces Reconsidered," *Traditio* 39 (1983): 447–55.

65. William Butler Yeats, "The Second Coming," in *The Variorum Edition of the Poems of W. B. Yeats*, ed. Peter Alt and Russell K. Alspach (New York: Macmillan, 1957), pp. 401–2.

66. Korzybski, *Science and Sanity: An Introduction to Non-Aristotelian Systems and General Semantics* (Lakeville, CT: International Non-Aristotelian Library, 1948), p. 58.

67. Ferster, *Chaucer on Interpretation*, p. 35.

68. For some recent views on the "Retraction," see James Dean, "Dismantling the Canterbury Book," *PMLA* 100 (1985): 746–62; David F. Marshall, "Unmasking the Last Pilgrim: How and Why Chaucer Used the Retraction to Close *The Canterbury Tales*," *Christianity and Literature* 31 (1982): 55–74; Gale C. Schricker, "On the Relation of Fact and Fiction in Chaucer's Poetic Endings," *Philological Quarterly* 60 (1981): 13–27; Douglas Wurtele, "The Penitence of Geoffrey Chaucer," *Viator* 11 (1980): 335–59.

69. In Boccaccio's *Teseida*, Chaucer's source for the "Knight's Tale," it is Arcite's experience after death that is described in terms of a journey into

space. Interestingly, Chaucer transfers the passage in presenting Arcite's death from the Knight's Tale to the end of the *Troilus*. See the note to lines 1807–27 in Benson, *Riverside Chaucer*, p. 1057.

70. Harley, "Maps, Knowledge, and Power," pp. 300–1.
71. Earlier versions of this essay were presented at meetings of the International Congress of Medieval Studies (1985), the American Library Association (1986), the Rocky Mountain Medieval and Renaissance Society (1987), and the Modern Language Association (1988), and at a lecture at Wake Forest University (1987). I would like to thank Brent Allison for his help in my initial cartographic explorations, Seamus Deane, Heather Dubrow, Duncan Harris, and Gregory Blake Smith for their tough and intelligent readings, and especially Julia Bolton Holloway for originally suggesting the possibility of a connection between *mappae mundi* and Theseus's amphitheater.

Geographies of Desire:

Orientalism in Chaucer's *Legend of Good Women*

SHEILA DELANY

The construction of woman as Other would seem the obvious target in a work so fitly titled for that purpose as the *Legend of Good Women* (1386). Elsewhere[1] I have argued that the socio-literary construction of gender is what Chaucer aims to deconstruct in his *Legend*, through a variety of rhetorical means and in the service of an ultimate (that is, historically unattainable but nonetheless "true") genderlessness such as that offered by St. Paul in his remonstrance to the Galatians, or by Augustine in his vision of the resurrection:

> There is neither Jew nor Greek, there is neither slave nor free, there is neither male nor female; for you are all one in Jesus Christ.
>
> (GALATIANS 3:28)

> For my part, they seem to be wiser who make no doubt that both sexes shall rise [at resurrection]. For there shall be no lust, which is now the cause of confusion. From those bodies, then, vice shall be withdrawn, while nature shall be preserved. And the sex of a woman is not a vice, but nature. It shall then indeed be superior to carnal intercourse and child-bearing; nevertheless the female members shall remain adapted not to the old uses but to a new beauty, which, so far from provoking lust, now extinct, shall excite praise to the wisdom and clemency of God, who both made what was not and delivered from corruption what He made.
>
> (CITY OF GOD, 22.17)

This essay first appeared in *Chaucer Yearbook* 1 (1992): 1–32. Reprinted by permission of the Edwin Mellen Press.

What I want to propose in this paper is another target than woman for the construction of otherness in the *Legend*: the foreigner, specifically the Middle Eastern, non-European Mediterranean or northern African foreigner, inhabiting what was called in Chaucer's day, and still is often called, "the Orient." I am indebted in this project to the provocative work of Edward Said, who distinguishes three meanings for the term *Orientalism*. The first, the academic study of the Orient from whatever disciplinary perspective, is relevant to my discussion to the extent it provides evidence for my reading of Chaucer. The second or "imaginative" meaning—"a style of thought based upon an ontological and epistemological distinction made between 'the Orient' and (most of the time) 'the Occident' "[2]—will accommodate most poets, including Chaucer. Further, though, I also want to claim Said's third definition— "a Western style for dominating, restructuring and having authority over the Orient" (p. 3)—for the fourteenth century, although Said (following Michel Foucault's notion of a discourse) located the starting point of this meaning as the late eighteenth century. It's doubtful whether meanings two and three really can be separated: whether the ontological/epistemological uses of the Orient can exist without accompanying and even generative material basis in colonialism (the Greeks in Asia Minor, Romans in North Africa, etc.). The concept is "historically and materially defined" in the late Middle Ages—which, in the Crusades, certainly had its "institution for dealing with the Orient" (p. 3).

Though I can't in the scope of this short paper fully display a medieval discourse on Orientalism, I hope at least to sketch its contours, and to show its operation in a fourteenth-century English courtly poem about love and gender. As we will see, the two versions of otherness—gender and geography—reinforce one another, though not necessarily in mechanical or predictable ways.

Let me begin, then, with material and institutional definition: land, commodities, social organization.

Joshua Prawer has articulated the colonial character of the European military presence in Palestine—*outremer*, the Holy Land, the Latin Kingdom of Jerusalem, won by Europeans in the First Crusade in 1099 and reconquered by the Muslims in 1291. This presence had broader motives than the doubtless sincere desire to salvage heathen souls and save one's own, even broader than the ambition of nobles and of ecclesiastical administrators to acquire fertile estates abroad or of the servile to gain their freedom there. The Orient included, for example, numerous Mediterranean port cities that opened "the Moslem hinterland to European penetration and inversely [brought] . . . a flow of Eastern wares to the European marts and fairs across the Alps"[3] from as far away as India, Africa and south-east Asia. As a market, the Orient took textiles and clothing, furs and leather, pearls, timber, iron and tin, metalwork of various kinds whether ornamental or armorial (along with wool, a British specialty for centuries), slaves (from non-Christian Slavic populations) and a great deal of hard currency. Pilgrimage was also, of course, major export business, especially lucrative for money-lenders, shipbuilders, seamen, hostellers and suppliers. As a resource the Orient gave oils, honey and wax, citrus and other fruits, wines, textiles (silks, brocades, cottons), ivory, glassware, dyes (used in painting as well as in the textile industry), grains, spices and especially sugar.

Socially, institutionally, the Crusades had a profound effect on European society; even for the Church they were more than a spiritual exercise. Christopher Tyerman writes of the lucrative crusade finance market, in which some ecclesiastical establishments had, by the thirteenth century, "emerged as major institutions of capitalist enterprise, acting as banker and financers as well as territorial empire builders."[4] The widespread desire to sell or mortgage in order to finance crusade created something like a real-estate boom in the thirteenth century, with what Tyerman calls "cut-throat competition" among lay and ecclesiastical purchasers to acquire available properties. The alienation of lands also created assorted problems for disinherited offspring and disendowed wives, who often had to pursue their rights in court.

There were other institutional consequences. A range of new taxes, with the necessary administrative apparatus (i.e., bureaucrats), came into being to support the Crusades. Privileges conferred upon the *crucesignatus* included exemption from interest, immunity from taxation and from court summonses, a debt moratorium, and protection for his family: nor were these privileges dependent upon immediate departure.

But let's bring generalities (material though they are) down to the particular. How important would the Orient be to an English courtier-civil servant of the late fourteenth century? Would it not seem remote to the point of utter irrelevance? And were the Crusades not already obsolete both as an ideal and as a military phenomenon?

In fact, Aziz Atiya describes the fourteenth century as "the age of the later Crusade in its fuller sense . . . the real age of propaganda for the Crusade."[5] This is because the military expansion of the Islamic Ottoman empire was taken very seriously indeed in Europe. As Thomas J. Hatton observed, "Europe buzzed with plans, preparations and half-hearted efforts to launch still another great expedition to the Holy Land. The need was real."[6] If England was not directly threatened by this expansion, some of its allies were. Though the major confrontations would occur in the 1390s, nonetheless there was plenty of concern and action during the preceding decade, when Chaucer played an active, if minor, diplomatic role in his country's international politics, and when the *Legend* was composed.

Certainly a very keen sense of east–west dynamic is revealed in the Monk's Tale, which has four of the five uses in all of Chaucer's work of the word *orient* (the other is in the Knight's Tale, 1494). Moreover, all four occur in context of Roman colonialism. Cenobia arouses the wrath of imperial Rome by conquering many kingdoms

> In the orient, with many a fair citee
> Apertenaunt unto the magestee
> Of Rome . . . (VII.2314–16),

while Caesar's rival Pompey is no less than thrice characterized as a campaigner in the "orient" (2681, 2685, 2693), with Caesar himself "the conqueror, / That wan al th'occident" (2673–74).

Given events of the day and Chaucer's role at court, it can scarcely surprise that the poet should incorporate into his work an awareness of the east-west confrontation threatening Europe. Nonetheless, as is often the cause with medieval authorial attitudes, particularly Chaucer's, the question of specific response is not clear-cut. I would endorse Paul Olson's observation that "Typically Chaucer does not lay into contemporary figures or social figures with an obvious jab. . . . Rather he circles the problem";[7] it is that circling we may observe in the uses of the Orient in the *Legend*.

Throughout the 1340s there were battles against the Turks, chiefly by Italians. A key date was 1353, when the Turks seized Gallipoli on the Hellespont and entered Europe. During the 1370s they took control in the Balkans, and in 1389 reached the Danube. All during the 1360s there were appeals for military help from rulers directly threatened by the Turkish onslaught: from the King of Hungary; from Constantinople; from the King of Cyprus and Jerusalem, Pierre de Lusignan.

The latter toured Europe trying to organize a crusade; he visited the English court in 1363–64 (a time for which we have no records of Chaucer's whereabouts). Lusignan managed to organize a temporarily victorious attack on Alexandria in 1365, in which he was assisted by a company of English knights. This event was commemorated in *La Prise d'Alexandrie* by Guillaume de Machaut, whose poetry Chaucer knew well and often imitated. It appears also in Chaucer's Monk's Tale, of which a stanza is devoted to

> worthy Petro, kyng of Cipre . . .
> That Alisandre wan by heigh maistrie, (VII.2391–98)

and again in Chaucer's description of his Knight, who is said to have participated in the battle of Alexandria and in numerous others, both with and against the Muslims, from the 1340s through the 1360s in Spain, Turkey and Morocco (Prol., 51–66).[8] We may note too—extending the geographical range—that the Wife of Bath has traveled to Jerusalem thrice (Prol., 463).

Among Lusignan's strongest proponents was Philippe de Mézières, former chancellor of the kingdom of Cyprus and, after the assassination of Lusignan in 1369, tutor to the young Charles VI of France. For four decades, Mézières propagandized the regaining of Jerusalem, and to that end he founded the Order of the Passion of Jesus Christ Crucified. He circulated documents calling for international support to the Order in 1368, 1384 and throughout the 1390s, winning twenty-two members from England.[9] Among them was Chaucer's friend and fellow-diplomat Lewis Clifford, who acted as intermediary between Chaucer and his admirer at the French court, Eustache Deschamps.

Another guest at the English court was Leo VI, King of Armenia. Expelled by the Mamelukes, who controlled Egypt and, intermittently, Palestine and Syria, Leo was in England in 1384–85—that is, just before the composition of the *Legend*. His aim was to forge a European alliance that would launch a crusade; this is why Mézières writes, in his *Songe du Vieux Pelerin* (1389), of "ladicte paix . . . par le tresvaillant Lyon, roy d'Armenie diligemment traictee et poursuite."[10] Leo's visit provoked what May McKisack calls "a glaring example of royal recklessness," for Richard II bestowed on Leo "lavish gifts and entertainment and an annual pension of £1000." She adds that according to one chronicler, the king

> was so liberal that he gave to all who asked him, dissipating the revenues of his crown so that he was forced to recoup himself by taxing his people.[11]

Following hard upon Leo's stay in England came the well-known Scrope-Grosvenor trial of 1385–86, in which Chaucer was called to testify. This was an armorial dispute over who had the right to display a certain heraldic figure. Tyerman observed that "at least fourteen individual crusaders either testified or were mentioned, their exploits of the previous twenty-five years stretching from Egypt to Lithuania" (p. 259), and Maurice Keen has proposed this collective dossier as Chaucer's model for his Knight.[12]

The official English policy toward the Crusades was not, in the 1380s, particularly supportive. (Richard II was a crusade enthusiast, but his major plans in this area—an Anglo-French project to repel the Ottomans and recover Palestine—did not commence until the 1390s.) In the late thirteenth and early fourteenth centuries, English kings had several times expropriated for their own use moneys raised by the papacy to fund crusades, and after 1336 no new mandatory crusade taxes were levied by the papacy in England (Tyerman, p. 253). It was consistent with the anti-papal and nationalistic policies of Edward III that, in contrast with the French, he declined to finance crusades even though individuals were permitted to do so themselves; hence English crusaders of the fourteenth century were privately financed through loans, mortgages or gifts, though by 1378 crusade bequests and legacies had virtually disappeared as a means of funding.[13] Indeed, Philippe de Mézières took the opportunity in his *Songe* (1.76–78) bitterly to denounce the English for (among other things) sabotaging French efforts to regain the Holy Land.

Yet despite the hands-off attitude of Edward III, and despite some criticism of the movement, recent scholars generally agree that both the theory and practise of crusade continued to enjoy a great deal of prestige in Chaucer's day:

> The crusade was very much in men's minds in England, and was a live issue in political society, among the highest and most influential in the realm, in the late 1380s and the 1390s. . . . Plenty of men went on crusade. (Keen, p. 57)

> Clearly it would be wrong to regard the crusade in the fourteenth century as an unpopular movement. There was a broadly based acceptance of the crusade . . . though criticism of what was happening in practise continued to be vociferous. (Housley, p. 239)

> Opposition to crusading was by no means widespread, and criticism of the ideal was even rarer. The crusade remained a practical and far-from-amateurish concern throughout the century. (Tyerman, p. 288)

Indeed, extremely practical. England may have taken a far less active role in regaining the Holy Land than could satisfy Philippe de Mézières, but it did nonetheless plan and launch two crusades of its own between 1382 and 1386, just preceding the composition of the *Legend*. These were quite similar campaigns, both of them designated "crusades"—equally opportunistically— by the Roman Pope Urban II because they targeted opponents of his, who professed loyalty to the rival pope in Avignon, Clement VII.

It is important to remember the decisive and disruptive impact in public life at every level that the crusade designation would carry. It meant sermons constantly preached for crusade, a national and multi-pronged fund-raising effort, new taxes and levies, the interruption of commercial shipping, and recruitment of armies (together with the popular protests provoked by these measures).

One of these campaigns was the May, 1383 invasion of Flanders: the crusade of Henry Despenser, Bishop of Norwich. Nominally its purpose was to ensure that the French did not force Flanders to support Clement. Richard Vaughan discerns an economic motive: to maintain free passage for English wool, which had been embargoed by the Count of Flanders.[14] J. J. N. Palmer sees instead a political motive: to use Flanders as a wedge against the French in the ongoing ("Hundred Years") war.[15] A distinctive feature of this crusade was the gross abuse of plenary indulgence: in return for contributions to the crusade, Urban offered full remission of sins for both living and dead. This offer contributed to what McKisack calls "the prevailing mood of national hysteria"; she writes of "the avidity with which the credulous of all classes, men and more especially women, sought to buy the plenary remissions" (p. 431). Olson suggests that the abusive ecclesiastical practises of this campaign are reflected in the Pardoner's Tale; he notes too that Chaucer's Squire—who has learned chivalry in Flanders—has evidently participated in it (pp. 203–7).

The campaign was a disgrace and a disaster in which cowardice, indiscipline and dysentery all played a part; Vaughan cites a chronicler who grimly joked that "percussit eos Deus in posteriora" (p. 29). The commander, Bishop Despenser, was impeached by Parliament and several captains were tried for treasonous surrender.

The other English crusade of the early 1380s was the political adventure in Castile planned for 1383 by John of Gaunt, Duke of Lancaster. It was not his first attempt to intervene in the dynastic affairs of that region, for ten years earlier John—in pursuit of his own claim to the Castilian throne—had led a campaign there which "has been rightly regarded, by all those who have described it, as one of the outstanding failures in Lancaster's chequered career as a military commander."[16] Negotiations for settlement dragged on through the 1370s, and by the early 1380s there was significant support in Parliament and in government for peace, despite John's intention to mount an expedition against Castile in 1383. In March of that year Pope Urban VI appointed John "standard-bearer of the Church in the coming crusade against the Trastamaran schismatics" (Russell, 348), for the Trastamaran ruler of Castile supported the Avignon Pope and was thus guilty of "the Clementist heresy." Although the plan eventually failed, nonetheless some English troops were dispatched to Spain, and it is not difficult to imagine that the cynically political deployment of crusade rhetoric must have been evident to many observers.

This was not, however, the end of the matter: once again, in 1385, the *chemin d'Espaigne* was brought to Parliament. This time the project was unanimously accepted, and by February 1386 "vast and widely publicized preparations were being made" (Russell, 408). These included the official propagation of crusade in England, fund-raising, a tournament at Smithfield at which Richard II presented John with a golden crown in anticipation of his coronation in Spain, and the arrest of commercial ships for diversion to the military campaign. (One can imagine the indignation of an experienced customs officer like Chaucer, whose twelve years in the post ended in 1386.) The invasion took place in July 1386; it ended two years later when John of Gaunt abandoned his claim to the Castilian throne in exchange for a large compensatory payment and the betrothal of his daughter Catalina to his former enemy. "Nor," as Russell remarks, "apparently, was his conscience greatly troubled by the thought that his daughter would be the bride of a heretic" (509), although the irritated Pope did eventually revoke all acts performed under his sponsorship of the ill-fated "crusade."

Crusade was thus a rather complex phenomenon in England just before 1386, composed as it was of grandiose schemes proposed by foreigners against the infidel in distant Arabic lands, and cynical adventures against other European Christians which had little effect besides draining the national treasury, already stressed by the war against France. That, at least, is how an ironically minded civil servant might have seen it, and I want to suggest that in the *Legend* Orientalism becomes a rhetorical device enabling Chaucer to do two things: to create a moral structure in the poem, and to offer veiled commentary on some aspects of English foreign policy. It becomes his negative pole, for certain qualities or behaviors associated with easterners become paradigmatic of flaws and vices which, while not confined to easterners, are nonetheless exemplified most dramatically in them, and certainly most memorably insofar as these figures are the stuff of western literary tradition.

As such, might not their presence in the *Legend* represent nothing more complicated than Chaucer's fidelity to his classical sources? Perhaps, but there are strong arguments to the contrary. Chaucer's freedom in altering his sources for political or other purposes is well known. Moreover, some of the stories—Dido, Cleopatra, the Roman Lucretia—already had blatantly political purpose, whether colonial or domestic. Finally, the prominence of Orientalist and crusade concerns at the English court during the several years preceding the composition of the *Legend*, especially the "crusades" of the magnates Despenser and Lancaster, precludes, I believe, a merely innocent or coincidental use of Oriental figures and themes.

As will be evident in what follows, the Oriental theme does not run consistently from start to finish of the work. I have not found it in the Prologue, in any substantial way, for instance, although some of the ladies named there in the balade—Helen,[17] Lavinia, Cleopatra—do come to Chaucer from literary works heavily laden with colonialist intent. The theme tends rather to surface intermittently in several of the legends.

Cleopatra

To begin his series, as Chaucer does, with Cleopatra is, first, overtly to undercut his numenous sponsors' demand for "good" women.[18] Second, it displaces the called-for theme of love with that of politics and the social order, specifically of colonialism gone soft. The cluster of images and concepts with which this first legend opens includes, in its first eight lines: king, governance, reigning queen, senator, conquering, realms and honor, custom, and having the world at one's obedience. After this opening movement setting a political theme, the hero is introduced: Antony, the "senatour" who is "sent . . . For to conqueren regnes and honour / Unto . . . Rome" (584–85). He does everything wrong. As a member of the ruling elite he becomes "Rebel unto the toun of Rome" (591); as a husband he abandons his wife; as a tactician he mortally offends Caesar, whose sister his wife is (592); as moral being he becomes not only an adulterer but a bigamist (594, 615).[19]

Antony does only one thing right: he is a very perfect gentle lover in the courtly style. So absolutely committed is he to his beloved that "al the world he sette at no value" (602); he is willing to die in her defense (602) and—best of all—the dependency bond is reciprocated (607). Chaucer underscores the erotic intensity of their love by inserting several tried and true phrases from the tradition of courtly lyric and romance: "desert . . . chyvalrye . . . gentilesse . . . discrecioun and hardynesse . . . And she was fayr as is the rose in May" (608–13). (This last phrase describing a swarthy North African queen must have evoked some little sense of irony in the keenly color-conscious medieval reader.[20]) We see that one can be an excellent lover and terrible at everything else, for erotic intensity certifies nothing at all. It can coexist with a wide range of moral deficiencies or even crimes; its standards can be met by immoral people. All that remains to Antony as a public person is his courage in battle, and this will be lost with his defeat at the battle of Actium—the "endlessly exemplary Actium," as Michel Foucault calls it[21]—after which he commits suicide.

Of what is Actium here exemplary? Here and elsewhere in the *Legends* it is the debilitating or depoliticizing effect of foreigners, Orientals, that I want to notice: their ability to distract a hero from his (in this case explicitly colonial) mission, generally through sensual and erotic pleasures. This sensuality could even corrode empires, according to Augustine, for just when "the Romans lived with greatest virtue and concord," the proconsul Manlius

> introduced into Rome the luxury of Asia, more destructive than all hostile armies. It was then that iron bedsteads and expensive carpets were first used; then, too, that female singers were admitted at banquets, and other licentious abominations were introduced. (*City of God*, 3.21)

The image of an enervating eastern sensuality against a properly masculine western energy, already ancient by the high Middle Ages, was reinforced when the Crusaders encountered eastern habits such as frequent bathing, the wearing of perfumes and make-up by men, the heavy use of spices in cooking, the abundance of jewelry worn by men and women.[22]

The story of Cleopatra is thus the other side of the coin to the romantic exoticism represented in the Squire's Tale. The Orient is no longer a realm of fantasy fulfilled but one of hope and ambition undone, for the Chaucerian version is a cautionary tale if ever there was one. But what does it caution against, or for?

Different possibilities exist. Terry Jones argues, correctly, that crusade was not officially approved of in England despite the participation of English knights in exotic campaigns. The reason, he suggests, is that the major focus of English foreign policy was the war against France, and then the defense of England's Scottish border. Perhaps, then, the Knight's adventures abroad show a less than patriotic commitment. Similarly, Alison's gadding about, even to holy places, might be suspect: need one go so far to show one's faith? It is a question the Wycliffites posed continually in their critique of pilgrimage. By this token Antony might be considered a negative exemplum in deserting his country for sybaritic pleasures and egoistic exploits abroad. His sad story might provide a very timely and distinctively English admonition against costly military adventures abroad—adventures such as those exhorted in the name of faith by Philippe de Mézières, or undertaken for profit by John of Gaunt. Even the above-cited reference in the Monk's Tale to "worthy Petro" could be ironic, for Lusignan was "notoriously immoral," had committed "deeds of the grossest cruelty," had incurred papal and episcopal censure and had broken feudal contract with his barons (Coopland, *Songe*, p. 64).

On the other hand, official—that is, royal and parliamentary—approval isn't necessarily the whole story. If Maurice Keen is right to assert that the number and status of persons taking up the banner in Chaucer's day made it impossible for crusade to look obsolete or disreputable, then the Orientalism shown in this and other legends might tend to affirm British or European aspirations abroad. Antony would still be a negative exemplum, of course, but the tactic would be to show the eastern adversary at its most alluring and therefore most dangerous. Thus the story might encourage not total abandonment of the crusade ideal but rather control of it, with the proper firmness abroad: a "Desert Storm" type of strategy.

Deciding between these positions is not simple. Nor does Hatton's hypothesis—that the Knight's Tale reflects the ultimately unachieved reconquest programme of Mézières—necessarily imply a positive attitude toward Orientalist projects. If Chaucer thought such plans unrealistic or fanatical (as some did), then the ironic or negative reading, for which there is ample grounding, would be appropriate.

It does seem to me that there is little in the conduct of the traveling heroes of the *Legend* to recommend foreign exploits. Yet if the *Legend*'s male figures do not provide a clearly virtuous standard of behavior, neither do they constitute an evidently or consistently villainous one. An aspect of Chaucer's above-mentioned attempt to collapse gender distinctions is precisely his representation of shared and equal folly. Cleopatra is reciprocally tempted by Antony; she loses as much as he does; she too abdicates her social responsibility as monarch in sheer subjective self-indulgence; she is far from lacking in courage. This is, therefore, a story of equals, a story without a victim.

Perhaps the Chaucerian point is that there is an "Oriental" tendency in all of us, which must be tamed if it can't be rooted out. (Surely Augustine himself, the North African latecomer to Christianity, is a prime instance of this ongoing effort.) To say as much is to acknowledge a very deep-rooted Orientalism: Said's definition two. For if, as Said claims, "European culture gained in strength and identity by setting itself off against the Orient as a sort of surrogate and even underground self" (p. 3), then the Oriental seducer or villain is an externalized aspect of the (European) self, and the east–west dynamic, in its literary representation, becomes a form of self-exploration in the interest of self-control. But not, after all, only *self*-control, for to be able to represent the unruly or the transgressive as Oriental is already to imply the desire to control the real Orient, a desire expressed not only in literary texts but, as indicated above, in social institutions.

Piramus and Thisbe

Chaucer's second legend is also an Oriental tale, as Ovid reminds us in the opening of his version (*Met.* 4.55–58), the main source of Chaucer's.[23] The setting is Babylon, specified in both texts as the city whose baked-brick walls were built by queen Semiramis. The eastern location is important to the ideological structure of the *Metamorphoses*, which, we recall, super-patriotically ends with the apotheosis and stellification of Caesar. Though there may well be irony in this ending, still the ebb and flow of Oriental ideas is very much in evidence in the Thisbe portion of the text. The tale occurs in a series exchanged by the daughters of Minyas. They, worshippers of Athena, are boycotting the festival of Asian Bacchus that has taken all the other women away from their proper domestic duties and off into the streets and woods. The Minyades stay indoors and spin, meanwhile telling cautionary tales of Oriental sensuality and excessive passion. Thus the narrators demonstrate the virtuous gender-behavior which their female character will fatally flout when she wanders into the woods to meet her lover. If Ovid has the Minyades transformed into bats because of their failure to acknowledge the power of Bacchus, this is his indirect critique of the repressive Augustan morality the tale itself overtly supports. The metamorphosis does not, in any case, alter the east–west conflict of values.

Babylon can scarcely portend any good to an author steeped, as Chaucer was, in the scriptural-Augustinian tradition. There Babylon is enemy of the chosen people and predecessor of Rome as archetypal city of man (cf. *City of God*, 18). It is in the patristic tradition too that Semiramis, formerly a much-honored military leader, becomes a prototype of feminine erotic evil: usurping man's prerogative to rule, murdering her husband to do so, committing incest with her son, and, in some texts, inventing trousers as female attire.[24] In the Man of Law's Tale, Chaucer gives us a closer view of such a figure: the Sultan's mother, who so far transgresses the bounds of femininity that she no longer qualifies as a woman. She is "feyned womman . . . serpent under femynynite . . . Virago"—and "Semyrame the secounde" (359–63). The polarities of Occident versus Orient and Christian law versus pagan law make up a basic structural principle in the Man of Law's Tale, and I think we may see it as developing ideas latent in the *Legend*.[25]

Although there is no western pole in the legend of Thisbe, the tale is already sufficiently defined by its context to make its point about the hazards of unbridled eroticism and unnecessary adventures abroad. Where "Cleopatra" makes that point in the arena of international politics, "Thisbe" domesticates it: she gives up no kingdom nor crosses the sea, but she disobeys her parents to wander from home at night. So, of course, does Piramus: again there is no victim, no disloyalty, but a double death freely chosen on both sides. The republican and humanist Boccaccio had already interpreted this medieval Romeo-and-Juliet as a warning against parental interference in adolescent love in the *De Claris Mulieribus* (c. 1360):

> Wicked Fortune sinned, as perhaps did their wretched parents. Certainly the ardor of the young should be curbed slowly, lest by wishing to oppose them with sudden impediments we drive them to despair and perdition. The passion of desire is without temperance, and it is almost a pestilence and fury in youth. We should tolerate it patiently . . . etc.[26]

For the courtier Chaucer, though—who held the lucrative wardship of two young men's marriages and had three offspring of his own—the pathetic Oriental tale maintains its original Ovidian purpose. The outcome affirms, after all, the wisdom of parents who protect their daughters "lest they diden som folye" (723). In Chaucer's hands humor or obscenity may neutralize pathos but not morality nor prudence. If the story—however amusing or pathetic— suggests that adventures far from home rarely turn out well, this is a sentiment with international as well as strictly domestic weight.

Dido and Aeneas

Another aspect of medieval Orientalism was the sexual immorality and "unnatural" behavior often attached to societies of the ancient Near and Middle East. Said gives several instances from Flaubert and other modern writers (e.g., p. 103). For the Middle Ages this immorality was a stock theme, carried in numerous ways. Some writers claimed that Muhammad devised a "plan of general sexual license as an instrument for the destruction of Christendom."[27] Some scholars glossed Mecca as "Mecha, id est adultera," playing on the Latin word *moecha*;[28] others explained the Islamic Friday holy day as due to the Muslims' worship of Venus, whose day Friday is.[29] Numerous lives of Muhammad carried the theme: in popular French poems, in chronicles of Spain or the Holy Land, in crusade histories, Dante commentaries, world-histories, or a *Roman de Mahomet*, they portrayed the founder of Islam as a sensualist, a lecher, an adulterer with eleven or twelve wives, innumerable mistresses and the virility of thirty men. For others the offense lay in the ancient royal institution of dynastic incest said by various authorities to have characterized Persian, Armenian and Egyptian society.[30] While incest plays no specific role in any of Chaucer's Oriental tales, he does have the Man of Law cite incest as the poet's reason for refusing to tell the stories of Canace or Antiochus. Though rejecting "swiche unkynde abhomynaciouns" (Man of Law's Tale, 88) as narrative material, Chaucer shows us that it was part of his general frame of reference about the Orient.

Some authorities believed that the Qur'an authorized anal intercourse with women, and intercourse during menstruation.[31] Moreover, the actual Islamic sanction of polygyny, of divorce or repudiation of wives, of extra-marital relations with slaves, and of prostitution ("temporary marriage" with a fee for the middleman, a practice continuing into the present) contributed to western perceptions of "the special lubricity of Muslims" (Daniel, 145). Nor were these perceptions limited to Muslims, but were generalized as "Oriental" attitudes.

In Chaucer's third legend, the hero and heroine are two of a kind: both of them worthy people with an impressive history, yet both of them deeply flawed, intensely self-indulgent, manipulative—and Oriental.

The figure Aeneas comes to Chaucer compromised in several ways. One is the conflict between the Virgilian and the Ovidian version of his behavior toward Dido: Chaucer had already confronted this disjunction in the *House of Fame*. Another is the Orientalist tradition about his culture, for Phrygia (Troy) was often represented as the site of debilitating sensuality and, more particularly, of effeminacy. This is adumbrated in the *Aeneid* when Dido's suitor Iarbus refers contemptuously to "Paris, with his semi-male retinue, oily-haired" (4.215–16: "Paris, cum semiviro comitatu . . . crinemque madentem"), or Turnus dismisses Aeneas as "half-male Trojan" (12.99: "semiviris Phrygis"). The idea persisted in medieval poetry and scholarship. When Ovid calls Paris a "Phrygian man" ("Phrygio viro," *Ars*, 1.54), this is glossed by a commentator as "Frigio. Trojana. vel debili. vel effeminatio."[32] In the *Roman d'Enéas* the accusation of homosexuality is used by Lavinia's mother to dissuade her daughter from the match with Aeneas. It is a long passage (8565–8621) full of explicit terminology ("traïtor," "sodomite") and obscene pun ("il n'aime pas poil de conin"); it uses cultural slander ("an ce sont Troïen nourri") and invokes the law of nature ("contre nature," "la natural cople").[33] In a non-literary context, the association of Oriental societies with homosexuality was helped along by papal propaganda justifying a Christian presence in Muslim lands with the story of Sodom and Gomorrah (Genesis 19). This well-known Biblical locus, usually interpreted as punishment for the sin of sodomy, was used by Pope Innocent IV as a model for Christian intervention against infidels, who inevitably violated natural law.[34]

Though the Chaucerian Aeneas is not shown to be homosexual, he is in a sense "effeminate" in spirit: far from sturdy in adversity. On arriving in Carthage, Aeneas is devastated to discover the fate of his people portrayed on a temple wall. He weeps aloud, wishing himself dead: "Allas, that I was

born! . . . No longer for to lyven I ne kepe" (1027–32). This is already unlike
the Virgilian hero, who weeps at the pictures but, like a proper leader, exhorts
his companion Achates to "be free of fear; this story will bring you some
good yet" (1.463: "solve metus; feret haec aliquam tibi fama salutem").

Heroic expectations continue to crumble when the hero and heroine are
brought together. Rhetorically, the anaphoric "and" (in eight out of eleven
lines, 1061–71) suggests—as it did with Criseyde (*Troilus*, II.449–69 or
II.1300 ff.)—the search for "an heep of weyes" of justification for desire.
Dido likes Aeneas not only for his story (as Desdemona would like Othello)
but for his looks as well. Moreover,

> for he was a straunger, somwhat she
> Likede hym the bet, as, God do bote,
> To som folk ofte newe thyng is sote. (1075–77)

She is, we see, vulnerable to appearance and newfangledness. Later Dido
will describe her motives this way: "For that me thynketh he is so wel
ywrought, / and ek so likly for to ben a man" (1173–74): motives scarcely
more elevated than those of a giddy adolescent.

At first, the queen's provisioning of Aeneas's fleet is no more than the
generous hospitality one would expect of a monarch—hospitality, perhaps,
such as had recently been displayed when Richard II welcomed Leo of
Armenia. Is it over-generous? The tell-tale anaphoric "And" (five times in
eight lines, 1090–97) again duplicates the piling up of goods and of reasons.
Aeneas thinks he has "come to paradys" (1103), and, with its spicery and
wines, its music and "amorous lokyng," its "riche beddes and . . . orne-
mentes," it certainly seems to be an Islamic paradise he has in mind.

In the next section, eight consecutive lines (1115–22) begin with "Ne,"
listing all the gifts Dido bestows upon Aeneas: not only hospitality but
horses, jewels, falcons, hounds, sacks of gold, cups of gold, and a great deal
of money. This money is a particularly discordant and distasteful note, for it
signals that Dido is engaged in a game of sexual and material power, attempting to buy the man she desires. Aeneas is her kept man: "And al is payed,
what that he hath spent" (1125). She gives too much materially, just as she
will shortly give too much of herself physically and emotionally. Chaucer has
Aeneas acknowledge the economic dimension when the narrator comments,

> Now laugheth Eneas and is in joye
> And more richesse than evere he was in Troye. (1252–53)

But this sexual economics will backfire, for paradoxically Dido sets herself up as victim by the too-generous giving; she allows herself to be used,

represents herself as "easy." The passivity which is the heart of her aggressive giving comes clear in Dido's interview with her sister. Twice she claims to hand over her life to Aeneas (1176, 1181), and she begs her sister to decide for her: "if that ye rede it me, / I wolde fayn to hym ywedded be" (1178–79). The moral abdication apparent here becomes general at the end, when Dido abandons her social responsibility as leader of Carthage in order to indulge her personal disappointment by committing suicide. Meanwhile, victim to her own subjectivity, Dido chooses to believe that she is wedded to Aeneas, though Chaucer's treatment of this topic, like Virgil's, makes it clear that the marriage exists only in her febrile imagination.[35]

As for Aeneas, we can scarcely trust him either. The Narrator assures us of the hero's dishonesty (1264–1302), then gives us the hero's dream of Mercury—which motivates his departure—only in the hero's verbal account of it, not, as in Virgil, on the diegetic level where we can see it for ourselves. This puts Aeneas's dream in the same category as Dido's pregnancy (1323): possibly true, possibly a hope or mistake, possibly a lie and desperate last resort. The detail of the pregnancy is imitated from Ovid, where it is equally ambiguous. "Forsitan," Ovid begins his sentence about the pregnancy: perhaps (*Her.*, 7.133). But this possibility creates a double bind. If it is false, then Dido is a liar. If it is true, she is a double murderer.

The despair felt by Aeneas at the beginning is acted out by Dido at the end. Less committed than Antony and Cleopatra, less innocent than Piramus and Thisbe, neither Aeneas nor Dido acquits him or herself admirably. Between these two Oriental figures there is little to choose, trapped as they are in their "own" subjectivity: that is, in traditions which incarnate the subjectivity of authors.

Hypsiplye, Medea and Jason

Jason is a questing hero from northern Greece who encounters two women on islands near Turkey. Though the actual distances are not extremely great, they sufficed to enable many writers to construct a typical Oriental motif: the hero from a relatively civilized (often western) place and with a mission, detained by a woman in a less civilized (often eastern) place. For when the *Argo* arrives from Greece, the women of Lemnos (according to tradition) couple with the treasure-seekers; some accounts claim that Hercules had to force his shipmates back to their duty. The Tegernsee commentary on Ovid's Epistle of Hypsipyle (*Heroides*, 6) says that Jason dallied and had frequently to be reminded of his mission.[36] As for Medea, her primitivism and provinciality are usually stressed: she is a sorceress in an outlying island. In *Heroides* Hypsipyle scornfully describes Medea as a barbarian (6.19, 81), and Medea herself deplores the fact that Jason considers her a barbarian (12.105).

The Oriental women we have seen in the *Legend* so far—Cleopatra, Thisbe and Dido—all commit suicide. Unlike them, the two represented here turn their violence outward, and not merely in disappointment, for both of them are associated with distinctively gory events. The women of Lemnos "withdrew their untamed necks from the yoke of men" (as Boccaccio puts it: Guarini, p. 33) and massacred all the men on the island. They excepted only King Thoas, whose life was spared by his daughter Hypsipyle before she took the throne. Though Boccaccio duly praises Hypsiplye for her filial piety, there is no comment about her complicity in the massacre or her failure to intervene against it—indeed, true to his project of rewriting woman good, or at least better, he exonerates Hypsipyle from the mysterious death of her ward Archemorus. These events, however, are firmly associated with Hypsipyle in accounts by Statius and Guido delle Colonne (Chaucer's primary source), and Chaucer inserts a genuine viciousness into Hypsipyle's prayer that the woman who has stolen Jason from her may lose him, kill her children by him, and also kill any other woman who loves him (1571–75). As for Medea, she does, of course, fulfill this prayer; but even before being abandoned by Jason she has embezzled her father's wealth and dismembered her brother in order to assist Jason's escape. Afterward she conspires against her father-in-law, and attempts to poison the king of Athens: events related by Boccaccio in *De Claris Mulieribus*, in the Ovid-scholia and elsewhere.

This grisly and violent material is conspicuous by its absence from the Chaucerian version; yet perhaps it makes its way implicitly into the frequent gender-role reversals found in the legend. An instance of what I mean occurs in the opening apostrophic denunciation of Jason:

> Thow sly devourere and confusioun
> Of gentil wemen, tendre creatures,
> Thow madest thy recleymyng and thy lures
> To ladyes of thy statly aparaunce,
> And of thy wordes farced with plesaunce, etc. (1369–73)

As sly devourer of tender creatures, Jason would seem to be an animal: perhaps a bird of prey, or the false fox that appears further along in this mini-prologue (1389–93). The imagery then turns to that of falconry: to reclaim is to call back the hawk, usually after it has taken its prey; the lure is a contraption made of leather and feathers which can be shaken to imitate a bird and thus attract the hunting bird back to the falconer. Jason is now the falconer, and the bird of prey is his lady, whom he lures with his good looks and other attractions. In this image Jason remains the superior and controlling figure, but the lady is neither victim nor prey. She is herself, as hawk, a trained and responsive partner in a hunting team; indeed the one who, rather than the falconer, directly commits violence. In this and other subtle ways does Chaucer deconstruct the gender-stereotypes of desire, affirming that violence and brutality are not exclusively masculine behaviors, nor is being victimized an exclusively feminine fate.

Greek Jason is no gentleman, to be sure: greedy, ambitious and manipulative he is. But what he learns of barbarism is taught him by two Oriental women.

Philomela

With the legend of Philomela, seventh in his series of nine, Chaucer reverses the usual alignment of sex and place of origin. Rather than a western or highly civilized hero and a barbarian or marginally located temptress, we are given two Athenian princesses, the sisters Procne and Philomela, and a villain, Tereus, who is not exactly Greek. Tereus is lord of Thrace, a territory to the extreme north and east of Greece, just below the Balkans and including the Bosporus and Constantinople. Tereus is thus very nearly a Turk, and when he travels to Athens he is said to go "into Greece." Much is made of the sisters' dangerous distance from home and, implicitly, from civilized norms of behavior. As indicated earlier on, this part of the world was fairly close to European concerns in the late fourteenth century, for in 1361 the capital city of Thrace, Adrianople, was captured by the Turks. It became a new capital of the Islamic Ottoman Empire and a base for its expansion into Europe via the Balkans. In this sense Tereus is, of all the fools and villains in the *Legend*, the one most easily associated with contemporary events and the Turkish threat.

Certainly Tereus is the worst of them all: incestuous adulterer, liar, rapist and mutilator—cannibal too, if we look at the Ovidian ending, which Chaucer omits. So terrible is he that his story offers an opportunity for Chaucer's Narrator to contemplate the problem of evil in the world, in the form of a prayer for theodicy:

> Thow yevere of the formes, that hast wrought
> This fayre world and bar it in thy thought
> Eternaly er thow thy werk began,
> Why madest thow, unto the slaunder of man,
> Or, al be that it was nat thy doing,
> As for that fyn, to make swych a thyng,
> Whi sufferest thow that Tereus was bore . . . ? (2228–34)

There is not much explicit Christian reference in the *Legend*, so this prayer stands out; though cast in a Platonic formula[37] it addresses a deity recognizably Christian in its eternity and creativity. In content it resembles Dorigen's prayer in the Franklin's Tale (V.865–93) challenging God's creation of "grisly feendly rokkes blak" and their ability to destroy mankind: "Why han ye wroght this werk unresonable?" It is, of course, no mere rhetorical question but one with answers amply provided by Catholic theology. Thus Chaucer deftly reintroduces the orthodox Augustinian perspective, which (as I argue in *Naked Text*) provides a backdrop to the *Legends* as a whole. It is interesting and not, I suspect, coincidental that he should do it here, at a point where his material most nearly recalls the present threat from an alien ideology.

Not everything that Europe knew about the Orient was legendary or stereotypical. There were efforts of serious scholarly documentation which featured major contributions by English scholars. These efforts included two translations (into Latin) of the Qur'an, one of them by the English-born Robert Ketton; this was widely diffused throughout Europe and used in missionary work through the seventeenth century.[38] There were also translations of Arabic treatises in science, history, philosophy and biography, done by Robert and other English and continental scholars. Peter Alfons—a Spanish Jew who converted to Christianity in 1106 and who lived in England as physician to King Henry I—produced a fairly balanced portrait of Islam in his "Dialogue of Christian and Jew"; William of Malmesbury (c. 1120) emphasized the monotheistic character of Islam; the English monk Matthew Paris discussed Islam in his *Chronica Majora*, and, writes J. J. Saunders, "we are surprised more by the accuracy than by the distortions of his picture."[39]

Some of this work was sponsored by Peter the Venerable, abbot of Cluny, starting in 1141. His purpose was defensive and polemical, to be sure, but his tactic was to understand the enemy so as to convert him: an "intellectual crusade," as d'Alverny put it. The premise was that this enemy offered no bizarre gallimaufry of deities (such as is represented in the *Chanson de Roland*, where the pagans worship Apollo, Tervagan, Mahomet, Jupiter, and many other figures) but rather a monotheistic faith with an ethics and a high intellectual tradition of its own, a faith which could, for just those reasons, pose a genuinely attractive alternative to Christianity. It is telling that Peter referred to Islam not as heathen worship but as a "heresy," indeed as a compendium of all previous heresies, implying that it was a deviation from truth but nonetheless in the same family, as it were, with Christianity. Mark of Toledo, who translated the Qur'an some decades after Ketton, considered Islam a "legem tertiam" blending features of Judaism and Christianity. The famous debate of 1254 in Karakorum, Mongolia, between the Flemish Franciscan William of Rubroek and representatives of three Asian religions—Nestorian Christians, Buddhists and Muslims—was predicated on an assumption of rationality, and indeed William won the debate with the Muslims as his allies at many points. In Chaucer's century, *Mandeville's Travels* opined that

> be cause that thei gon so ny oure feyth thei ben lyghtly converted to cristene
> lawe whan men preche hem And schewen hem distynctly the lawe of Ihesu
> crist & whan men tellen hem of the prophecyes. (Chapter 16)

The similarities, beyond monotheism, are that Islam too is a revealed religion dependent on a sacred book, it too respects Moses and Jesus, it too has angels and saints and prophets.

The scholarly approach was as determined as any other to extirpate Islam, though preferably by persuasion than by force of arms. To that end, while no liberal or tolerant program, it did recognize the need for accuracy and for respect of the considerable virtues of Islam. This is not, however, the tradition that Chaucer chose to embody in his work. The Oriental theme was particularly available in the few years just preceding the composition of the *Legend* because of a confluence of episodes and of demands being made on English finances and foreign policy: the 1383 Despenser crusade; John of Gaunt's Spanish crusade project of 1383–86; the presence of Leo of Armenia at court in 1384–85; the 1384 propaganda campaign of Mézières; the Scrope-Grosvenor trial of 1385–86; the glamorous appeal of crusade to many English knights and nobles. Chaucerian Orientalism seems to revert to older attitudes: to a model at once patristic and vulgarized, one which maintained the idea of a sinister and insidious Orient, and which the poet was able to turn to the uses of subtle commentary on events of his own day.

Chaucer was able to deconstruct gender difference *sub specie aeternitatis*: Christianity gave him the way to do so. The same possibility did not exist for an alien ideology embodied in Orientals who, though exposed to Christian truth, rejected it. Woman isn't *eternally* Other; the infidel is.

Notes

1. In *The Naked Text: Chaucer's Legend of Good Women* (Berkeley) [1994]. The present discussion of Orientalism is also drawn from the book [especially pp. 164–86]. My summary of the Pauline–Augustinian position should not be taken to mean that I propose Chaucer was "woman's friend" (as Gavin Douglas would call him in the sixteenth century), for to deconstruct gender categories is not necessarily to reject them out of hand. The significant distinction is between ideal/absolute and social/contingent arenas of value.
2. Edward Said, *Orientalism* (New York, 1979), p. 2.
3. Joshua Prawer, *The Latin Kingdom of Jerusalem: European Colonialism in the Middle Ages* (London, 1972), p. 352. I do not discuss the institutions which the Crusaders exported to Palestine in establishing the Kingdom of Jerusalem; Prawer does so in *The Latin Kingdom* and in *Crusader Institutions* (Oxford, 1980). For much of the material in these paragraphs I am indebted to Prawer, *The Latin Kingdom*, and to Robert S. Lopez and Irving Raymond, *Medieval Trade in the Mediterranean World* (New York, 1955).
4. Christopher Tyerman, *England and the Crusades, 1095–1588* (Chicago, 1988), p. 206. See Chapter 8 for information in this and the next paragraph.
5. Aziz S. Atiya, *Crusade, Commerce and Culture* (Bloomington, 1962), pp. 92, 94.
6. Thomas J. Hatton, "Chaucer's Crusading Knight: A Slanted Ideal," *Chaucer Review* 3 (1968): 77–87.

7. Paul A. Olson, *The Canterbury Tales and the Good Society* (Princeton, 1986), pp. 49–50.

8. For a detailed, if contentious, analysis of this figure and his exploits, see Terry Jones, *Chaucer's Knight: The Portrait of a Medieval Mercenary* (London, 1983).

9. G.W. Coopland, ed., *Philippe de Mézières: Letter to King Richard II* (Liverpool, 1975): Introduction, pp. xxxiii–xxxiv. The letter, dated 1395, proposes peace between France and England as a necessary prerequisite to winning back the East. Another project of Mézières was his campaign to have the Feast of Mary's Presentation in the Temple—long a major event in the Greek church despite its apocryphal origin—included in the Latin liturgy: cf. William E. Coleman, ed., *Philippe de Mézières' Campaign for the Feast of Mary's Presentation* (Toronto, 1981). Coleman speculates that Mézières hoped to establish an ecumenical, then a military, alliance with the Byzantine Christians against the Turkish threat. The campaign included an anonymous sermon (dated about 1372) on Matt. 24:27: "Exit ab oriente et paret usque in occidentem."

10. Book 1, chapter 78. The *Songe* has been edited by Coopland, 2 vols. (Cambridge, 1969).

11. May McKisack, *The Fourteenth Century, 1307–1399* (Oxford, 1959), p. 441.

12. Maurice Keen, "Chaucer's Knight, the English Aristocracy and the Crusade," in *English Court Culture in the Later Middle Ages*, ed. V. J. Scattergood and J. W. Sherborne (London, 1983).

13. Norman Housley, *The Avignon Papacy and the Crusades, 1305–1378* (Oxford, 1978), p. 236.

14. Richard Vaughan, *Philip the Bold: The Formation of the Burgundian State* (Cambridge, MA, 1962), p. 28.

15. J. J. N. Palmer, *England, France and Christendom, 1377–99* (London, 1972), pp. 21–22.

16. P. E. Russell, *The English Intervention in Spain and Portugal in the Time of Edward III and Richard II* (Oxford, 1955), p. 204. Lancaster's claim was based on his 1371 marriage to Costanza, daughter of Pedro I of Castile and Leon.

17. I argue in *The Naked Text* that this name ought to be read as denoting not Helen of Troy, as scholars have always automatically assumed, but *la belle Hélène* of Constantinople, eponymous heroine of a well-known fourteenth-century romance. The work—to my knowledge unedited—is framed as an anti-Saracen tale of papal and imperial politics.

18. Cleopatra is among the most consistently negative figures in the western tradition, as Beverly Taylor has shown in "The Medieval Cleopatra: the Classical and Medieval Tradition of Chaucer's *Legend of Cleopatra*," *JMRS* 7 (1977): 249–69.

19. Although the *Riverside Chaucer* remarks that the pair are married "only in the accounts of Vincent of Beauvais and Boccaccio" (p. 1066, note 594), there is a source for this detail much closer to home: Higden's *Polychronicon* (3.44). There the monk writes, "Antonius repudiata sorore Caesaris quam duxerat, Cleopatram reginam Aegypti superduxit, cui et Arabiam dedit." One notes that the same verb, *duco*, is used of both partnerships. Trevisa, displac-

ing Cleopatra's name into the wrong clause, nonetheless preserves the relationship in translating, "Antonius putte from hym his wife Cleopatra, Cesar
his suster, and wedded the quene of Egipt, and yaf hir Arabia." The question
whether Chaucer considered this unsanctioned marriage, and others in the
Legend (and in other of his works) to be morally and legally binding, is debatable; however, this is tangential to my argument here because the characters
do consider it so.

20. On medieval color-consciousness, see the collection *Les couleurs au Moyen
Age* (Aix-en-Provence, 1988) and the bibliography on color in R. E. Kaske,
ed., *Medieval Christian Literary Imagery: A Guide to Interpretation* (Toronto,
1988), pp. 172–81. Color symbolism has been studied in connection with *Sir
Gawain and the Green Knight*; cf. Robert Blanch, "Games Poets Play: the
Ambiguous Use of Color Symbolism in *SGGK*," *Nottingham Medieval Studies* 20 (1976): 64–85, and Joseph F. Eagan, "The Import of Color Symbolism
in *GGK*," *St. Louis University Studies*, ser. A, Humanities, 1.2 (1949): 11–86.

Outstanding as an instance of high-medieval color-consciousness linked with
Orientalism is the remarkable Gahmuret-prologue to Wolfram von Eschen-
bach's *Parzival* (1198–1212). The Angevin knight Gahmuret (the hero's father)
marries a beautiful and virtuous black Moorish queen, Belacane. Much is made
of the color difference, as in this description: "If there is anything brighter than
daylight—the queen in no way resembled it. A woman's manner she did have,
and was on other counts worthy of a knight, but she was unlike a dewy rose: her
complexion was black of hue"; *Parzival*, trans. Helen Mustard and Charles
Passage (New York, 1961), Book I, p. 14. Belacane bears a son, Feirefiz
Angevin, who is dappled black and white "like a magpie."

In the *Chanson de Roland*, it is only when he sees the Ethiopian troops—
"la neire gent" from "une tere maldite" (laisse 143), blacker than ink and with
nothing white about them except their teeth—only then does Roland admit:
"Now I know truly that today we will die" (laisse 144).

21. In "Theatricum Philosophicum," *Language, Counter-Memory, Practise*, ed
Donald F. Bouchard (Ithaca, NY, 1977), p. 172.

22. Prawer, "The Roots of Medieval Colonialism" in *The Meeting of Two Worlds.
Cultural Exchange between East and West during the Period of the Crusades*,
ed. Valdimir P. Goss and Christine V. Bornstein (Kalamazoo, MI, 1986).

23. Besides Ovid, Chaucer also used the twelfth-century *lai* of Thisbe inserted
into the fourteenth-century *Ovide Moralisé*: S. Delany, "The Naked Text:
Chaucer's 'Thisbe,' the *Ovide Moralisé*, and the Problem of *Translatio Studii*
in the *Legend of Good Women*," *Mediaevalia* 13 (1989 for 1987): 275–94.

24. For a formidably thorough study of the evolution of the Semiramis legend,
see Irene Samuel, "Semiramis in the Middle Ages: The History of a Legend,"
Medievalia et Humanistica 2 (1943): 32–44. The detail about trousers occurs
in numerous places, including Orosius, Godfrey of Viterbo, Boccaccio's commentary on Dante's *Commedia* and Hidgen's *Polychronicon*.

25. See S. Delany, "Womanliness in the *Man of Law's Tale*," *Chaucer Review* 9
(1974), reprinted in *Writing Woman* (New York, 1983); also "'Loi' and 'Foi'
in the Man of Law's Introduction, Prologue and Tale," *Mediaevalia* 8 (1985
for 1982): 135–49.

26. Translated by Guido A. Guarino as *Concerning Famous Women* (New Brunswick, NJ, 1963), p. 27.

27. R. W. Southern, *Western Views of Islam in the Middle Ages* (Cambridge, MA, 1962), p. 30.

28. Marie-Thérèse d'Alverny and Georges Vajda, "Marc de Tolède, Traducteur d'Ibn Tumart," *Al-Andalus* 16 (1951): 99–140, 259–307; this from p. 261.

29. Norman Daniel, *Islam and the West: The Making of an Image* (Edinburgh, 1960), p. 145.

30. The authorities include St. Jerome, Clement of Alexandria, Diogenes Laertius, Quintus Curtius; cf. A.H. Krappe, "La Belle Hélène de Constantinople," *Romania* 63 (1937): 324–83. In "Domesticating the Exotic in the *Squire's Tale*," *ELH* 55 (1988): 1–26, John M. Fyler relates incest to the romance rhetorical tropes of doubling and repetition, via their shared analogous concern with same and other, as well as their effect of forcing decisions about identity and discrimination. He argues that the tale shows that "reintegration—the quest of romance—is not fully achievable, that the other finally resists integration with the self" (p. 12).

31. Daniel, Appendix E, "Res turpissima."

32. Ralph Hexter, *Ovid and Medieval Schooling: Studies in the Medieval School Commentaries . . .* (Munich, 1986), p. 75, n. 197. The gloss is in the twelfth-century Hafn. 2015 ms., a continuous commentary on the *Ars*. Hexter notes further that Ganymede, the passive homosexual boy butler of the gods, was Phrygian (pp. 198–99). A debate between Ganymede and Helen of Troy on the respective merits of homosexual and heterosexual love is the topic of a well-known medieval poem, the "Altercation Ganimedis et Helene," edited with commentary, by Rudolf Lenz, *Mittellateinisches Jahrbuch* 7 (1972): 161–86. At least two thirteenth-century mss. of it are in England, one bound with the standard rhetorical work of John of Garland, the other part of the library of Bishop Thomas Bekynton (fifteenth century).

33. *Eneas: Roman du XIIe siècle*, ed J. -J. Salverda de Grave, 2 vols. (Paris, 1968). There is a translation by John A. Yunck (New York, 1974). The wordplay is on "conin": rabbit/cunt.

34. James Muldoon, *Popes, Lawyers and Infidels: The Church and the Non-Christian World, 1250–1550* (Philadelphia, 1979), pp. 11; 165, n. 34.

35. I have made this argument in more detail in *The Naked Text*, Chapter 5. See, to the contrary, H. A. Kelly, *Love and Marriage in the Age of Chaucer* (Ithaca, NY, 1975), passim.

36. Hexter, p. 252: "apud eam moratus esset, sue reminiscens legationis sociorumque crebris obediens monitis, iter inceptum peregit," etc.

37. Karl Young, "Chaucer's Appeal to the Platonic Deity," *Speculum* 19 (1934) shows that Chaucer could have found the material in the *accessus* to a *Metamorphoses*-commentary, or in the *Ovide Moralisé*.

38. Marie-Thérèse d'Alverny, "Deux traductions latines du Coran au Moyen-Age," *Archives d'histoire doctrinale et littéraire du Moyen Age* 22–23 (1947–48): 69–131. Also Dorothee Metlitzki, *The Matter of Araby in Medieval England* (New Haven, CT, 1977), 30–35 on Ketton, and the rest of

Chapter 2 for other medieval English Arabists. In *The Arabic Role in Medieval Literary History: A Forgotten Heritage* (Philadelphia, 1987), Maria Menocal also covers much of this material. She argues the need to revise our paradigm of the Arabic presence in Europe, and she examines its influence on courtly love lyric in particular. In "The *Canterbury Tales* and the Arabic Frame Tradition," *PMLA* 98 (1983): 237–51, Katharine Slater Gittes traces the lineage of frame stories from the Indian *Panchatantra* through its eighth-century Arabic translation (retitled *Kalilah and Dimnah*); this was the model for Peter Alfons's famous *Disciplina Clericalis*, which in turn influenced Boccaccio's *Decameron* and which Chaucer refers to several times in the *CT*. But cf. comments in "Forum," *PMLA* 98 (1983) and 99 (1984).

39. J. J. Saunders, "Matthew Paris and the Mongols," in *Essays in Medieval History Presented to Bertie Wilkinson*, ed. T. A. Sandquist and M. R. Powicke (Toronto, 1969), p. 116.

Worlds Apart:

Orientalism, Antifeminism, and Heresy in Chaucer's Man of Law's Tale

SUSAN SCHIBANOFF

Although the Man of Law's Tale comes fifth in the order of the Canterbury tales in all but one manuscript,[1] readers often detect something initiatory about this performance. The Host's astronomical calculation of date and time in the Introduction to the tale sounds like a "new beginning" to Derek Pearsall,[2] and Cooper speculates that the Introduction, which implies that the storytelling has not yet begun, may once have stood at the head of all the tales, following the General Prologue.[3] Cooper also finds that the lawyer's tale of Custance, the Christian missionary bride, "certainly makes a new start":

> after the ever more sexually active women of the first fragment comes the saintly Emperor's daughter ... [;] after the vagaries of Fortune and the frenzied human disorder of the preceding tales comes a story that insists throughout on the providential control of events.[4]

V. A. Kolve has also written on the initiatory nature of the Man of Law's tale, arguing, as does Cooper, that it provides the overall work "a new beginning"[5]: in contrast to the secular romance and bawdy fabliaux that constitute the first four tales told by the Knight, Miller, Reeve, and Cook, the austere story of Custance's trials and tribulations reorients the direction of the *Canterbury Tales*, heading it for the first time towards its pilgrimage goal. In Kolve's view, the Man of Law's tale encodes a Chaucerian "self-correction,"[6] a kind of interim palinode before the final Retraction, which serves the end of "clarification and renewal—for the *communitas* as much as for the individual Christian soul."[7] As Chaucer's spokesperson, Kolve's Man of Law rallies the faithful by presenting them the narrative of Custance's spiritual journey to emulate in their own travel to Canterbury.

The reading I shall develop here also detects something new and initiatory about the Man of Law's tale, but proceeds from my perception of a different kind of novelty in the narrative: the story of Custance presents Chaucer's sole

---

This essay first appeared in *Exemplaria* 8 (1996): 59–96. Reprinted by permission of Pegasus Press, University of North Carolina, Asheville, NC 28804.

textual confrontation with medieval Christianity's strongest religious rival, Islam, and it contains his only reference to the prophet Muhammad and to the Qur'an. My question from the start has been to interrogate why, at this particular juncture in the *Canterbury Tales* and nowhere else, Chaucer turns our attention to an alien faith, to a faraway place, to a distant time.

I shall argue that the Man of Law uses a discourse of orientalism[8] to issue a clarion call for unity—not among the general *communitas* of the faithful but specifically among the Christian men of his audience. What the lawyer endeavors to remedy by means of his tale is not so much the licentious disorder that characterizes the opening stories as it is the overt divisiveness that has broken out among their narrators, starting with the Miller's "quiting" of the Knight and continuing into the Reeve's angry retort to the Miller and the Cook's possible jab at the Host. As Lee Patterson notes,[9] this dissension takes the form of class antagonism, and the Miller's disruption proves to be the most "explicitly threatening" of all the discord that occurs on the pilgrimage.

The lawyer's strategy, I shall maintain, is to deflect attention from potentially explosive class rivalry by confronting the fractious men of fragment I with another world, another time, ultimately with the Other, in order to forge a sense of community—that is, fraternity—among them. Gradually but inexorably the Man of Law works to build an airtight case against the Other. It is a project that Chaucer eventually subverts by exposing its self-interested hypocrisy; like Patterson, I hear in the Man of Law "the voice of orthodoxy"[10] from which Chaucer dissociates himself. Yet, in the remaining Canterbury tales, Chaucer creates no subsequent voice persuasive enough to undermine the Man of Law's authority, discredited as it may be.

My reading also proceeds from my observation that the Man of Law constructs the Other in tightly intertwined guises in his tale—as Saracen or Muslim, as woman, and as heretic—and that the lawyer repeatedly performs a reductive rhetorical maneuver in order to induce Christian fraternity among the pilgrims. In locating orientalism at the heart of the Man of Law's treatment of the Muslim, I must take issue with such critics as Morton W. Bloomfield, who in 1952 judged the tale to be tolerant of cultural and religious diversity. Focussing on Chaucer's sense of history, Bloomfield also remarks that the narrative of Custance goes beyond its source to present matters from the "Mohammedan point of view" and to give credibility to Saracen deliberations concerning the sultan's impending conversion and marriage.[11] Elaborating upon Bloomfield's reading, Roger Ellis more recently argues that the tale offers a "sympathetic presentation of Islam" by virtue of Chaucer's "heterodox understanding" that the "experience of faith [is] remarkably *similar* no matter what the formal system created to contain it":

> The [Man of Law's] narrative hints at this heterodox understanding when it gives *similar* terms to Christian and Muslim to describe the experience of

their own faith. The Muslim law is "sweete" [II.223], and the Christian "deere" [II.237], to its followers.[12]

Contra Bloomfield and Ellis, I maintain that the Man of Law is not sympathetic but hostile to Islam and that an altogether orthodox antipathy rather than "heterodox understanding" motivates the lawyer's implication that Islam imitates Christianity. The Man of Law renders Islam threatening not by depicting it as different from Christianity—as idolatrous—but by revealing its dangerous closeness to his own religion. He employs what I shall call the "rhetoric of proximity" to figure Islam as an insidious heresy that mimics Christianity.[13] In doing so, the lawyer avails himself of a popular medieval tradition regarding Islam's relationship to Christianity, albeit one unsupported by canon law.

I shall further argue that the Man of Law's hostility extends beyond religion to gender—specifically, to woman. In holding this view, I join with feminist critics who have commented upon the tale's misogyny for several decades now. Their analyses have largely centered upon Custance's passivity. Although for many readers Custance's lack of action and agency constitutes her Christian virtue, Sheila Delany has defined the problematic nature of this behavior: in the Man of Law's handling, it becomes less an emblem of laudable Christian suffering than a model for female submission.[14] Similarly, Priscilla Martin sees the tale as one of decidedly female—rather than Christian—suffering that endorses the tyranny of husband over wife.[15] So too does Elaine Tuttle Hansen remark upon Custance's resemblance to the "archetypally passive" woman who "put[s] the love of a man above all other responsibilities, even above life itself," in direct consequence of which she must endure "great suffering."[16]

Custance's passivity indeed offers little cause for feminist celebration, but my concern here will be to define the functional role it is made to play in the Man of Law's narrative. Not only does Custance's behavior provide a model of female submission, but it helps the Man of Law reach a more fundamental goal in his tale: to establish and maintain woman's difference from (inferiority to) man, her otherness. The Man of Law's overriding aim, I shall suggest, is to preserve and enhance such difference—between women and men, East and West, Islam and Christianity, ultimately between western patriarchal culture and the Other. That his rhetoric renders Muslims and women interchangeable and thus dehumanizes them is of no consequence to the lawyer; indeed, such reductiveness facilitates his creation of Christian fraternity. And what this tale-teller most fears—similitude—he exploits to realize this objective.

I

In his exploration of the homosexual as Other, Jonathan Dollimore establishes that such anxiety concerning sameness or proximity and such appropriation often go hand in hand in western culture.[17] Dollimore argues that the system of binary oppositions, so basic to western thought, finds similarity the "most disturbing of all forms of transgression": "the outlaw . . . as inlaw, and the other as proximate [prove] more disturbing than the other as absolute difference."[18] At the same time, ironically, the most effective way to maintain this system of polar opposition, which always favors the dominant party, is to figure its collapse—in particular, to depict the Other as potentially similar, the outlaw-as-inlaw.

The roots of this strategy of threatening proximity lie in patristic thought. In Augustine's theodicy, Dollimore notes, the figuration of evil as proximate to good—indeed, as intimate with good—leads to a strengthening of their binary opposition, for it means that "one must necessarily and always seek to distinguish the good from the evil": "as Augustine says, one knows evil only through good. From here it is a short step to knowing good by always and vigilantly distinguishing it from evil."[19] The perception that evil may masquerade as good causes the vigilant Christian continually to separate the two, to redefine and resituate evil as absolutely other. What I call the rhetoric of proximity, which draws the Other dangerously near by suggesting its similitude or "intimacy," ultimately serves the monitory purpose of displaying evil's disturbing likeness to good; it sounds the alarm, so to speak, that mobilizes the faithful to repel evil into a clearly delimited position as Other. The rhetoric of proximity thus plays an indispensable role in maintaining rigid binary oppositions by temporarily destabilizing them.

The simultaneous fear and exploitation of similitude that Dollimore detects in Augustine's theodicy surfaces in two later medieval discourses of domination, those of heresy and of antifeminism. Heresy was perceived— and represented—as an attack on the religious community from *within* itself as opposed to the challenge posed by the non-belief of those who subscribed to contrary religious doctrines.[20] In canon law, the heretic (from Greek *haerein*, to choose) is one who keeps the name of Christian but chooses to doubt or deny some part of the faith, whereas the infidel rejects a religion never professed and the pagan remains ignorant of Christian religion.[21]

As "outlaws" rather than "inlaws," non-believers—pagans or infidels— posed the lesser threat to Christianity. Clearly defined as Other, non-Christians occupied a stable, unambiguous position. Ironically but perhaps logically, medieval Christianity could show an ecumenical and charitable attitude to virtuous heathens and good pagans, preferably long dead ones; Langland, Dante, and Chaucer all accord such figures as Trajan and Troilus a final resting place in heaven, if not ultimate salvation.[22] Good Saracens, the heroic figures of the *chansons de geste*, are dubbed "pagans," and, Norman Daniel observes, "there is a persistent effort to link them with the pagans of the ancient world,"[23] while evil Saracens are denied this relatively benign status.

By their definition as wayward "insiders," heretics, however, evoked a different response. Their insidious proximity to the dominant faith created a

dangerous instability that demanded resolution, not complacency or tolerance. Typically, that resolution took one of two forms: the heretic was either
reassimilated into the fold or altogether driven from it, clearly branded as
other through excommunication or a worse fate. Condemned as a relapsed
heretic, Joan of Arc, for instance, had but two choices: abjuration or the
stake.[24] The heretic's "perversion"—or choice to turn away from true belief
or doctrine—must either be eliminated (made orthodox or "straightened
out") or exaggerated for all to recognize clearly.

While actual heretics such as Joan of Arc were subjected to attempts to
clarify (and nullify) their ambiguous position, the concept of heresy, person-
ified in Satan, might also serve useful ends and thus remained integral to
Christian thought. As Augustine argued in the *City of God*, "heresies are necessary, to show which of you are in sound condition."[25] The arch-heretic,
Satan, was similarly "necessary" to strengthen the faithful by reminding
them of unseen enemies that lurked nearby. Of the two high-water periods of
Christian heresy, the earlier centuries of the patristic era and the last three
centuries of the Middle Ages, the first no doubt resulted from the historical
struggle that took place to define Christian dogma and defend it against its
competitors. The second period, however, may have resulted from the
Church's attempt to envision itself as persecuted, as "imitator Christi," when
in fact it no longer had strong rivals in western Europe.

Steven Kruger has suggested that the Church sought to downplay its situation as "an enormously powerful institution" in the later Middle Ages by
imagining itself as beset by enemies bent on its destruction, thus "deny[ing]
its own power and claim[ing] the moral high ground of the persecuted."[26] If
the late medieval Church did seek to present itself as marginalized, then the
heretic, by definition a foe so similar as to be nearly invisible, offered it a
unique opportunity, for the Church might posit the threat of heresy with
impunity and thus rally the faithful to its defense. As Augustine had earlier
noted, heresies are "necessary" for delimiting and preserving the Christian
communitas.

The discourse of medieval antifeminism also feared yet traded upon
similitude, specifically, woman's proximity to man. Patristic interpretation of
the dual account of woman's creation in Genesis provides an early example
of this simultaneous anxiety and exploitation. Genesis contains two etiolo-
gies of woman, the first in 1:27: "And God created man [*hominem*] to his
own image: to the image of God he created him, male and female he created
them."[27] As R. Howard Bloch observes, this passage implies the contemporaneous "creation of man and woman, undifferentiated with respect to
their humanness, and whose equality is attested by a common designation
[*homo*]."[28] The second—and more familiar—account of Eve's creation from
Adam's rib (Genesis 2:7–22) accords man chronological and ontological priority over woman, who is called "*virago*" "because she was taken out of

man" (Genesis 2:23). Despite the apparent differences between these accounts, both could be (and were) interpreted by medieval exegetes as arguments for woman's essential lack of similitude (hence inferiority) to man.

For instance, in *De Genesi ad litteram*, Augustine couples the egalitarian creation story of Genesis 1:27 with Genesis 1:28, which expresses God's command about fecundity ("increase and multiply"). Genesis 1:28 defines the purpose of woman's creation (in 1:27) as generative, Augustine argues. Woman was created to help Adam beget children, and woman's role in generation is passive, opposite from and inferior to man's active role. Therefore, woman is different from (less perfect than) man, regardless of the cotemporality of their creation. So too, of course, in Augustine's interpretation of the second creation story of Adam's rib, Eve—*virago*—has a status dependent upon Adam, formed from his body and after him. Aquinas and other later medieval authorities also read both creation accounts as justification of the binary opposition of man and woman, expressing the widespread anxiety about similitude that fuels antifeminist discourse.[29]

At the same time, however, the story of Adam's rib was expropriated to implicate woman's alarming propensity to elide differences between the sexes and encroach upon male status. While the term *virago* initially indicated Eve's derivational and inferior status, her "otherness" from Adam, by the later Middle Ages it could also refer to woman's perverse desire to take over male roles and claim similitude to him. Throughout the Middle Ages, the term occurs pejoratively to denote a "mannish" woman, as the *OED* records, a bold, impudent, or wicked woman, a termagant and scold. And the reason the virago evoked such cultural scorn was because, as Gavin Douglas phrased it, she transgressed traditional gender roles by "exersand a mannis office."[30]

The virago became a standard monitory topos of later medieval antifeminist satire and discourse. Boccaccio's *Corbaccio*, for instance, warns its (implied) male audience that women's "appetite for mastery" knows no bounds. Women desire the accoutrements of power—crowns, girdles, ermines, and costly clothes—as ill-disguised "weapons to combat [their husbands'] mastery and vanquish it," "contriving with all their might to seize control" from their "wretched husbands" and become "mistress and ruler" of the house.[31] Like man or "mannish" but not quite man—"mistress and ruler": Boccaccio thus situates his virago in the disturbingly unstable position of proximity to man, the "outlaw" posing as "inlaw." Such ambiguous intimacy, Dollimore argues, leads to calls for resolution by the dominant party. Unlike the heretic, who theoretically might abjure the status of outlaw or Other and rejoin the faithful, medieval woman could not put aside her sex and literally become male. Thus, the patriarchal solution to the threat of her proximity was to reestablish woman's distance from man, to reinscribe her as inferior and subordinate to him, which Augustine, Aquinas, and others repeatedly did.

Ultimately, the rhetoric of proximity that devolves from patristic thought serves the agenda of western binary ideology, for its figuration of woman and heretic as, respectively, "mannish" and pseudo-Christian creates intense pressure to resituate them as clearly distant or Other, be it passive helpmate or member of Satan's perverse legions. As I shall next argue, so too does medieval orientalism employ the discourse of similitude to misrepresent Islam as a crisis of proximity—as a Christian heresy—that demands response and resolution not tolerance.[32]

II

In Said's view, the discourse of medieval orientalism sought to "domesticate the exotic" through analogy:

> since Christ is the basis of Christian faith, it was assumed—quite incorrectly—that Mohammed was to Islam as Christ was to Christianity. Hence the polemic name "Mohammedanism" given to Islam, and the auto- matic epithet "imposter" applied to Mohammed.[33]

The purpose of such rhetoric, Said maintains, was to establish Islam as both a misguided and inferior "version of Christianity," the "Orient and the Orien- tal [as] repetitious pseudo-incarnations of some great original (Christ, Europe, the West) they were supposed to have been imitating."[34]

Said speculates that the strangeness of Islam was deliberately rendered familiar—analogized—by western Europeans in the Middle Ages in order to mute and hence control the threat of this new religion:

> If the mind must suddenly deal with what it takes to be a radically new form of life—as Islam appeared to Europe in the early Middle Ages—the response on the whole is conservative and defensive. Islam is judged to be a fraudulent new version of some previous experience, in this case, Christian- ity. The threat is muted, familiar values impose themselves, and in the end the mind reduces the pressure upon it by accommodating things to itself as either "original" or "repetitious."[35]

Said bases his paradigm of domestication on European response to Islam in the early Middle Ages, yet Dollimore's theory of transgressive proximity would appear to illuminate more satisfactorily the dynamics of orientalism in the high and later medieval periods.[36] That is, the western rhetoric of proxim- ity troped the familiarity of Islam in these latter eras not to mute the threat of the new religion to Europe, but to intensify it, to increase rather than reduce the "pressure" it created upon the occidental mind. Islam was commonly misrepresented as a heresy, a viper all the more dangerous for its proximity to Christianity's bosom, its intimacy with the "true" faith.[37] To heresy, the medieval Christian mind could never accommodate itself; in one way or another—by conversion or extinction—the pressure posed by the heretic as proximate Other had to be released.

The creation of such pressure through the falsification of Islam as a Christian heresy appears to have taken on a new urgency in the period of the Crusades. Although such earlier authorities as John of Damascus (ca. 675–ca. 749) viewed Islam as the last and greatest of the Christian here-sies,[38] it was Peter the Venerable (1092–1156) who made a concerted attempt to forge Christian "weapons" against the heresy of Islam, as Southern phrases it (39). In theological terms, canon law denied that Islam was a heresy. Norman Daniel clarifies the issue: canon law recognized that, unlike a heretic, a Muslim had not been baptized and therefore was "not liable to penalties for leaving the church."[39] In what Sheila Delany calls the "rational-scholarly approach" to Islam, this distinction is sometimes observed; Mark of Toledo, for instance, regards Islam as a *legem tertiam* that combines fea-tures of Judaism and Christianity yet evidently remains a separate religion.[40] And respect for the rationality of Islam, if not a willingness to grant its autonomous status, would seem to undergird the repugnance some Christians experienced over the forced conversion of Muslims. Delany cites William of Tripoli and thirteenth-century Dominican and Franciscan missionaries who "believed in the principle that God is not pleased by forced worship."[41] And Dana Carleton Munro charts the development of a generally more positive and accurate European approach to Muslims beginning in the thirteenth cen-tury, due in part, he speculates, to increased contact between East and West and to the appearance of a new enemy, the Byzantines.[42]

Yet, Munro notes, a stronger counter-tradition of antipathy to Islam exists throughout the Middle Ages: the majority of Christian clergy remained hostile, especially during the high propaganda periods preceding new Cru-sades.[43] And Delany discusses the deep roots of later medieval (Chaucerian) orientalism. Founded on patristic and popular attitudes "older than the ratio-nalistic one that had developed since the twelfth century," this antipathetic tradition "maintained the idea of a sinister, immoral, insidious Orient."[44] The notion of an "insidious" Orient had as its corollary, I would argue, the premise that Islam was a Christian heresy, an internal perversion of the puta-tively true faith. Learned men promoted this view, and some apparently rec-ognized at the same time that it was a falsification, as is the case with Peter the Venerable. Peter, who wrote his *Summa totius haeresis Saracenorum* for the purpose of acquainting Europeans with Islam so that they might resist it, opens his work by arguing that Islam is the greatest, the most formidable, of all the Christian heresies, as had his predecessor, John of Damascus. But, James Kritzeck notes, Peter immediately subjects his choice of terms to scrutiny, questioning whether a body of religious doctrine that originated outside, not within, the Church could be called a "heresy":

> I cannot clearly decide whether the Mohammedan error must be called a
> heresy and its followers heretics, or whether they are to be called pagans.
> For I see them, now in the manner of heretics, take certain things from the
> Christian faith and reject other things; then—a thing which no heresy is
> described as ever having done—acting as well as teaching according to
> pagan customs.[45]

In the end, Kritzeck comments, while Peter left the decision up to his readers
whether to call Islam a Christian heresy or a distinct pagan faith, he himself
chose to view it as a heresy.

Daniel maintains that the western image of Islam as the "culmination or
summit of all heresy" was widespread, if by no means universal, for many of
Peter's contemporaries adopted the term casually and carelessly in spite of
canon law: "neither at Cluny nor elsewhere did polemists take the canonical
position into account."[46] Some authorities saw no real distinction between the
Muslim and the heretic and treated them as equivalents, even if they were
aware that Muslims had not entered the Catholic faith and thus could not
renounce it.[47] The popular western notion that Islam was carved out of Christian dogma took different literary forms, often fantastic in conception:

> [T]here were stories that associated Muhammad with the New Testament
> heresiarch Nicholas; others that supposed him to have been under the influ-
> ence of, or actually to have been, a Roman cardinal or cleric, frustrated in
> his ambition, who perverted his own converts to spite the Roman Church;
> together with the poems of Waltherius, du Pont, and before them Hildebert,
> all these presuppose that Islam arose in a Christian people, "derelicta fide
> catholica."[48]

The effect of the polemical decision by Peter and others to mischaracter-
ize Islam as a Christian heresy was, in Daniel's words, to find a place for it
within the "family of Christian error,"[49] to present it as an erroneous faith that
Christians could see only as a perversion of their *own* truth. In particular,
Islam's denial of Christ's divinity was considered the most blasphemous part
of its heretical falsehood. Yet Islam did accept Christ as a prophet, and the
western rhetoric of proximity contained several tropes to acknowledge that
the Qur'an mixed truth with untruth, honey with poison. Perhaps more than
anything else, this recognition of the Qur'an's "sweetness," its "truth" about
Christ, positioned Islam in what Dollimore would call the "permanently
unstable" position of intimacy with Christianity and hence demanded resolution. Typically, Christian polemicists and other western writers suggested
that the problem posed by Islam's proximity might be solved in one of two
related ways: either by fully assimilating Islam to Christianity or by exposing
it as a diabolical plot and altogether rejecting it. In either case, the intent was
to eradicate Islam from the West and insure Christian hegemony. Even the

relatively more benign "scholarly" tradition, Delany observes, "was as determined as any other to extirpate Islam."[50]

An example of what Daniel sees as the assimilative approach occurs in William of Tripoli's *Tractatus de statu Saracenorum* (c. 1271), which encourages Muslims to think that "they themselves were in a fair way to becoming Christians."[51] A later work expressing the same viewpoint but addressed to a Christian audience is Mandeville's *Travels*. It opens its discussion of the Saracens with an enumeration of the beliefs and doctrines shared by the Qur'an and the Scriptures, stressing the infancy narrative and Christ's status as a prophet. It then solves the "problem" of Islam's proximity to Christianity by seeing in it an opportunity for evangelizing:

> because [the Saracens] go so nigh our faith, they be lightly converted to Christian law when men preach them and shew them distinctly the law of Jesu Christ, and when they tell them of the prophecies.[52]

Daniel points out that favorable western commentary on the closeness of Islam to Christianity always had the ulterior motive of conversion, just as praise of a Saracen—usually the token figure, Saladin—served the satirical purpose of exhorting Christians to live up to the ideals of their own faith. After all, the rationale went, if a Muslim could achieve virtue, a Christian should strive to do at least as much.

The inverse western response to the challenge of the Qur'an's "truth" was to expose it as Muhammad's trick to deceive innocent Christians, as does an anonymous Cluniac commentator:

> In the first chapter (i.e., surah II) [Muhammad] immediately praises prayers and alms, that is, under the appearance of seeming good he may entice the unwary to believe him. Notice throughout the whole book that, with marvellous cunning, when he is going to say something ungodly, or recalls having said it, he soon puts in something about fasting, or about prayer, or praising God.[53]

Yet another metaphor that unmasks Muhammad's fraud, in which he is characterized as offering the unwary "deadly poison" within a "sweet apple," analogizes the Prophet to the ultimate instigator of the heresy of Islam: Satan. Often, the link between Christianity's arch-heresiarch, its first and chief pervert, and Muhammad is asserted more baldly. For Peter the Venerable, Muhammad is simply "this Satan," one who advanced all previous heresies, a nefarious task to be "wholly completed by Antichrist, according to diabolical intention." William of Tyre phrases the relationship in familial terms: Muhammad is the "first-born of Satan." As Satan had seduced Eve, Muhammad "seduced" the Orient. Jacques de Vitry combines all these motifs in his condemnation of Muhammad:

[L]ike another Antichrist and the first-born son of Satan, transfigured like
Satan into an angel of light, Muhammad, upheld by God's great anger and
special displeasure, with the co-operation of the enemy of the human race,
perverted . . . more people than any other heretic before his time.[54]

In this case, the difficulty posed by Islam's proximity to Christianity was
not soluble by subsuming its followers within the community. Instead,
Islam's "poison" had to be exposed and expelled. Characterized as the first-
born son of Christianity's initial and chief pervert, Muhammad was distinctly
cordoned off as absolutely Other, beyond the pale, even if the rhetoric of
proximity would continue its inherent work of resituating Islam dangerously
close to Christianity only to inspire yet more intense acts of resolution. In
practice, these acts were often violent: "it is evident that Christendom recognized a relationship which aimed primarily at the destruction of Islam, and in
which missionary endeavor held a subordinate place."[55] Even as late and supposedly liberal a cleric as Robert Holcot (d. 1349) argued the right to kill
Muslims who refused to convert. If Christian attempts at conversion fail,
Holcot reasons, then the community is justified in protecting itself from the
dangerous element that threatens its integrity, just as "a putrid member must
be cut off from the natural body."[56]

Holcot's diction figures Islam not as an external foe, but as infection, an
internal corruption of the natural body of the community; and the communal
body must act to rid itself of this deadly venom. As I shall next trace, the narrative movement of the Man of Law's Tale enacts a similarly oscillating
paradigm of medieval orientalism, for it tropes Islam's "sweetness"—its intimately heretical relationship with Christianity—only to reveal the poison
within that calls for a communal act of expulsion. Although Paul E. Beichner
has concluded that Chaucer's secular lawyer "must have known much canon
law in so far as it touched upon civil law and things temporal,"[57] such knowledge would not necessarily have impeded the Man of Law's orientalist project, for any number of medieval religious authorities chose to ignore canon
law and present Islam as a heresy. I shall further argue that the lawyer constructs woman's otherness on the same model and that his invention bears
fruit in the Epilogue, which features the detection of yet a third Other, a local
and contemporary heretic, in the most disturbing position possible, within
the very ranks of the Canterbury pilgrims.[58]

III

Based upon a section of Nicholas Trevet's Anglo-Norman *Chronique* (ca.
1334) and, probably, John Gower's adaptation of it in his *Confessio amantis*,
the lawyer's narrative of Custance follows the main outlines of its sources.[59]
In all three versions, the saint-like Christian woman is first pledged in mar-

riage to the sultan of Syria on condition that he, a Muslim, convert to her religion. The sultan's mother takes deep offense at her son's conversion and has him murdered, exiling Custance at sea. Custance eventually washes ashore in Northumbria and in due course weds its pagan monarch, Aella, who also converts. Fiercely opposed to her son's action, Aella's mother engineers Custance's second exile. Set adrift again, this time with her infant son, Custance makes her way back to Rome, and her lot finally begins to improve as she and her child are reunited with Aella and with her father, the emperor of Rome.

Although Trevet, Gower, and Chaucer relate the same basic set of events, each shapes the narrative to different ends—respectively, to biography, moral exemplum, and orientalist polemic—and this molding is foreshadowed in each version's development of the initial episode. Taking the role of biographer, albeit of a pseudo-historical narrative, Trevet opens his life of Constance with claims to historical accuracy; he alludes to the different sources (various chronicles, including the ancient one of the Saxons) he has drawn upon, some of which conflict with one another concerning Constance's genealogy. Trevet sorts out the matter and then reconstructs Constance's family tree, identifying her father, mother, and son, and recounting details of Constance's early years with her parents.[60]

Gower's narrator, Genius, however, characterizes his tale in advance as moral exemplum, not as history or biography. Genius terms the Constance narrative a "tale of gret entendement" (*CA* 2.584)[61] and offers it as an example of correct behavior in response to envy and detraction. He too begins the tale with reference to Constance's early years in Rome, but truncates the discussion of sources and focusses instead on the worthiness of Constance's father, the emperor Tiberius Constantius, and Constance's own good name, setting the stage for the attacks by Envy and Backbiting in the guise of the two evil mothers.

Unlike Trevet and Genius, whose first episodes feature Constance, the Man of Law initially ignores her, casting his opening focus instead upon the group of Syrian merchants that has travelled to the Christian community of Rome either for business or leisure ("for chapmanhood or for disport," II.143). Whatever the merchants' motivation, their passage from Syria to Rome is unremarkable, historically no doubt a commonplace occurrence given the physical proximity of the two Mediterranean locations. Their merchandise ("chaffare," II.138) may be novel, but in themselves the merchants evoke little curiosity. In fact, the Man of Law goes out of his way—beyond Trevet and Gower—to underline the extent to which the Syrians exhibit western values and attitudes. He observes that the merchants are not merely rich and successful, but trustworthy and honest ("sadde and trewe," II.135). These are indeed good men, as seen through western eyes. Like Mandeville, the Man of Law searches for commonalities; at least at the outset of his tale, he makes no mention of the cultural and religious differences—the *disparitas cultus*[62]—between Syrians and Romans. Instead, the Man of Law works to establish the closeness, both geographically and culturally, between the two as his opening act.

His next move is to recount how these merchants come to learn of Custance's reputation for goodness and beauty and carry word of it back to their ruler, the sultan. Here the lawyer's emphasis is more upon the "traffic" between the groups of men—the Romans who sing Custance's praises and the Syrians who heed it—than it is upon Custance herself, who has not yet actually appeared in the tale.[63] No cultural or other barriers prevent the Syrians from recognizing and appreciating western—Roman—goodness and beauty as soon as they hear reports of them. Forthwith, the merchants load their ships, catch a glimpse of the "blisful mayden" (II.172) for themselves, and return home as Custance's ambassadors.

In contrast, Trevet and Genius's merchants are clearly delineated as Other the moment we encounter them: they are presented as pagan or heathen traders who have arrived in Rome. Trevet identifies their origin as the great Saracenland, wherever that vague region might be ("marchauntz paens hors de la graunde sarazine," *Chron.* 5), while Genius specifies their homeland as "Barbarie" (*CA* 2.599),[64] and both narrators maintain an emphasis upon the foreignness of the newcomers. Indeed, the merchants' visit to Rome immediately arouses Constance's curiosity, and she seeks them out to learn of their land and of their religious beliefs. Upon discovering that the merchants are heathens ("paens," *Chron.* 5), she sets to preaching them the Christian faith. Her instruction is so forceful that in short course the foreign merchants renounce, in Genius's words, their "false goddes" (*CA* 2.610), convert, and receive baptism. They then return to their land. The episode is brief and aptly summed up in the marginal annotation of Trevet's manuscript (Arundel 56): "conuersio paganorum" (*Chron.* 5). Significantly (and accurately, according to canon law), Trevet considers his Saracens to be pagans, unbaptized non-believers, rather than heretics—unambiguous outlaws rather than outlaws posing as inlaws.

As the Chaucerian narrative continues, however, so does its emphasis upon the commonalities between Syrians and Romans, culminating in the voluntary and altogether effortless conversion of the former to the latter's faith. Hearing from the merchants of Custance's great "noblesse" (II.185), the sultan sets his heart upon the emperor's daughter and to that end assigns his privy council the task of discovering some remedy for his lovesickness.[65] His advisors consider several cures, including magic and deception, but conclude that the only relief for the sultan's malady is to wed Custance. At this point, the issue of cultural diversity throws a brief shadow across the lawyer's narrative: the sultan's councilors doubt that a Christian emperor would allow his daughter to marry under "Mahoun's" law "by cause that ther was swich diversitee / Bitwene hir bothe lawes" (II.220–21).

But the hurdle raised by this "diversitee" is easily overcome, for the sultan soon waves aside his own faith and vows to convert in order to wed Custance. Like Mandeville, whose Saracens may be "lightly converted," the Man of Law stresses the ease with which the sultan comes to terms with Custance's religious differences by speeding the narrative along: "what nedeth gretter dilitacioun?" (II.232), the narrator asks as he quickly runs through the negotiations that take place between Syrians and Romans, condensing greatly this part of Trevet's story. In short space, the Man of Law brings both sides to agreement—"they been accorded" (II.238). Sounding again the note of commonality between Muslims and Christians—"this same accord was sworn on eyther side" (II.244)—the Man of Law succinctly draws this section of his narrative to a close: "this is th' ende" (II.255). The followers of Muhammad's "lawe sweete" take up the parallel "lawe deere" of Christ, and every Christian is instructed to pray that Christ look favorably upon the union between the new convert and his bride. By implication, the Man of Law figures the sultan's religious faith as but a variation of Christianity, and his conversion requires little effort. The sultan's conversion also seems not to demand the sacrament of baptism; or, if it does, the lawyer has the ceremony performed discreetly offstage in order to mute the actual differences between Islam and Christianity as the canonists saw them.

The unique congruity that Chaucer's narrator establishes between the law of Islam and Christianity, Syrians and Romans, in the first part of the story of Custance gains emphasis from the disparity he creates between different religions and cultures in the second part, which relates Custance's further adventures in sixth-century England, specifically, in the Northumberland ruled by King Aella upon whose shores Custance's boat washes up after her exile from Syria. The first note the Man of Law strikes in this second episode is one of cultural difference: upon her discovery by the Saxon constable, Custance begs for mercy "in hir langage" (II.516), which, of course, is not the tongue of Saxon Britain, but a "maner Latyn corrupt" (II.519), or Italian.[66]

By contrast, Gower's Genius altogether sidesteps the matter of linguistic difference at this point in the narrative and takes poetic license to allow the Roman woman to communicate with her Saxon hosts. Trevet's Constance knows several languages, including Saxon, and she speaks the constable's tongue ("en sessoneys," *Chron.* 13) so well that she raises his hopes that perhaps she is one of his own race, maybe the daughter of a Saxon king from abroad, from Germany, Saxony, Sweden, or Denmark. Speaking her own language and no other, the lawyer's Custance, however, is too foreign-sounding to excite such expectations in her hosts. By unexplained means, she manages to make herself understood, yet the Man of Law establishes the dominant note of diversity between Latin and Saxon culture early in this episode.

Evidently, Custance is also foreign-looking to her new Saxon acquaintances. Aella's mother, Donegild, opposes the marriage of her son to Custance not because, as in Trevet, she envies her daughter-in-law's marvellous beauty ("merueilouse beaute," *Chron.* 25), goodness, and purity, or, as in Gower, because she fears her new in-law will displace her (*CA* 2.648), but because it seems to her an insult that her son should wed "so straunge a creature" (II.700) as Custance. Unlike the Syrian sultan, who was smitten with Custance's physical beauty, or at least with the report of it, Aella appears largely unaware of or unaffected by Custance's charms. The Saxon king marries Custance, the Man of Law explains, because Christ wills it, a motivation unique to the lawyer's version of the tale:

> And after this Jhesus, of his mercy,
> Made Alla wedden ful solempnely
> This hooly mayden, that is so bright and sheene;
> And thus hath Crist ymaad Custance a queene.

> (II.690–93)

The Man of Law sounds the note of cultural estrangement again as he turns his attention to the religion of Custance's Saxon hosts. Unlike Trevet and Gower's accounts, which merely remark that Constance comes to shore in a heathen land, the Man of Law's Tale depicts sixth-century England in greater detail as a land conquered by pagans ("payens," II.534, 542), who have driven all but a few Christian Britons into Wales. Those native Christians who do remain must practice their religion secretly, shielding it from the "hethen folk" (II.549) who now rule the realm. Unlike the parallels between the "sweete lawe" of Islam and the "deere" one of Christianity that the lawyer created earlier, he establishes no close ties between Custance's faith and that of Aella's people. Indeed, as the Man of Law comments, the constable's wife Hermengyld takes a liking to Custance in spite of her religion, not because of it:

> This constable and dame Hermengyld, his wyf,
> Were payens, and that contree everywhere,
> *But* Hermengyld loved [Custance] right as hir lyf.

> (II.533–35; ITALICS MINE)

The Saxon conversion to Christianity in the second part of the Man of Law's narrative is also configured differently than was that of the Syrians in the first part. In the earlier episode, the sultan's councilors "by wey of resoun" (II.219) lead their lord to see that he must convert in order to have Custance; however inadvertently, the sultan's advisors themselves further the Christian agenda. The pagan Saxons, however, require overt external agency to persuade them to accept the truth of Custance's faith, and Custance herself helps effect the initial conversions. After Christ converts Hermengyld (II.538–39), Custance emboldens her to perform his will and restore sight to the blind Briton (II.566). When the astonished constable questions this miracle, Custance expounds upon "oure lay" (II.572) until he too converts. Aella's conversion also requires acts of divine intervention, in the form of the mysterious hand that knocks down Custance's accuser and a disembodied voice that declares her innocent of his false charge of murder. These two events lead the Saxon king (and "many another," II.685) to convert, followed by Aella's marriage to Custance. Unlike the Syrians, the pagan Saxons do not bring about their own conversion; rather, they capitulate to a wondrous and frightening display of divine power and might, abetted by Custance herself.

Thus, in contrast to the distant pagan Saxons, the Muslims of the Man of Law's tale indeed appear "nigh" unto Christianity, as Mandeville would have phrased it, and the lawyer's efforts to situate Islam close to Christianity culminate in the proposed dynastic merger between Romans and Syrians when Custance and the sultan are to marry. But, as the rhetoric of proximity dictates, at exactly this juncture the Man of Law reveals the corruption within Islam that calls for its violent repositioning as Other. Upon learning of her son's conversion and negotiations to wed Custance, the sultaness herself feigns conversion and requests the honor of holding a banquet for her son and his Roman guests. At the banquet, the sultaness reveals her malice; her men slay all the Christians, both Syrian converts and Roman visitors, and set Custance adrift. Not only is the impending union between Custance and the sultan averted in this act, but it leads to the separation of the two cultures and religions, for Custance's father, emperor of Rome, later retaliates against the sultaness and her entire country of Muslims. Roman forces invade Syria and "brennen, sleen, and brynge [its inhabitants] to meschaunce/ Ful many a day" (II.964–65). As the Man of Law observes, it is certainly "heigh vengeance" (II.963) that Christians exact upon Muslims.

In their retaliation upon Islamic Syria, the Romans reverse—and thus complete—the lawyer's narrative paradigm that began in similitude. They enact his warning that proximity may harbor and disguise danger, and they model one extreme resolution of the unsettling ambiguities they perceive in such intimacy. This solution takes the form of eradicating the corruption that lurks near Christianity, if not within its very family, and resituating Islam in its radically opposite (and inferior) position as Other. The Syrians literally disappear from the Man of Law's narrative at this point, enabling the tale to proceed to its joyous conclusion of reuniting Custance with her *western* family, her Saxon husband, Aella, and her Roman father, and to end on a note of dynastic succession in the observation that Custance and Aella's son, Maurice, became a model Christian emperor. As Margaret Schlauch identifies it, this "recognition scene" is typical of Greek romance,[67] but I would suggest that it functions in the Man of Law's narrative to draw round the wagons—western Christian defenses—against a now clearly defined oriental Other.

If the Man of Law partly shapes his narrative to provide an etiology of British Christianity, aligning its origins with the dynastic line that begins in the new emperor, Maurice, he also contrasts this successful merger with the disastrous and aborted union between East and West. Whether or not many fourteenth-century English people had actually met Muslims, or so-called Saracens, such narratives as the Man of Law's must have informed their response to them. But this reinscription of the oriental as Other does not complete the lawyer's cultural work, for he also employs the cautionary discourse of transgressive proximity to create a second outsider in his tale—this one, however, known personally to every Englishman: woman.

IV

Islam may stalk the boundaries of Christianity in the Man of Law's Tale, but closest to its center lurks the primal transgressor, Satan, the heresiarch of whom Muhammad is but a shadow, or, as medieval writers phrased it, "first-born son." Furthermore, the lawyer's narrative couples Satan with an equally alarming figure to the medieval patriarchal mind, woman, through whose agency the "father of lies" exclusively operates to undermine Christianity. Woman, Syrian as well as Saxon, not only imitates Satan's deceptive means but, as the Man of Law exposes her, presents the ultimate menace: although distanced and putatively stabilized in ancient and medieval philosophy and science as man's binary opposite, she schemes to obscure these differentiating marks and become, if not actually male, like man—"mannysh" (II.782), as the lawyer phrases it. Such "mannishness" is the more threatening transgression the Man of Law wishes to reveal, for he presents it as having plagued the entire world—Occident as well as Orient—from its inception, from Eve through Semiramis to the sultaness and Donegild, and, by extension, to the lawyer's own era.[68] Compared to woman, Islam is an analogous but localized and recent problem.

As Satan's agents, women in the Man of Law's Tale work against both Christianity and patriarchy through deception and infiltration. In both the Syrian and Saxon episodes, women are in-laws—actual or intended mothers-in-law of Custance—who are at the same time Dollimore's "outlaws." Their transgressive acts originate in response to Custance's intrusion of a foreign religion into their worlds, but, as the Man of Law presents it, these women also plot to usurp the traditionally masculine power of rulership for themselves.

Outraged that her son has abandoned "Makometes lawe" (II.336) in order to marry Custance, the sultaness vows to die rather than also take up the "newe lawe" (II.337) of Christianity. She wishes to reestablish the Qur'an as the law of the land and thus to escape the pains of hell for renouncing Muhammad. So too does Trevet's sultaness act out of concern that her son's conversion imperils the future of Islam in Syria (*Chron.* 8). Yet the Man of Law alone creates a desire for conventionally male power in his sultaness, inventing for her a scene that anticipates the council in hell in book 2 of Milton's *Paradise Lost*, with the sultaness playing the role of Satan as he schemes to regain his former might and glory. She assembles her Syrian "conseil" and harangues its members with rhetorical questions about the evils of forsaking "Mahoun," promising to keep them safe if they swear allegiance to her (II.330–43) and recruit their friends to do so. Unlike Trevet and Gower's figure, the lawyer's sultaness works to establish a political power base in opposition to that of her son. Albeit smaller, her council rivals her son's, for, the Man of Law pointedly observes, in her murderous enterprise the sultaness means to usurp her son's rule: "she hirself wolde al the contree lede" (II.434).

Like Satan, the sultaness enacts her transgressive desire deceptively, feigning conversion to Christianity and good will to Custance in order to entrap and assassinate the sultan and his retinue of converts. Such counterfeit proximity comes in for its share of rhetorical vituperation by the Man of Law, who castigates the sultaness as the scorpion who, for all her flattery of Christianity and Custance, fully intends to "stynge" them (II.403–5). So too does the Man of Law associate the sultaness with the primal transgressor, the source of all evil: she is the "welle of vices" (II.323), "roote of iniquitee" (II.358), "nest of every vice" (II.364), and a serpent disguised as woman "lik to the serpent depe in helle ybounde" (II.360–61). Yet the sultaness's most egregious sin is not that she impersonates Satan, for, the Man of Law remarks, it is Satan who makes women his instrument when he wishes to beguile, as he did with Eve (II.365–71). Instead, the sultaness's ultimate danger is that she would be like man; she is, as the Man of Law alone styles her, "Virago," "Semyrame the secounde" (II.359).

In the Middle Ages, Semiramis was known as the militant queen of ancient Syria (or Assyria) who built Babylon's walls and later became notorious for sexual depravity, including incest with her son, the sin for which Dante consigns her to the second circle of hell. As Johnstone Parr argues, however, more pertinent to the Man of Law's Tale than Semiramis's sexual aberration is the legend that she usurped the throne from her husband, King

Ninus, whom she had assassinated after he attended a banquet she arranged for him.[69] Alternatively, as Boccaccio relates the legend in *De claris mulieribus*, after King Ninus had died from an arrow wound, Semiramis prevented her young son from ruling and "retain[ed] for herself the great kingdom of her husband."[70]

Boccaccio also offers a detailed account of how Semiramis managed to expropriate unto herself the conventionally masculine prerogative of rulership after Ninus's death. With "feminine wiles," Boccaccio explains, she "masqueraded as a man and pretended to be her own son":

> Semiramis's face looked very much like her son's; both were beardless; her woman's voice sounded no different from her young son's; and she was just a trifle taller, if at all. Taking advantage of this resemblance, she always wore a turban and kept her arms and legs covered. . . . Lest the novelty of her garb shock her countrymen, Semiramis decreed that everyone should dress in this fashion.

Having proven her abilities as a ruler, Semiramis later revealed her actual sex, almost as if, Boccaccio speculates, "she wanted to show that in order to govern it is not necessary to be a man, but to have courage." For this "marvelous subterfuge," Semiramis gained the admiration of all those who looked upon her, and she not only retained the lands acquired by her husband, but added Ethiopia and India to them, restored Babylon, and built other new cities, Boccaccio concludes.

Semiramis's pretense as a man and her usurpation of masculine privilege do not, however, finally escape Boccaccio's censure, for he ends his portrayal of her with a dire warning concerning the sexual confusion such masquerades cause in men. It is believed, Boccaccio reports, that the "manly-spirited" Semiramis, "constantly burning with carnal desire," gave herself to many men, including her own son, Ninus, "a very handsome young man," by which description Boccaccio means to suggest the son's effeminacy: "as if he had changed sex with his mother, Ninus rotted away idly in bed, while she sweated in arms against her enemies." Women who take over traditionally male roles, Boccaccio implies, not only threaten men's power and prerogatives but confuse their very sexual identities, indeed, confound even sexual perversity itself. Like the woman-man of medieval homophobic discourse,[71] Ninus plays the passive or female role, yet he does so in heterosexual intercourse with his mother, the man-woman: "Oh, what a wicked thing this is!" Boccaccio complains, "something more beastly than human."[72]

The Man of Law points to the sultaness's relationship to Boccaccio's figure in the epithet "virago" that he couples with "Semiramis" (II.359). As the fifteenth-century poet Gavin Douglas defined the term, a *virago* is not simply a large or quarrelsome woman, but like Juturna in the *Aeneid*, "a woman exersand a mannis office."[73] To be sure, the lawyer's sultaness is but "Semi-ramis the secounde," a pale reflection of the cross-dressed transgressor Boccaccio had constructed. Unlike her notorious predecessor, the sultaness does not literally impersonate a male ruler, nor does she commit incest (the "unkynde abhomynacion," II.88, the Man of Law earlier ruled out as potential subject matter for his tale), but she too would take "mannis office" of rulership into her own hands.

Impersonation does occur, however, in the second episode of female deception in the Man of Law's narrative, that in which King Aella's mother, Donegild, masquerades in writing as her son.[74] Having intercepted a letter to Aella informing him that Custance has given birth to their child, Donegild substitutes a letter proclaiming Custance to have borne a monstrous creature. (Such offspring implies that Custance is an "elf," II.745, an evil spirit in the form of a woman.) Donegild next intercepts the return letter from Aella, which voices his compassionate acceptance of the fabricated news, and substitutes her own missive, which directs that Custance and her son are to be exiled from the country, set adrift in the sea. On the authority of this forged letter, the constable sadly carries out what he believes to be Aella's wishes and banishes Custance and her child. For her traitorous male masquerade, the Man of Law excoriates Donegild and rhetorically links her perverse "mannishness" to the ultimate pervert, Satan: "Fy, mannysh, fy!—o nay, by God, I lye— / Fy, feendlych spirit . . . !" (II.782–83).

Donegild's arrogation of male power extends beyond the fact that she impersonates King Aella to the mode by which she actually does so: she takes up the pen, traditionally a male instrument in the Middle Ages, and forges a letter from him. Trevet's narrative also specifies that his Domild intercepts and reads Aella's message and substitutes the counterfeit one she writes herself. Gower, whose interest is to exemplify the evils of envy, not of "mannishness," suppresses Domild's literal inscription of the letters. She commissions others to do the actual writing: "Sche hath [Aella's] lettres overseie / And formed in an other weie" (*CA* 2.1011–12). But the Man of Law restores the proscribed "mannish" agency of Trevet's Domild, putting the pen back into his Donegild's hand, so to speak. When Aella returns and finds his wife and child exiled contrary to his express orders, his supposed letter of banishment is reexamined and the hand that wrote it identified (II.890). Presumably this hand is Donegild's, for Aella at once slays his mother for her "cursed dede" (II.891).

The Man of Law also recasts Donegild's motivation for opposing Custance into the virago's, rather than invoking the traditionally female reasons earlier writers named. Trevet imputes Domild's hostility to her envy and jealousy of Constance's "goodness and holiness and marvellous beauty" (*Chron.* 24), and Gower ascribes it to the conventionally female verbal sins associated with envy—"bacbitinge" (*CA* 2.1281) and "false tunge" (*CA* 2.1299). The

Man of Law, however, names malice and tyranny (the latter, implicated twice, II.696 and 779) as the dominant causes of Donegild's hostility to Custance. Tyranny in particular is an "unwomanly" trait to the Man of Law's way of thinking. Earlier in his narrative, he established that it stands opposed to humility, the Virgin Mary's preeminent virtue in the later Middle Ages,[75] and perhaps Custance's dominant quality as well: "Humblesse hath slayn in [Custance] al tirannye" (II.165), the lawyer observes early in his tale.

As male impersonator, writer, and would-be tyrant, Donegild is indeed "mannish" to patriarchal eyes, like the sultaness, another "Semiramis the secounde." In the Man of Law's deployment, the rhetoric of proximity brings these two maternal figures perilously close to man, blurring the traditional hierarchical arrangement of distinct binary opposition between the sexes. As was the case with the proximate Muslim, such ambiguous "intimacy" calls for violent clarification, which in due course the lawyer's narrative supplies: both the Roman emperor, who dispatches the sultaness and Aella, who kills Donegild, move decisively to reestablish male dominance over—distance from—woman.

Yet the sultaness and Donegild's attempted appropriation of so-called male roles evokes a further—and perhaps more forceful—resituation of woman as man's submissive opposite. Against these viragoes and the transgressive women who serve as their exemplars, from Semiramis back to Eve, the Man of Law advances Custance. Unlike the "mannish" woman, who crowds the preserve of maleness, Custance is repeatedly differentiated as female Other throughout the narrative. In fact, I would argue that Custance plays an integral role in the Man of Law's project to construe and expose woman's insidious desire to achieve similitude to man. Custance is not only an emblem of submissiveness, as Delany observes, but a reassuring symbol of all that is not-man. At crucial points in his narrative, the lawyer uses Custance to reinforce woman's proper difference from man, a task he has rendered urgent by his exposure of woman's perverse desire and ability to mask her outlaw status and masquerade as inlaw, as man.

V

The Man of Law shapes his presentation of Custance not to offer a biography of her but to focus on her relationship to male power, divine and human. Unlike Trevet's history and Gower's exemplum, which start with the birth and early years of Constance and end with her death, the lawyer's narrative truncates this cradle-to-grave coverage and frames our exposure to Custance between two scenes: her departure from and eventual return to Rome, where Custance is reunited with her husband and her father. In the first episode, in which Custance bids farewell to her parents, she arises "ful pale" (II.265) and weeps at the prospect of leaving her home for a strange land and an arranged marriage to a husband whose "condicioun" (II.271) she does not know. Furthermore, marriage itself is presented pejoratively here: Custance is to "be bounden under subjeccioun" (II.270) to a husband. If we expect any active resistance on Custance's part to the designs patriarchal authorities—father, husband-to-be, church, or state—have on her life, we soon find that Custance serves a different purpose in the Man of Law's narrative. She stands to articulate reassuring asymmetries between the sexes, not troubling congruities. Accordingly, Custance's first words in the lawyer's narrative not only signal her acquiescence to her father's plans to marry her to the sultan, but enunciate the basic dissimilitude between men, born to rule, and women, destined to serve:

> "Wommen are born to thraldom and penance,
> And to been under mannes governance,"

Custance remarks (II.286–87). The Man of Law's tale ends with an image of subjection that mirrors this opening scene. Upon the death of her husband, Aella, Custance returns to Rome to live with her father. Finding him, "doun on hir knees falleth she to grounde" (II.1153). By word and by gesture, Custance's role in the lawyer's tale is to represent and validate woman's difference from man, her humble position literally beneath him.

Accordingly, Custance's response to the adversities that men—her father, the false knight who accuses her of murdering Hermengyld, and, as she is tricked into believing, Aella—visit upon her is silence or submission. To the emperor's wish that she marry the sultan, Custance quickly succumbs: "I moste anoon, syn that is youre wille" (II.282), a sentiment the Man of Law echoes ("But forth she moot," II.320). In the face of the false accusation that Custance has murdered Hermengyld, Custance loses her voice altogether, and the Man of Law must speak for her:

> Allas! what myghte she seye?
> For verray wo hir wit was al aweye.

> (II.608–9)

As the lawyer points out, Custance cannot defend herself; she has no mortal "champion," and unlike "mannish" women such as Semiramis, she does not know how to "fighte" (II.631–32). Instead, Custance assumes her properly female—submissive—posture. She falls upon her knees and prays for Christ's aid, which is forthcoming. Exiled with her son by, she believes, Aella's decree, Custance takes it all in "good entente" (II.824), once again kneeling down to request Christ's succor. Reunited in Rome with Aella, whom she still believes commanded her and her child's cruel exile, Custance stands as "dumb as a tree" (II.1055), only to swoon twice at Aella's feet before he clears himself of guilt. Throughout the narrative, Custance's silence and her humble postures—kneeling, fainting—implicitly reiterate her different status from man.[76]

So too does Custance explicitly assert the difference between human and divine. As she is about to be exiled from England, Custance, again kneeling, first prays to Christ and then to Mary to take pity on her infant son, Maurice, also condemned to banishment. Despite the clear parallels between these two mothers, Custance emphasizes that there is "no comparison" (II.846) between the Virgin's woe and her own:

> "Thow sawe thy child yslayn bifore thyne yen,
> And yet now lyveth my litel child parfay!"

> (II.848–49)

It is, of course, Custance's very refusal to analogize her experience—to man or to god—that distinguishes her from the virago, be it the sultaness Donegild, Semiramis, or, ultimately, Eve, through whose "eggement / Mankynde was lorn, and damned ay to dye" (II.842–43), Custance prompts us to recall.

Yet at the same time that Custance stands opposed to the sultaness and Donegild, she is allied to them, for together these female figures define the full range of woman in medieval antifeminist thought, from Eve to the second Eve, Mary. Accordingly, the Man of Law never brings Custance into actual confrontation with her female opponents the way she is brought into conflict with her male adversaries.[77] Instead, Custance is yoked in juxtaposition to the viragoes, her humble and "womanly" behavior serving as a corrective gloss on their "mannishly" tyrannical actions. Thus, following the farewell scene (invented for the Man of Law) in which Custance declares woman to be born to slavery and man's governance (II.246–322), the lawyer inserts the episode in which the sultaness plots to usurp the governance of her country from her son (II.323–85). And with the account of Custance's wedding night (including the narrator's sententious decree that wives must suffer "in pacience," II.710, their husbands' sexual advances[78]) and of the subsequent birth of Maurice, the Man of Law pairs the scene in which Donegild employs a traditionally masculine agent—the phallic pen—to enact her own desires and "depaternalize" her son by misleading him into thinking Maurice was fathered by a demon.

Neither the sultaness nor Donelgild slays Custance, for the obvious reason that her absence would halt the tale. At the same time, however, one might observe in this narrative pattern the interdependence of the female characters as the Man of Law situates them. In their "mannishness," their transgressive proximity to man, the sultaness and Donegild provide patriarchal interests justification for creating and venerating the figure of Custance, the clearly distanced female Other. The former figure, the virago, is used to promote the establishment of the latter, and while both the sultaness and Donegild are eventually eradicated from the narrative, the rhetoric of proximity might readily supply a host of substitutes, beginning with Eve, to continue justifying a Custance.

VI

My interpretation of the Man of Law's narrative as a cautionary fable of transgressive proximity suggests a way of reading the disputed Epilogue to the tale.[79] As I shall argue here in conclusion, this endlink mimics the tale proper and performs its own corrective act of resituation. Having heard the lawyer's tale of unseen enemies who lurk nearby, the Host and the Shipman join forces to echo its narrative dynamic: they fabricate yet a third type of transgressor within their ranks and then silence him.[80]

In the Epilogue to the Man of Law's tale, Harry Bailly turns to the Parson and "for Goddes bones" (II.1166) requests of him the next tale. The Parson rebukes Harry for swearing so sinfully, and the Host, alluding to the aversion to oaths among Lollards, retorts with a charge of heresy: "I smelle a Lollere in the wynd" (II.1173). Although Harry is prepared to entertain a performance by "this Lollere" (II.1177), the Shipman is not. " 'That shal he nat!' / Seyd the Shipman, 'Heer schal he nat preche' " (II.1178–79). The Shipman blocks the Parson's tale on the grounds that this heretic Lollard might corrupt the faithful.

Although Lollardy, an actual heresy in canon law, and Islam, popularly regarded as heretical in spite of Church law to the contrary, were perceived as distinct, nevertheless Harry's accusation of the Parson seems more than casually related to the Man of Law's narrative. For one, Harry's jibe about the Parson's Lollardy constitutes Chaucer's exclusive reference to this contemporary English heresy, and it seems more than coincidental that it should follow the Chaucerian tale most concerned with the religious enemies within the Christian family as well as Chaucer's sole references to Islam, so often positioned as a heresy in the later Middle Ages. Not only does the reference to Lollardy localize heresy in a geographical and temporal sense, literally bringing it home to fourteenth-century England, but the term "Lollard" made possible a pun that situates this particular heretic especially close to the faithful, in fact, almost inseparably interspersed among them. In his objection to the Parson's tale, the Shipman employs this pun: "[the Parson] wolde sowen som difficulte, / Or springen cokkel in our clene corn" (II. 1182–83).

Medieval etymology derived "Lollard" from Latin *lollium*, or weed, and Lollards were likened to the tares sown among the wheat in Matthew's parable (13:24–30).[81] In that parable, an enemy sneaks into a man's field and sows weed seed among the wheat seed, unbeknownst to the field's owner until the blades spring up and reveal the corruption of his crop. But not until harvest can the farmer remove the tares, for were he to eradicate the weeds earlier he would also uproot his wheat. Both the etymology of "Lollard" and the verses in Matthew lie behind the Shipman's accusation of the Parson, which likens the cleric to the enemy in the parable of the wheat and tares, one who infiltrates the faithful and sows heresy. By means of his own rhetoric of proximity, then, the Shipman succinctly sums up one lesson he has learned from the Man of Law's cautionary fable: even in one's own field, one must be ever vigilant, for cockle may masquerade as corn and corrupt the true "clene" crop.

As facetious as Harry Bailly's accusation of heresy may be, it contains a similar note of alarm in that it is leveled specifically against the Parson. Many have commented on the apparent ineptness of charging not only a pilgrim cleric but this particular parson with Lollardy; Lollards frowned upon pilgrimage, and the tale that the Parson tells is, in Benson's words, "perfectly orthodox."[82] But the point of implicating the idealized Parson in Lollardy is, I think, precisely its illogicality. The accusation gives voice to medieval anxieties about the very nature of heresy, the fear of its uncanny, demonic ability to insinuate itself into the most disturbing and unlikely locations imaginable.[83] In Harry's case, this means within the Canterbury pilgrimage, indeed, amongst the very group responsible for guarding the faithful from such infiltration, the clergy. Like the Shipman, the Host has learned well another lesson the Man of Law's tale preaches: the Other is more transgressive the closer it approaches.

As Kolve argues, the lawyer's performance does attempt to reorient the direction of the Canterbury fictions. What I suggest the tale motivates, however, is not a return to the austere and vigorous commitment to Christ of the early Church, but the sense of a common vested interest among English men who, thanks to such narratives as the lawyer's, imagine themselves crowded on several fronts by the proximate Other—the woman, the heretic, the Oriental. At one and the same time, the tale of Custance provides the catalyst for the development of such a bond among the men who travel to Canterbury and locates its historical origin in the Saxon past of Aella's Northumberland.

The new praxis we see develop among the Canterbury pilgrims in the endlink bears witness to the effectiveness of the lawyer's rhetoric. Instead of squabbling amongst themselves, as did the fractious men of fragment I, the Host and Shipman join forces to perform a communal act of ousting, resituating the Parson as heretical Other. Just as masculine identity appears to demand a clearly delineated female Other,[84] so Christian identity rests upon the perception of a clearly inscribed religious Other, the heretic Lollard. Not by chance is this the sole occasion on the pilgrimage when the Shipman constructs both a communal and piously Christian identity for himself: "we leven alle in the grete God" he proclaims (II.1181).

The Shipman's profession of religion helps define the cultural work the Man of Law's tale of Custance has accomplished. But it also interrogates the lawyer's project, for the sailor's newfound Christian conscience must strain audience credulity. The Shipman's expression of religious devotion in the endlink has already been compromised by what we have heard about his maliciousness in the General Prologue, information valorized by the fact that Chaucer the pilgrim enunciates it. With uncharacteristic bluntness, Chaucer there introduced the Shipman as one who pays no heed to "nyce conscience" (I.398), who is not above stealing from merchants and dispatching his enemies to watery graves. This suggests that what the Shipman has found in the Epilogue is not Christ but men of his own stripe and that he has found such fraternity in opposition to the Other as the lawyer constructs that layered figure in his tale. The Man of Law's Tale exposes, hence questions, a central dynamic of patriarchal Christianity by which the *communitas* that develops in the Epilogue is achieved in response to a tale of exclusion and subordination, a tale that situates men and women, East and West, worlds apart.[85]

VII

A brief epilogue to this article is also in order, however, for no matter how deeply Chaucer may implicate the *communitas* the Man of Law has created, it is also true that Chaucer preserves this group's hegemony as the pilgrimage proceeds. Its authority is challenged on several occasions, most evidently by the Wife of Bath's resistance to playing the role of man's binary opposite, by the Pardoner's attempt to lure the Host away from his peer group, and by the Squire's effort to narrate a tale of eastern origin, quite possibly one that meant to rewrite the story of Custance.[86] Yet the fraternal ties that emerge in the Man of Law's Epilogue hold firm against these and other challenges: the Clerk, Merchant, and Franklin come together to rebut the Wife of Bath; the Knight reintegrates both the Pardoner and the Host into the fold; the Squire's tale fizzles out and the Franklin takes the young man under his paternal wing. No matter how clearly Chaucer exposes the Man of Law's dehumanizing rhetoric, the lawyer's tale nevertheless remains a pivotal narrative, for it catalyzes the originary act of solidarity among the Christian men of the Canterbury pilgrimage. That bond of western brotherhood proves to be a privileged defensive wall. The other pilgrims—and the Other—may strain against it, but they are not allowed to breach it.

Notes

1. As Helen Cooper, *The Structure of the Canterbury Tales* (Athens: University of Georgia Press, 1984), 121, notes, "the manuscripts, with remarkable consistency, place [the Man of Law's Tale] after fragment I and the Cook's Tale, whether the tale ascribed to the Cook is the Chaucerian fragment or *The Tale of Gamelyn*." The one exception appears to be Hengwrt, but, Cooper observes (121 n. 11), Hengwrt "has a misplaced quire at this point."
2. Pearsall, *The Canterbury Tales* (London: Unwin Hyman, 1985), 286.
3. Cooper, *Structure*, 63, 120.
4. Ibid., 121.
5. V. A. Kolve, *Chaucer and the Imagery of Narrative: The First Five Canterbury Tales* (Stanford, CA: Stanford University Press, 1984), 296.
6. Ibid., 368.
7. Ibid., 297.
8. 1 use the term *orientalism* in the sense that Edward W. Said does, to indicate "a Western style for dominating, restructuring, and having authority over the Orient," *Orientalism* (New York: Pantheon Books, 1978), 3.
9. Lee Patterson, "'No Man His Reson Herde': Peasant Consciousness, Chaucer's Miller, and the Structure of the *Canterbury Tales*," in *Literarcy Practice and Social Change in Britain, 1380–1530* (Berkeley: University of California Press, 1990), 124. Patterson reiterates the nature of the Miller's explicit threat in *Chaucer and the Subject of History* (Madison: University of Wisconsin Press, 1991), 246.
10. Patterson, "No Man His Reson Herde," 124.
11. Bloomfield, "Chaucer's Sense of History," *JEGP* 51 (1952): 309. Note the use of "Mohammedan" even in modern scholarly discourse.
12. Roger Ellis, *Patterns of Religious Narrative in the Canterbury Tales* (Totowa, NJ: Barnes & Noble, 1986), 146; italics mine.
13. Recent exploration of Chaucer's treatment of Islam is similarly skeptical concerning Chaucer's (or the Man of Law's) sympathy. See, for instance, Glory Dharmaraj, "Multicultural Subjectivity in Reading Chaucer's *Man of Law's Tale*," *Medieval Feminist Newsletter* 16 (1993): 4–8. Sheila Delany, *The Naked Text: Chaucer's Legend of Good Women* (Berkeley: University of California Press, 1994), remarks that Chaucer availed himself of the "patristic/popular mythos of the ever-threatening Orient" in the *Legend* (230), even though the poet is not a "raving warmonger" on the subject of the forced conversion of Muslims (185–86).
14. Sheila Delany, "Womanliness in the *Man of Law's Tale*," *ChauR* 9 (1974): 62.
15. Priscilla Martin, *Chaucer's Women: Nuns, Wives, and Amazons* (Iowa City: University of Iowa Press, 1990), 139.
16. Elaine Tuttle Hansen, *Chaucer and the Fictions of Gender* (Berkeley: University of California Press, 1992), 196.
17. Jonathan Dollimore, *Sexual Dissidence: Augustine to Wilde, Freud to Foucault* (Oxford: Clarendon Press, 1991), 131–48. In Dollimore's terms, "similarity" or "proximity" indicates the intimate relationship that exists between supposedly opposite binaries. Such "intimacy" ultimately stems from the

Christian anti-dualistic notion of evil as good's privation, not good's opposite, of vice as the perversion rather than antithesis of virtue. Evil and vice are thus "the more dangerous and potentially subversive for being in intimate relation with good" (141).

While I employ Dollimore's ideas of "transgressive proximity" and the "perverse dynamic" to theorize issues of gender, race, and religion in Chaucer, Glenn Burger has applied these concepts to (homo)sexuality; see his "Kissing the Pardoner," *PMLA* 107 (1992): 1142–56. Just as the Man of Law conflates the Muslim, woman, and the East, so are homosexuality, heresy, and Islam frequently coalesced in medieval thought. See, for instance, John Boswell, *Christianity, Social Tolerance, and Homosexuality* (Chicago: University of Chicago Press, 1980); Michael Camille, *The Gothic Idol: Ideology and Image-Making in Medieval Art* (Cambridge: Cambridge University Press, 1989), 90–92; Steven F. Kruger, "Claiming the Pardoner: Toward a Gay Reading of Chaucer's Pardoner's Tale," *Exemplaria* 6 (1994): 133 n. 45; Jeffrey Richards, *Sex, Dissidence and Damnation: Minority Groups in the Middle Ages* (London: Routledge, 1990), 148; and my "Mohammed, Courtly Love, and the Myth of Western Heterosexuality," *Medieval Feminist Newsletter* 16 (1993): 27–32.

18. Dollimore, 15.
19. Ibid., 138.
20. See Bernard Cullen, "Heresy," *Dictionary of the Middle Ages*, ed. Joseph R. Strayer (New York: Charles Scribner's Sons, 1985) 6: 202–4.
21. Ellen C. Shannon, *A Layman's Guide to Christian Terms* (New York: A. S. Barnes, 1969), s.v. "heresy."
22. On the virtuous pagan and salvation of the heathen in medieval literature, see R. W. Chambers, "Long Will, Dante, and the Righteous Heathen," *Essays and Studies* 9 (1923): 50–69; T. P. Dunning, "Langland and the Salvation of the Heathen," *Medium Aevum* 12 (1943): 45–54; Thomas G. Hahn, *God's Friends: Virtuous Heathens in Later Medieval Thought and English Literature* (Ph.D. thesis, University of California Los Angeles, 1974); and A. J. Minnis, *Chaucer and Pagan Antiquity* (Cambridge, England: D. S. Brewer, 1982), 55–56 and 61–67.
23. Norman Daniel, *Heroes and Saracens: An Interpretation of the Chansons de Geste* (Edinburgh: Edinburgh University Press, 1984), 263. Daniel notes exceptions to the treatment of Islam as heresy in the poetic tradition (*chansons de geste*) which calls Saracens "pagans" and views them as "non-Christian communities" (131). See also Antonio Franceschetti, "On the Saracen in Early Italian Chivalric Literature," *Comparative Literature East and West: Traditions and Trends; Selected Conference Papers*, ed. Cornelia N. Moore and Raymond A. Moody (Honolulu: College of Languages, Linguistics and Literature, University of Hawaii, 1986), 203–11. More typically, however, the Saracen is misrepresented not as heroic pagan but as evil heretic, as I discuss below. On this latter depiction, see William Wistar Comfort, "The Literary Role of the Saracens in the French Epic," *PMLA* 55 (1940): 628–59, and C. Meredith Jones, "The Conventional Saracen of the Songs of Geste," *Speculum* 17 (1942): 201–25.

24. Joan's "heresy" was her wearing of male attire, deemed idolatry, as I discuss in "True Lies: Transvestism and Idolatry in the Trial of Joan of Arc" (in *Fresh Verdicts on Joan of Arc*, ed. Bonnie Wheeler and Charles T. Wood [New York: Garland, 1996], 31–60).

25. *City of God* 16.2, cited and translated by Dollimore, *Sexual Dissidence*, 139.

26. Steven Kruger, "Racial/Religious and Sexual Queerness in the Middle Ages," *Medieval Feminist Newsletter* 16 (1993): 35. Late medieval heresy, of course, did more than offer the church an excuse to self-marginalize; it voiced social protest and called for reform, particularly of the institution it attacked as overly materialistic or endowed. With respect to the Man of Law's seemingly irrelevant tirade against poverty in the prologue to his tale, it is interesting to note that scholars now see voluntary poverty as the common practice of late medieval heresies, including Lollardy. For instance, Gordon Leff, *Heresy in the Later Middle Ages: The Relation of Heterodoxy to Dissent, c. 1250–c. 1450* (New York: Barnes & Noble, 1969), 1: 9, calls the veneration of poverty "one of the hallmarks of most heretical movements." The Man of Law casti-gates involuntary rather than elective poverty, yet any kind of anti-materialism may well be a threatening "heresy" to this lawyer who specializes in real estate transactions. Heretical or not, poverty evokes the lawyer's self-serving contempt; see Chauncey Wood, *Chaucer and the Country of the Stars* (Prince-ton, NJ: Princeton University Press, 1970), 192–244, and Paul A. Olson, *The Canterbury Tales and the Good Society* (Princeton, NJ: Princeton University Press, 1986), 90–91.

27. I cite the Douay–Rheims translation of the Old Testament (New York: P. J. Kennedy, 1950).

28. R. Howard Bloch, *Medieval Misogyny and the Invention of Western Romantic Love* (Chicago: University of Chicago Press, 1991), 22.

29. Kari Elisabeth Borresen, *Subordination and Equivalence: The Nature and Role of Woman in Augustine and Aquinas*, trans. Charles H. Talbot (Washing-ton, DC: University Press of America, 1981), 17–21 and 157, discusses both Augustine's reading of Genesis 1:27 in the context of 1:28 and Aquinas's use of *De Genesi ad litteram*. See also Prudence Allen, *The Concept of Woman: The Aristotelian Revolution, 750 BC–AD 1250* (Montreal: Eden Press, 1985), 223–25, on the dual creation account.

30. Cited by Larry D. Benson, ed., *The Riverside Chaucer*, 3rd ed. (Boston: Houghton Mifflin, 1987), 860 n. 359. All quotations of Chaucer's text are from this edition and cited parenthetically by fragment and line number in my text.

31. Boccaccio, *The Corbaccio*, trans. and ed. Anthony K. Cassell (Urbana: Uni-versity of Illinois Press, 1975), 25.

32. In addition to the work of Said, Daniel, Southern, and others cited specifi-cally in these notes, several studies generally inform my discussion of medieval western attitudes to Islam: Jeremy Jones, "Christianity and Islam," *The Oxford Illustrated History of Christianity*, ed. John McManners (Oxford: Oxford University Press, 1990), 163–95; Rana Kabbani, *Europe's Myths of Orient* (Bloomington: Indiana University Press, 1986); Benjamin Z. Kadar, *Crusade and Mission: European Approaches Toward the Muslims* (Princeton, NJ: Princeton University Press, 1984); Bernard Lewis, *The Arabs in History*

(1950; rpt. New York: Harper, 1967); Maria Rosa Menocal, *The Arabic Role in Medieval Literary History: A Forgotten Role* (Philadelphia: University of Pennsylvania Press, 1987); and W. Montgomery Watt, *The Influence of Islam on Medieval Europe* (Edinburgh: Edinburgh University Press, 1972).

33. Said, *Orientalism*, 60.

34. Ibid., 61–62.

35. Ibid., 59.

36. The period of the Crusades might well produce a different dynamic of orientalism, yet Norman Zacour, *Jews and Saracens in the Consilia of Oraldus de Ponte* (Toronto: PIMS, 1990), 22, maintains that "even during periods of truce with Islamic states, the tension between Christians and those Muslims who lived within Christian territory remained severe."

37. R. W. Southern, *Western Views of Islam in the Middle Ages* (Cambridge, MA: Harvard University Press, 1962), 39, observes that Islam, in fact, "never made the slightest appeal in Europe," and, if accurate, one of the reasons for this failure, I would suggest, is the success of the rhetoric of proximity.

38. Cf. Daniel J. Sahas, *John of Damascus on Islam* (Leiden: Brill, 1972).

39. Norman Daniel, *Islam and the West: The Making of an Image* (Edinburgh: Edinburgh University Press, 1960), 187. In *The Arabs and Medieval Europe* (London: Longmans, 1975), 254, Daniel further notes that "although theoretically Islam was identified as the sum of ancient heresies, it was never actually treated as a heresy until the sixteenth-century Inquisition was able to lay its hands on *baptized* Moriscos" (italics mine). Daniel also observes that Islam was never associated specifically with particular heresies of the high Middle Ages, e.g., Albigensians, Waldensians (*Arabs*, 246–47). The charges of heresy against Islam are painted broadly—"sum of all heresies," "sink of all heresies," etc. These accusations are rhetorical, not theological, meant for popular consumption, not for ecclesiastical court (cf. Daniel, *Arabs*, 246).

40. Delany, *Naked Text*, 184.

41. Ibid., 185.

42. Munro, "The Western Attitude toward Islam during the Period of the Crusades," *Speculum* 6 (1931): 329–43.

43. Ibid., 343.

44. Delany, *Naked Text*, 186.

45. Text and translation are from James Kritzeck, *Peter the Venerable and Islam* (Princeton, NJ: Princeton University Press, 1964), 143–44.

46. Daniel, *Islam*, 187. The notion of Islam as Christian heresy lingers, implicitly or explicitly, in some of the earlier scholarship I have cited above, as, for instance, in Southern's statement: "But in fact the heresy of Mahomet—if it was a heresy—never made the slightest appeal in Europe" (*Western Views*, 39).

47. Norman Zacour, *Jews and Saracens*, 42, cites the lack of distinction between Muslims and heretics in Oraldus's consilium 51. Oraldus (d. 1337?) also equates Jews with Saracens and heretics. See also Peter Herde, "Christians and Saracens at the Time of the Crusaders: Some Comments of Contemporary Medieval Canonists," *Studia Gratiana* 12 (1967): 359–76.

48. Daniel, *Islam,* 83–84.

49. Ibid., 184.

50. Delany, *Naked Text,* 185.

51. *Islam,* 263. Munro, "Western Attitude," 341–42, summarizes William's account.

52. *The Travels of Sir John Mandeville,* ed. A. W. Pollard (New York: Dover, 1964), 91.

53. Translated by Daniel, *Islam,* 164.

54. This passage from Jacques de Vitry, and the preceding quotations of Peter and William, are translated by Daniel, *Islam,* 185.

55. Daniel, ibid., 123.

56. Translated by Daniel, *Islam,* 322.

57. Paul E. Beichner, "Chaucer's Man of Law and *Disparitas Cultus,*" *Speculum* 23 (1948): 75.

58. Chaucer's lawyer exhibits other signs of an obsession with the theme of internal corruption. In the Introduction to the tale, his apparently irrelevant refusal to narrate stories of incest—specifically, Canacee's sinful love for her brother and Apollonius's for his daughter—first suggests the motif. Interestingly, Chaucer's source for the story of Canacee in the Squire's Tale, which hints at the incest in V.668, may be an oriental tale; see *Riverside Chaucer,* 890.

59. The extensive scholarship on the sources of Chaucer's tale of Custance is summarized by David Raybin, "Custance and History: Woman as Outsider in Chaucer's *Man of Law's Tale,*" *SAC* 12 (1990): 72–73, and by A. S. G. Edwards, "Critical Approaches to the *Man of Law's Tale,*" in *Chaucer's Religious Tales,* ed. C. David Benson and Elizabeth Robertson (Cambridge, England: D. S. Brewer, 1990), 87–90. See also Peter Nicholson, "*The Man of Law's Tale:* What Chaucer Really Owed to Gower," *ChauR* 26 (1991): 153.

60. For lack of a better text of Trevet, which is under preparation by the Chaucer Library, I have relied upon Margaret Schlauch's edition of Oxford MS Magdalen 45 in W. F. Bryan and Germaine Dempster, eds., *Sources and Analogues of Chaucer's Canterbury Tales* (1941; rpt. New York: Humanities Press, 1958), 165–81, and Edmund Brock's dual-language edition of British Museum Arundel 56 in F. J. Furnivall, Edmund Brock, and W. A. Clouston, eds., *Originals and Analogues of Some of Chaucer's Canterbury Tales* (1872; rpt. London: N. Trubner, 1887), 1–53. Quotations from Trevet, or Brock's translations, in my text are cited as *Chron* by page number from Brock's edition.

61. For Gower's *Confessio amantis,* I use the edition by Russell A. Peck (New York: Holt, Rinehart, Winston, 1968), cited by book and line number in my text as *CA.*

62. See Beichner, "*Disparitas Cultus,*" 72.

63. In somewhat different contexts, R. A. Shoaf, "'Unwemmed Custance': Circulation, Property, and Incest in the Man of Law's Tale," *Exemplaria* 2 (1990): 287–302, and Laurel L. Hendrix, " 'Pennannce profytable': The Currency of Custance in Chaucer's Man of Law's Tale," *Exemplaria* 6 (1994): 141–66, view Custance as a token of exchange between men, as does Patterson, *History,* 285.

64. The Man of Law's Custance echoes this place name, II.281.

65. The sultan's sudden and intense passion for Custance, a woman he has never seen, is an orientalist motif in that it analogizes the sultan to the lovesick knight of western romance whose beloved remains afar, although it might also be seen to stereotype the sultan as the sensualist eastern potentate.

66. *Riverside Chaucer*, 861 n. 519. See John A. Burrow, "'A Maner Latyn Corrupt,'" *Medium Aevum* 30 (1961): 33–37. The Man of Law earlier finessed the problem of how Custance spoke with her new compatriots and inlaws-to-be, implying that Syrian and Roman understood one another unaided.

67. Bryan and Dempster, *Sources and Analogues*, 160.

68. My interpretation is indebted to Delany's important early reading of the way in which women define one another in the Man of Law's tale ("Womanliness," 67–71), and to Jill Mann, *Geoffrey Chaucer* (Atlantic Highlands, NJ: Humanities Press, 1991), 130–31, for a similar reading of how "mannishness" is made to gloss "womanliness" in the tale.

69. Johnstone Parr, "Chaucer's Semiramis," *ChauR* 5 (1970): 57–61.

70. Boccaccio, *Concerning Famous Women*, trans. Guido A. Guarino (New Brunswick, NJ: Rutgers University Press, 1963), 5. All subsequent quotations of this translation are from pages 5 and 6.

71. On the topos of the woman-man, see Monica McAlpine, "The Pardoner's Homosexuality and How It Matters," *PMLA* 95 (1980): 8–22.

72. On the Man of Law's concern with incest, see note 58.

73. Cited in *Riverside Chaucer*, 860 n. 359.

74. On the forged letter as female stratagem, see Joan Ferrante, "Public Postures, Private Maneuvers: Roles Medieval Women Play," in *Women and Power in the Middle Ages*, ed. Mary Erler and Maryanne Kowaleski (Athens: University of Georgia Press, 1988), 217–18.

75. On the figure of the humility Madonna in medieval art and thought, see my "Botticelli's *Madonna del Magnificat*: Constructing the Woman Writer in Early Humanist Italy," *PMLA* 109 (1994): 196–97.

76. On the one occasion when Custance does act physically to defend herself, against a would-be rapist, the Man of Law mutes her personal agency and emphasizes God's role in protecting her (II.918–45). Significantly, this aggressor who has hidden himself on Custance's ship is a heretic, "a theef, that had reneyed oure creaunce" (II.915).

77. After Trevet's sultaness assassinates her son and all the Saracen converts, she first tempts and tortures Constance, who refuses to renounce her faith, and eventually exiles her (*Chron.* 11). Gower's Genius compresses this episode, but personally involves the sultaness in arranging Constance's banishment (*CA* 2.705–6), whereas unspecified Syrians, appearing to act on their own volition, set Custance adrift in the Man of Law's tale.

78. Neither Trevet nor Gower's Genius mentions the need for female submission to male sexual desire.

79. The Epilogue occurs in thirty-five manuscripts of the *Canterbury Tales* and is absent in twenty-two. As Benson explains, part of the debate over the Epilogue concerns whether it was written to follow the Man of Law's (putatively earlier) tale of Melibee or his current narrative of Custance. Finding the last three lines of the Epilogue more suitable to the Melibee than to the tale of

Custance, Benson deems it "likely that the Epilogue was composed to follow the Man of Law's (then) Tale of Melibee" (*Riverside Chaucer*, 862). The reading of the Epilogue I develop here, however, discovers more thematic linkage between it and the tale of Custance than the Melibee, suggesting that, even if the Epilogue was originally crafted to follow the latter, its appropriateness to the former motivated its retention in the majority of manuscripts. Also disputed is the name of the speaker of line 1179 (see *Riverside Chaucer*, 863 n. 1179); with Benson and most other editors, I take it to be the Shipman.

80.   The contagiousness of creating racial/religious Others is apparent to Zacour: Oraldus blends "into a single class all those outside Catholicism, among whom the only distinctions worth noting are their respective relations to orthodox Christianity. All the stronger, therefore, the propensity for grouping Jews and Muslims together, despite their myriad differences" (*Jews and Saracens*, 21). See note 47, above.

81.   *Riverside Chaucer*, 863 n. 1183. The term *Lollard* probably derived in actuality from Middle Dutch *lollaerd*, according to Eilert Ekwall, "A Twelfth-Century Lollard?" *English Studies* 28 (1947): 108–10.

82.   *Riverside Chaucer*, 863 n. 1173.

83.   Zacour, *Jews and Saracens*, 12–13, points out that Lateran IV required both Jews and Muslims to wear distinctive clothing, live in separate quarters, etc., all of which, I would argue, evidences (as well as created) the xenophobic fear about infiltration in the later Middle Ages that Chaucer portrays in the Epilogue.

84.   On the formation of Christian male identity based on aggression towards women in medieval Castile, see Louise Mirrer, "Representing 'Other' Men: Muslims, Jews, and Masculine Ideals in Medieval Castilian Epic and Ballad," in *Medieval Masculinities: Regarding Men in the Middle Ages*, ed. Claire A. Lees (Minneapolis: University of Minnesota Press, 1994), 169–86.

85.   My point about the "mob psychology" of the Epilogue holds regardless of which male pilgrim speaks line 1179 and whether the assignment is authorial or scribal (see *Riverside Chaucer*, 863 n. 1179).

86.   Dorothee Metlitzki, *The Matter of Araby in Medieval England* (New Haven, CT: Yale University Press, 1977), 153–54, discusses the relationship between the Man of Law's tale and the Squire's tale.

Chaucer and Englishness

DEREK PEARSALL

This lecture has its origins in a number of occupations I have been engaged in and preoccupations I have had over the past few years. One is a talk I gave at a conference in Minnesota some years ago on 'Strangers in Late Fourteenth-Century London'.[1] The conference topic was 'Strangers in the Middle Ages', and I found the idea of 'the stranger' a very fruitful one for thinking about concepts of community identity and national consciousness. Another influence has been my own life as an Englishman working in the United States for the last thirteen years, and living there for part of the year as a stranger (a 'resident alien'), with the thoughts about Englishness that such an existence has been bound to provoke, whether out of a desire to exercise them or to exorcise them. And of course, since I am always 'doing' Chaucer, there was inevitably the desire to associate any thoughts about Englishness that came my way with the poet who occupied a large portion of my time, and to find out whether Englishness was in any way important in his writing.

I spent the whole of the academic year 1996–97 in England, and 'Englishness' was a subject that it was impossible, during that year, not to go on thinking about, in day-to-day life, in attending to the news, in voting in the general election—the whole question of what constitutes a sense of national identity, a sense of nationhood, the idea of a national community—with maybe the added excitement that comes from examining something that seemed to be in a state of morbid decay, or at least changing rapidly in the aftermath of the cold war. I even did a little sociological research—of a not too strenuous kind—asking my friends in England what they thought 'Eng-

This essay was read as the Sir Israel Gollancz Memorial Lecture at the British Academy, 26 March 1998. It first appeared in print in *1998 Lectures and Memoirs, Proceedings of the British Academy*, 101 (Oxford and New York: Oxford University Press, 1999), 77–99. Reprinted by permission of the British Academy.

lishness' consisted in. I received an enormous variety of answers, including the categorical answer that there was no such thing, and I could find no consensus among those who thought there was. Tolerance, a sense of humour, a taste for understatement and irony, a love of gardens, standoffishness, excessive consciousness of class, prudishness, prurience, hypocrisy—these are only some of the traits that were mentioned, not all of them, as will readily be seen, forms of complacent self-congratulation.

However, the fact that the concept of 'Englishness' proved amorphous, that there were a number of shifting mythologies of Englishness competing for attention and promoted by a variety of more or less interested parties, did not make the idea of Englishness, and the desire to think about it and investigate it, any less pressingly important. And I was aware that there was at least one consistent strain in the answers to my question, even when people seemed to be putting forward completely different viewpoints, and that was the universal tendency to define 'Englishness' in terms of what it was or what it was not in relation to a presumption of national identity in other countries. So the English have a sense of humour where the Germans have only Teutonic belly-laughter, the English are sexually stunted where the French are open and frank, the English are standoffish and snobbish where the Americans are friendly and neighbourly. Or, as it might be, vice versa, since the truth-content of all these generalisations is about equal with their opposites, which is to say, nil. Nevertheless, these opinions are passionately held to, and, what is more, necessarily held to, since it seems to be a law that communities, including national communities, are chiefly constituted not through their sharing in the possession of certain unique and intrinsic qualities but through the exclusion from those communities, on one pretext or another, and sometimes quite arbitrarily, of those who are perceived not to belong to them.

This, in its implications, is not an entirely happy conclusion, but the strength of its claim on us may be demonstrated by placing side by side two quotations which together, I think, constitute a paradigm of social cohesion and exclusion, of national consciousness and xenophobia. The first quotation is from *Survival in Auschwitz*, by Primo Levi:

> Many people—many nations—can find themselves holding, more or less wittingly, that 'every stranger is an enemy'. For the most part this conviction lies deep down like some latent infection; it betrays itself only in random, disconnected acts, and does not lie at the base of a system of reason.[2]

Despite his experiences at the hands of some of them, it is clear that Levi has a quite optimistic view of the many people, the many nations, that he speaks of. He describes the origin of the enmity towards strangers, the exclusion and often vilification of outsiders which informs the more rabid forms of nationalistic consciousness, as a form of deviance from a normally healthy state, as a potential flaw or weakness, like vulnerability to infection. What he does not take account of, or wish to take account of, is the possibility that what he calls the 'infection' is not some rottenness in the system, but part of what makes the system work, indeed part of a 'system of reason'.

The second quotation is from George Simmel, in a 1908 essay on 'Der Fremde' which is very familiar to students of sociology as a classic early statement of the structuralist view of the 'construction' of strangers,[3] a view that provides an important working hypothesis in analyses of group-identity by scholars as widely different in their approaches as the Norwegian anthropologist Fredrik Barth, the French linguist Emil Benveniste, and the American social historian John A. Armstrong.[4] The stranger, says Simmel, is 'an organic member of the group, both outside it and necessary to its efficient working. . . . Mutually repulsive and opposing elements here compose a form of joint and interacting unity.'[5] A stranger is one who is identified as 'other' in relation to a group that perceives itself or desires to define itself as the opposite of that 'other', that is, as 'one'. The concept of the stranger is thus vital to the creation and preservation of communities. Where a community feels itself to be under threat, the otherness of strangers will be thought of as potentially menacing, and hostility towards them will grow or be fomented. The threat may be perceived to be economic (as for instance in a shortage of jobs because of immigrants) or political (as for instance in a threat to national security because of the presence of non-nationals). Even where there is no clearly identifiable threat to a community, one may have to be invented, and continually reinvented, often in the form of demonised racial or religious 'others', in order to preserve the integrity of that community.

Turning now to Chaucer, with this paradigm in mind, one can first use the Chaucer text as a linguistic data-base from which to derive a taxonomy of 'stranger-hood', an understanding of the system through which words mark the boundaries that strengthen a given community's consciousness of its identity. Take the word *strange*. Chaucer uses the adjective *strange* or *straunge* quite frequently, with a range of meanings that are illustrated also in the Middle English word *straunger*. *Straunge*, first, means 'foreign, from a country not one's own, from abroad', without connotation of odd or weird, and is applied thus to the warriors who come from all over the near east and the far east to fight in the lists for Palamon or Arcite in the Knight's Tale. Theseus and his court entertained them, we are told,

> And made revel al the longe nyght
> Unto the straunge lordes, as was ryght.[6]

Such strangers are not necessarily hostile, but they are not unlikely to be so disposed, like the 'strange nacion' that Constance fears, in the Man of Law's Tale (II.268). Second, *straunge* means 'not a member of one's social group', as more narrowly but still quite broadly defined. The 'straunge folk' that Prudence warns Melibeus against in Melibee (*Canterbury Tales*, VII.1245) are people from outside their circle of friends: all such people one is to be wary of. Thirdly, and in a somewhat narrower sense, *straunge* is used to refer to people who are not members of one's family or household or who are not friends of the family. Such a meaning is to be understood when Criseyde tearfully reproaches Pandarus for encouraging her to get embroiled in a love affair. How can she trust 'straunge', she says (using the plural adjective as a substantive) when the one she took to be her best friend betrays her in this way (*Troilus and Criseyde*, II.411). Finally, and in the most strict construction, *straunge* is used to refer to people who are not members of one's family, in the sense of blood-relatives. In the Clerk's Tale, people are worried that 'a straunge successour' may take Walter's heritage if he has no heir (IV.138): they mean someone who is not a member of the ruling family. January has the same concern in the Merchant's Tale lest his heritage 'sholde falle / In straunge hand' (IV.1439–40) if he does not marry and get an heir.

There was, one might say, a disposition in the language to reinforce and solidify relations within groups.[7] One could call it, pessimistically, a linguistic architecture of xenophobia, or one could, in a better mood, call it a linguistic embodiment of the principle of community, but it seems embedded in the language through which that community expresses and identifies itself. The word *disposition*, borrowed from the language in which medieval people talked about one's 'disposition' in relation to the stars, is a useful one, since it avoids the suggestion of a determinism in language so rigid that escape from the prison-house is impossible. But it may be optimistic to think so, since escape is at the least very difficult, and certainly the views of Chaucer on the subject of 'strangers' were to some extent already formed in the language he inherited.

The language thus reinforced those ideological systems by which communities identify themselves and exclude others. And one can go on from there, to other kinds of evidence, in documents and records as well as literary texts, to show that linguistic systems of exclusion and community identity-formation operated at every level. If one looked, for instance, at some of the realities that surrounded late fourteenth-century Londoners like Chaucer, one would find that from the point of view of London citizens a large number of their fellow-Londoners were, as far as the record went, 'foreigners' (in the language of the records, usually *forinsecus*), being poor, unenfranchised and condemned to perform only the most menial tasks needed by society.[8] There were also the 'foreigners' who came from out of town to sell their goods. These people were a menace to the citizens, since they tended to undercut monopolistic price-fixing, and they needed to be excluded, not just controlled. The guild and municipal records are full of the city's attempts to do so. Langland is conscious of the painful lives of at least some of these people ('the wo of this wommen that wonyeth in cotes'),[9] but in principle he is hostile to them, whether in the person of the humble workers (characterised as

layabouts) who frequent Glutton's tavern, or as the hated 'regraters' or unau-
thorised retail-dealers.[10] In Chaucer the principle of exclusion operates so
fully as to make them all in effect invisible, unless we find them among the
riff-raff of petty criminals who dwell in the 'suburbes' of the city in the
Canon's Yeoman's Prologue (VIII.657–61).

Immigrants from other parts of England, who were urgently needed to
replenish a declining population and provide workers for London's rapidly
expanding cloth-industry, constituted another class of foreigners. They were
of course a particular target for Londoners' hostility and scorn, and those
from Norfolk, close enough to London to be an important source of immigrants and yet far enough away to be utterly foreign, seem to have come in
for more than usual abuse. In having the Reeve, perhaps the nastiest person
on the pilgrimage, come from Norfolk, Chaucer is certainly playing on Londoners' contempt for *parvenu* immigrants from that area, a hostility the more
virulent since they came to London in such numbers.[11]

There seems no reasonable way of finding subversive self-contradiction
at the heart of Chaucer's project here, in the modern post-structuralist fashion, and it should not be a matter for surprise that a great poet like Chaucer
should follow so readily the linguistic fault-lines of class and regional prejudice, either in excluding whole classes of people from his poetry and making
them invisible, or in selecting a particular class for abuse. It is, in a way,
inevitable that he should do so: it is a structural principle of the language, and
in the formation of the communities that identify themselves in that language. The principal thing that establishes a Londoner as a Londoner, then as
now, or an Englander as an Englander (or a New Yorker as a New Yorker), is
their scorn of those who do not belong to the group that marches under the
banner of that sign. Obviously, the group will have some intrinsic and objectively definable qualities as well; but these are less important in identifying
the group than the structure of boundary-markers, or 'linguistic border
guards', as Armstrong calls them.[12] Thus for Barth the 'critical focus of
investigation' is 'the ethnic *boundary* that defines the group, not the cultural
stuff it encloses', while Armstrong deplores the tendency of theorists of
nationalism to look for ' "essences" of national character instead of recognizing the fundamental but shifting significance of boundaries for human
identity'.[13]

The historical realities of Norfolk-hood to which Chaucer refers are
relayed to us in a characteristically literary way, as part of a fictional narrative of experience, and with allusion to what had become a familiar topos of
anti-Norfolk satire.[14] And a similar point can be made about Chaucer's literary encapsulation of the most murderous outbreak of anti-immigrant hostility
in London history. There had been spectacular street-killings of 'alien merchants' from Italy in 1370 (Nicholas Sardouche) and 1379 (Janus Imperial),
as much the product of a general hostility towards foreigners as of economic

jealousy, but these were sporadic events, not part of a pattern.[15] The 'merchant strangers' were rich men, and there were not many of them. The case was different with the Flemish immigrants who had settled in London in quite large numbers to work for low pay in the London cloth-industry: they were systematically persecuted by the authorities with specially oppressive regulations, and pursued by their fellow-Londoners with hostility and suspicion. There were of course economic motives for hatred, fear and suspicion, and a different account from mine might want to place more stress on those economic causes, and on the fomenting of ethnic hostility by employers in order to divide employees and prevent them making common cause. There is evidence that this did happen,[16] but the attribution of agency in such matters to the repressive apparatus of authority is perhaps too easy and comfortable an explanation.

The massacre of the London Flemings took place on Friday, 14 June 1381, the day when the villagers and craftsmen from Kent had their rebellion hijacked by the London rabble. Excited by their successes at the Tower and the Savoy, the rioters fell upon the group that they were structured to hate even more than they hated their oppressors, and the massacre that followed is described in every one of the chronicles of the Peasants' Revolt.[17] Chaucer's account of the massacre is well known. It forms a brilliant comic climax to the Nun's Priest's Tale, and it provides a superlative example of Chaucer's readiness to allow his poetry to flow in the ideological currents of his age and to 'literaricize' its nasty realities.

> Ran Colle oure dogge, and Talbot and Gerland,
> And Malkyn, with a dystaf in hir hand;
> Ran cow and calf, and eek the verray hogges,
> So fered for the berkyng of the dogges
> And shoutyng of the men and wommen eeke
> They ronne so hem thoughte hir herte breeke.
> They yolleden as feendes doon in helle;
> The dokes cryden as men wolde hem quelle;
> The gees for feere flowen over the trees;
> Out of the hyve cam the swarm of bees.
> So hydous was the noyse—a, benedicitee!—
> Certes, he Jakke Straw and his meynee
> Ne made nevere shoutes half so shrille,
> Whan that they wolden any Flemyng kille,
> As thilke day was maad upon the fox. (VII.3383–97)

We share Chaucer's sense of fun with more than a slight uneasiness, along with a further sense of embarrassment that our uneasiness may be dictated by prudently self-serving assumptions of political correctness. But there is no doubt what Chaucer is doing. The lines are brutally trivialising and also cruelly suggestive of the glee that some Londoners may have felt at the fortuitous removal of a public nuisance by an equally contemptible rabble. It's dog eat dog, and a humorous good riddance. There may be some parody, in the passage, of Book I of Gower's *Vox Clamantis*, where Gower portrays the rebels as a rabble of domestic animals run wild,[18] but the effect of this would only be to make Chaucer's appeal more cliquish, and the Flemings more expendable, as part of a literary joke.

Of course, there are ways in which the sense of unease, which many have described themselves as experiencing in reading the passage, can be alleviated.[19] One is simply to relieve Chaucer of any responsibility, historically, for his text by pointing to his role as a mere 'author function' within his text, and to his 'text' as an array of floating signifiers. Another is to recall that Chaucer deliberately diffuses authorial responsibility in the *Canterbury Tales* by assigning the tales to different tellers, himself merely ventriloquizing their voices. One can also argue, with the Nun's Priest's Tale as with the Prioress's Tale, that the context reverses the apparent direction of the meaning of the passage: in other words, the narrator is in some way inadequate, and the views that the narrator puts forward, or that are embodied in the tale that is told, are ironically undercut because of our recognition of that inadequacy. So the lines in the Nun's Priest's Tale are a repudiation of the views of those who take them to be crudely dismissive of the lives of these unimportant and objectionable people. These three views could be summed up, in the manner of Wayne C. Booth,[20] as the 'Go away, author, you don't exist' position, the 'Come back, author, all is forgiven' position, and the 'It's all someone else's fault' position.

There seems, though, little point in continuing to complain about this passage, or in *blaming* Chaucer, or in attempting further to salvage Chaucer for modern liberal sentiment. He lived when he did, shared the mentality of his age, flattered the prejudices of the class that sponsored him, even if at times with a deodorising dash of ironic self-reflexivity. What is more important is to recognise how susceptible Chaucer has been, partly through his readiness to aestheticise difficult social realities, to modern attempts to appropriate him for a variety of ideologies of 'Englishness', with all that that term implies of xenophobia.

It would be sobering to think that part of the reason for the extraordinary popularity of Chaucer in the last two centuries has been that his writing confirmed and nourished, in the subtlest and wittiest and most pleasing ways, an Englishness that his readers could feel comfortable with, an Englishness that was rooted in insularity and therefore in a prejudice, implicit or explicit, against 'strangers'. In other words, the xenophobia which is a special point of pride in the proclaiming of English national consciousness—the 'wogs begin at Calais' theme—has historically been nourished by a reading of Chaucer which has found in him all the qualities that the English want to think of as peculiarly their own. The idealisation of Chaucer as the poet of a particular kind of Englishness makes his poetry serviceable to deriving forms and manifestations of national consciousness, some of them obnoxious.

The point I have to make here is that this idealisation of Chaucer as the poet of Englishness has little or no basis in his poetry. Chaucer has been described above as participating fully in contemporary linguistic and other structures of community identity-formation. These structures can be thought of as a series of interconnected circles of common interest, most of them to do with some sort of class affiliation. They are circumscribed or defined by the manner in which they exclude those who are deemed not to belong within the circle. An individual will belong, or perceive himself to belong (for 'self-ascription' is a vitally important element in the making of these communities[21]—they are, in Benedict Anderson's phrase, 'imagined communities'[22]), within a number of these circles, and particular medieval individuals that we now might lump together under some common label like middle-class or bourgeois will belong within different sets of circles. Chaucer's situation, both real and imagined, is very different from Usk's, and from Hoccleve's, and from Gower's, more subtly different than from Langland's or from Lydgate's, but no less remarkably different.

But with all this said, there is one circle of common interest which Chaucer never seems desirous of moving in or even recognising, and that is England. I am conscious that the nation is a more complicated phenomenon than the forms of community-identity that I have so far been talking about, but the structural paradigm I originally set out still works, I think. Scholars are generally agreed that the most important period in the development of the English nation and of the idea of the English nation was the sixteenth century. Richard Helgerson and Alan G. R. Smith have argued this case from their different points of view, and Liah Greenfield has put it even more strongly: 'The original modern idea of the nation emerged in sixteenth-century England, which was the first nation in the world': most recently, Andrew Hadfield, Gerald Hammond, and Claire McEachern have attempted to identify the emergent moment of English nationhood in relation to particular texts.[23] The Reformation was clearly important in identifying an England for the first time fully isolated from Catholic Europe, and John Bale and John Foxe both speak of England as the nation of the elect; Bale personifies England the nation as 'widow England' in *King Johan* (the dead husband is the true British church, put away at the time of the Augustinian conversion).[24] And the renewed Spanish threat towards the end of the century, as well as the highly successful personal rhetoric of majesty devised by and for Elizabeth, clearly gave some spur to the celebration of the Protestant nation in the *Faerie Queene* and the portrayal of the nation embodied in the monarch in

Henry V. In both cases, assertion of difference, of identity through opposition, seems to me the decisive factor in welding together different elements making for a sense of national community.

Even so, these are only preliminary moves in the making of the modern nation-state, which seems to have come into existence, along with the ideology of nationalism, in the late eighteenth and early nineteenth centuries; in fact, Elie Kedourie, Ernest Gellner, and E. J. Hobsbawm would go so far as to argue that nations are produced by the ideology of nationalism, working on, transforming, even inventing pre-existent forms of national identity.[25] This may be so, but there are decisive material changes at work too. If we accept the definition of the nation offered by Anthony D. Smith, 'a named human population sharing an historic territory, common myths and historical memories, a mass, public culture, a common economy and common legal rights and duties for all members',[26] then it seems obvious that the early to mid-nineteenth century must be the crucial period of development, since the articulation of nationhood can only become truly national when there are the beginnings of an adequate system of communication and information-dissemination, namely the railways and the newspapers.

But English medieval scholars have not been content to be left out of this exciting new game, and there have been various attempts to identify medieval moments of emergent English nationhood. A recent book by Thorlac Turville-Petre points to the years 1290–1340 as a time when what he calls 'national feeling' and 'the expression of national identity' come into prominence.[27] Certainly there are a number of writers at this time—the Kentish author of the romance of *Arthour and Merlin* ('Freynsche use this gentil man / Ac everich Inglische Inglische can'), the northern author of the biblical history of the *Cursor Mundi* (written in English 'For the love of Inglis lede, / Inglis lede of Ingland')—who argue vigorously that English should be the language of England, and who seem therefore to be promoting a kind of linguistic nationalism, calling into existence an as yet shadowy nation.[28]

Language, it is true, is an important part of national identity; indeed, a nation can hardly begin to exist in any terms until it is perceived as a community of people who speak the same language.[29] But the remarks of these authors, about England and the English language, and further of Robert Mannyng, Robert of Gloucester and the author of the *South English Legendary*,[30] are evidence only of fragmentary, sporadic, regional responses to particular circumstances, not of a wave of English nationalism sweeping the country. These writers are culturally under-capitalised: this is not where great changes will be initiated. There may be a temptation to relate these phenomena, in terms of the structural paradigm, to the baronial opposition to Henry III, which, since the barons took special exception to the French courtiers that Henry III had surrounded himself with (in his attempt to emulate Louis IX as a European monarch), may look like some assertion of Englishness. But it was not: the leader of the barons was Simon de Montfort, a Frenchman who spoke no English, and what the barons wanted, as always, was not England for the English but England for themselves, and more of the say to which they felt themselves entitled in the national councils.

Turville-Petre points also to other evidences of national identity that were emerging at this time. Of one of them—geographical integrity—it is hardly necessary to speak, since England, with or without Scotland and Wales, had always had the advantage over places that were not islands of being immediately recognisable as a territorial unit, a *there*. But to the establishment of nationhood on the basis of a national history, or the history of a race, there were severe obstacles. The foundation history of the island was that of the Britons, and the hero was Arthur, who had made all his reputation slaughtering the cruel and treacherous and uncivilised people who were now the English. Geoffrey of Monmouth had got round this, in a way, by treating the story as the legitimation of serial invasion and conquest and thus flattering his Norman patrons, but this could not be a happy answer for long (and of course for the more austere student of history it was an extremely gloomy answer right from the beginning).[31] Geoffrey's successors came up with a variety of strategies for dealing with the problem. The author of *Arthour and Merlin* quite simply calls the Anglo-Saxons Saracens and asserts that Arthur's Britons are the people we now call the English. The others just went away. Robert Mannyng invented a whole episode in which the Anglo-Saxon conquerors are conquered by a Briton called Engle who lands at Scarborough and turns the vile Saxons into a fine handsome people called the English, named after himself, of course.[32]

When English did take over as the spoken and written language of the vast majority of English people during the latter part of the fourteenth century, there was unexpectedly little trumpeting of national identity, perhaps because England was not at the time at war with France. Chaucer did of course choose to write in English, and it is to his influence and example that some large part in the rapidity of the linguistic shift must be ascribed; and he does talk about 'the king's English' in the prologue to the *Treatise on the Astrolabe* ('And preie God save the king, that is lord of this langage', line 56), thereby acknowledging a bond between the monarch and the language which Henry V was to find extremely useful as an instrument of policy. A national language is an important constituent element in national identity, as I have said, but in itself it is more of an enabling condition than a determining characteristic. Chaucer's idea in using English was in any case not to assert an independent national identity but to enable England to take its place among those more advanced nations of Europe—France and Italy—

that had already an illustrious vernacular. English is part of Chaucer's European project. As Elizabeth Salter says, 'His use of English is the triumph of internationalism.'[33]

Of national feeling or a sense of national identity—whether it has to do with ideas of national or racial history, with England as a land, with ideas of national character, or with opposition to some hostile national other—I find little or nothing in Chaucer. The framework story of the *Canterbury Tales* is set in England—'And specially from every shires ende / Of Engelond to Caunterbury they wende' (General Prologue, 15–16)—and this is an important innovation. England is being fully *recognised*, so to speak, perhaps for the first time, as a real place. But it is not a place for which we are encouraged to feel a particular affection, as a beloved land or heritage-site, and the pilgrims and the people who inhabit those of the *Canterbury Tales* that are set in England[34] are on the whole a pretty unsavoury lot. The Flemings are killed by an English mob, but the massacre as Chaucer alludes to it is not an outburst of national feeling; the Londoners are a rabble, and just as contemptible, to the observing eye of the would-be patrician, as their victims. Chaucer's references to Arthurian legend are patronising and faintly contemptuous, as to a bad joke that has grown stale with repetition.[35]

The reading of Chaucer as the poet of Englishness did not properly develop until the nineteenth century, though there was a time in the early fifteenth century when he played a part in a political programme of national legitimation. At this time Henry V did indeed make strenuous efforts to encourage the use of the English language in official documents as part of a programme to promote a sense of English national identity which would be triumphantly symbolised in his own person as monarch. He encouraged the use of English in the Chancery, so that by the end of his reign, a few short years, English was the norm in Chancery documents where at the beginning it had been the exception.[36] When in 1422 the London Company of Brewers made their famous decision to keep their records in future in English instead of French, they made a point of saying that they were proud to do so because of the encouragement Henry V had given to the English language.[37] Henry also, while still Prince of Wales, set Lydgate on his way translating the vast Latin prose history of Troy into English, not just because it was an exemplary story of chivalric exploits (it took Lydgate some while to find that it wasn't), but because it seemed to the king a slur on England and the English language that the greatest story of antiquity should be represented in Latin and French but not properly in English.

> Bycause he wolde that to hyghe and lowe
> The noble story openly wer knowe
> In oure tonge, aboute in every age,
> And y-writen as wel in oure langage

As in Latyn and in Frensche it is.[38]

Chaucer, meanwhile, was recruited to the national cause as the founder of the newly elegant and prestigious English ('the firste fyndere of oure faire langage') that was to embody the aspirations of nationhood, and was acclaimed thus in lavish terms by Hoccleve and Lydgate.[39]

Henry V's motives in encouraging the use of English are clear. He considered that a nation's language is to some extent an embodiment of its identity (and he made this explicit in the instructions he gave to the English ambassadors at the council of Constance in 1415—'The peculiarities of language', he told them, 'are the most sure and positive sign of a nation in divine and human law'),[40] and he wanted that identity reinforced in every way that he could, not just to integrate the national effort in the war against France, but to ensure that that sense of identity was focused and symbolised in the person of the king. The French campaign of 1415 was, in some measure at least— like the encouragement of English in official and literary circles—an assertion of the unified identity of nation, language and king. The whole episode is in fact a striking example of what John Armstrong, in his book *Nations before Nationalism*, describes as the operation of the state in the production of the nation, and it is where Henry V bears for a moment a striking resemblance to Kemal Ataturk. Such operations will depend for their permanence on the resources that are put into them and the degree of cultural penetration that an administration can achieve.[41]

Henry's campaign on behalf of the national language was powerfully influential, at a certain level, while it lasted, but it died with him, or before him, when the immediate circumstances that prompted it had passed away. Indeed, the legacy of the dual kingdom of England and France with which he burdened his brothers and his son was one that worked against any exclusively English sense of national identity.[42] There is a good deal of 'nationalistic' anti-French propaganda in the English poetry of the fifteenth century,[43] evidence of the role that the French had played since the twelfth century (and have continued to play) as the principal agents of English national self-construction, always available to stand for everything that the English do not want to be, according to a structural pattern that seems impervious to political accommodations.[44] But the idea of the nation in these poems is only imperfectly articulated, and the story of English nationhood in the fifteenth century, as in the thirteenth and fourteenth, is one of local manoeuvres, of surges of enthusiasm slopping back into indifference, of historical contingencies and short-lived glories.

Chaucer is certainly seen in the fifteenth century as the founder of English poetry, as the first to give high status to English as a literary language, but this is a specialised claim for the poetry of a cultural elite and has only indirectly to do with English nationhood. And even when the narrative of nationhood begins to be more fully told, Chaucer plays no significant part in it at first.[45] In the sixteenth century Chaucer is seen against a classical or Italian background, as a writer who has given English poetry respectability, brought it to a point where it can claim some place among the great poetries of Europe. In the seventeenth century he is decried as old and obsolete, or blamed for having corrupted English by importing whole cartloads of foreign words. Dryden praises Chaucer memorably in the Preface to the *Fables* (1700), and is proud that Chaucer was an Englishman, but his highest commendation, as befits a neo-classical commentator, is reserved for Chaucer's portrayal of 'our Fore-fathers and Great Grand-dames' as they are representative of a universal human nature.[46] Elsewhere in the eighteenth century there are a few references here and there to Chaucer and other early poets as 'old British oaks',[47] but this is a patronising, not an idealising, version of his Englishness. The first allusions I find to Chaucer's Englishness as an embodiment of a permanent and idealised national identity are in the immediate aftermath of the Napoleonic wars, which most scholars of nationalism, as I have said, take to be an extremely significant period in the development of that national spirit of identity.

Linda Colley, in her book *Britons*, describes the Napoleonic wars as the climax of a period when 'Great Britain was made out of that remarkable succession of wars with France'.[48] Her thesis is substantially the one I have stated:

> Men and women decide who they are by reference to who and what they are not. Once confronted with an obviously alien Them, an otherwise diverse community can become a reassuring or merely desperate Us. This was how it was with the British after 1707. They came to define themselves as a single people not because of any political or cultural consensus at home, but rather in reaction to the Other beyond their shores.[49]

So it was that the threat of invasion in 1803 was met by the assertion of the changelessness of British identity:

> ... Let them see
> How unchanged the British name.
> Let the ruffians know that WE
> ARE IMMUTABLY THE SAME ...
> Shew them that age to age bequeaths
> The British Character complete.

Britain has a kind of immune system which immediately comes into operation with the threat of foreign bodies—

> All Party diff'rence would at once be o'er
> Soon as a HOSTILE FRENCHMAN trod the shore.[50]

The French meanwhile, in accordance with what was by now a very old tradition, are characterised as all the things the British are not—frivolous,
unstable, immoral, deceitful, hypocritical, over-sexed and at the same time
effeminate.

And it is now for the first time that Chaucer becomes, not just an English
writer, but a representative of the nation in its idealised self-imaging form, an
agency in the nationalistic production of the idea of the nation. Robert
Southey, for instance, says in 1814 that 'strong English sense and strong English humour characterize his original works'.[51] An anonymous writer in the
Retrospective Review for 1824 speaks of Chaucer's poetry as 'an essential
portion of the authentic history of his country . . . of the history of the
national mind'.[52] Another anonymous writer in the *Edinburgh Review* of
1837—and these writers are just as important in representing and conveying
these broad shifts in consciousness as better-known writers—says that though
Chaucer was indebted to French and Italian writers, he was above all 'a
national poet formed by national circumstances, and appealing to a nation'.
'It was in Chaucer that the literary spirit of the English people, vigorous, simple, and truthful, found its voice, [in] a poetry especially robust, catholic, and
manly.'[53] A Scots writer, James Lorimer, in a review of Nicolas's edition of
Chaucer in the *North British Review* for 1849, says of Chaucer:

> He lived among a people possessing in the highest degree those distinctive
> features, that sharp and prominent nationality which distinguishes the pre-
> sent inhabitants of England from every other people . . . joyous and exuber-
> ant reality . . . hatred of 'humbug' . . . [a spirit] that though it was
> revolutionary in appearance, it was conservative at heart. . . .[54]

The Great Exhibition of 1851 marks something of an epoch in the development of national self-consciousness. It was a powerful stimulus to national
pride, and the beginning of an increasingly self-glorifying and by implication
xenophobic form of nationalism. Chaucer is not readily available for appropriation to the more extreme forms of late Victorian jingoism, but he continues to be loaded on to the bandwaggon of the new Englishness: as Carolyn
Collette shows, writers 'sought to place Chaucer himself as a sign of preeminent Englishness at the heart of nineteenth-century English life'.[55] For H.
H. Milman, author of the great *History of Latin Christianity* (1853), Chaucer is

> resolutely, determinately, almost boastfully English. . . . The creation of
> native poetry was his deliberate aim; and already, that broad, practical,
> humorous yet serious view of life, of life in its infinite variety, that which
> reaches its height in Shakespeare, has begun to reveal itself in Chaucer.[56]

J. R. Green, in his *Short History of the English People* (1874), one of the most important and influential and widely disseminated nineteenth-century works of popular history, speaks of Chaucer as having 'the sturdy sense and shrewdness of our national disposition. . . . The genius of Chaucer was . . . English to the core.'[57] One of the fullest statements of this view of Chaucer's Englishness comes from another Scotsman, Alexander Smith, writing on the poet William Dunbar in 1863. He finds Chaucer like the novelist Fielding:

> In both there is constant shrewdness and common sense, a constant feeling of the comic side of things, a moral instinct which escapes in irony, never in denunciation or fanaticism; no remarkable spirituality of feeling, an acceptance of the world as a pleasant enough place, provided good dinners and a sufficiency of cash are to be had, and that healthy relish for fact and reality, and scorn of humbug of all kinds . . . which . . . we are accustomed to call *English*.[58]

It is the poet Swinburne who identifies in Chaucer (1880) 'the great gift of specially English humour' combined with 'the inseparable twin-born gift of peculiarly English pathos'.[59]

One can of course recognise different degrees of discernment in the qualities in Chaucer that are selected for admiration, or at least detect signs that some people have actually read some of his poems. But sometimes hysteria takes over, even in otherwise sensible people. 'He hates Friars, because they are not English and not manly', says F. D. Maurice (1866),[60] and Matthew Browne, in a book called *Chaucer's England* (1869), rants on and on: 'Who is an Englishman more English than Chaucer?'; the *Canterbury Tales* 'contain more Englishness than any other poem in the language'.[61] Conscious that he should explain what this Englishness consists in, Browne tells us that Chaucer is bluff, open, manly, solid, well-balanced, genial, common-sensical, *normal*, the qualities, he says, that have made the English the best colonists and missionaries in the world. What is extraordinarily important in all this is not the imputation of these qualities to Chaucer—there are available, after all, for a literary work, only different kinds of misinterpretation[62]—but the appropriation of Chaucer, as the possessor of these qualities, to a particular kind of jingoistic national pride—especially given that Chaucer is, *historically*, in his own time, and in his own view of things, above all a European rather than an Anglocentric poet, as Elizabeth Salter has so eloquently made clear to us.[63]

None of the American writers of the period, of course, say anything of this kind in their commentaries on Chaucer—Thoreau, Longfellow, Lowell, Child. Their silence concerning Chaucer's 'Englishness' is not surprising; but there is something else. American writers were developing their own kind of national consciousness, and it differs in an interesting way from the English kind. The English kind is xenophobic and exclusive; the American kind is transcendental and inclusive. Americanness is a superior form of being, but it is one to which all human beings, of any race, may aspire, even if they do not live in the United States. Crèvecoeur, in his *Letters from an American Farmer* (1782), spoke of Americanness as an essential though latent quality inherent in individuals which a new political and geographical environment merely encouraged to reveal itself,[64] while Whitman, in the Preface to *Leaves of Grass* (1855), speaks of 'the Americans of all nations at any time upon the earth'.[65] This is a different notion from the idea of England, so powerful in the late nineteenth century, as the country of God's chosen people, with a divine mission to bring the values of Englishness to the barbaric peoples of Africa and Oceania, the lesser breeds without the law. This is the imposing of a will and consciousness upon others, or upon the Other; the American version is the unforced realisation of an ideal Americanness within oneself.

I am not arguing that Chaucer's facetious dismissal of the Flemings of 1381 was in itself an example of the contempt for foreigners that was needed to define English nationalism. My argument is that Chaucer has been read or misread, or lent himself to being read, in ways that have helped nourish a particular form of xenophobic national consciousness. It appears in muted form in some English critics of Chaucer in the twentieth century. F. R. Leavis avoided Chaucer, but amongst his followers there was a strong tendency to import his special brand of Anglo-centricity ('If one is uneducated in one's own literature one cannot hope to acquire education in any serious sense by dabbling in, or by assiduously frequenting, any other')[66] into the reading of Chaucer. It is there in John Speirs, who argues '(on the evidence of the unity of English literature since Chaucer) that there has been *one* complex English organic community from the thirteenth century';[67] it is there too in Ian Robinson, who considers that 'by seeing England whole, by seeing the connection between the parts, Chaucer created the whole he saw', and that his achievement was 'the creation of a national literature, a place where a nation can begin to find and recognize itself'.[68] An expedition to the remoter heights of lunacy would find G. K. Chesterton. 'Chaucer is the father of his country', he says, dizzyingly, 'rather in the style of George Washington'. In a final vision, he sees him as the primordial giant of Albion, 'with our native hills for his bones and our native forests for his beard'.[69]

The history of the attempt to make Chaucer serviceable in the cultivation of a certain kind of national pride is worth recovering. The purpose is not to prove that national pride is always a bad thing[70]—it has an important role in creating a sense of community in times of danger (though one would assume that this role is withering away as far as England is concerned, to be replaced by some sense of European unionhood or, less hopefully, by smaller and more viciously competitive tribal loyalties). Nor is the purpose to prove that

Chaucer was xenophobic. It doesn't matter: if it did, one could say that, though he shared the attitudes towards outsiders that prevailed in the communities he belonged to, there is no English poet who is *less* interested in England as a nation. What I am arguing is that Chaucer, through the aestheticisation and ironisation, characteristic of his poetry, of social and political issues relating to the identity of communities, lent himself to appropriation. The point of talking about Chaucer and Englishness, or rather the imputation of Englishness to Chaucer (the 'nationalization' of Chaucer), is to show how the apparently non-political and non-aligned writing of a great poet can become the instrument of an unrelated and historically powerful ideology.

Notes

1. This talk, which provides material for the early part of this lecture, is now published as 'Strangers in Late Fourteenth-Century London' in *The Stranger in Medieval Society*, ed. F. R. P. Akehurst and S. Cain Van D'Elden, *Medieval Cultures*, Volume 12 (Minneapolis, 1997), pp. 46–62.

2. Primo Levi, *Se questo e un uomo* (1958), trans. S. Woolf as *Survival in Auschwitz: The Nazi Assault on Humanity* (1960; New York, 1993). The quotation is from the 'Author's Preface', added in the later editions, p. 9 in the 1993 edn.

3. G. Simmel, 'Der Fremde' ('The Stranger'), translated in *Introduction to the Science of Sociology*, ed. R. E. Park and E. W. Burgess, 3rd edn. (Chicago, 1969), pp. 322–27.

4. F. Barth, Introduction, in *Ethnic Groups and Boundaries: The Social Organisation of Culture Difference*, ed. F. Barth (Boston, 1969), pp. 9–38 (see p. 15); E. Benveniste, *Indo-European Language and Society*, translated from the French, *La vocabulaire des institutions Indo-Européennes* (Paris, 1969), by E. Palmer (Coral Gables, FL, 1973), pp. 289–304; J. A. Armstrong, *Nations before Nationalism* (Chapel Hill, NC, 1982), pp. 4–6.

5. Simmel, 'Der Fremde', p. 322. Cf. Armstrong, *Nations before Nationalism*: 'Groups tend to define themselves not by reference to their own characteristics but by exclusion, that is, by comparison to "strangers"' (p. 5). Benveniste explains how the ethnic group is defined by exclusion (*Indo-European Language and Society*, p. 299, though I prefer here the translation provided by Armstrong, p. 5): 'Every name of an ethnic character, in ancient times, was differentiating and oppositional. There was present in the name which a people assumed the intention, manifest or not, of distinguishing itself from neighbouring peoples. . . . Hence the ethnic group often constituted an antithetical duality with the opposed ethnic group.'

6. *Canterbury Tales*, I.2717–18. Chaucer quotation and citation is from *The Riverside Chaucer*, ed. L. D. Benson (Boston, 1987).

7. The structure of Indo-European words of non-kinship social relation can only be understood, says Benveniste (*Indo-European Language and Society*, p. 294), by 'starting from the idea that the stranger is of necessity an enemy, and correlatively that the enemy is necessarily a stranger' (cf. Levi, in n. 2, above).

8. The information in this paragraph is mostly from S. L. Thrupp, *The Merchant Class of Medieval London* (Chicago, 1948), pp. 3–16, and is more fully treated in Pearsall, 'Strangers', pp. 48–50.

9. William Langland, *Piers Plowman: An Edition of the C-Text*, ed. D. Pearsall, York Medieval Texts, second series (1978), C.IX.83.

10. *Piers Plowman*, C.VI.362–75; C.III.82, C.VI.232.

11. See T. J. Garbaty, 'Satire and Regionalism: The Reeve and His Tale', *Chaucer Review*, 8 (1973), 1–8.

12. Armstrong, *Nations before Nationalism*, p. 8.

13. Barth, *Ethnic Groups and Boundaries*, p. 15 (his italics); Armstrong, *Nations before Nationalism*, p. 4. Gerald Newman, in *The Rise of English Nationalism: A Cultural History 1740–1830* (New York, 1987), lays the usual stress on 'the importance of *aliens and outsiders* in the formation of group consciousness' (his italics), and reinforces the point by adding: 'This consciousness does not simply form itself, as an ineluctable fact of the natural world' (p. 55).

14. See T. Turville-Petre, *England the Nation: Language, Literature and National Identity 1290–1340* (Oxford, 1996), p. 142.

15. See A. Beardwood, *Alien Merchants in England 1350 to 1377: Their Legal and Economic Position*, Mediaeval Academy of America, Monograph Series, No. 3 (Cambridge, MA, 1931), pp. 80–84; *Select Cases in the Court of King's Bench, under Richard II, Henry IV and Henry V*, Vol. VII, ed. G. O. Sayles, Selden Society, 88 (London, 1971), pp. 15–21, 40–41; P. Strohm, 'Trade, Treason, and the Murder of Janus Imperial', *Journal of British Studies*, 35 (1996), 1–23.

16. See Pearsall, 'Strangers', p. 57, and n. 40.

17. See especially the account in the reliable *Anonimalle Chronicle*, quoted in translation in R. B. Dobson, *The Peasants' Revolt of 1381* (1970; 2nd edn., 1983), p. 162.

18. See S. Justice, *Writing and Rebellion: England in 1381*, The New Historicism: Studies in Cultural Poetics, 27 (Berkeley, Los Angeles, and London, 1994), p. 217.

19. Paul Strohm, for instance, in *Social Chaucer* (Cambridge, MA, 1989), argues that the 'troubling social implications' of the passage are evaded through the dehistoricizing effects of the tale's stylization (p. 165).

20. W. C. Booth, *A Rhetoric of Irony* (Chicago, 1974), p. 37.

21. 'Self-ascription' is the term used by Barth, *Ethnic Groups and Boundaries*, pp. 13–15, to describe how people declare themselves to belong to this or that group, even though there may be large differences, objectively considered, within it. V. H. Galbraith, 'Nationality and Language in Medieval England', *Transactions of the Royal Historical Society*, 4th series, 23 (1941), 113–28, puts it crisply: 'A nation may be defined as any considerable group of people who believe they *are* one; and their nationalism as the state of mind which sustains this belief' (p. 113). Cf. also Armstrong, *Nations before Nationalism*, p. 291.

22. B. Anderson, *Imagined Communities: Reflections on the Origins and Spread of Nationalism* (1983; revised edn., 1991), p. 6.

23. R. Helgerson, *Forms of Nationhood: The Elizabethan Writing of England* (Chicago, 1992); A. G. R. Smith, *The Emergence of a Nation-State: The Commonwealth of England 1529–1660* (1984; 2nd edn., 1997); L. Greenfeld, *Nationalism: Five Roads to Modernity* (Cambridge, MA, 1992), p. 14; A. Hadfield, *Literature, Politics and National Identity: Reformation to Renaissance* (Cambridge, 1994); G. Hammond, 'How They Brought the Good News to Halifax: Tyndale's Bibles and the Emergence of the English Nation State', *Reformation*, 1 (1996), 11–28; C. McEachern, *The Poetics of English Nationhood 1590–1612*, Cambridge Studies in Renaissance Literature and Culture 13 (Cambridge, 1996).

24. See Hadfield, *Literature, Politics and National Identity*, pp. 57–59, 77–78.

25. E. Kedourie, *Nationalism* (1960), p. 9; E. Gellner, *Nations and Nationalism* (Ithaca, 1983), pp. 48–49; E. J. Hobsbawm, *Nations and Nationalism since 1780: Programme, Myth, Reality* (Cambridge, 1990, 2nd edn., 1992), p. 9.

26. A. D. Smith, *National Identity* (1991), p. 14.

27. Turville-Petre, *England the Nation*, p. v. Turville-Petre refers (pp. 24–25) to other studies that have argued similarly for the existence in the Middle Ages of some strength of national identity and awareness. See especially B. Guénée, *States and Rulers in Later Medieval Europe*, translated from the French (1971) by J. Vale (Oxford, 1985).

28. Turville-Petre, *England the Nation*, p. 21.

29. Not all scholars accept the primary importance of a common language to a sense of national identity: see Armstrong, *Nations before Nationalism*, p. 241. But England seems a special case, even though the weight of Galbraith's reservations about the 'national' status of the English language at this particular period ('Nationality and Language', pp. 114, 124) must be acknowledged.

30. Turville-Petre, *England the Nation*, pp. 14–19.

31. See L. W. Patterson, 'The Romance of History and the Alliterative *Morte Arthure*', chapter 6 in his *Negotiating the Past: The Historical Understanding of Medieval Literature* (Madison, WI, 1987), pp. 197–230.

32. See Turville-Petre, *England the Nation*, pp. 76–99, 125–27.

33. E. Salter, 'Chaucer and Internationalism', *Studies in the Age of Chaucer*, 2 (1980), 71–79 (see p. 79).

34. Namely, the three *fabliaux* of Fragment I (Miller's Tale, Reeve's Tale, Cook's Tale), the two coarse anecdotes of Fragment III (Friar's Tale, Summoner's Tale), the Nun's Priest's Tale and the Canon's Yeoman's Tale. The Man of Law's Tale is set partly in an oddly antique Anglian Britain, and the Wife of Bath's Tale in the faery-infested Britain of King Arthur.

35. See Wife of Bath's Tale (III.857, etc.), Squire's Tale (V.95, 287), Nun's Priest's Tale (VII.3212).

36. See J. H. Fisher, 'Chancery and the Emergence of Standard Written English in the Fifteenth Century', *Speculum*, 52 (1977), 870–99; M. Richardson, 'Henry V, the English Chancery, and Chancery English', *Speculum*, 55 (1980), 726–50; J. H. Fisher, 'A Language Policy for Lancastrian England', *PMLA*, 107 (1992), 1168–80.

37. See Richardson, 'Henry V', pp. 727, 739–40; Fisher, 'A Language Policy', pp. 1171–72.

38. *Troy-Book*, ed. H. Bergen, Early English Text Society, Extra Series 97, 103, 106, 126 (1906–20), *Prologue* 111–15.

39. See particularly Lydgate, *Troy-Book*, II.4697–700. The quotation in the text is from Hoccleve, *The Regement of Princes*, ed. F. J. Furnivall, Early English Text Society, Extra Series, 72 (1897), 4978.

40. F. R. H. Du Boulay, 'The Fifteenth Century', in *The English Church and the Papacy in the Middle Ages*, ed. C. H. Lawrence (New York, 1965), p. 211, cited in Richardson, 'Henry V', p. 741. J. -P. Genet, in 'English Nationalism: Thomas Polton at the Council of Constance', *Nottingham Medieval Studies*, 28 (1984), 60–78, makes it clear that Henry's pronouncement was not just a declaration of abstract principle but a strategic move in the debate that was taking place at the Council concerning the relative voting power to be given to the different national delegations. The French delegation was scornful of the English claim to parity (e.g., in terms of number of bishoprics) and the English were anxious about the ambiguous status of the 'Britain' they claimed as the nation (*natio anglicana sive britannica*, p. 74).

41. Armstrong, *Nations before Nationalism*, pp. 129–30. For the problems in identifying the 'state' with the nation, see Genet, 'English Nationalism', p. 77.

42. See L. Patterson, 'Making Identities in Fifteenth-Century England: Henry V and John Lydgate', in *New Historical Literary Study: Essays on Reproducing Texts, Representing History*, ed. J. N. Cox and L. J. Reynolds (Princeton, NJ, 1994), pp. 69–107.

43. See V. J. Scattergood, *Politics and Poetry in the Fifteenth Century* (1971), pp. 41–99. He comments on the increase of 'nationalistic feeling' in the poetry of the period (p. 42).

44. See Newman, *The Rise of English Nationalism*, p. 75: 'A consciousness of France as England's military, commercial and diplomatic enemy was one of the foundation stones of the national mind' (see also p. 124).

45. The survey that follows is based on the invaluable collections of material in C. F. E. Spurgeon, *Five Hundred Years of Chaucer Criticism and Allusion* (Chaucer Society, 1908–17, in 5 parts; in 3 vols., Cambridge, 1925), and D. Brewer, *Chaucer The Critical Heritage*, 2 vols. (1978).

46. Dryden, Preface to the *Fables*, quoted in Spurgeon, *Chaucer Criticism and Allusion*, I.279.

47. John Hughes, in his edition of Spenser (1715): see Spurgeon, I.340.

48. L. Colley, *Britons: Forging the Nation 1707–1837* (New Haven, CT, and London, 1992), p. 7.

49. Colley, *Britons*, p. 6.

50. These two quotations are from popular broadsides of 1803, cited by S. Cottrell, 'The Devil on two sticks: Franco-phobia in 1803', in *Patriotism: The Making and Ummaking of British National Identity*, ed. R. Samuel, 3 vols. (1989), I.259–74 (pp. 263, 261).

51. Southey, in a review of Chalmers' *English Poets*, quoted in Spurgeon, II (Part ii), 67.

52. Spurgeon, II (Part ii), 155.

53. Spurgeon, II (Part ii), 220; Brewer, *Critical Heritage*, I.315.

54. Brewer, *Critical Heritage*, II. 90.

55. C. P. Collette, 'Chaucer and Victorian Medievalism: Culture and Society', *Poetica*, 29–30 (1989), 115–25 (p. 115).

56. Spurgeon, II (Part iii), 24. The role of Shakespeare in the production of this new ideology of nationhood is of course another and more important story.

57. Spurgeon, II (Part iii), 118.

58. Brewer, *Critical Heritage*, II.126. It is interesting confirmation of the paradigm of 'construction through difference' to see 'humbug' singled out again (as by Lorimer, above) as specially un-English, when non-English people would normally perceive the opposite to be true.

59. Spurgeon, II (Part iii), 131.

60. Spurgeon, II (Part iii), 83.

61. Matthew Browne [a pseudonym for William Rands], *Chaucer's England*, 2 vols. (1869), pp. 47, 49–50. Browne's insistence on Chaucer's 'manliness', which we have seen before, is remarkable: George Meredith speaks of Chaucer likewise (1851), egregiously: 'Tender to tearfulness—childlike, and manly, and motherly; / Here beats true English blood richest joyance on sweet English ground' (Spurgeon, II [Part iii], 3).

62. At the same time, it is striking that Langland, whose views of community identity-formation we have seen to be shaped in the same way as Chaucer's, should be so much more resistant to appropriation: he has been misread, but not, I think, misread so against the grain as Chaucer.

63. See 'Chaucer and Internationalism' (note 33, above); also her *Fourteenth-Century English Poetry: Contexts and Readings* (Oxford, 1983), pp. 120–40.

64. J. Hector St. John de Crèvecoeur, *Letters from an American Farmer*, Introd. by M. T. Gilmore (1971), Letter III, pp. 43–44.

65. Walt Whitman, *Leaves of Grass*, ed. H. W. Blodgett and S. Bradley (New York, 1965), p. 709.

66. F. R. Leavis, 'How to Teach Reading', in *Education and the University* (1943), pp. 105–34 (p. 134).

67. J. Speirs, *Chaucer the Maker* (1951), p. 16.

68. I. Robinson, *Chaucer and the English Tradition* (Cambridge, 1972), p. 283.

69. G. K. Chesterton, *Chaucer* (1932), pp. 15, 216.

70. The power of nations to 'inspire love, and often profoundly self-sacrificing love', is spoken of by Benedict Anderson, in *Imagined Communities*, p. 141. He conveys a vivid intuitive sense of that power by contrasting the experience of standing before the 'Tomb of the Unknown Soldier' with the imagined experience of standing before the 'Tomb of the Unknown Marxist' (pp. 10–11).

Index

303

List of Contributors

Suzanne Conklin Akbari is Associate Professor of English and Medieval Studies at University of Toronto.

Kenneth Bleeth is Professor of English at Connecticut College.

Sheila Delany is Professor of English at Simon Fraser University.

Vincent J. DiMarco is Professor of English at University of Massachusetts, Amherst.

Louise O. Fradenburg is Professor of English and Comparative Literature at University of California, Santa Barbara.

John M. Fyler is Professor of English at Tufts University.

Katharine Slater Gittes is Professor of English, Emerita, at California Polytechnic State University, San Luis Obispo.

Kathryn L. Lynch is Katharine Lee Bates and Sophie Chantal Hart Professor of English at Wellesley College.

Dorothee Metlitzki was Professor of English at Yale University.

Derek Pearsall is Gurney Professor of English, Emeritus, at Harvard University.

Susan Schibanoff is Professor of English and Women's Studies at University of New Hampshire, Durham.

Sylvia Tomasch is Professor of English at Hunter College, City University of New York.

For Product Safety Concerns and Information please contact our EU
representative GPSR@taylorandfrancis.com
Taylor & Francis Verlag GmbH, Kaufingerstraße 24, 80331 München, Germany